Democracy, governance, and economic performance

Changing Nature of Democracy

Note to the reader

The United Nations University Press series on the *Changing Nature of Democracy* addresses the debates and challenges that have arisen as "democratic" forms of governance have blossomed globally. The march of democracy has defined the close of the twentieth century; the fulfillment of individual and collective aspirations, good governance, and the nurturing of civil society form the benchmark of political organization. However, democracy defies a universal model, and the definition of democracy continues to be elusive. Moreover, the performance of democracy often fails to live up to its promise. This series explores two areas. Firstly examined is the theoretical discourse of democracy, such as the tension between procedure and substance, the dialectic between principles and institutions, the challenge of reconciliation and peace-building in democratic transition, the balance between universal and communitarian notions of democracy, between participation and efficiency, and between capital and welfare. Secondly, the series explores how these themes and others have been demonstrated, with varying effect, in a number of regional settings.

Titles currently available:

The Changing Nature of Democracy edited by Takashi Inoguchi, Edward Newman, and John Keane

The Democratic Process and the Market: Challenges of the Transition edited by Mihály Simai

Democracy, Governance, and Economic Performance: East and Southeast Asia edited by Ian Marsh, Jean Blondel, and Takashi Inoguchi

Democracy, governance, and economic performance: East and Southeast Asia

Edited by Ian Marsh, Jean Blondel, and Takashi Inoguchi

United Nations University Press

TOKYO · NEW YORK · PARIS

United Nations University Press
The United Nations University, 53-70, Jingumae 5-chome,
Shibuya-ku, Tokyo, 150-8925, Japan
Tel: +81-3-3499-2811   Fax: +81-3-3406-7345
E-mail: sales@hq.unu.edu
http://www.unu.edu

United Nations University Office in North America
2 United Nations Plaza, Room DC2-1462-70, New York, NY 10017, USA
Tel: +1-212-963-6387   Fax: +1-212-371-9454
E-mail: unuona@igc.apc.org

United Nations University Press is the publishing division of the United Nations University.

Cover design by Joyce C. Weston

Printed in the United States of America

UNUP-1039
ISBN 92-808-1039-1

Library of Congress Cataloging-in-Publication Data

Democracy, governance, and economic performance : East and Southeast Asia / edited by Ian Marsh, Jean Blondel, and Takashi Inoguchi.
     p.   cm.
   Includes bibliographical references and index.
   ISBN 9280810391
   1. Democratization—East Asia. 2. Democratization—Asia, Southeastern. 3. East Asia—Politics and government—1945. 4. Asia, Southeastern—Politics and government—1945. 5. East Asia—Economic conditions—1945. 6. Asia, Southeastern—Economic conditions—1945. I. Marsh, Ian. II. Blondel, Jean, 1929. III. Inoguchi, Takashi. IV. Title.
   JQ1499.A91   D446   1999
    338.95—dc21   99-050732

Contents

Tables and figures

Tables

Figures

Acronyms

ABIM	Angkatan Belia Islam Malaysia (Malaysian Islamic Youth Movement)
AKAR	Angkatan Keadilan Rakyat (People's Justice Movement) (Malaysia)
APU	Angkatan Perpaduan Ummah (Community Unity Movement) (Malaysia)
ASEAN	Association of Southeast Asian Nations
BBC	Bangkok Bank of Commerce
Bhd	Berhad (limited company) (Malaysia)
BN	Barisan Nasional (National Front) (Malaysia)
BOC	Board of Election Canvassers (Philippines)
CDF	Countrywide Development Fund (Philippines)
COMELEC	Commission on Elections (Philippines)
CPP	Chart Pattana (National Development Party) (Thailand)
CTP	Chart Thai (Thai National Party)
DAP	Democratic Action Party (Malaysia)
DBM	Department of Budget Management (Philippines)
DFI	Direct foreign investment
DJP	Democratic Justice Party (South Korea)
DLP	Democratic Liberal Party (South Korea)
DP	Democratic Party (South Korea)
DPP	Democratic Progressive Party (Taiwan)
EMS	European Monetary System

ENA	Ecole nationale d'administration (France)
EOI	Export-oriented industrialization
GDP	Gross domestic product
Gerakan	Gerakan Rakyat Malaysia (National People's Movement) (Malaysia)
GNP	Grand National Party (South Korea)
GNP	Gross national product
GO	Governmental organization
Golkar	Golongan Karya (Functional Group) (Indonesia)
GP	Green Party (Taiwan)
HICOM	Heavy Industries Corporation of Malaysia
HKMA	Hong Kong Monetary Authority
ILO	International Labour Organisation
IMF	International Monetary Fund
IPF	Indian People's Front (Malaysia)
ISA	Internal Security Act (Malaysia)
ISI	Import substitution industrialization
ISIS	Institute of Strategic and International Studies (Malaysia)
IT	Information technology
KBL	Kilusang Bagong Lipunan (New Social Movement) (Philippines)
KMT	Kuomintang (National Party) (Taiwan)
Korpri	Korps Pegawai Negeri Republik Indonesia (Indonesian Civil Servants Corps)
Lakas-NUCD	Lakas ng Tao–National Union of Christian Democrats (Philippines)
LAMMP	Laban ng Makabayang Masang Pilipino (Struggle of the Nationalist Filipino Masses)
LAMP	Labian ng Masang Pilipino (Struggle of the Filipino Masses)
LDP	Labang ng Demokratikong (Struggle of Democratic Filipinos)
LDP	Liberal Democratic Party (Malaysia)
LEDAC	Legislative-Executive Development Advisory Council (Philippines)
LP	Liberal Party (Philippines)
MCA	Malaysian Chinese Associates
MIC	Malaysian Indian Congress
MIDA	Malaysian Industrial Development Authority
MIER	Malaysian Institute of Economic Research
MNC	Multinational corporation
NAMFREL	National Movement for Free Elections (Philippines)

NAP	New Aspirations Party (Thailand)
NCNP	National Congress for New Politics (South Korea)
NDRP	New Democratic Republican Party (South Korea)
NEP	New Economic Policy (Malaysia)
NGI	Non-governmental individual
NGO	Non-governmental organization
NIC	Newly industrializing country
NKP	New Korea Party
NP	Nationalista Party (Philippines)
NP	New Party (Taiwan)
NPA	New People's Army (Philippines)
NPC	Nationalist People's Coalition (Philippines)
NPP	New Party for the People (South Korea)
NRP	National Reunification Party (South Korea)
OEC	Omnibus Election Code (Philippines)
OECD	Organisation for Economic Co-operation and Development
OFWs	Overseas Filipino workers
PAP	People's Action Party (Malaysia)
PAP	People's Action Party (Singapore)
PAS	Parti Islam SeMalaysia (Pan-Malaysian Islamic Party)
PBB	Parti Pesaka Bumiputera Bersatu (United Bumiputera Party) (Malaysia)
PBDS	Parti Bingsa Dayak Sarawak (Sarawak Dayak People's Party) (Malaysia)
PBRS	Parti Bersatu Rakyat Sabah (United Sabah People's Party) (Malaysia)
PBS	Parti Bersatu Sabah (United Sabah Party) (Malaysia)
PDI	Partai Demokrasi Indonesia (Indonesia Democratic Party)
PDP	Philippine Democratic Party
PDS	Parti Demokratik Sabah (Sabah Democratic Party) (Malaysia)
PMP	Partido ng Masang Pilipino (Party of the Filipino Masses)
PNB	Partido ng Bayang (People's Party) (Philippines)
PNB	Permodalan National Bhd (National Equity Corporation) (Malaysia)
PO	People's organization (Philippines)
PPCRV	People's Pastoral Council for Responsible Voting (Philippines)
PPD	Party for Peace and Democracy (South Korea)
PPP	Partai Persatuang Pembangunan (United Development Party) (Indonesia)

PPP	People's Progressive Party (Malaysia)
PR	Proportional representation
PRC	People's Republic of China
PRM	Parti Rakyat Malaysia (Malaysian People's Party)
PRP	Philippines Reform Party
RDP	Reunification Democratic Party (South Korea)
ROC	Republic of China (Taiwan)
SAP	Social Action Party (Thailand)
SAPP	Sabah Progressive Party (Malaysia)
SAR	Special Administrative Region (Hong Kong)
SEDCs	State Economic Development Corporations (Malaysia)
Semangat	Parti Melayu Semangat 46 (Spirit of '46 Malay Party) (Malaysia)
SF	Socialist Front (Malaysia)
SMI	Small and medium industries
SNAP	Sarawak National Party (Malaysia)
SNTV	Single non-transferable vote
SUPP	Sarawak United People's Party (Malaysia)
TAIP	Taiwan Independence Party
TEPU	Taiwan Environmental Protective Union
TNC	Transnational Corporation
UDP	United Democratic Party (Malaysia)
ULD	United Liberal Democrats (South Korea)
UMNO	United Malay National Organization (Malaysia)
USNO	United Sabah National Organization (Malaysia)
WTO	World Trade Organisation

Preface

In the late 1980s and the early part of the 1990s, a number of polities of East and Southeast Asia firmly engaged in a democratization process. At the same time and largely because of this process, a number of prominent regional leaders asserted that such a development was contrary to "Asian values" and would affect negatively the economic performance of the countries concerned. As it turned out, the economic performance of the countries of the region was affected, not by democratization, but by the globalization of the world economy and in the first instance by the financial consequences of this globalization: thus the downturn struck more a country such as Indonesia, which had not democratized, than a country such as Taiwan, which had fully democratized.

At the beginning of the third millenium as at the beginning of the 1990s, whatever the extent of the financial crises, the same question remains, equally urgent and equally daunting: does democratization affect economic perforamce negatively and, more specifically, does it affect economic performance negatively in the particular context of East and Southeast Asia? Such a question has not so far attracted the full attention of scholars, perhaps because too little emphasis was placed, after World War II, on the weight of political factors in socio-economic development: as a matter of fact, the converse relationship, that which relates democratization to previous economic performance, has been studied in an increasingly sophisticated manner since S. M. Lipset first raised the matter in the early 1960s in *Political Man*. Now, however, with regional leaders stating emphatically that democratization would have an ill effect on the well-being of citizens, the problem of relating economic performance to democratization has to be directly confronted. The aim of this book is therefore to provide at least some elements of answer to the question, even if it is naturally recognized that the short duration of the democratization process and the small number of countries concerned must mean that conclusions can only be tentative.

This work would not have been possible without the help of scholars from the region and in particular of those who agreed to undertake the difficult task of writing country chapters on the basis of a commonly agreed framework. We are truly grateful to all of them. We wish to thank the United Nations University for its generous financial support, one of us, Takashi Inoguchi, having been associated with that university at the time the project started. We are also indebted to the University of Malaysia and to Jomo Kwame Sundaram for having organized the first meeting of the group of contributors at Kuala Lumpur in January 1997. We are especially grateful to the Shizuoka Research and Education Foundation for the generous funding and hospitality which it provided for our second meeting at Hamamatsu in March 1997. We thank the academic institutions to which we belonged during the whole or part of the period, the European University Institute in Florence, the University of Siena, Colorado College in Colorado Springs, the University of Tokyo, and the Australian Graduate School of Management of the University of New South Wales in Sydney, for having provided us with greatly needed facilities such as e-mails, faxes, and telephones, as these were obviously essential instruments for the completion of a collaborative enterprise such as this. We are most grateful to Professor Martin Shefter of Cornell University for allowing us to reproduce the figure which appears in his *Political Parties and the State* (Princeton, N.J.: Princeton University Press, 1994): the analysis which he conducts in this volume has helped us markedly in the development of our conceptual framework.

We learnt much while undertaking this study, both about the concrete political, social, and economic life of the countries concerned and about comparative politics and administration: we hope that readers, too, will find that this volume helps to assess, not just whether democratization does affect economic performance, but, perhaps even more importantly, what democratization practically consists of at the level of party development in particular, as well as what economic performance entails in terms of economic governance.

Florence, Tokyo, and Sydney, October 1998

Introduction

1

Economic development v. political democracy

Jean Blondel, Takashi Inoguchi, and Ian Marsh

Until the financial crisis of 1997, the economic success of the countries of East and Southeast Asia was widely regarded as the economic "miracle" par excellence of the last decades of the twentieth century. This success had represented the first sustained experience of economic modernization by non-Western states. It had occurred at a pace unprecedented in Western experience. It was associated, in a number of states, with a distinctive pattern of economic governance. From the late 1980s, democratization was also progressively introduced, renewed, or consolidated in a number of states: Korea, Taiwan, the Philippines, and Thailand. The compatibility between democracy and economic development had already been a lively question because of the publicly expressed views of some regional leaders, notably Lee Kuan Yew and Dr. Mahathir. The events of the late 1990s give this relationship new significance. The financial crisis raises fresh questions about the distinctive patterns of economic governance that had been adopted in a number of states. It places in a new context political developments that were already in train in Korea and Thailand. It reframes the political outlook in other affected states, particularly Indonesia, but also perhaps Malaysia and Hong Kong.

The question of the compatibility between democracy and economic development first arose in the context of the extraordinary growth rates achieved by regional states. Their development up until 1997 surpassed by far by the rapidity of the "miracles" which Western Europe had known after World War II; it is perhaps even more surprising than the

Japanese miracle in that, in Japan, as in Western Europe, the existing economic infrastructure and industrial base surely accounted at least for part of the rapid growth of the second half of the twentieth century: there seemed no equivalent in the countries of East and Southeast Asia. Further, despite exclusions and rent seeking, these high rates of growth have generally been accompanied by diminishing income inequalities (World Bank 1993; Abbeglen 1994; Amsden 1989; Clifford 1997; Wade 1990). The countries included in this study fully belonged to the "developing" group in the 1950s: they were not more "advanced" than the bulk of the countries of South America, for instance.

One key difference between East and Southeast Asian countries and Western Europe and Japan was the character of their political life. Up to the mid-1980s at least, these polities either had been ruled continuously by authoritarian or semi-authoritarian governments or had had periods of liberal rule interspersed with periods of dictatorial, often military, government. Korea, Thailand, Burma, and the Philippines belonged to the second category; the first included two subsets, those which allowed a modest degree of dissent, albeit in some cases at the cost of considerable harassment of the dissenters, and those in which no dissent at all was allowed. The first subset included Malaysia, which was the "least illiberal," Singapore, and Indonesia; the second included all the other polities of the area, that is to say Taiwan, the countries of the Indochinese peninsula (Vietnam, Cambodia, and Laos), and last but not least, China. Hong Kong had always occupied a somewhat peculiar position, since it was a crown colony in which a degree of personal freedom was recognized but representative institutions were almost wholly non-existent.

This picture began to be altered in part from the second half of the 1980s. On the one hand, there was no political change in China, Vietnam, and Laos; authoritarian rule remained strongly entrenched in Burma; moves towards representative government began to take place in Hong Kong but these were overshadowed by uncertainty concerning political life after the retrocession of the colony to China; finally, there was very little political change in Malaysia, Singapore, and Indonesia. On the other hand, in Korea, the Philippines, and Thailand, authoritarian rule appeared to be on the way out as a result of the replacement of dictatorial presidents or prime ministers by new leaders elected on a pluralistic basis; most remarkably, the strong single-party system under which Taiwan had been ruled since World War II came to be replaced, without a crisis of regime and without major conflict, by a functioning and apparently well-structured system, at first of two parties, and subsequently of three parties; finally, but on a seemingly very fragile basis and under much United Nations pressure, Cambodia moved from a most brutal dictatorship and from years of foreign occupation to a liberal democratic system based on party pluralism.

As a result, the political map of East and Southeast Asia came to be composed in the 1990s of three groups of countries: first, those which had remained strongly authoritarian and where there were no signs of change – China, Vietnam, Laos, and Burma; second, those which had formally adopted liberal democratic institutions, but remained in practice authoritarian although they typically tolerated a limited amount of dissent – Malaysia above all, but also Singapore and Indonesia; and third, those which had become democratic – Korea, Taiwan, Thailand, and the Philippines, to which Hong Kong and Cambodia might be added, for different reasons but possibly only for a time (Alagappa 1995; Cheng and Haggard 1992; Anek 1996; Morley 1993; Taylor 1996; Bell 1995; Rodan 1996).

These developments suggested that a process of democratization was under way, as a result of which the countries of the area were becoming comparable to Western Europe, North America, and Japan, not merely economically but politically as well. There were shadows in this picture, however. To begin with, as was just noted, only about a third of the countries of the area were undergoing a process of democratization, while another third were liberal democratic formally only, and those of the last group were not democratic at all. Second, it was not clear how far democracy was "consolidated" – to adopt an expression that is widely used in the study of new democracies – in those countries in which the democratization process had taken place. In other parts of the world during the same period, the results were somewhat mixed. Democratic consolidation seemed to have been achieved in many Latin American countries and in much of Central Europe; but the same conclusion could not be reached with respect to most of what was Yugoslavia, much of what was the Soviet Union, and large parts of Africa. There was therefore still a question mark with respect to those countries of East and Southeast Asia which were undergoing a democratization process.

The political future of the area is therefore far from clear. Even if we leave aside the group of countries which are fully authoritarian, there is considerable uncertainty as to what will be the direction in which Malaysia, Singapore, Indonesia, as well as indeed Hong Kong will move, if they move at all. Doubts about the future of democratization become even greater as one takes into account the fact that in the first three countries of this group, the view has been put forward by members of the political establishment that liberal democracy is merely a Western European concept and that "Asian values" are far better adapted to the societies of the area. In different ways, Mahathir, Lee Kuan Yew, and Suharto have at one time or another propounded the notion that they had adopted a political model which suited their countries well and that there was no need to move, indeed no virtue whatsoever in moving, towards the Western model.

Moreover, the question of "Asian values" became to an extent a screen or an ideological front for the markedly more down-to-earth view according to which the introduction of liberal democracy in East and Southeast Asia is incompatible with sustained economic development. Events of 1997 give this issue an especial edge.

This second, down-to-earth concern is, in reality, a markedly more serious attack against the introduction of liberal democracy than the argument about "Asian values." The validity of the "Asian values" argument hinges on citizens holding these values and, given that they did hold them in the past, on their continuing to hold them at present; there is no evidence which firmly demonstrates whether these values prevail or not, but there are indications that they are not, to say the least, universally shared in the area. For instance, a study undertaken among Taiwanese citizens shows that liberal democratic values have gained substantial ground and are becoming markedly more widespread than "Asian values" (Parish and Chi-hsiang Chang 1996, 27–41). Thus, there is some ground for doubting whether the "Asian values" argument can be sustained for long even in those countries in which it has been put forward by "authoritative" sources; this is all the more so given that, in other countries of the area, the argument has not been put forward or has been, as in Taiwan, firmly rejected by the relevant authorities.

The more down-to-earth claim that democratization impedes economic growth cannot be as easily combatted. Admittedly, the strength of this argument depends also ultimately on the citizens believing in it, but the extent to which the citizens are likely to do so does not rest solely nor even principally on the values held by these citizens: the judgement passed by citizens on these matters rests primarily on impressions about the situation in other countries – for instance in the West – as well as on the extent to which there are worries about the uncertainty which tends to characterize periods of political change. What citizens are therefore asked to do is to assume either that politics and economics are so distant from each other that a change in political arrangements will have no effect on economic life, or that the new politics will produce a group of leaders who will be as concerned with economic growth and as able to steer the economy in the direction of economic growth as their predecessors. This is manifestly asking much of citizens and it is understandable that some at least should not be willing to accept the validity of either of these two assumptions.

Given that the view that liberal democracy impedes economic development has manifestly important political consequences, it is rather strange that there should not have been systematic efforts to look at the problem in the East and Southeast Asian context; as a matter of fact, the problem has been studied primarily in the Latin American context. Rather than examining whether liberal democracy might impede economic growth, most of the work devoted to East and Southeast Asia has been concentrated on the converse problem, namely whether economic growth favours democratization or not. There has thus been a study on the political role of elections in East and Southeast Asia; there is also much theoretical and empirical literature on the links between economic governance and economic growth: but there is no recently published work on the possible influence of democratization on economic performance. What the present study attempts therefore to do is to start filling this gap in the literature by looking at the relationship between politics and economic performance in two of the three groups of countries which were identified earlier: those countries which did democratize their political life since the mid-1980s (Korea, Taiwan, Thailand, the Philippines, and Hong Kong); and those countries which remained relatively authoritarian in the context of a formally liberal democratic structure (Malaysia, Singapore, and Indonesia).

There seemed to be little point in examining the strongly authoritarian countries in which there was no change at all in political arrangements, although these may have undergone substantial alterations of the economic structure and management; on the other hand, it is essential to examine both the countries in which a move towards liberal democracy has taken place and those in which relatively liberal arrangements coupled with a rather authoritarian interpretation of these arrangements have resulted in little political change. There is manifest scope for an opening up of these latter political systems and they may well be gradually affected by the same process of democratization as the countries of the other group: the events of 1998 in Indonesia suggest that some move in this direction may indeed be taking place; conversely, not all those countries in which the process of democratization has taken place may see this process consolidated. Above all, the comparison between the two groups will provide at least some of the evidence required to assess whether the introduction of a liberal democratic system is likely to impede economic growth. Thus this study covers eight countries: five from the first group, Korea, Taiwan, Thailand, the Philippines, as well as Hong Kong, which has naturally peculiar characteristics; and three from the second, Malaysia, Singapore, and Indonesia. Given the serious difficulties encountered by the pluralistic Cambodian regime and given that this regime was installed to a substantial extent at the behest and under the pressure of the international community and was not primarily the result of an internal evolution towards liberal democracy, it was not felt appropriate to analyse Cambodia as it was not clear to what category it would have belonged, absent the external pressure.

Democracy, authoritarianism, and economic growth

The view that democracy can impede growth – indeed, that it does impede growth – has been based on a number of arguments, typically made in relation to Latin America and typically more in the form of hypotheses than of empirically based conclusions (Sirowy and Inkeles 1990, 126–57). These conclusions are also to an extent contradictory: "Some empirical studies have found no significant relationship between economic development and democracy. Others have observed a strong impact of democracy on growth. Yet others have ascertained only a weak positive effect of freedom on growth, or have discerned a negative influence of freedom on growth" (Feng 1997, 393–94). Feng notes that three hypotheses have been put forward, which relate to the dysfunctional consequences of premature democracy; to the inability of democracies to implement policies for rapid growth; and to the incapacity of pervasive state involvement (Sirowy and Inkeles 1990, 129; Feng 1997, 392). Feng's own empirical study, on the other hand, is a systematic attempt to look at the relationship between growth, democracy, and political stability in 96 countries; but it relates only to the 1960s and the 1970s and it does not specifically identify East and Southeast Asia: it is therefore impossible to know how far the area behaved at the time in the same manner as Latin America or Africa. Moreover, the conclusions which Feng draws are somewhat mixed: on the one hand, it appears that democracy "tends to have a negative but weak impact on growth" (Feng 1997, 403); but it also appears that "overall ... democracy promotes growth indirectly by inducing major regular government change and inhibiting irregular governmental change" (ibid., 414).

Three further points can be made in favor of the argument that democracy impedes growth. One is that, at least until 1997, economic growth has been lower in Western industrialized countries than in East and Southeast Asia, and that following 1997, the restoration of growth requires authoritarian leadership. Another is that at least some forms of democracy are unstable in terms of the personnel which is at the head of the executive and that there is no way of ensuring that there will not be instability, as many changes of government result from the vagaries of the electoral fortunes of the political parties. A third argument has to do with the inefficiency of decision-making in democracies which results from the multiplication of demands, many of them contradictory, and from the fact that decision makers are constrained to take advice and consult widely because of the prevailing ethos.

The first of these arguments does not constitute a foolproof case that democracy cannot be associated with rapid economic growth, while the other two are merely hypotheses which need to be tested. It is true that Western democracies have had low rates of economic growth in the last decades of the twentieth century: but it is also true that, apart from East and Southeast Asia and even if one leaves aside the special cases of the ex-Communist countries, economic growth tends to be rather low everywhere; it is indeed lower in parts of Africa and of Latin America than in the West. Authoritarianism is clearly no recipe for growth: as a matter of fact, as was just noted, empirical studies dealing with Latin America have come to contradictory conclusions in this respect (O'Donnell and Schmitter 1986; Feng 1997, 395).

Moreover, while the argument is about rates of economic growth, it must nonetheless be noted that economic development as a whole is highly correlated with liberal democracy (Lipset 1983; Lipset, Seong, and Torres 1993; Marks and Diamond 1992; Moore 1995; Vanhanen 1990; Vanhanen 1997). The richer countries are also by and large democracies. There are exceptions, but these are more due to the fact that poorer countries tend to be democratic (India and many states of the New Commonwealth) than to the fact that richer countries tend to be authoritarian, the only examples of the latter correlation being the states of the Arabian peninsula. The wealth of democracies may be accounted for in large part by their past development and by the fact that they exploited substantial segments of the rest of the world: admittedly, this finding often led to the conclusion that economic development was at the origin of the move towards liberal democracy and not vice versa; but we are confronted here with a correlation and the direction of influence is problematic. What is certainly the case is that stable institutionalized democracies are unquestionably not associated in the main with low living standards.

The question of the relative instability of the political leadership and of the ministerial personnel in democratic and authoritarian governments has several facets. As is noted by Feng, succession is more regular in democracies than in authoritarian states (Feng 1997, 398); on the other hand, there is noticeable instability in some democratic countries, typically as a result of the inchoate or undisciplined character of parties in parliament. Moreover, electoral upsets change both the governmental personnel and governmental policies: what was done by one team may be undone by the next, a point which was repeatedly made in connection with Britain in the 1970s, but which lost much of its validity subsequently (Kellner and Crowther-Hunt 1980, 211–12).

Yet cases of major reversals of policies are a small minority, as are cases of weak governments which last only a few months, in the majority of Western countries. This is not only because, by a fortunate accident, in many democracies, governments of the same party or parties are returned to office by the electors; it is also in part because most parties are sufficiently well organized and disciplined to prevent governments from disintegrating; and because many governments follow in broad terms the policies of their predecessors, even if they do not belong to the same parties. As a matter of fact, major policy changes are almost as likely to occur during the lifetime of a government as from one government to the next: circumstances, such as economic downturns, have forced Western European cabinets of both Right and Left to alter their course markedly, a clear-cut example being that of the Socialist government in France in 1983.

Meanwhile, the uncertainty which characterizes the tenure of authoritarian rulers is typically greater than that of democratic governments. Not just the accidents of death, but the incidence of coups have rendered rather bumpy the political history of authoritarian nations, except when these have remained traditional. But traditional states are becoming very rare and are in any case of no interest from the point of view of assessing what the future of East and Southeast Asian polities is likely to be.

The high turnover of ministers, as distinct from that of governments and of their leaders, has been a matter of major concern in a number of democracies, admittedly; but this high turnover is in no way a characteristic of democracies alone. The turnover has been very high in Korea or Indonesia – as high as in Belgium or Italy; it has not been lower in Taiwan than in Germany or Austria; nor has it been lower in Singapore than in Switzerland. Overall, the turnover of ministers and of heads of governments has been more rapid in the developing world than in the West: the turnover was least rapid of all in communist states, but, with that exception, the stability of the political personnel has been greater in Western liberal democracies as a class than elsewhere in the world (Blondel 1985).

The suggestion that decision-making is hampered in democracies by the open character of political debate and by the large amount of consultation which takes place in these regimes has been a matter of concern in the West: it was common in the 1970s to declare that Western polities suffered from "overload" (Rose 1980). Yet this point is relevant to the question of economic growth only if two further points are also valid. First, it has to be demonstrated that decision-making is necessarily more rapid when there are few actors operating behind closed doors. Blockages may also occur in such situations, and it has therefore to be found empirically whether, by and large, the delays and blockages which occur in authoritarian regimes are less marked and less troublesome for the economy than those which occur in democratic polities. One might hypothesize that there are likely to be variations in this respect, given the well known fact that there are variations among democratic regimes. Second, it is not clear that economic growth benefits necessarily from speedy decision making. Japan and Sweden are examples of countries in which decision processes are slow: yet neither the first case nor even the second constitute instances of low economic growth over the long term. It may well be more valuable from the point of view of economic growth that decisions be arrived at after a very careful consideration of alternatives and in a climate of consensus than that they should be taken speedily.

The problems posed by the analysis of economic growth in East and Southeast Asia

Economic growth, economic governance, and the role of values

As is well known and as was pointed out at the outset, until 1997 East and Southeast Asia were the region of the globe in which economic growth was highest. Over the 25 years between 1965 and 1990, the eight countries of the area grew by an average 6.5 per cent a year, as against 2 per cent or less in the rest of the developing world and 2 per cent in the West (Hughes 1995). This same trend continued into the 1990s. In 1995, for instance, the growth of GDP ranged from 9.1 per cent in Singapore to 4.9 per cent in Taiwan, with Malaysia and Thailand very close behind Singapore with respectively 8.8 and 8.5 per cent.

The financial sector collapse that began in Thailand in March 1997 and progressively spread to Indonesia, Malaysia, the Philippines, and Korea raises fresh questions about the impact of democratization on growth. The existence of different political regimes in these states constitutes one relevant fact: two countries were democratizing and two remained authoritarian (or quasi-authoritarian). A more detailed analysis of causality and of dynamics is required. Meanwhile it could be argued that East and Southeast Asian states continued on the same trajectory which had been theirs previously out of some kind of inertia, and that growth might subsequently be impaired as a result of the continuous pursuit of democratization.

To argue along these lines entails adopting one or both of two standpoints about the relationship between liberal democracy and economic growth, however. The first standpoint is in turn composed of two parts. On the one hand, it suggests that liberal democratic arrangements may have a negative impact on the characteristics and the role of the bureaucracy, on the grounds that the bureaucracy might be prevented from steering the economy with the same degree of autonomy in a democratic context as under authoritarian rule. On the other hand, to be convincing, this standpoint must also demonstrate that the bureaucracy does have a direct effect on economic performance, a matter which is also problematic. Economic development has been rapid in East and Southeast Asia, but it is not axiomatic that this rapid economic development has been due to the action of the bureaucracy.

The systematic examination of the validity of this standpoint entails, therefore, that the possible effect of the bureaucracy on growth be carefully ascertained. Although this does not constitute an alternative to such an examination, some prima facie evidence suggests that, in East Asia, in Singapore, and to a lesser degree in other states of Southeast Asia, the bureaucracy has been particularly proactive in contrast to what it has been in the rest of the world. Most economists and other analysts do indeed accept that as a result and to a varying extent, these countries have profited from what can be described as a favourable governmental climate (Hughes 1995, 98; Weiss 1997, 2). Hughes speaks of "governments" playing a major role: what is meant by "governments" in this case is manifestly not merely the 20 or 30 ministers but the whole administrative apparatus. Another way of referring to this element is to speak, as Weiss and others do, of "strong states." This means that government departments, on the one hand, are able to implement policies because they have "penetrative" and "extractive" power, and can "negotiate" with economic actors – to use Weiss's expressions – and, on the other hand, that they also pursue active policies (Weiss and Hobson 1995, p. 7). These implementation characteristics are by and large uncommon in the Third World, and they make East and Southeast Asia more akin to Western countries; however, as Western countries, by and large, have not tended to pursue a truly active economic policy, the role of the bureaucracy is appreciably larger in East and Southeast Asia than in the West (except, most noticeably, for France where the role of the state has been large over lengthy periods). Thus one cannot deny the tendency for the bureaucracy to be strong, obviously to a varying degree, in the region, by comparison with other regions of the world; and although it is not proven that the impact of this steering of the economy by the bureaucracy has been crucial to economic development, it is difficult to believe that this steering did not play some part. If this is the case, it becomes essential to discover whether the introduction of a liberal democratic framework would indeed have a negative impact on the action of the bureaucracy.

The second standpoint about the relationship between liberal democracy and economic development is concerned with "Asian values": it is suggested that a key reason why East and Southeast Asian countries should have grown so rapidly is that their populations held values likely to favour economic growth. It could then be argued that, as liberal democracy is likely to undermine these values, the effect of democratization would be a decline in economic growth. In such an interpretation, liberal democracy would not be detrimental to economic growth because of its structural arrangements, but because of the values which it instils.

This second standpoint is the more insidious because it is almost impossible to test its empirical validity. It seems always plausible to suggest that the values held by sets of individuals have an effect on their behaviour, but the connection between the two elements is at best hard to demonstrate. In fairness, this type of connection has not been made merely in East and Southeast Asia: it has often been made, for instance, with respect to those Westerners who had a "Protestant ethic" by comparison with those who did not. Yet the fact that a similar argument was made in the West to the one about "Asian values" does not make the latter more acceptable. In reality, it is by now well established, to begin with, that the determination of what constitute values and what constitutes a prevailing culture in a given country is a highly complex task (Hofstede 1980). To be able then to assess what impact such values and such a culture may have on the behaviour of whole populations is manifestly highly speculative. It is therefore more appropriate to concentrate here on the two elements that make up the first standpoint, according to which liberal democracy may impede economic growth: the possible negative effect of liberal democracy on the ability of the bureaucracy to be proactive; and the effect which a proactive bureaucracy may have on economic growth.

The question of economic globalization

In the last decades of the twentieth century, a further phenomenon may have come to disturb, and thus may have rendered more complex, the relationship between the political regime and economic growth: the possible impact of economic globalization on the economies of individual states. The period during which the countries of East and Southeast Asia were experiencing rapid economic growth was one in which a large number of physical and psychological barriers to the movement of goods, and even more of capital, from state to state and from region to region, were diminishing. Consequently, states have clearly lost some or perhaps even much of their power over economic governance and, if this power had an effect on economic development, globalization could have important consequences for that development.

Yet there is no clear indication as to what the effect of globalization on economic governance or economic growth might be; consequently, it is difficult to determine whether and, if so, how far the relationship between liberal democracy and economic performance is likely to be affected. An extensive empirical and theoretical literature now exists which reviews the scale and significance of economic globalization and the extent to which it might induce convergence between the economic strategies of individual states, and reduce the opportunities for economic governance. International capital flows impose new constraints on states, as the Mexican experience in 1982 and 1994 and the East and Southeast Asian experience in 1997 have demonstrated. Pressures for convergence between states in such areas as competition policy and intellectual property regimes arise, amongst other sources, from the IMF and the World Trade Organisation. The OECD has been promoting a standard code for DFI. Various studies of the Japanese economy suggest that the state cannot maintain its earlier activist or leadership role (Emmott 1989). The causes and consequences of the financial crisis for economic governance and for democratization will be explored in later chapters. Here more general considerations bearing on the impact of economic globalization on state sovereignty are briefly summarized.

The notion that nation states will be inexorably driven to a common economic pattern under the influence of international forces seems at best a half-truth, however. On the one hand, there is indeed convergence between countries in the goals and purposes of their policies: most want a minimally successful economic performance; there is also convergence in some of the economic constraints. Where FDI is a primary element in economic development, regulatory and prudential arrangements in the financial sector need to retain the confidence of international investors. In addition, relations between states and firms are shifting. More businesses, both large and medium-sized, are internationalized (Dunning 1993; Strange 1995). States are faced with more footloose firms and they need to redefine their own attractions and to discover new forms of negotiating leverage. For example, Peter Evans (1996, 465) suggests that this posed a major challenge for the Korean state.

On the other hand, "new institutional economics" is a powerful source of theoretical arguments against convergence at the institutional or attitudinal level. In this theory, institutions are the key determinants of longer-term economic performance. These are "the humanly devised constraints imposed on human interaction. They consist of formal rules, informal constraints (norms of behaviour, conventions, and self-imposed codes of conduct), and their enforcement characteristics. They consist of the structure that humans impose on their dealings with each other" (North 1991, 3). Convergence around economic purposes between states is likely to be associated with institutional diversity. This is because, if states try to imitate what they perceive to be the successful practices of others, they will mostly be able to do so only in functionally equivalent ways. Path dependence determines this outcome.

Further, in this perspective, states remain important arenas for the formation of ideas, choice sets, and motives. Because of the particularity of language and norms, the pervasive influence of path dependence, and genuine uncertainty, elite and public opinion in particular states is no less "bounded" than its reciprocal, the "bounded rationality" of individuals. This means that between states, the reality will likely be interdependence and the management of difference, miscomprehension or incomprehension – not economic interdependence, progressive political, cultural understanding, and institutional homogeneity.

Other authors, having explored the extent to which TNCs remain embedded in particular host cultures, argue that nation states continue as significant actors with significant opportunities to influence economic outcomes (Hirst and Thompson 1996; Drache and Boyer 1996; Berger and Dore 1996; Dunning 1993). All acknowledge that the role of the state is being transformed: the question is how much leverage does it retain and what forms might this leverage take?

In practice, in any particular society, culture, institutions, and markets coexist in a mutually conditioning, contingent pattern. There is no such thing as capitalism with a big C: there are many capitalisms, differing from country to country (Hollingworth, Schmitter, and Streeck 1994; Hollingworth, Rogers, and Boyer 1997; Crouch and Streeck 1997). Further, if states try to imitate what they perceive to be the successful practices of others, they will mostly only be able to do so in functionally equivalent ways. Any more than partial convergence is thus unlikely; perhaps more accurately, convergence on some dimensions will bring into sharper focus differences on others. The reality will be interdependence and the management of variety, not interdependence and progressive homogeneity.

The Japanese example

Assuming therefore that economic globalization constrains but does not negate the capacity of states to steer the economy, the question of the relationship between liberal democracy, economic governance, and economic performance does continue to need to be explored. In this respect, the Japanese example is obviously highly relevant, for four reasons. First, Japan has clearly been and continues to be a "strong state" in the double sense which was given to this term earlier. Second, Japan has been a strong state as well as a democracy: this shows that the two elements are not incompatible. Japanese democracy may be different in some respects from both Anglo-American and Continental democracies, but it is a democracy on the basis of all the criteria which are typically adopted. Third, the example of Japan has manifestly been followed, first in East Asia, and subsequently to a degree in Southeast Asia, as the metaphor of the "flying geese" pattern so aptly suggests. Finally, Japan's economy was characterized until the early 1990s by a rate of economic growth which was of the order of magnitude of the rate achieved by East and Southeast Asian countries. This shows that liberal democracy is fully compatible with a high rate of economic growth. Admittedly, the rate of growth has slowed down markedly in Japan since the early 1990s. But whatever its causes, such a slowdown cannot be regarded as being due to the institutionalization of democracy, since it occurred after over forty years of uninterrupted democratic life and indeed despite two very severe oil shocks which also markedly affected the economies of Western European countries.

Given the generally accepted view that a strong state has been a key element in enabling East and Southeast Asian countries to achieve high rates of growth, and given that the Japanese example shows that there exists a path which allows for the combination of democracy and high growth, a path which may well imply adopting the formula of the strong state, what has to be determined about East and Southeast Asia becomes clear: are the states of the area likely to retain their strong state characteristics and yet also maintain their democratic features?

Is there a future for the strong state in East and Southeast Asia?

The strong state is sometimes felt to be at risk in East and Southeast Asia on the grounds that civil servants will not be able to operate as effectively in a democratic context as in an authoritarian framework. This conclusion is far from axiomatic: it is likely to be true only if there is no desire to achieve consensus between state actors and economic actors. It may be that such a consensus will be difficult to achieve in some of the states of the area because a tradition of consensus has not existed so far. Bureaucracy in Korea is sometimes said to wish to impose authority rather than to build collaboration, unlike Japanese bureaucracy (Clifford 1997). On the other hand, such a pattern of behaviour is unlikely to characterize Malaysia, for instance, as consensus arrangements have typically been in place in that country. They have even been regarded as a necessity in the context of the complex ethnic relationships which have prevailed there.

What needs to be investigated, therefore, is whether the strong state can be expected to remain in place, given either that consensual decision-making processes already exist, or that the hierarchical mode is likely to be replaced by consensual types of relationships between the relevant actors. As our discussion will show, only if and where such a consensual mode is regarded as highly unlikely to prevail in view of the attitudes of the governmental and/or the economic agents can serious doubts be entertained as to the survival of the strong state in the context of democratic institutionalization. This question is even more pertinent in the wake of the financial crisis.

Liberal democracy and the role of parties

We have so far begun to explore the problems relating to the analysis of economic governance and looked at the ways in which different institutional structures may affect the extent to which the bureaucracy is able to steer the economy of a given country. A parallel exploration needs to be undertaken in relation to the democratization process. A liberal democratic system cannot be maintained unless it is buttressed by a network of institutions, some of which are typically established by a constitution while others are set up independently of the constitution. Executives, legislatures, and courts fall in the first category; the second category includes above all the political parties, but it is also composed of a large number of other groups and organizations.

The political parties are by far the most important of all these institutional structures of either category. On the one hand, executives and legislatures cannot function effectively without the political parties giving life to and structuring debates leading to policy initiatives and policy developments; on the other hand, the representation of the people cannot take place meaningfully unless parties organize that representation. Interest groups are of course critical in this process as well, but it is on the parties that these groups focus either directly or indirectly, since they have to put pressure on the parties in the legislature or on those party leaders who are in the executive if they want to see their policies adopted. Thus parties are the nerves of the political system: they provide the crucial link between citizens and government.

As parties are so critical in ensuring that the liberal democratic system is put in place and functions effectively, it is naturally by examining the characteristics of the parties that one can assess the extent to which the democratization process is taking shape in a given polity. A first question which arises is, naturally, how far parties are genuinely free to be established and to develop: this is a sine qua non, but it is not a sufficient condition. The parties which are established have to be both truly lively and truly viable if they are to fulfil their role. The liveliness of parties means that these are well implanted across the nation and that they can be regarded as being truly representative; the viable character of parties means that they must be sufficient large and consequently not too numerous: only if this is the case can parties be effective both at the level of the executive and at that of the legislature in order to support the government or to oppose it. Unless these roles are fulfilled, the parties cannot be regarded as ensuring that a liberal democratic system is truly implemented; if they are fulfilled, on the other hand, the democratic process will take place in a smooth and regular manner.

In order to be able to begin at least to assess whether a liberal democratic system is likely to impede economic growth, three questions have to be addressed generally: these will be the object of the first part of this study. First, given that the existence of an effective liberal democracy depends on the presence of lively parties and of a viable party system, chapter 2 will examine the characteristics which parties and party systems must possess to enable a liberal democratic system to function effectively. Chapter 3 will then turn to the analysis of the forms which state institutions must take if they are to steer the economy, as well as of the extent to which such a steering can be expected to have a direct effect on economic growth. Chapter 4 will bring these two points together by considering the relationships which must exist between parties and bureaucracy, if both are to be able to fulfil their tasks efficiently and thus to ensure that active governance takes place and liberal democracy flourishes.

The second part is devoted to case studies of the eight countries forming part of the two groups of East and Southeast Asian countries identified earlier, namely the five countries in which a move toward liberal democracy has taken place, Korea, Taiwan, Thailand, the Philippines, and Hong Kong (but not Cambodia); and the three countries in which some of the structures of democracy have been put in place but the practice of democracy leaves much to be desired, Malaysia, Singapore, and Indonesia. These case studies provide the empirical evidence on the basis of which conclusions, however tentative, can be drawn about the way in which, in practice, the parties have come to develop, the bureaucracy is performing, and a new relationship between parties and bureaucracy may be taking shape. Such a conclusion concerns both the polities whose political system has been markedly altered, and those in which no change had taken place by the late 1990s but where some change might take place in the opening decades of the twenty-first century.

The third part consists of a concluding chapter which synthesizes the evidence presented in the country studies and evaluates comparatively the degree of democratic consolidation and the outlook for economic governance. Regarding democratic development, the evidence suggests that parties and/or party systems remain underdeveloped in most cases, despite some pathbreaking structural changes in the early 1990s. Similarly, in relation to economic governance, only Korea, Taiwan, and Singapore displayed appropriate institutional capacities, and Korea's state capacity was significantly weakened in the mid-1990s, although the financial crisis may facilitate its reconstitution. The states of Southeast Asia that espoused economic leadership mostly lacked well-developed institutional capacities.

The general theme of this study – political development, economic governance, and their linkages – is not yet common in the scholarly literature on the region. Yet the states of East and Southeast Asia constitute a fertile comparative setting for exploring this nexus. Democratization occurred, or was consolidated, in a number of states in the early 1990s (e.g., Korea, Taiwan, and Thailand). But irrespective of the level of democratization, economic performance has been a primary source of political legitimacy in all states. Yet the levels of economic development vary markedly – with Korea, Taiwan, Hong Kong, and Singapore progressively turning to technological innovation as its primary engine. The other states (the Philippines, Thailand, Indonesia, Malaysia) have based development primarily on incorporation in regional/global production systems.

The political and policy-making institutions surveyed in this study must now frame and implement state responses to the financial crisis. Outcomes will be determined, on the one hand, by the capacity of political systems to sustain popular support, and on the other, by the capacity of institutions to rework dysfunctional economic arrangements. These two features are the central focus of the following analysis, which thus contributes essential information for estimating futures for regional states.

REFERENCES

Abbeglen, James (1994), *Sea Change: Pacific Asia and the New World Industrial Center*, The Free Press, New York.

Alagappa, Muthiah (ed.) (1995), *Political Legitimacy in Southeast Asia: The Quest for Moral Authority*, Stanford University Press, Stanford, Calif.

Amsden, Alice (1989), *Asia's Next Giant: South Korea and Late Industrialization*, Oxford University Press, New York.

Anek, Laothamatas (ed.) (1997), *Democratisation in East and Southeast Asia*, Silkworm Books, Chiang Mai.

Bell, Daniel, A. David Brown, Kanishka Jayasurya, and David Martin Jones (1995), *Towards Illiberal Democracy in Pacific Asia*, Macmillan, London.

Berger, Suzanne and Dore, Ronald (eds.) (1996), *National Diversity and Global Capitalism*, Cornell University Press, Ithaca, N.Y.

Blondel, J. (1985), *Government Ministers in the Contemporary World*, Sage, London and Los Angeles.

Cheng, Tun-Jen and Haggard, Stephan (eds.) (1992), *Political Change in Taiwan*, Lynne Reiner, Boulder, Colo.

Clifford, Mark (1997), *Troubled Tiger*, rev. ed., Butterworth-Heinemann, Singapore.

Crouch, C. and Streeck, W. (1997), *Modern Capitalism versus Modern Capitalisms: The Future of Capitalist Diversity*, Oxford, Oxford University Press.

Drache, D. and Boyer, R. (eds.) (1996), *States against Markets*, Routledge, London.

Dunning, J. (1993), *The Globalization of Business*, Routledge, London.

Evans, Peter (1996), "Review of States and Economic Development," *American Political Science Review* 90(2).

Feng, Y. (1997), "Democracy, Political Stability, and Economic Growth," *British Journal of Political Science* 27, pp. 391–418.

Hirst, P. and Thompson, G. (1996), *Globalisation in Question*, Polity Press, Cambridge.

Hofstede, G. (1980), *Culture's Consequences*, Sage, London and Los Angeles.

Hollingworth, J. Rogers and Boyer, Robert (eds.) (1997), *Contemporary Capitalism: The Embeddedness of Institutions*, Cambridge University Press, Cambridge.

Hollingworth, J., Schmitter, P., and Streeck, W. (eds.) (1994), *Governing Capitalist Economies*, Oxford University Press, New York.

Hughes, Helen (1995), "Why Have East Asian Countries Led Economic Development?" *Economic Record* 71(212), pp. 88–104.

Kellner, P. and Crowther-Hunt, Ld (1980), *The Civil Servants*, Macdonald, London.

Lipset, S. M. (1983), *Political Man*, Heinemann, London.

Lipset, S. M., Seong, K. R., and Torres, J. C. (1993), "A Comparative Analysis of the Social Requisites of Democracy," *International Social Science Journal* 136, pp. 155–75.

Marks, G. and Diamond, L. (eds.) (1992), *Reexamining Democracy*, Sage, London and Los Angeles.

Moore, M. (1995), "Democracy and Development in Cross-National Perspective: A New Look at the Statistics," *Democratisation* 2(2), pp. 1–19.

Morley, James W. (ed.) (1993), *Driven by Growth: Political Change in the Asia-Pacific Region*, New York, M. E. Sharpe.

North, Douglass (1991), "Towards a Theory of Institutional Change," *Quarterly Review of Economics and Business* 31(4), pp. 3–11.

O'Donnell, G. A. and Schmitter, P. C. (1986), *Transitions from Authoritarian Rule*, Johns Hopkins University Press, Baltimore.

Parish, W. L. and Chi-hsiang Chang, C. (1996), "Political Values in Taiwan: Sources of Change and Constancy," in Hung Mao Tien (ed.), *Taiwan's Electoral Politics and Democratic Transition*, M. E. Sharpe, Armonk, N.Y., pp. 27–41.

Rodan, Gary (ed.) (1996), *Political Oppositions in Industrialising Asia*, Routledge, London, 1996.

Rose, R. (1980), *The Challenge of Governance: Studies in Overloaded Politics*, Sage, London and Los Angeles.

Sirowy, L. and Inkeles, A. (1990), "The Effects of Democracy on Economic Growth and Inequality: A Review," *Studies in Comparative International Development* 25, pp. 16–57.

Strange, Susan (1995), "The Defective State," *Daedalus* 124(2), pp. 55–75.

Taylor, R. H. (ed.) (1996), *The Politics of Elections in Southeast Asia*, Cambridge University Press, New York.

Wade, Robert (1990), *Governing the Market: Economic Theory and the Role of the Market in East Asian Industrialization*, Princeton University Press, Princeton, N.J.

Weiss, Linda (1997), "Globalization and the Myth of the Powerless State," *New Left Review*, no. 225, pp. 3–27.

——— (1998), *The Myth of the Powerless State*, Cornell University Press, Ithaca, N.Y.

Weiss, Linda, and Hobson, John (1995), *States and Economic Development: A Comparative and Historical Analysis*, Polity Press, Cambridge.

World Bank (1993), *The East Asian Miracle, Economic Growth and Public Policy*, Oxford University Press, New York.

Parties, party systems, and economic governance

2

The role of parties and party systems in the democratization process

Jean Blondel

Parties are the central institutions of modern liberal democratic countries. Whatever may be said – and has repeatedly been said – about their shortcomings, parties are crucial to the functioning of these societies as they are the only organizational structures to have been discovered (so far) through which the views, attitudes, and sentiments of the people can be conveyed to the top decision makers and through which potential leaders can be nominated and subsequently appointed. Indeed, as key agents of the democratic process, parties fulfil three main functions: they provide a permanent link between citizens and government; they set out policies which are proposed to electors and implemented by governments; and they are the means by which politicians are selected for office.

As a matter of fact, parties are also critically important to political life in authoritarian regimes, most of which have operated, in particular since World War II, on the basis of single-party or near single-party systems. Evidence for the importance of parties in these regimes can be found most clearly in communist states; but examples are also numerous among Third World authoritarian regimes, from Mexico to Zimbabwe and pre-1985 Taiwan. The single-party or near single-party system has been the institutional means by which dictators have been able to control their countries for years on end: there could not be any better proof that parties play a key part in all types of modern societies, both liberal and illiberal.

Parties are therefore the instruments par excellence which organize the relationship between people and government in modern political systems; but, given that political parties exist, or at least one political party exists, in authoritarian states, they must have some distinctive characteristics when they operate in the context of a liberal democratic system. These distinctive features do not relate only, nor perhaps even primarily to the internal structure of parties, but also to the shape of the party system. As was indicated in the previous chapter, parties have to be considered from two main standpoints. First, if they are to be truly representative, parties must have solid roots in the population: a "lively" party cannot be just a clique concentrating its activities in the capital of the country. Second, in order to be able to make an impact on political life and not merely be debating societies, parties must form part of a "system." There must be a number of them; they must relate to each other and yet be autonomous from each other; and their total number must be sufficiently small to ensure that the system is efficient in terms of decision-making (Blondel 1995).

While the first of these two broad features, that which relates to the structure of the parties, needs to be examined in any polity where parties exist, the second feature, which relates to a number of parties independent from each other, can be found only if these parties are able to operate freely – especially, but not exclusively, in the context of elections. There must therefore be a constitutional framework formally establishing a number of freedoms, and the practices of the regime must follow the principles of the constitution. Parties play a key part in this respect as they can ensure by their behaviour and by their sheer existence that the constitutional framework is respected. To use the currently fashionable expression, democracy will be "consolidated" – that is to say be stable and immune from coups, attempted coups, and other forms of authoritarian rule – if, but only if, a pluralistic party system exists in which two or more parties freely compete: indeed, liberal democracies are often defined by the fact that they have a pluralistic party system. On the other hand, such systems cannot exist unless the characteristics of these political systems enable parties to compete freely. There is thus reciprocal reinforcement, so to speak, of the constitutional guarantees by the parties and of the parties by the constitutional guarantees.

Thus, to determine the extent to which democracy has become "consolidated" in East and Southeast Asia, we need to examine, first, how far constitutional arrangements and practices allow for the development of a pluralistic party system; second, whether the parties are structured in such a way that they are true instruments of popular representation; and third, whether autonomous parties exist and whether they form a party system in which their number is sufficiently small for the decision-making process to be efficient.

Constitutional arrangements, political practices, and the development of a pluralistic party system

To be able to function freely and autonomously, parties have to operate in a milieu which recognizes their existence and allows them to develop their activities in the ways they wish. A number of conditions have therefore to be fulfilled, relating to the way parties can conduct their affairs, not just during election periods but at other times; they concern, for instance, the facilities which parties need to enjoy to be able to have access to the media. The political system must treat parties in an even-handed manner: rules and practices must be such that equality of treatment is approximated. The aspects of the political system which are therefore directly involved in enabling parties to act freely and independently are, first, the constitutional framework; second, the electoral system; and third, the way the media report (and may affect) political life.

The role of the constitutional structure

Constitutional arrangements have a direct impact on party development. First and foremost, there has to be a constitution and that constitution has to be applied. Second, the constitution must allow for the unimpeded development of parties. Restrictions on the right of some types of parties to exist and act freely are always dangerous, even in the case of parties which are illiberal and undemocratic; if there are to be any restrictions, these must be precisely and limitatively defined. Third, liberal constitutions themselves also affect the characteristics of parties in two main ways.

In the first place, the constitutional provisions regarding the relationship between executive and legislature have an effect on parties, especially as a by-product of the major distinction between presidential, semi-presidential, and parliamentary systems, though that effect may not be as profound as was believed up to the 1990s: largely on the basis of American experience, presidentialism was then widely regarded as leading to a reduction in the cohesion of parties (Linz 1990; Shugart and Carey 1992). Two main arguments have been put forward which have probably some, but only some, general validity. On the one hand, internal party divisions seem fostered by the fact that several presidential candidates of the same party compete against each other, often for long periods, in order to win the official nomination. Indeed, in the United States, this competition is particularly strong and long because of the primaries; parties are obviously divided internally as a result and the scars may never be entirely healed. By contrast, leadership battles in parliamentary systems are shorter and tend to take place, not merely among party members only, but even often exclusively within the leadership groups. One East and Southeast Asian exception is Malaysia, perhaps somewhat surprisingly, as all members of the United Malay National Organisation (UMNO) participate in the election of their leader. Moreover, the sharp separation between executive and legislature which is characteristic of the presidential system seems also to contribute to reducing party cohesion. In parliamentary systems, the cabinet's existence depends on the continued support of the legislature: this fosters party discipline as it is a big step, and one which is obviously taken rarely, for the backbenchers of the majority party or parties to vote against the government when they know that their vote is likely to bring that government down. Reciprocally, to avoid trouble, the cabinet is likely to woo the members of the parliamentary majority by all the means at its disposal. The relationship between government and majority is therefore likely to be close in a parliamentary system; on the other hand, since, in presidential systems, the chief executives and their cabinets do not depend for their survival on the legislators, their links with these legislators are likely to be more distant. However, while these tendencies seem true in the American context, lack of party cohesion is not universal in presidential systems: in Venezuela, Chile, and Argentina, for instance, parties have displayed a marked degree of discipline in Congress (Mainwaring and Scully 1995, 17–19; Coppedge 1994).

The second way in which the constitutional structure affects parties is by decentralizing the territorial structure of the state. The impact of this is particularly large in federations, but it also exists as a result of other forms of territorial decentralization, at least when that decentralization is genuine, and specifically when local or regional bodies are popularly elected. Thus, although decentralization is often conceived primarily as an administrative device, it has inevitably political implications and these implications cannot but affect parties to an extent, in particular because candidates for the top positions in the decentralized bodies have to be selected as well as because these bodies have to take important decisions concerning local or regional matters. This is likely at a minimum to lead from time to time to conflicts with the central organs of the parties.

Federalism is regarded as a particularly strong form of decentralization, but in practice, federalism varies widely in content. Some federal countries leave little scope for the component bodies, whether they are states, provinces, regions, or cantons. This is in particular the case in Austria or Venezuela; in the United States, Canada, Belgium, or Switzerland, on the other hand, the component units are powerful, as are the "communities" into which Spain has been divided since the 1970s. The Australian federation is an intermediate case, as is Malaysia, which is the only federal country in East and Southeast Asia. Indeed, while, in the least decentralized countries which have just been mentioned, there are identical parties across the federation, this is not the case in Canada and Belgium; interestingly, an analogous development has taken place in Malaysia, where the Sabah and Sarawak parties are different from those of continental Malaysia. Parties are nominally identical in the United States and Switzerland, but only because in each component body – state or canton respectively – they are almost entirely independent: in the United States and to a large extent in Switzerland the autonomy of each state or cantonal party is such that it is not clear whether it is justified to refer to these parties as together forming a single national unit.

The impact of the electoral system

Constitutions sometimes determine the broad characteristics of the electoral system; in the majority of cases, they do not. Yet the electoral system has a major impact on the structure and on the relative strength of parties, and therefore on the party system, both in the legislature and, indirectly, in the population as a whole, whether this impact is deliberate or not. The deliberate impact is often due to systematic discrimination against some parties, especially opposition parties: this discrimination includes malpractices relating to the composition of electoral lists and harassment at all times and during election campaigns in particular; the short duration of election campaigns also belongs to this category, a practice which in Southeast Asia is characteristic of Singapore and Malaysia. Behaviour of this kind prevents the parties from developing a genuine representative structure, and by tilting the balance in favour of the governmental parties, it also prevents the party system from becoming truly institutionalized.

Another common way in which some parties – not necessarily only the government parties – can enjoy unfair advantages consists of a variety of forms of corruption, ranging from the outright buying of votes by some candidates to the distribution of favours in a more or less concealed manner by some of the parties (more frequently the government parties) to groups of electors in particular districts. While corrupt practices cannot be altogether eradicated by the provisions of electoral systems, the silence of the law in this respect manifestly results in these practices remaining unchecked. The widespread development of corruption – as well as the widespread belief that corruption takes place – have an obvious effect on the standing of the political parties among the population. Moreover, this behaviour tends to reduce the ability of the parties to become institutionalized, as it often results from the action of wealthy individuals and especially from that of persons who rapidly amassed large fortunes in periods of high economic growth and who intend to use their fortunes to influence politics to their advantage. Not surprisingly, therefore, corruption has played a major part in electoral practices in many countries, whether undergoing a process of democratization or not, including in the countries of East and Southeast Asia (Taylor 1996).

Yet even the complete elimination of anti-opposition harassment and of corrupt practices, if it were possible, would not solve entirely the problems arising from the need to ensure that all parties be treated fairly, as some of these – typically the government parties – have privileged access to resources. Attempts have therefore been made increasingly in a variety of countries, principally in the West, to remedy this resource inequality by distributing public funds to political parties, typically on the basis of the results obtained by these parties at elections (Alexander 1989). Whether this policy achieves real fairness is debatable and has been debated: existing parties clearly have an advantage over new parties, as funds are distributed on the basis of previous results; moreover, parties would appear to be less likely to want to make efforts to mobilize citizens if their administrative costs are guaranteed by public funds. Overall, the pros and cons of public financing in countries undergoing a process of democratization are finely balanced. On the one hand, in cases where new parties are started by politicians from one of the main centres and in particular from the capital, these politicians often have limited followings outside these centres and they should therefore make special efforts to develop the activities of their parties at the local level if these parties are to have a strong and loyal electorate. It may be preferable not to provide finance automatically in these circumstances even if, as a result – especially when they belong to the opposition – these parties find it difficult to make ends meet. On the other hand and conversely, there may be parties that are purely local and operate on the basis of favours distributed locally without much attention being addressed to national politics. As the public financing of parties tends naturally to reinforce their central organs, the incidence of corrupt practices at the local level may be reduced if the parties are publicly financed, provided the distribution of these public funds takes place in a fair manner; the leaders of these localized parties may become in the process more concerned with national affairs.

The various practices which have just been described do not of course affect only the structure of the parties: they affect also the party system. Corrupt practices are indeed aimed at modifying patterns of voting behaviour. Party systems are naturally also markedly modified as a result of the mechanics of electoral systems, since these have a direct effect on the allocation of seats in parliaments and on the procedure by which presidents are elected: thus the "first-past-the-post" system strongly exaggerates majorities while this is not so, or at least not so much the case, with proportional representation, especially if it is based on large districts (Duverger 1954; Rae 1967; Lijphart 1994; Leduc, Niemi, and Norris 1996; Farell 1997; Norris 1997); but, as has been pointed out in the literature, the mechanics of seat allocation or the methods of electing presidents have an indirect effect on the way electors vote, partly because they are aware, at least in a broad manner, of the effects of electoral systems and partly because the parties field candidates bearing in mind the characteristics of the electoral system. Given that governments are naturally also aware of these effects, they are likely in many cases to try to ensure that the system of seat allocation which is adopted is the one most favourable to them. There is no doubt, for instance, that the maintenance of the first-past-the-post system in Malaysia has helped the governing coalition in that country to obtain much larger majorities than would have been obtained under a PR system; there is indeed little doubt that this situation may have led electors to believe that the ruling coalition could not be defeated. The same conclusion can be drawn, indeed more forcefully, in relation to Singapore.

The role of the mass media

The precise effect of the mass media on political behaviour is a subject of much controversy. It is widely believed, in Western countries at least, that the immediate effect of the media is not as large as was originally assumed and indeed that television in particular has tended to be helpful in improving political knowledge (Halloran 1970; De Fleur and Ball-Rokeach 1982; Blumler 1983; Blumler and Gurevitch 1995). Yet, while the immediate effects can be measured, for instance in the context of an election, the longer-term impact of the media is markedly more difficult – probably impossible – to assess adequately.

Even if one does not take sides in this controversy, it can at least be suggested that fairness in reporting will help to strengthen party development and to render the battles between parties fairer, especially the electoral contests. This has implications for the behaviour of the media both between elections and during election campaigns. However, what fairness consists of varies depending on the way the media are organized: what is critical in this respect is not whether these are privately or publicly owned, but whether they are closely linked to parties or not. If they are closely linked to parties, as is or was often the case with the press but is less common with radio and occurs rarely with television, it is not "unfair" that they should, within limits, present the point of view of the party to which they are linked. Fairness is maintained if all the parties – or at any rate those which have a substantial following – possess newspapers, radio, or even television stations and can thus carry on their contests in a pluralistic atmosphere. If the media are "independent," on the other hand, fairness implies that the coverage given to all the parties by each of the organs of the press, radio, or television be balanced and that this should be the case at all times and not only during election campaigns. Paradoxically, perhaps, this requirement is more difficult to achieve with the press than with radio or television, partly because the tradition of a party-based or at least of an ideologically based press is strong, and partly because, probably as a result, those who write in newspapers, professional journalists and occasional contributors alike, find it less justified to be constrained by the need to present a balanced view.

While a fair organization of the media thus depends in principle on whether these are party-based or "independent," and not on the distinction between private and public ownership, this distinction does have important and typically serious consequences. Particularly outside the West and Japan, radio and television stations, at least, have been established in a context in which the funds available to the private sector were relatively limited and where, at the same time, authoritarian governments have been adamant to dominate and indeed control completely what was being said and what was being printed. This was often achieved by establishing a government monopoly of radio and television, on the one hand, and, on the other, by introducing censorship, controlling the distribution of paper, and/or giving to the newspapers of the ruling party or parties marked advantages over others, for instance in terms of advertising. Even though the impact of these arrangements cannot be assessed even in broad terms, let alone be measured, it seems inconceivable that it should be not be substantial, especially in the long run, and that it should not affect markedly the views of citizens about the actions of the government and the reactions of the opposition: indeed, the citizens may not even come to know what are the standpoints of the opposition parties.

The behaviour of the media at election times is of course critical, although it has to be regarded as being only an element in the role which they play in political life. This is particularly so because, almost certainly, especially in recent years under international pressure, the electronic media have often had to provide a relatively balanced presentation of the different parties and of the different candidates, when there are presidential contests. Thus, while it is clearly valuable that there should be fairness in the reporting of election campaigning on television, it is at least as important that there should be the same amount of fairness on radio – in particular on local radio – and in the press, a mode of behaviour which is perhaps less likely to occur as these are less open to international scrutiny. Moreover, the ownership of the media by the parties may be used to restrict access, as seems to have occurred with the KMT in Taiwan. Parties and candidates which do not benefit from a balanced coverage are therefore likely to suffer markedly, if the only occasion, or the main occasion at least, on which there is fairness in the media is in the course of election campaigns and on television only, while during the rest of the time and in the other media there is domination by the government.

The internal structure of parties and the democratization process

A favourable constitutional, electoral, and media environment is a pre-requisite for parties to be able to develop. If such an environment exists, parties have an opportunity to play a full part in the political life of their country; but this condition is not sufficient. There are well-known examples of countries in which liberal democratic rule has existed for decades and yet parties have not become strong. This has been the case, for instance, in France where, even since the advent of the Fifth Republic, let alone before, parties have been relatively weak and shaky. It has also been the case in many Latin American countries, Brazil in particular, where parties have to be described as inchoate. In the United States, too, parties have long tended to be almost empty shells and have become even more so in the last decades of the twentieth century. By contrast, parties in most of Continental Europe, but also in some Latin American countries, such as Costa Rica, Venezuela, Chile, or Argentina, have been strong, even very strong.

Mass parties v. parties of "notables"

In a democratic context, parties will tend to be strong if they have a stable relationship with their supporters in the electorate, a relationship which has been classically referred to as "party identification" (Budge, Crewe, and Fairlie 1973). This relationship also needs to exist in a national context if the parties are to be key agents of the democratization process – the parties which benefit from such an identification on a national basis being nationwide mass parties. Although claims about these parties have been exaggerated, especially with respect to the size of the membership and to the involvement of the members, nationwide mass parties are characterized by a well-implanted structure, with a network of provincial or regional organizations culminating in the national bodies (Duverger 1954). These parties contrast sharply with their opposite, which have been referred to as "cadre" parties in the translation of Duverger's work, but which should more aptly have been labelled parties of "notables":

parties without a developed formal structure whose base is constituted by well-known local figures, often landowners, but also professional people such as lawyers, doctors, and occasionally teachers. The appeal of these notables to electors is of a "clientelistic" character.

In traditional societies parties have often been led by notables, but these have been on the decline. While parties had this character in Western Europe in the nineteenth century, they have been progressively replaced by nationwide mass parties. Elsewhere, they have sometimes remained in existence during the modernization period, but they have also often disappeared. In many cases they went under as a result of the overthrow of the political system, for instance by a coup, when military rulers abolished party activity, at least for a while, or when strong leaders established a single-party system.

All these scenarios have taken place in East and Southeast Asia. In Thailand and the Philippines parties of notables have tended to remain in control; in Taiwan, there was single-party rule dominated for decades by a "charismatic" leader, before the democratization process led to the gradual decline of the role of that party; in Korea, the regime oscillated between near single-party government under military tutelage, and a pluralistic system in which notables played a large part. If full democratization were to take place in Malaysia and Singapore, the evolution would probably be similar to that of Taiwan, as the existing ruling parties of these two countries are well structured; in Indonesia, the "weight" of Golkar in the nation has been at best rather uneven and its future has become increasingly uncertain as a result of the fall of Suharto.

Social cleavages and the legitimation process of mass parties

For nationwide mass parties to emerge and be strong, two developments have to take place in succession. First, these parties need to be sustained by a broad social cleavage. In a celebrated article first published in 1970, Rokkan showed that a number of cleavages had been dominant in Western Europe in the nineteenth and early twentieth centuries, and that these cleavages had remained identical for at least a generation; indeed, the same cleavages have continued to play a significant part during yet another generation (Rokkan 1970). These cleavages relate to what can be described as "communal patterns of relationships." The most ancient among them is the tribal or clientelistic cleavage, which has given rise to locally based traditional parties of notables. Subsequently, as a result of changes in the social structure and of movements of population, further communal patterns of relationships began to prevail, based on ethnicity, religion, or class. These are the cleavages which have given rise to mass parties, typically of a nationwide character (Blondel 1995, 101).

The part played by these cleavages has been significant across the world, especially the industrial world. Thus the class cleavage and the religious cleavage have been at the origin of many parties across most of Western Europe and the Old Commonwealth, as well as in Japan, Israel, and some Latin American countries, Chile in particular; the ethnic cleavage, sometimes associated with the religious cleavage, has also been influential in many societies. Meanwhile, even the tribal or clientelistic cleavage of parties of notables has continued to play some part in modern societies, specifically in areas where feelings of local identity have remained strong and where local leaders are regarded as embodying and defending forcefully the interests of the area. These "communal" cleavages do not automatically lead to the establishment of parties, admittedly, as the conditions described in the previous section must be such that parties can develop freely and "naturally," but where these conditions obtain, nationwide parties are likely to begin to emerge from these patterns of relationships.

Yet a second characteristic has to exist for the mass parties to come to be fully "in orbit," so to speak. The loyalty to the group – ethnic, religious, or class based – has to be gradually transferred to the party so that the electors come to view the party, and not the "parent" group, as representing them. Time has therefore to elapse for the legitimation of the party to occur. If this process is not interfered with, by a coup or as a result of forms of authoritarian rule, the transfer of legitimacy takes place and the mass parties acquire a legitimacy of their own independently of the group from which they originated (Blondel 1995, 133–36). It is during that period that these parties establish their organization and acquire "members," a development which does not occur in the more clientelistic parties of notables as these remain dependent on their local leaders who do not see the need for and even do not want to create a formal organization which could constitute a challenge to their own power.

The partial erosion of support for mass parties in industrial societies and the emergence of "issue" parties

Starting in the 1960s, however, first in America and subsequently elsewhere in industrial societies, some erosion of the traditional loyalties to the mass parties began to occur, while, occasionally, new parties emerged without being based on social cleavages. Both these new parties and the established ones started to seek support on the basis of issues – environmental questions, for instance – as these issues were held to be relevant to some groups of electors.

Such a (partial) move from cleavages to issues as a basis for support has led to the suggestion that parties were becoming "producers" of "political goods," in the way that firms are producers of commercial goods: electors would come to choose among the parties as they choose among commercial products (Downs 1957). However, this change is unlikely ever to be complete as a party does not merely sell products but administers a country, and therefore needs loyalty to overcome the ups and downs of its fortunes which will inevitably result from time to time from its policies. Indeed, this loyalty is needed even in order to enable the party to "sell" its policies and its programmes and especially to do so over a substantial period: the same is also true of firms which have to enjoy at least some customer loyalty if they are to remain in business for long periods. Yet the move from cleavages to issues has led to an erosion of support for mass parties and consequently to what has been described as a greater "volatility" at elections, from one party to another, from established parties to issue-based parties and vice versa, and from participation to abstention (Pedersen 1983).

Four types of parties and the development of parties in East and Southeast Asia

A key distinction has therefore to be drawn among three main types of parties: mass parties which originate from an ethnic, religious, or class-based cleavage and which are in general national in character; traditional parties based on tribal or clientelistic loyalties, typically of a local nature; and issue-based parties set up without the support provided by one of the social cleavages, which tend to be small and often highly unstable. To these three types must be added a fourth, that of parties wholly created by a popular leader: such a development has characterized many countries in the process of democratization in the second half of the twentieth century, particularly in Africa. These distinctions are important in terms of the patterns of electoral behaviour, of the types and strength of the leadership, and of the importance given to ideology and policies.

Of these four types, the mass party is the one most likely to provide a basis for genuine democratization: mass parties should therefore come to prevail in East and Southeast Asia if the region is to consolidate its democratic development. Yet mass parties will not emerge unless there are broad national cleavages on which they can be based and unless time is allowed to elapse for these mass parties to go "into orbit." Neither of these two conditions can easily be fulfilled.

There are substantial differences across the region in this respect, admittedly. In Malaysia, the major parties have been established on the basis of an ethnic-cum-religious cleavage: were a move towards full democratization to take place in the country, the existing parties would constitute a natural basis for the consolidation of democracy. Differences of a "national" character appear also to account to a large extent for the division between the two main parties of democratic Taiwan: this is likely to lead to the consolidation of the regime. On the other hand, in Korea, the Philippines, and Thailand, the basis of party divisions appears to be primarily clientelistic and unstable alliances are likely to continue to prevail, while the future of parties in Singapore and Indonesia remains highly uncertain so long as no move towards full democratization is made.

Leadership

The nature of the leadership is markedly affected both by the nature of the parties and by the constitutional arrangements. The way succession takes place, the extent of stability of cabinets, and the power of leaders differ depending on whether the country has mainly mass parties, parties of notables, issue parties, or parties established by leaders on the basis of their popularity. Leadership characteristics differ also profoundly depending on whether the regime is parliamentary or presidential, especially within the parties which come to belong, if only from time to time, to the government.

Leadership suffers in those parliamentary systems in which parties are numerous or internally divided: in such cases, governmental instability is chronic and the effective power of leaders is limited or uncertain. The number of candidates for the leadership of the parties and of the government is large, either because the parties are small and there are many of them or because, when there are few of them, they are markedly divided internally, typically into factions of a local or regional character. Leadership battles tend to be fought either in or around a parliament which is jealous of its prerogatives: it is in parliament that governments are made and unmade, laws are passed, and the budget is adopted. Leadership is therefore mostly ad hoc, is typically transient, and emerges on the basis of deals struck to solve problems as they arise. In East and Southeast Asia, Thailand has typically suffered from weak parties operating in the context of a parliamentary system.

On the other hand, leaders are likely to be strong and to remain in office for long periods in parliamentary systems in which parties have a large electoral support and are national in character. Leadership contests within such parties may occasionally be tense, but they are likely to be resolved quickly, at least in the party or parties which belong to the government. If these party leaders are even only moderately successful in the conduct of public affairs, they are likely to enjoy considerable autonomy while in office, especially when one party is large enough to form the government on its own; they are often, but not always, less powerful and less autonomous if they are in a coalition, since they have then to strike compromises with their partners, unless one of the partners in the coalition is dominant as is typically the case in Germany. An example of strong parliamentary leadership in East and Southeast Asia is provided by Malaysia, where leadership contests within the major Malay party, UMNO, have occasionally been tense, but where these contests have in no way affected the power of leaders once they were elected.

Presidential systems render problems of leadership succession and stability less dependent on the nature of the parties – at least, on that of the party to which the president belongs. Fixed terms thus ensure that the chief executive remains in office even where parties do not have a national appeal, for instance if they are divided nationally because they are clientelistic; fixed terms also ensure that leadership contests in the party which controls the executive occur (normally) only towards the end of the tenure period and not at random intervals. Yet, with localized clientelistic parties, the number of candidates for the presidential nomination and for the subsequent presidential election may be very large and none of these candidates may come to obtain a substantial proportion of the votes, as has occurred in the Philippines, especially in 1992, at the second election after the ouster of Marcos: the result may well be a loss of authority of the chief executive. Thus the presidential system brings about solutions to only some of the problems resulting from the absence of well-established and disciplined parties, as a president who cannot rely on the support of a stable national party base experiences continual difficulties with the legislature. In East and Southeast Asia, Taiwan is the one fully liberal democratic presidential country in which parties are sufficiently well established for the chief executive to be able to enjoy strong and loyal support.

Ideologies, programmes, and policies: "Programmatic" and "representative" parties

Parties obviously differ sharply in their approach to policy-making. At one extreme, there are parties which wish to bring about a comprehensive programme of reforms; at the other, there are parties which are essentially concerned with managing the status quo; in between, many parties hope to implement their policies but also have an eye on their popularity. Parties can thus be divided into three broad groups from the point of view of their programmes and policies. Those that have a clear ideology which they try to implement can be labelled "programmatic"; those which tend to be mainly concerned with ensuring that they keep the support of their electors have been labelled "catch-all" by adherents of the commonly held view that the era of ideology has ended (Kirchheimer 1966; Bell 1961), but which could perhaps better be termed "representative"; and those which have no fixed policies at all can be described as "inchoate." The first group includes the mass parties as they were originally conceived, in particular on the Left; the second group is composed of the representative mass parties; and the third group includes among others the parties which tend to be clientelistic and within which local leaders play a major part.

Governmental programmes and policies can suffer where parties are inchoate, especially in the context of parliamentary systems, but also in presidential systems. There is likely to be obstruction on their part, or at least much objection to a strong policy line. On the other hand, parties which are highly programmatic are often viewed as rigid, a situation which may arise (and has often been criticized for being likely to arise) with strongly organized mass parties, in particular those of the Left (Michels 1911/1962).

As a matter of fact, such a rigidity of programmatic parties in a pluralistic Western context is more a myth than a reality: while it could be found sometimes to exist when these parties were in the opposition, it has always been rare when the same parties came to be in government. To an extent, the erosion of support suffered by many Western European parties has accelerated the move towards the abandonment of ideological purity and of programmatic rigidity, but even without their social base being eroded, indeed well before ideology was said to be in decline, the mass parties of Western Europe displayed flexibility. They did so for two main reasons. First, as we noted, the leadership of governing mass parties is typically able to enjoy considerable autonomy, in part because the victory of the party is often due to the leader's popularity. This feature does not date solely from the second half of the twentieth century but can be observed already in the nineteenth century, in Britain for instance, and it is common in successful mass parties. While there may be internal opposition and even major conflicts within these parties, leaders who are victorious at the polls are likely to be able to impose their views. Second, mass parties have had from very early on to take into account the mood of the electorate and in particular of that fraction of the electorate which appeared to have been most instrumental to their victory. This led to Western European mass parties being viewed as "catch-all" instead of ideological; but, while the expression was coined in the middle of the twentieth century, the phenomenon had in reality begun to occur earlier.

Representative mass parties, as we have termed the "catch-all" parties, are thus more flexible than the programmatic mass parties. They are therefore valuable instruments for governmental policy-making in the countries in which the bureaucracy plays a key, if varying, part in economic governance, as in the case of East and Southeast Asia. While parties which are internally divided because of their inchoate or clientelistic character, and because of the large number of competing leaders and subleaders which characterizes them, are unable to maintain a consistent policy line, representative mass parties with highly visible leaders are most likely to strike compromises designed to secure their global interests. These interests consist, indeed, in part simply in implementing their programme; they also consist in ensuring that they stay in power, as this is a sine qua non if they are to even begin to implement their programme.

Flexible representative mass parties have therefore to become the norm in East and Southeast Asia if democratization is to proceed smoothly in the area and take into account at least the broad sentiments of the population. Such parties cannot be established artificially where broad social cleavages do not give rise to them, however. By the late 1990s, Taiwan was the only country of the area in which the process of democratization was taking place with parties which had this representative character. Elsewhere, therefore, difficulties can be expected to arise. The only hope would be for clientelism to decline gradually, for localised parties to "gel," so to speak, as these become less concerned with local problems and feel obliged to adopt and stick to a national policy line. This development is perhaps not very likely but it could occur if some at least of the party leaders were to recognize that, for their countries to remain stable and democratic, the parties must have a well-developed structure within the population and endeavour to promote policies broad enough to appeal to substantial sections of the electorate and yet flexible enough to be realistic. Alternatively, the party leaders might feel that broad national policies are a way of consolidating their personal appeal on more secure foundations.

Party systems

The two forms of party competition

The process of democratic consolidation implies not only that parties be strong and lively but that they form a system in which no component is so dominant that the others become satellites or are marginal; for the extent of liveliness of the party structure itself has an impact on the extent of institutionalization of a pluralistic party system. If the parties are weak and almost inchoate, the party system is also weak; if, at the other extreme, one of the parties is so strong that it overshadows all the others, the party system is not pluralistic. For the party system to be both lively and pluralistic, the parties have to be strong, but not overwhelmingly so.

Moreover, for the party system to be genuinely pluralistic, there has to be real competition among its components. Competition can vary between two extremes. It can be in effect a state of war between strongly opposed "armies" when the parties are so close to the social cleavages from which they emerged that they have no wish to appeal to electors linked to other cleavages: thus ethnic or religious parties may merely be the mouthpieces of the ethnic or religious groups from which they proceed. At the other extreme, competition may resemble the contests in which firms engage in order to sell their products. This is likely to occur when each party is anxious to attract new electors by propounding programmes and policies which may appeal to those who were previously their opponents. In reality, most mass parties tend to follow an intermediate course between these two extremes: they wish to retain their traditional supporters while also making inroads into the territory of their competitors. Thus, for the electors, issues come to play a part alongside loyalty to a group.

The evolution of mass parties from support based on loyalty to support based on both loyalty and issues has clear advantages for the development of a stable party system. Given the loyalty which electors still feel for "their" parties, the party system is likely to become institutionalized and to display a low level of volatility. In particular, there are unlikely to be party splits in which some sections of one organization leave in order to join another, an occurrence which, on the contrary, tends to be found rather frequently among localized clientelistic parties: it is the absence of basic national group loyalties which accounts for the many splits which have taken place in the democratizing countries of East and Southeast Asia, for instance in Thailand, in Korea, or in the Philippines, and even to some extent in Taiwan. The limited character of the basic loyalties to broad social groups renders leaders and subleaders less hesitant to divide their parties and to attempt to form new ones.

On the other hand, only if there is a mix of group-based loyalties and of support based on issues can a party system function efficiently. If parties are almost entirely oriented to a strong cleavage of a communal character, of an ethnic or religious kind in particular, tension is likely to be high among the parties and the pluralistic regime may be difficult to maintain and may be overthrown. This kind of tension has often characterized "plural societies," a large number of which have succumbed to military regimes or to single-party dictatorships, in particular in Africa but also in Asia (Rabushka and Shepsle 1971; Vanhanen 1997). In reality, the difficulties experienced by Belgium and Canada in attempting to overcome their ethnolinguistic problems show that tensions of this kind are not confined to countries at a lower level of socio-economic development. On the other hand, although Malaysia stops somewhat short of being fully a liberal democracy, a degree of pluralism has been maintained in the context of a society in which deep ethnic conflicts could have taken place and might have resulted in a full-blown dictatorship being installed.

The consolidation of liberal democracy appears to require a move away from a type of party system configuration in which each component is tied to a broad social cleavage towards one in which the weight of these cleavages is balanced by the part played by issues. The party system must therefore go successively through two phases. It must first be established on the basis of broad social groups or groupings giving each party a stable support in the relation to the others; then, the link between parties and social groups has to be loosened somewhat so that genuine competition takes place among the parties, each of which then becomes anxious to gain the votes of middle-of-the-road electors who are not or no longer wholly committed to total loyalty to the social group to which they belong. Moreover, the move from the first to the second phase should not be so slow that each party finds it hard to leave the orbit of its original cleavage, a difficulty which has been experienced in Northern Ireland for decades and may be in the process of being experienced in Malaysia. If the move from the first to the second phase takes place relatively rapidly, on the other hand, the system will be institutionalized qua system, that is to say the population will view the parties as being in genuine, but "civilized" and fair competition, and the conditions for the consolidation of democracy will be met. There is then interplay between the parties as the influence of social cleavages on the parties declines; instead of there being a state of war between organizations fearing each other and viewing each other as dire enemies, there will merely be contests. Yet past loyalties will remain sufficiently strong between at least many of the voters and "their" parties for fluctuations in the electoral fortunes of the parties belonging to the system to remain relatively small.

Types of party systems

Pluralistic party systems depend therefore on the nature and the strength of the social cleavages in the country, as well as on the structure, leadership, and programmatic standpoints of the parties which compose them. Yet party systems also differ from each other, and differ markedly, as a result of both the number and the basic electoral support of those component organizations which can be deemed to be "significant," that is, able to play an effective part in the policy-making process of the country. Naturally, the more parties there are in a legislature, the smaller they are in size and the larger is the number of significant parties. Indeed, if the policies and programmes of very small parties are such that these come to be strategically placed in the configuration of the overall system, these small parties, too, may be significant even where there are few large ones: thus small nationalist parties have sometimes benefited from such a position in Western Europe, Britain, and Spain, for instance. Yet the number of significant parties remains relatively small in consolidated liberal democracies: it ranges from two or three to perhaps six or seven.

If number and relative size are taken into account, pluralistic party systems can be divided into four broad types: two-party systems, two-and-a-half-party systems, multi-party systems with a dominant party, and multi-party systems without a dominant party. In the first group, two more or less equal parties dominate the scene, Britain being a case in point. In the second, there are two large parties and a much smaller third one, but this third party often holds the balance of power: this has been for a long time the situation in Germany. In the third group, there are four or five significant parties, but one of them is as large or almost as large as all the others together, a configuration which has been characteristic of several Scandinavian countries, and in particular of Sweden. Finally, in the fourth group, there are the same number of truly significant parties, but all of them are of about equal strength and are therefore rather small, Switzerland being the archetype in this category. This fourfold classification was first developed for Western party systems, but it has also tended to correspond in broad terms, to party system configurations not just in Western countries, but in other democracies, in particular Japan, Israel, and most Commonwealth and Latin American democracies (Blondel 1968; Blondel 1995, 170–72; Sartori 1976).

Admittedly, in countries in the process of democratization, especially outside the Commonwealth, and particularly in the early stages of this process, there has often been a single party or a party which is so dominant that it overwhelms all the others and treats them either as irrelevant or as satellites: this was the case for a long time in Mexico. As such a dominant single party should decline before the party system becomes genuinely pluralistic and comes close to one of the four categories which have just been described, the democratization process always takes time: in Taiwan, for instance, the evolution began in the second half of the 1980s and was not complete by the late 1990s. In the intervening period, during which the strength of the "controlling" single party is eroded but is still large, that party continues to hold an "abnormal" position in the party system configuration.

In the East and Southeast Asian context, the party systems of the countries in the process of democratization have remained volatile as the electoral fortunes of the components of these systems have been subject to wide fluctuations. Taiwan is the exception: it is slowly moving towards a two-and-a-half-party system or towards a multi-party system with a dominant party. In Korea, the Philippines, and above all in Thailand, on the other hand, the institutionalization of the party system seems still rather remote: the consolidation of democracy seems therefore also somewhat problematic in these countries. Admittedly, there were no signs at the end of the twentieth century suggesting that the democratic process might be halted; but there were no signs either that a stable party system was about to be established. This is manifestly due to the fact that, in these three countries, in contrast to Taiwan, parties have not been based on a national social cleavage and the bond between some of the parties and their electors has typically been clientelistic and localized.

Adversarial v. consociational party systems

The cases of Malaysia and to a lesser extent of Singapore suggest that party systems can move from the first phase to a different second phase, however, with important implications for the structure and composition of the national government. The process of consolidation of democracy which has been described so far assumes that the party system must remain competitive because politics is inherently conflictual: the pluralistic context merely "civilizes" and "domesticates" these conflicts. In such a model of liberal democratic politics, the relationship between the parties is adversarial. This is the model which has characterised Anglo-Saxon countries in general and Britain in particular (Finer 1975; Lijphart 1984).

The other model of pluralist liberal democracy is based, not on competition, but on association or "accommodation," as Lijphart has labelled it (Lijphart 1977). Instead of behaving as firms do in a market, parties can decide to collaborate. When leaders of the main social groups recognize that none of them can win and indeed that attempting to be victorious would be dangerous for the very existence of the polity because the cleavages are fundamentally exclusive, competition seems inappropriate and the solution seems to be to move towards a "consociational" model, sometimes described by Lijphart as "consensual" – probably exaggeratedly, as not all the parties, not even all the significant parties, typically belong to the arrangement. Such a model has been shown to characterize a number of Continental countries, in particular Belgium, the Netherlands, Switzerland, and, with variations and intermittently, Austria (Lijphart 1984).

Indeed, as the links forged in this manner are very strong, it has come to be suggested that the parties formed in reality a cartel aiming by a variety of means at remaining indefinitely in (or very near) power. One of these means is the distribution of substantial amounts of public funds to the political parties, those belonging to the cartel being the largest beneficiaries since they happen also to be the largest parties (Katz and Mair

1995). While the concept of a party cartel may be somewhat exaggerated, it does highlight the fact that the same parties tend to work together to run a country and, in doing so, help each other to maintain the influence which, for decades, they have come to exercise.

As a matter of fact, the adversarial and the consociational models are in reality two extreme poles of a continuum: consolidated party systems can take many intermediate forms, depending on whether the system is wholly adversarial (as two-party systems often, but not always, are) or wholly consociational (as multi-party systems are more likely to be but are not always). In a certain sense, the Malaysian experiment partakes of both models and is truly intermediate: there is both an opposition to the governmental coalition and a consociational coalition composed of parties representing the key social cleavages in the society. This is indeed why it is difficult to determine whether Malaysia is to be regarded as being in the process of consolidating democracy or remains outside the democratic framework altogether. The parties, at least the main parties which belong to the governmental coalition, are manifestly institutionalized; yet the accommodation which takes place among these parties is accompanied by a variety of practices which make it very difficult for parties not belonging or not wanting to belong to that coalition to compete with it on fair terms. So long as this occurs, it is difficult to conclude that the consolidation process has truly taken place. Yet this does not mean that accommodation and consociationalism do not constitute a route towards this consolidation process, as the evidence from a number of Western countries clearly indicates, especially where it seems very difficult, if not impossible, to reduce the intensity of broad social cleavages within the population and therefore their effect on the relationship between electors and "their" parties.

Parties are tools: they can be used to foster democracy, but they can also be used – and often are used – to prevent democracy from being established. Although they then appear to forge a link between people and government, this is at best in order to mobilize the population in the full military sense of the word rather than in order to achieve representation. Yet lively and functioning parties are needed if democracy is to be established and consolidated, though the ways in which they help to consolidate democracy are complex and rather tortuous. Parties cannot consolidate democracy if they are not themselves institutionalized, that is to say if they do not have profound roots in the society as a result of which they come to be genuinely in communication with their electors, and thus both represent them and are able to lead them. For this to be achieved, however, parties have to be truly distinct from each other. The link between a party and its supporters is strong only if these supporters are very disinclined to join other parties; they will be disinclined to do so if they are markedly opposed to these parties. At the same time, liberal democracy cannot function unless the parties tolerate each other and indeed come to collaborate with each other over at least some matters. Hence the key difficulty which the question of consolidation of democracy poses: there must be enough opposition among the parties for loyalties to be strong, but there must also be enough toleration for a climate of liberalism to prevail.

This contradictory pull is encapsulated in the party system, as this determines both the differences and the links which exist among the parties. These links can be stronger or looser. The mode may be one of accommodation or one of adversarial politics; but the accommodation must not be so close that parties form a cartel and come to dominate the society. Nor should the adversarial practices be so brutal that the party system is in constant danger of breaking up and of giving way to the authoritarian domination of one party over the others.

There is an inevitable tension in the process of consolidation of democracy. This tension is accentuated if another element is present in the equation, the goal of economic development. For the party system to enable economic development to take place regularly and at a rapid pace, a number of constraints have to be imposed on the nature and character of the battles which the parties fight. The parties have to respect certain policy objectives and they have to be prepared to extend accommodation to a different organ of the policy-making process, the bureaucracy. As economic development has been for decades the number one goal which the polities of East and Southeast Asia have pursued, the democratization process is unlikely to be successful in these countries unless the parties truly make that goal their own. We must therefore examine the characteristics of economic governance in the East and Southeast Asian context before considering whether there is truth in the idea that liberal democracy might impede economic development.

REFERENCES

Alexander, H. E. (1989), *Comparative Political Finance in the 1980s*, Cambridge University Press, Cambridge.
Bartolini, S. and Mair, P. (1990), *Identity, Competition, and Electoral Availability: The Stabilisation of European Electorates 1885–1985*, Cambridge University Press, Cambridge.
Bell, D. (1961), *The End of Ideology*, Collier, New York.

Blondel, J. (1968), "Party Systems and Patterns of Government in Western Democracies," *Canadian Journal of Political Science* (June), pp. 180–203.
—— (1995), *Comparative Government*, Prentice-Hall, London.
Blumler, J. (1983), *Communicating to Voters*, Sage, Los Angeles.
Blumler, J. and Gurevitch, M. (1995), *The Crisis of Public Communication*, Routledge, London.
Budge, I., Crewe, I., and Fairlie, D. (eds.) (1973), *Party Identification and Beyond*, Wiley, London.
Coppedge, M. (1994), *Strong Parties and Lame Ducks: Presidential Patriarchy and Factionalism in Venezuela*, Stanford University Press, Stanford, Calif.
De Fleur, M. L. and Ball-Rokeach, S. (1982), *Theories of Mass Communication*, Longmans, New York.
Downs, A. (1957), *An Economic Theory of Democracy*, Harper, New York.
Duverger, M. (1954), *Political Parties*, Wiley, New York.
Farrell, D. (1997), *Comparing Electoral Systems*, Prentice-Hall, London.
Finer, S. E. (1975), *Adversarial Government*, Oxford University Press, Oxford.
Halloran, J. D. (ed.) (1970), *The Effects of Television*, Panther Books, London.
Katz, R. S. and Mair, P. (1995), "Changing Models of Party Organisation and Party Democracy: The Emergence of the Cartel Party," *Party Politics* 1, pp. 5–28.
Kirchheimer, O. (1996), "The Transformation of the Western European Party Systems," in J. La Palombara and M. Weiner (eds.), *Political Parties and Political Development*, Princeton University Press, Princeton, N.J.
Leduc, L., Niemi, R., and Norris, P. (eds.) (1996), *Comparing Democracies: Elections and Voting in Global Perspective*, Sage, Thousand Oaks, Calif.
Linz, J. (1990), "The Perils of Presidentialism," *Journal of Democracy* 1(1), pp. 59–69.
Lijphart, A. (1977), *The Politics of Accommodation*, University of California Press, Berkeley, Calif.
—— (1984), *Democracies*, Yale University Press, New Haven, Conn.
—— (1994), *Electoral Systems and Party Systems*, Oxford University Press, Oxford.
Lipset, S. M. (1983), *Political Man*, Heinemann, London.
Mainwaring, S. and Scully, T. R. (eds.) (1995), *Party Systems in Latin America*, Stanford University Press, Stanford, Calif.
Michels, R. (1962), *Political Parties* (1911), Free Press, New York.
Norris, P. (1997), "Choosing Electoral Systems: Proportional, Majoritarian and Mixed Systems," *International Political Science Review* 18(3), pp. 297–312.
Ostrogorski, M. (1902), *Democracy and the Organization of Political Parties*, Macmillan, New York.
Pedersen, M. (1983), "Changing Patterns of Electoral Volatility in European Party Systems 1948–1977: Explorations in Explanation," in H. Daalder and P. Mair (eds.), *Western European Party Systems*, Sage, Los Angeles, Calif.
Rabushka, A. A. and Shepsle, K. A. (1971), *Politics in Plural Societies*, Merrill, Columbus, Ohio.
Rae, D. (1967), *The Political Consequences of Electoral Laws*, Yale University Press, New Haven, Conn.

Rokkan, S. (1970), *Citizens, Elections, Parties*, Universitetsforlaget, Oslo.

Sartori, G. (1976), *Parties and Party Systems*, Cambridge University Press, Cambridge.

Shugart, M. S. and Carey, J. M. (1992), *Presidents and Assemblies*, Cambridge University Press, New York.

Taylor, R. H. (1996), *The Politics of Elections in Southeast Asia*, Cambridge University Press, Cambridge.

Vanhanen, T. (1990), *The Process of Democratisation: A Comparative Study of 147 States, 1980–1988*, Crane Russak, New York.

3

Economic governance and economic performance

Ian Marsh

This chapter considers economic governance both as a kind of ideal type and as it has occurred in the states of East and Southeast Asia. Three issues are explored. The first is the link between economic governance and economic performance. Theories that specify causalities deductively and empirical studies that do so inductively are reviewed and potential causal links are operationalized. Second, using these categories and variables as a framework, the actual practice of economic governance in a number of East and Southeast Asian states is sketched, essentially as an indicative exercise. Third, the extent to which patterns of economic governance are common amongst states of the region is assessed and the principal pressures affecting this activity are summarized. This will enable us, in the next chapter, to consider the impact of democratization on economic governance.

Until the financial reverse of 1997, the states of East and Southeast Asia had a remarkable record of economic achievement. The 1997 crisis began in the financial sector and affected those states with greatest dependence on foreign investment (Thailand, Indonesia, Philippines, Malaysia) and/or with extensive short-term borrowings (Korea). The predatory possibilities of Korea's chaebol had already been recognised (Evans 1995; Clifford 1997; Ernst 1996). Similarly, the role of "money politics" in Malaysia, of predation and rent seeking in Indonesia, and of corruption in Thailand were acknowledged (e.g., Gomez and Jomo 1997; Gomez 1998). These structural conditions were not the only elements in the crisis. Other ingredients included: the enthusiasm with which financial institutions lent funds to regional companies and intermediaries; change in the relative competitiveness of affected states (particularly following China's 1995 devaluation); and the capacity of states to upgrade technologically in step with rising wage rates (Thurow 1998; Radelet and Sachs 1997; Wade 1998). Later analysis may identify other causes. The immediate consequence is a reduction in the expectations for growth in the affected states and in the region as a whole (World Bank 1998). The IMF has required affected states to implement budgetary, financial sector, and other institutional changes. The medium-term outlook depends on how individual political systems absorb the twin pressures of recession and institutional change. More distantly, a Chinese devaluation or a slump in Japan would compound the difficulties of adaptation.

Yet productive capacity of East and Southeast Asia remains strong. The region as a whole has dominated global output of a variety of manufactured products. For example, in 1994, regional production amounted to over 60 per cent of world production of radio–tape players, VCRs, bicycles, microwave ovens, colour TVs, air conditioners, refrigerators, watches, and ships, and just under 40 per cent of world production of automobiles and steel manufactures (*Nikkei Weekly*, 3 October 1994). Export-led industrialization has been the engine of economic development. In turn, this has stimulated the growth of domestic capital, infrastructure, and consumer goods markets, culminating in the 1997 bubble.

Save for Hong Kong, government has taken an active part in economic management in all the states of industrializing Asia (Stiglitz 1996). The experience of Japan provided a model for Taiwan and Korea (Kim et al. 1995). The different circumstances of Southeast Asian states have circumscribed Japan's relevance to them. Economic globalization, manifested vividly in the events of 1997, is a constraining element. This is the context for exploring the links between economic governance and economic performance. On the basis of varying perspectives drawn mainly from economics but also from political science and from such eclectic approaches as business strategy, a substantial body of empirical work about economic governance in regional states has emerged. However, comparison and synthesis is difficult, not least because of different premises and different methodologies. Nevertheless, recent developments in institutional and evolutionary economics have begun to provide a link, and a common framework can perhaps be explored. In particular, the latter theorizes the causal linkage between economic governance and economic performance, albeit at a high level of generality. Meanwhile, the empirical literature suggests some of the detailed elements – although the events of 1997 suggest its incompleteness.

One threshold difference in economic governance between individual states of the region arises from the duration and level of their economic performance and the primary source of investment. In this perspective, the eight states covered in this study fall into three categories. The first group is composed of Singapore, Korea, Hong Kong, and Taiwan. These states have enjoyed sustained growth, at least since the seventies; all four remain significant global competitors in electronics, computing, and information technology (IT), and are seeking positions in advanced technology sectors: with the exception of Singapore, indigenous firms, not DFI, have been the engine of development. In this group, Korea alone was immediately affected by the 1997 crisis. The countries of the second category, Malaysia, Indonesia, and Thailand, experienced accelerated development after the Plaza Accords of 1986. To a large degree these states have become production sites for industries from Japan. They remain underdeveloped by comparison with those of the previous group: even if they sustained growth rates of 7 per cent p.a., it would have taken Malaysia 17 years, Thailand 22 years, and Indonesia 46 years to achieve Korea's 1990 per capita income (MacIntyre 1994a, 16). Finally, the Philippines is in a third category as its experience of development dates from the early 1990s. All the states in the last two groups were implicated in the 1997 crisis.

Economic governance and economic performance: Theory

The state as a distinctive learning environment

Studies of economic performance based in neoclassical economics discount the role of the state beyond the establishment of a liberal market system, appropriate fiscal and monetary settings, and skills development (Krugman 1994): these deductive analyses therefore contest the link between economic governance and performance. Studies which emphasize the role of state institutions typically generalize from empirical appraisals of arrangements and are therefore essentially inductive. However, evolutionary and institutional economics have added new dimensions to the case for asserting that there is a causal link between economic governance and economic performance on the basis of a framework consistent with the historical record of optimal solutions often ignored; efficient solutions rarely replicated; decline experienced as often as development; and limited convergence between states and between firms from different states.

Both evolutionary and institutional economics share the premise that the actors (firms, state agencies, politicians, citizens) make their choices on the basis of bounded rationality and genuine uncertainty: path dependence thus becomes a key influence in development. In addition, institutional economics focuses on transaction costs, which are indeed held to be the decisive influence in long-term performance. Douglass North proposes "adaptive efficiency" as the relevant norm. This embodies "the willingness of a society to acquire knowledge and learning, to induce innovation, to undertake risk and creative activity of all sorts, as well as resolve problems and bottlenecks of the society through time" (North 1992, 80).

Jettisoning the neoclassical model of choice opens up the issue of the genesis and propagation of the motives and ideas which guide business firms, citizens, organized interests, the political leadership, and the bureaucracy. According to North, the state and the political system more generally influence what actors identify as relevant information and how they gather, process, and act on the latter (North 1992, 76, 111).

Transaction costs are also critical causal variables. These arise in measuring the valued attributes of what is being exchanged, of protecting rights, and of enforcing agreements. The polity is the setting in which trust (an informal constraint) and credible commitments (a formal constraint) can be mobilized: the level of trust and credible commitments, among others, determines the transaction costs to be faced by firms in the market.

There are thus at least four broad ways in which economic governance might contribute to economic performance: first, actions contributing to the generation of ideas, choice sets, and motives; second, actions reducing transaction costs; third, actions stimulating creativity, innovation, and skills; and, fourth, actions inhibiting and/or correcting government failure.

A critical threshold concerns the characteristics of the state as a learning system and of the polity as a learning environment. To play an effective part in economic performance, the state must constitute a setting in which, despite bounded rationality and uncertainty, distinctive information can be gathered and distinctive perspectives framed (Kelm 1996; Marsh 1995). If the information and perspectives generated from the state cannot be distinguished from those of private actors, the state's role is obviously weakened, if not even negated; its capacity for leadership and for acting as a catalyst in selective interventions is markedly affected.

The state's learning and teaching capacities arise from two broad sources. The first is the public policy agenda: it is the deposit of an extended historical process, which largely determines the questions addressed in technical analysis and the context in which this occurs. Perhaps more importantly, this process also determines pertinent values. In turn, the public policy agenda affects the spatial and temporal comprehensiveness and reach of the state's information gathering and judgements. It also affects the state's conception of its dissemination and mobilization task.

The second source of distinctive state capacities arises from the institutions through which the broader community and particular interests are mobilized and information is disseminated. These, too, are historical deposits. The presence and impact of these two factors can be explored comparatively and empirically (Hall and Taylor 1996; Steinmo et al. 1993). In general, the scope of politics and the role of the state in strategic socio-economic developments is the basis for differentiating the information generated and the perspective formed by private and public actors.

Third, the different conceptions of their role held by different states can be assessed through such factors as the economic, social, and other issues on the public agenda, the temporal horizon within which perspectives are framed, and the range of values and remedies conventionally recognized as relevant: these are the "ideas in good currency" (Schon 1971).

Fourth and finally, depending on how the state construes its role, it might be expected to have different motives from those of business organizations in gathering information and framing perspectives. Indeed, how the state construes its role may be an important constitutive element in the formation of business motives, ideas, and choice sets.

The state is not only an agent of scanning and discovery: it is also a constitutive setting for the formation of the motives, choice sets, and ideas of private actors. The state is a kind of learning system within which private actors are situated and in which they participate. Both through the distinctive information and perspectives it gathers and through its specific authoritative role in information dissemination and interest and citizen mobilization, the state is an important potential influence on the motives, ideas, and choice sets of private actors, whether they are individual citizens or business firms. The state's impact on these relationships is brokered by both a variety of media and a host of intermediary associations and institutions.

Developmental state theory

These propositions about the causes of longer-term economic performance and about the distinctiveness of the state as a learning environment provide a link to the inductive literature on what are termed "developmental states." At the core of developmental states is an elaborate practice of economic governance. Descriptions of economic governance are available in the literature on "governed markets" (Wade 1990), "governed interdependence" (Weiss and Hobson 1995), and "embeddedness" (Evans 1992, 1995). These studies deal with state penetration of, or "embeddedness" in the surrounding society and specifically with business-government relations, as well as with "state steering" capacities. Broader community mobilization on behalf of developmental goals has also been mentioned as an additional causal element in longer-term economic performance (Campos and Root 1996). These concepts suggest ways in which the abstract notion of economic governance might be operationalized.

Business-government collaboration

Evans (1995) identifies at least three criteria for effective collaboration between business and the state: the forums available for interaction; the sources of influence at the disposal of the state; and the capacity of business to participate in these exchanges. The first criterion is constituted by the modes of exchange: it refers to the institutional arrangements through which interaction between government and business takes place. Japan, for instance, the paradigm case, is characterized by deep formal and informal exchanges (Okimoto 1989; McMillan 1996). Arrangements that are more or less elaborate and more or less collaborative have been identified in the other states of the area.

The second criterion is constituted by the resources available to the state to influence behaviour in its exchanges with business. These include coercive, indirect, and cooperative instruments. Legal authority provides coercive influence; the ability to allocate capital or specific tax or subsidy arrangements might constitute indirect influence; and provision of valued information constitutes the third source of influence. Commentators have pointed to a move from the former to the latter modes as relationships develop from a directive towards a more collaborative pattern. States with collaborative business-government relations possess an array of deliberative councils.

The third criterion concerns the extent to which business is organized in associations. These might be more or less independent from the state, but organization and representation are essential for effective interaction: an atomized business sector would not be able to enter into or maintain ordered relations.

The role of labour, which has not generally been treated as a partner of equivalent standing to business, might also be noted. For example, in Japan, after initial unrest, integration was largely accomplished at the firm level through enterprise unions. Wage decisions are co-ordinated through the annual *Shunto* round (Sako 1997). Analogous arrangements exist in Singapore, Taiwan, and Thailand. Korean labour relations are more turbulent, and unions are handled differently in Indonesia and Malaysia.

State autonomy

Economic governance also involves what is termed state autonomy. If the state is to play a catalytic role, it must display a capacity for independent strategic and tactical planning. This process might be more or less collaborative and more or less iterative; but the requirement that the state be able to take an independent view of its strategic economic priorities is fundamental.

Evans (1995) enumerates three conditions for state autonomy to be realized without rent seeking. The first is constituted by strategic institutions (see also Wade 1990, 322–23). Directing institutions must be able to evaluate longer-term economic priorities and propose goals, at least as a contribution to a subsequent debate. The state must have at its disposal institutions that can frame a view about its desired economic future. This has been the classic role of MITI in Japan. The second condition is bureaucratic prestige, which is required to render a public service career valued and respected and therefore able to attract talented and qualified recruits. In Confucian states, this prestige is grounded in a tradition of bureaucratic social leadership; in other cases equivalent arrangements need to be present. The third condition is bureaucratic integration: talented bureaucrats might otherwise be attracted to extend their personal power or their "turf" at the expense of larger public goals. An *esprit de corps* and a sense of common purpose strong enough to counteract these tendencies needs to exist in the elite bureaucracy: this could be maintained through socialization, in more material ways, or both.

There is a fourth condition of state autonomy, moreover, as the three features which have just been described could be present in states in which there are no strategic economic or structural aims: manifest economic priorities are a sign that such aims exist. These priorities might emerge in three areas at least: the identification and orchestration of action relating to growth sectors (from the perspective of employment, output, or trade); the identification and orchestration of action for the development and commercialization of new technologies; and the elaboration of mechanisms designed to ease the difficulties of declining industries. Empirical studies attest to activities of all three of these types in Japan (Tilton 1996), although there is disagreement with respect to the second of these types (Callon 1995).

Technology development has been particularly significant in contributing to regional economic growth. The state has played a part, more or less directly, in its stimulation (Hobday 1995; Matthews 1997a). Reverse engineering has been an effective catching-up strategy (Magaziner and Patinkin 1995, 235–50), and Wade (1992) judges this to have been central to the economic success of the states of the area: "late industrialisation . . .

has been a political process shaped by the exigencies of mastering (and learning) already existing technologies." This strategy has become less effective because of the impact of microelectronics on both product and production processes (Bernard and Ravenhill 1995, 171–209; Hobday 1995). Innovation has been found to pose special challenges to particular states (e.g. Korea, Ernst 1996).

Shared growth

Shared growth as a distinctive feature of states of the area is noted as an important feature in a number of studies; income distribution data also point to the relative success of this strategy (World Bank 1993; Campos and Root 1996). This strategy has been said to result from the need for legitimacy on the part of the political leadership, as Wade states: "What should be at the heart of a politics of economic growth [is] rulers' and would be rulers' calculations, that is how they attempt to secure support, by what mix of policies designed to appeal to which groups, with what political success, and at what political cost" (1992, 309).

Economic governance and economic performance: Practice

If we concentrate on institutional analysis, four broad factors accounting for economic performance can be identified: the development of appropriate ideas, choice sets, and motives; the minimization of transaction costs; the encouragement of innovation, creativity, and skills; and the minimization and subsequent correction of governmental failure. These four factors provide the basic headings for the following survey of East and Southeast Asian practice. The subheadings within each of the four basic headings are drawn from the developmental state analysis.

Hong Kong is not considered in detail because of the distinctive character of its approach to policy-making. As a matter of fact, two studies of Hong Kong's future economic strategy reach contrary conclusions about what the state should do, one recommending an active and selective role (Berger and Lester 1997) and the other pressing for the maintenance of the existing approach (Enright et al. 1996).

Ideas, choice sets, and motives

According to Garrett and Weingast, the capacity of ideas to facilitate co-operation is a function of three factors, "i) the gains to be expected from co-operation among a relevant set of players, ii) an idea which expresses these gains from co-operation, and iii) a mechanism devised to translate the idea into a shared belief system so as to affect expectations and hence behaviour" (1993, 203–5).

Ideas might be deployed at both national and sectoral levels. At the national level, the state might champion longer-term socio-economic objectives and mobilize popular support on their behalf; this might be expected to influence the expectations of individual citizens and their understanding of the steps which have to be taken in order that the desired outcomes be achieved. In particular, linkages between the national and the global economy might be better understood and the implications accepted. Meanwhile, the potential positive-sum character of the national socio-economic project might be articulated and its terms affirmed. These points would be expressed in terms appropriate to the particular political culture or other sources of normative authority; they would have to be substantiated by technical analysis.

At the sectoral level, these broad purposes would need to be translated into programmes: similar outcomes in terms of ideas, choice sets, and motives might be stimulated in this way. The process would have to be collaborative and reciprocal: commitment would thus be built and the process of adaptation eased. While unanimity would be neither achieved nor expected, a majority coalition would be established and maintained.

Ideas, choice sets, and motives at the national level

At least five elements of governance might contribute to the development of ideas, choice sets, and motives at the national level: the establishment of strategic social and economic goals; elite economic agencies responsible for defining and refining these goals; leadership consensus; active advocacy; and appropriate outcomes.

STRATEGIC SOCIO-ECONOMIC GOALS

There is evidence of the adoption of broad socio-economic goals by all states, though with varying degrees of explicit articulation. For example, according to Kim, in Japan, "the idea of catching up and surpassing the West (*oitsuke, oikose*) was generally accepted throughout the population, including by the elite of the ruling party.... It was the pervasive anxiety arising from *fuan* (insecurity) that helped mobilise the people.... The state adopted the principle of shared growth" (Kim et al. 1995, 515).

In the case of Korea, Campos and Root suggest, "For economic growth to be a substitute for legitimacy it had to be transformed into a symbol.... that symbol in Korea was ... double digit GNP growth ... the Korean score in the race to catch up with Japan" (1996, 34). In relation to Singapore, Khong (1995, 112) suggests that Lee sought "to legitimise his rule through the promise of economic performance" and Cheng and Haggard suggest that Taiwan adopted the principle of shared growth from 1949 (1992, 22). Similar conditions existed in Southeast Asia. In Thailand, Sarit justified his 1958 coup as essential for both security and development; MacIntyre suggests that Suharto also sought legitimacy by promising economic growth (1994b, 242); in Malaysia's case, Gomez and Jomo suggest that redistribution has been given priority over growth (1997).

ELITE AGENCIES

In emulation of Japan's MITI, elite agencies concerned with the strategic economic or socio-economic outcomes have been set up in every state. Their effectiveness, however, varies widely. Strong agencies include Singapore's Ministry of Trade; Korea's Economic Planning Board, and since 1995 the Ministry of Finance and the Economy (Lee 1997); and Taiwan's Council of Economic Planning and Development and the Industrial Structure Bureau in the Ministry of Economic Affairs. Parallel agencies can be identified in Southeast Asian states, but various studies suggest they are much less well insulated from political pressures and/or much less authoritative in the public policy process than those noted above (Gomez and Jomo 1997; MacIntyre 1994). In Malaysia, strategic policy-making is concentrated in the Economic Planning Unit in the Prime Minister's Department. This has a staff of around 80 professionals, of whom 90 per cent have at least a master's degree. The Institute of Strategic and International Studies (ISIS) is a quasi-independent think tank associated with the government; it was particularly active in the development of the broader "2020" vision, and is also the co-ordinating agency with the peak national business organization, the Malaysia Business Council.

Indonesia's strategic agencies include the National Planning Agency (Bappenas), the Ministry of Finance, and the Investment Co-ordination Board. An Agency for Strategic Industries was established in 1984; its role has since expanded to managing state-owned strategic industries in the areas of transportation, information, telecommunications, and electronics.

There are four elite agencies in Thailand: the National Economic and Social Development Board (NESDB), the Bank of Thailand, the Board of Investments, and the Bureau of the Budget in the Ministry of Finance. The NESDB was established in 1959 and is directed by a 15-member committee including key public executives, the governor of the Bank of Thailand, the secretary-general of the Civil Service Commission, the director of the Bureau of the Budget, the director-general of the Fiscal Policy Office, the secretary-general of the NESDB, and nine members appointed by the Cabinet. There is also a Joint Public/Private Sector Consultative Committee (NJPPCC), established in 1980 by the NESDB, which identifies issues affecting economic development. Finally, in the Philippines, the elite agencies include the Department of Finance, the central bank, the Department of Trade and Industry, and the National Economic Development Authority (Velasco, this volume; also Rivera 1996).

The central strategic agencies in each state are responsible for the preparation and dissemination of longer-term plans. With the exception of Thailand, the Philippines, and Indonesia, projections are based on industrial structure outcomes, not economic magnitudes; they will therefore be examined in the next section. Singapore has begun to experiment with scenario planning as the basis for a revision of its development strategy (Schwartz 1991).

In states where strategic agencies are strongest, government service continues to be an elite activity associated with high social prestige. In Japan, law graduates from Tokyo University constitute 14 per cent of the applicants but 35 to 40 per cent of the intake. Similarly, in Korea, 55 per cent of the intake comes from Seoul National University and 45 per cent from two prestigious Seoul high schools; engineers predominate in Taiwan's Industrial Development Bureau; and Singapore rewards its civil servants well, with "public sector salaries ... higher on average than private sector salaries and higher than salaries of equivalent senior officials in the US" (Campos and Root 1996, 143).

The relationship between the elite bureaucracy and the political leadership varies between states. In relation to Japan, Inoguchi suggests that "the national bureaucracy does not seem to be ready to relinquish its power.... it is the only feasible agent for making the body politic reasonably cohesive" (1997). The situation in East and Southeast Asia varies in this respect. In Korea, public policy power is concentrated in the president's hands and the bureaucracy plays a less independent role than in Japan, although Matthews suggests bureaucratic authority may be reasserted in the wake of the financial crisis (1998). Taiwan and Singapore are intermediate between Korea and Japan.

In Southeast Asia, the situation is again different. For example, in Thailand the bureaucratic elite is distant from political influence, as a result of civil service traditions established under the absolute monarchy, while parliament has a minimal role in determining public spending, even though elected politicians are influential in implementing policies. This division of roles between executive and legislators has given technocrats scope to pursue a conservative macroeconomic agenda. These "tend to distrust the line ministries, believing that they are dominated by narrow bureaucratic and political interests" (Christenson et al. 1993, 24). Endemic corruption at these levels and continuing military influence did impede economic development until the collapse of 1997. (Suchit 1996;

Anek 1996). The independent standing of the Bank of Thailand was compromised in a corruption scandal in 1996. In the Philippines, the elite bureaucracy has retained its autonomy.

LEADERSHIP CONSENSUS

Taiwan, Korea, Thailand, Malaysia, and the Philippines all have political opposition parties, none of which opposes the strategy of economic growth and all of which support an activist state. In Singapore and Indonesia, the opposition is not significant, as was already indicated in the previous chapter.

ACTIVE ADVOCACY

Detailed evidence of the steps taken within each state to mobilize the society on behalf of developmental objectives remains to be gathered. Before the financial crisis, and ostensibly at least, Malaysia appears to have gone furthest by elaborating three components, a "vision," ten-year outline plans, and a five-year operating plan. In 1991, *Vision 2020*, adopted by the government, envisaged the country to be by that year a fully developed society. This was supported by an Outline Perspective Plan for the 1990s, covering macroeconomic prospects, sectoral targets, and human resource development, which identified the major steps required for the 2020 goals to be realized. This Outline Plan is supported by a Five-Year Plan, which details the macroeconomic and sectoral targets needed to implement the larger objectives as well as social balance and ethnic issues; educational issues, including the needs for professional, technical, and related workers; and the desired R & D levels (0.5 per cent in the mid-1990s). Detailed evidence on how popular support is mobilized for these objectives has still to be gathered.

APPROPRIATE OUTCOMES

One of the distinctive features of the region's experience has been the association of economic growth with diminished income inequality (Campos and Root 1996; World Bank 1993). The point is to some extent disputed, however: Evans acknowledges the general participation of the population in the prosperity in Taiwan and Korea, but suggests that a cloak of legitimacy has been given in this way to narrower interests and to "a kind of Gramscian hegemony in East Asia" (1992, 181). In Indonesia's case, Mochtar suggests that economic growth "has benefited the urban and modern sectors considerably while marginalizing the rural and traditional ones" (Mochtar 1995, 277). Campos and Root argue about Thailand that "underinvestment in postprimary education had a negative effect on income distribution in the 1980s as the economy shifted to more skill-based activities" (1996, 59); a rural movement, the "Assembly of the

Poor," mobilized 15,000 people for a camp and vigil in Bangkok (*Sydney Morning Herald*, 27 January 1997). In Malaysia, partisan interests have been especially favoured (Gomez and Jomo 1997). Thus aggregate findings supporting the view that there has been shared growth may mask significant regional or sectoral variations, and more detailed evidence is required.

Ideas, choice sets, and motives at the sectoral level

Sectoral mobilization is the second activity through which ideas, choice sets, and motives might be influenced. Mobilization at this level is required to implement broader national objectives and it involves selective intervention. At least four processes contribute to this outcome: the establishment of appropriate institutional and planning processes; the establishment of sectoral priorities; the introduction of specific incentives; and business-government collaboration.

SECTORAL AGENCIES

Except for Thailand, the Philippines, and Indonesia, the states of the area have institutional arrangements covering the key dimensions of industry strategy formulation and implementation. In figure 3.1, three fields are covered: industrial strategy, technology strategy, and industrial-cum–trade policy implementation.

In Korea, as in Japan, key strategic agencies are supported by external policy think-tanks. In Singapore, the Economic Development Board has played a key part (Schein 1996). It operates as an enterprise, maintaining 22 international offices and taking initiatives in identifying gaps in industry clusters or new sectors where investment is desired, discovering suitable multinational corporations to meet these needs, and approaching firms to solicit interest. It is also the key agency in charge of implementing Singapore's programme of expansion in the region, boosting the role of local firms, and broadening the part played by its SOEs. In Malaysia, the major co-ordinating bodies are the National Economic Consultative Council and the National Development Planning Committee. Large powers are concentrated in the prime minister's hands; industrial policy is the responsibility of the Ministry of Trade and Industry; the Malaysian Industry Development Authority (MIDA) co-ordinates foreign investment.

SECTORAL PRIORITIES

The sectors targeted by Korea, Taiwan, and Singapore (as in Japan) build from existing activity and reflect the linkage between the economic prosperity of these states and the growth of global trade in manufactures (figure 3.2).

	Japan	Korea	Taiwan	Singapore
Industry Strategy (Peak Agency)	• Industrial Structure Council • Industrial Policy Bureau MITI (237 staff) • MITI Research Institute (46 staff)	• Economic Planning Board (Ministry of Finance) • Korean Development Institute	• Council for Economic Planning and Development (CEPD) • Nominates strategic industry/export sectors	• Ministry of International Trade and Industry
Technology Strategy	• Agency of Industrial Science and Technology (AIST – 3,537 staff, 6 programmes, 25 target fields (1995)	• Ministry of Science and Technology (MOST) • Korea Advanced Institute of Science and Technology • 9 main research centres • Implementation through HANPs (Highly Advanced National Projects)	• IDB nominates development-targeted lead products (69 in 1994) • Industrial Technology Research Institute (ITRI – 8 major subunits)	• National Science and Technology Board (administers National Technology Plan) – R & D Target 2% GDP) – 40 Researchers per 10,000 – Administers 52 BICC R & D Funds
Industry Policy/ Trade Policy	• Industrial Structure Council • 14+ Deliberation Councils • MITI – International Trade Policy Bureau (236 staff) – Basic Industries Bureau (208 staff) – Industry Location (177 staff) – Machinery and Information Industries (200 staff) – Consumer Goods Industries	• Ministry of Trade Industry and Energy (MOIE) • Korean Institute of Economics and Technology • Trade Policy/Export Promotion by Kotra (100 International Trade Centres) • Major Centres – Korea Institute of Science and Technology – Korean Research Institute of Bioscience and Biotechnology – Korea Institute of Energy Research – Korea Institute of Machinery and Metals – Electronic Research Industry	Industrial Development Bureau (Ministry of Economic Affairs)	• Economic Development Board (22 international offices) • Trade Development Board (1995 – 5 missions, 29 trade fairs)

Figure 3.1 **Institutional structures for industry strategy in Japan, Korea, and Taiwan**

Japan	Korea	Taiwan	Singapore
Microelectronics	Biotechnology	Communications	Aerospace
Biotechnology	New materials	Consumer electronics	Biotechnology
New materials	Aeronautical engineering	IT	Chemicals
Telecommunications	Oceanography	Semiconductors	Precision engineering
Commercial aircraft	Fine chemicals	Precision machinery and automation	A third petrochemical cracker
Machine tools	Informatics	Aerospace	Electronics
Robotics	Environmental audit	Advanced materials	Disk media
Computers	Precision manufactures	Speciality chemicals and pharmaceuticals	Precision engineering equipment and components
		Speciality medical devices	
		Pollution control	

Figure 3.2 **Targeted emerging industrial sectors in Japan, Korea, Taiwan, and Singapore** (Sources: Thurow 1996, 67 [Japan]; *Technical Transfer Week*, 26 June 1996 [Korea]; Matthews 1977b, 300 [Taiwan]; Economic Development Board, http://www.sedb.com.sg [Singapore])

Japan	Singapore	Taiwan
Information	RHQs	Asia Pacific Regional Operations Center
Consumer credit	Logistics	Sea/air transportation
Advertising	Lifestyle	Financial services
Education	Health	Telecommunications
Security	Communications/information	Media enterprises
Temporary staff placements	Education services	
Music	TV broadcast	
Fitness	Multimedia content	
Design		
Homes for the aged		
Home cleaning		

Figure 3.3 **Targeted services sectors in Japan, Singapore, and Taiwan** (Sources: Economic Planning Agency, http://www.epa.go.jp [Japan]; Economic Development Board Web Site http://www.sedb.com.sg [Singapore]; Council for Economic Planning and Development 1995, http://www.cepd.gov.tw [Taiwan])

There is substantial overlap between the nominated sectors. This is a consequence of the facts that regional firms have established global positions in some sectors such as electronics, and that production in these sectors is regionalized. In some cases, too, this overlap is the consequence of emerging global market sectors such as biotechnology, or of a desire to build national participation in an established sector, such as aircraft and aerospace. The selection criteria nominated by Taiwan are typical. These include strong market potential, production which is technology-demanding but not energy dependent, high value added, and a pivotal industrial position (Matthews 1997b). Explicit strategies for service sector development have been identified in figure 3.3 for Singapore, Taiwan, and Japan. Expected outcomes for sector size and growth are set in relation to both manufacturing and service target sectors; performance can thus be assessed.

The Japanese policy of preserving a bureaucratic role in the development of the industrial structure is particularly relevant because of the economic maturity of the country. It is envisaged that the Ministry of Finance will maintain financial and monetary control and that MITI will extend its role to include telecommunications; MITI also wishes not merely to foster individual industrial sectors but to be concerned with the overall industrial environment (*Nikkei Weekly*, 30 June 1997). Japanese agencies continue to give a strong lead in identifying growing sectors. The list established by MITI of these sectors (see figure 3.4) is notable for the fact that it covers emerging technologies as well as domestic manufacturing and service sectors, the outlook for market size and employment levels being specified for the last two of these.

Malaysia has targeted multimedia as an area for growth in value-added activity, the focus being the "Multimedia Super Corridor," of which the prime minister, Mahathir, has been the most active advocate. This is envisaged to provide an advanced communications infrastructure between Kuala Lumpur and a new urban centre, Cyberjava. Government investment of between US$8 billion and US$15 billion had been foreshadowed before the financial crisis. The corridor aims at hosting companies to provide multimedia content, such as digitally produced special effects and video games; by May 1997 (but before the financial crisis had fully developed), over 900 companies had made a bid to participate in the corridor (*Nikkei Weekly*, 5 May 1997).

In Thailand, Indonesia, and the Philippines, the established economic bureaucracies have sought to manage only macroeconomic aggregates, although before his downfall, President Suharto had supported family members and Technology Minister Habibie in favouring particular sectors or activities. In Indonesia, the Pelita VI strategic plan (1994–95) involved a further relaxation of restrictions on foreign investment and a reduction of tariffs. Investment has been concentrated on textiles, tourism, shoes, food processing, and timber products.

SECTORAL INCENTIVES

Targeted incentives are a direct method used to influence sectoral activity. Research and development, automation, training, and new ventures in particular are thus singled out for special benefits and concessions in the policies of Taiwan, Singapore, and Malaysia (Sicklen 1997).

BUSINESS-GOVERNMENT COLLABORATION

Business-government collaboration can contribute directly to the dissemination of ideas, choice sets, and motives; it can also contribute indirectly, as we shall point out later, to the reduction of transaction costs. This kind of collaboration has been mentioned as a particular feature of the development process. In Japan, it has been extensively documented, for instance by Okimoto, who notes: "Much of the crucial negotiation that goes into industrial policy-making takes place behind the scenes in what might be called an intermediate zone between the public and private sectors. It would be hard to formulate and implement Japanese industrial policy if the labyrinth of personal relationships in the intermediate zone did not exist." He adds: "Instead of labelling Japan a strong state [it would be] more accurate to call it a 'societal,' 'relational,' or 'network' state ... whose strength is derived from the convergence of public and private interests and the extensive network ties binding the

Technologies	Services		Domestic Sectors				
	Market size (Y trillion)			Market size (Y Trillion)		Employment (1000's)	
New materials	Information	6.17	25.00	Housing: renovation, building housing for the aged	1	4	30	90
Superconductivity	Consumer credit	13.69	24.00	Medical and welfare services: nursing equipment	38	91	3,350	3,690
Biotechnology	Advertising	6.35	10.00	Lifestyle and culture: leisure and lifelong learning businesses	8	19	1,220	1,760
Micromachinery technology	Education	3.60	5.40	Urban development: development of deep underground environments	5	16	60	150
Electronics/information	Security	1.75	2.86	Environment: recycling, waste disposal	15	37	640	1,380
Femosecond technology	Temporary staff placement	0.93	1.59	New energy sources: generating electricity from waste materials	2	7	40	130
Accelerated biofunction technology	Music	0.56	0.95	Information and communications: electronic trading	38	126	1,250	2,440

Figure 3.4 **Targeted growth sectors in Japan** (Sources: AIST, *Annual Report 1996* [Technologies]; MIT [*Nikkei Weekly*, 3 June 1995] [Services]; MIT [*Nikkei Weekly*, 2 December 1996] [Domestic sectors])

Optical topographic imaging system	Fitness	0.35	0.60	Distribution	36	132	490	1,440
Digital hearing aids	Design	0.19	0.33	Employment services	2	8	60	100
Unassisted excretion	Homes for the aged	0.06	0.16	Internationalization: convention services and translation	1	2	60	100
Stereotactic cancer treatments	Home cleaning	0.03	0.12	Business support services: technology assessment	17	29	880	1,260
Renewable energy technology				New manufacturing technology	14	41	730	1,530
Fossil fuel utilization				Biotechnology	1	10	30	150
Energy transfer				Aviation and aerospace	4	9	90	150
Environment management								

Figure 3.4 **(cont.)**

two sectors" (Okimoto 1989, 104). The practice of *amakudari* (retirement from public service to a senior private-sector position) fertilizes contact between the state and the business sector. The transmission of information and the formation of perspectives are thus influenced in both directions, as will be examined in the next section.

In Korea, relations between the state and the chaebol were identified before 1997 developments as a threat to continued growth (Clifford 1997; Evans 1995). The economic dominance of these conglomerates was remarkable, with the 50 largest organizations contributing 93 per cent of GDP in 1983 (Lim 1996, 2). As Evans notes: "Korea is pushing at the limit at which embeddedness can be concentrated without partial predation" (1992, 158), while financial liberalization, to the extent that it has occurred, has not been used to curb the chaebols' power (Kong 1995). Dieter Ernst (1996) has noted the dysfunctionality of chaebol strategies for upgrading technology in the critical electronics sector. In Taiwan, on the contrary, the business sector is dominated by small and medium-sized enterprises, while large enterprises are mostly state-owned. As a result, the top 50 firms contributed only 32 per cent of GNP in 1983. One study suggests that organized business had developed close relationships with the dominant party, the KMT (Shiau 1996).

There are differences among the states in the character of relations with the bureaucracy. Kong observes that relations between bureaucrats and business in Korea are, in contrast to Japan, "vertical, secretive, and exclusionary" (1995, 636). For Taiwan, Evans notes that "weak links to private capital threaten the state's ability to secure full information ... and efficient implementation" (1992, 158).

In Southeast Asia, the situation is more problematic. In Thailand, business-government collaboration is thoroughly institutionalized for established industries, but it coexists with endemic corruption (Anek 1992). In Malaysia, the institutional apparatus came to acquire a quasi-developmental pattern fairly late, especially with the Malaysian Business Council which was set up in 1991. But according to Bowie, "direct personal access is a *sine qua non* for obtaining partnerships in privatised government operations and infrastructure projects" (Bowie 1994, 189). In Indonesia, "traditional patrimonialistic or clientelistic patterns of political participation endure in the business community.... State-allocated monopolies are the key to business success" (MacIntyre 1994b, 243). In the Philippines, President Marcos's crony coalition was significantly weakened with the restoration of democracy. This was confirmed by the course of the Lakas-LDP coalition from April 1995 to November 1996.

Following the events of 1997, pressure for more transparent rules, administrative processes, and a non-corrupt regulatory infrastructure have come from the IMF and foreign investors.

Transaction costs

Transaction costs arise in measuring the valued attributes of what is being exchanged, of protecting rights, and of enforcing agreements. They are pervasive in economic activity and can result from patterns of culture; failure of governance, markets, or co-ordination; limitations of ideas; and genuine uncertainty. Steps which might be taken to reduce those transaction costs which stem from limitations of ideas and from uncertainty have already been discussed. Governance can affect transaction costs both formally and informally and both directly and indirectly: for example, the regime of property rights might be more or less formalized and more or less comprehensive. The 1997 financial crisis points to deficiencies in the affected states. Similarly, social trust might be based on a mix of formal agreements on such matters as wage outcomes, indirect programmes such as welfare and training arrangements, and tacit understandings on matters such as norms of authority and hierarchy (Redding 1996).

Regarding market failures, it is important to note that these are endemic. Dunning identifies five categories of endemic failure: (1) those arising from uncertainties concerning supply and/or demand, for instance concerning future prices and qualities of inputs, future demand conditions, and the behaviour of competitors; (2) those arising from externalities associated with transactions, for instance environmental consequences; (3) those arising from effects of scale where optimum production may influence price; (4) those arising from high start-up or fixed costs and low or zero production costs, as in telecommunications; and (5) those arising from chronic rigidity, as in labour and capital goods markets (Dunning 1993). At the same time, it is necessary to distinguish between dysfunctional and positive market failures. For example, when innovation and technology development are the engine of economic growth, market failures differentiate opportunities for gain: this creates incentives for innovation (Kelm 1995).

So far as failures of co-ordination are concerned, governments can reduce these, for instance, by initiating co-ordination focused on more remote and less certain global markets and by announcing changes in industry structure. Thus in December 1996, the Korean Ministry of Information and Communications presented a strategy for development of what it termed the "infocommunications" subsector. The programmes covered developments in existing product lines up to 2001 and in emerging technology beyond 2000. In each product category, global market size and Korean market share were specified precisely. The global telecommunications equipment market was estimated to grow to US$1.2 trillion by 2000. The telecommunications gear industry was expected to grow from US$929 million in 1997 to US$1.048 trillion by 1999; meanwhile, Korean telecommunications companies exported US$26 billion worth of goods in 1997 and were expected to export US$59 billion worth by 2001. Production and export goals for the software industry by 2001 were established at US$20 billion and US$2.5 billion respectively: it was estimated that 500 new software companies would need to be created if this target was to be met.

Government investment in R & D activities of 1.9598 trillion won (approx. US$1.7 trillion) by 2000 was predicted. A joint public-private project involving the commercialization of a future public land-mobile telecom service (FPLMTS) cellular technology was announced: this project is designed to enable Korean industry to supply the next generation of wireless communication services, including voice, data, and video, which is expected to replace cellular services from 2000.

In general, transaction costs can be reduced through processes which ensure repeated interactions between key participants. As North states: "The most likely empirically observable state in which contracts are self-enforcing is that in which parties to an exchange have a great deal of knowledge of each other and are involved in repeat dealings.... In such a world the measured costs of transacting are very low" (1992, 55).

In a discussion of the characteristics of Japan as a "network state," Moon and Prasad argue that "the factor influencing economic performance is not state dominance or bureaucratic competence, but continued interactions between public and private organisations." These arrangements diminish transaction costs through "extended bounded rationality, reduced opportunism and uncertainty, reduced small number indeterminacies, better information, and a group-oriented atmosphere" (1994, 360–86). Dore notes the contribution of interaction to the diminution of transaction costs in framing longer-term business strategies in Japan (1996, 367). The role of the state has progressively changed from being directive to being collaborative, with information playing increasingly a key part (Wang 1995, 568–69).

In the context of a discussion of formal public- and private-sector consultation and other patterns of interaction in Korea and Taiwan, Hawes and Liu suggest that

[states] can reduce transaction and information costs as well as provide collective goods. They do this by reducing bureaucratic red tape, by pooling information, by reducing the need for regulation, and by increasing the efficiency of decision-making. The collective goods produced by these institutions may include market information, sectoral co-ordination, bargaining leverage, or a myriad of other factors that have helped to make Southeast Asia internationally competitive in an expanding range of products and services. (1993, 656)

Sabel embellishes this theme in discussing exchange in Japan. He argues that transaction costs are reduced by building from, and making explicit, the shared or common interests of the parties. This arises from

institutions that make discussion of what to do inextricable from discussion of what is being done and the discussion of standards for apportioning gains and losses inextricable from apportionment.... discrete transactions among independent actors become continual joint formulations of common ends in which the parties' identities are reciprocally defined.... These institutions transform transactions into discussions, for discussion is precisely the process by which parties come to reinterpret themselves and their relation to each other by elaborating a common understanding of the world." (1994, 231–74)

Transaction costs increase as governmental capacities – including law and order, administration, ports, harbours, transports, banking, and customs – diminish. These capacities have been found to be much less embedded in the states of Southeast Asia than in those of East Asia. In 1994, MacIntyre reached a cautious, even pessimistic, conclusion about the general condition of economic governance in the region: "Limited capacities and insulation of Southeast Asian state institutions are likely to be a serious constraint on economic performance" (1994a, 17). The events of 1997 seem to vindicate this judgement. Ethnic pressures differentiate the political circumstances of Malaysia, Indonesia, and Singapore from those of Korea, Taiwan (and Japan) (Jesudasan 1996). Overseas Chinese dominate the business sector in Southeast Asian states: in Malaysia, they account for 36 per cent of the population but control 61 per cent of companies in terms of market capitalization; in Indonesia, for 3.5 per cent of the population and 68 per cent of companies; and in Thailand, for 10 per cent of the population and 81 per cent of companies (East Asia Analytical Unit 1995).

The dependence of Southeast Asian states on DFI is a contextual factor differentiating their experience from that of the states of East Asia. Moreover, the instruments available to the former states for economic governance are different from those available to Japan in the 1950s and to Korea and Taiwan in the 1960s and 1970s, in particular because of U.S. bilateralism and because of the advent of the World Trade Organisation (Strange 1996).

The 1997 financial crisis in Thailand, Korea, Indonesia, Malaysia, and the Philippines, at least in part, reflected a perception by international investors that transparency and other prudential arrangements in the financial sector were inadequate. The precise conditions and circumstances in each state remain to be evaluated. A systematic collection and analysis of data relating to transaction costs remains to be undertaken.

Creativity, innovation, and skills

Economic governance can foster innovation and skills through compulsory education and through programmes which encourage research and development.

The emphasis on compulsory schooling in the states of the area and the success of these states in achieving skills development in fields such as mathematics and computing have been thoroughly documented (World Bank 1993). The experience of Southeast Asian states may again have to be distinguished from that of East Asia: Thailand, in particular, has achieved lower rates of educational participation and retention.

In relation to research and technology, the states of East Asia all have active strategies based on lead agencies, clear performance goals, targeted technologies, and elaborate arrangements for public–private sector co-operation: Hobday (1995) and Mathews (1997a) document these points for the electronics sector. Japan's commitment is clear, with total spending in these fields of approximately US$75 billion, or US$97 per labour force member, in 1993: this figure was higher than that of the United States, where expenditure was only US$76 per labour force member. Korea would have to spend 60 per cent of its entire GDP to achieve a similar level of expenditure (Kong 1995).

All the states of the area have clear development targets, following the model of Japan's Agency for Industrial Science and Technology, which set technology priorities in 15 areas in 1995. Thus, in 1994, and within the framework of its nominated 10 sectors, Taiwan's Industrial Development Bureau selected 69 components and products as "development targeted lead products" (DTLP). The criteria for selection were high added value, good development potential, contribution to competitiveness of downstream products, and import replacement. These 69 products were estimated to have a near-term production value of US$11 billion rising to US$50 billion early in the twenty-first century. Firms seeking to develop their products were eligible for a 50 per cent subsidy for development costs and a subsidized loan for the balance; the government owns 50 per cent of any resulting intellectual property.

The Korean government also launched a programme designated "Highly Advanced National Project" (HANP) which is intended to select and develop strategic industrial technology requiring nationwide R & D investment. Two categories of HANPs have been selected. The first group, the Products Technology Development Project, concerns technologies for specific products which have or will have a substantial share in the global industrial markets; the second group, the Fundamental Technology Development Project, concerns core technologies; products resulting from both projects should be available by 2001. Fourteen HANPs were set up in 1995.

The effectiveness of technology transfer programmes in Southeast Asia is less clear. Japanese companies, as the principal investors, are also the principal potential source of such transfers. State action can be seen in programmes designed to achieve linkage between investing firms, local enterprises, and local citizens. Moore's judgement is cautious: "Japan's record of technology transfer has improved in the 1990s. . . . While more advanced technology has been transferred, this does not necessarily bode well for the emerging NICs since this kind of export-oriented production is often highly reliant on imported inputs, automated manufacturing processes, and foreign management" (1996, 24; also Bernard and Ravenhill 1995).

Government failure

There is a familiar litany of arguments against state action. Purposive action is a powerful source of co-ordination and selective action has special advantages, but as Kelm observes, selective action "has inherent disadvantages as a generator of incentives" (1995, 63). In markets, he argues, "the unconscious force of natural selection operates only on the basis of achieved results without taking the individual circumstances affecting these results into account" (55). In contrast, purposive state action always introduces evaluation and assessment and the problem of withdrawing support from unsuccessful ventures.

A number of findings derived from the transposition of assumptions originating in the neoclassical model of economic activity to the political sphere suggest that, even in an imperfect world, action by the state is unlikely to be preferable to market-based decisions because of the knowledge needed for effective state action. "Misapplication, abuse, interest group capture, mistaken targeting, and bungling can bring about economically undesirable outcomes" (Murtha and Lenway 1994, 120). Such a list suggests a taxonomy of governmental failures which might also allow for remedial practices to be documented.

There are indeed numerous studies of governmental failure in East and Southeast Asia (Callon 1996; Islam 1994). There is also extensive empirical evidence of corruption: bribery scandals have caused political crises in Korea and Japan, for instance, while corruption is acknowledged to be endemic in Thailand and Indonesia, and Gomez (1998) regards rent seeking as pervasive in Malaysia.

But the weight of evidence, at least up until the early 1990s, and at least in East Asia, favours an opposite conclusion. The developmental state, conceived as an ideal type, was the antidote to government failure. Bureaucratic capture, at least until the early 1990s, had been resisted through elite recruitment and the prestige attaching to public service. Bureaucratic authority was reinforced, at least in Korea and Taiwan and at least through the 1980s, by a capacity to influence capital allocations and to initiate tax audits (Rodrik 1995). But there were also marked contrasts between states. For example, in a comparison with Japan, Kong observed: "The divergence of state and business interests originated in the 1980s. . . . five years after democratization a smooth partnership of the Japanese type has yet to materialize" (Kong 1995, 636–37).

The East and Southeast Asian experience also illustrates the extent to which a state can absorb corruption and (episodic) government failure and still foster development. The causal relationship seems contingent. Aoki identifies a variety of remedies for government failure in both East and Southeast Asia. He cites instances of corruption which had positive effects (Aoki et al. 1996, 14–18).

The financial crisis of 1997 also challenges the earlier findings of persistent government failure. The first point to note is that factors other than government failure might be introduced to explain this crisis. An obvious market failure occurred at the level of the international financial system. Total short-term fund flows by commercial banks to East and Southeast Asia escalated from US$24 billion in 1994 to US$53 billion in 1996. In 1997, the flow was reversed by US$74 billion (Wade 1998). The eagerness of commercial banks to lend coincided, in Korea's case, with a partial liberalization of its financial markets that occurred as a condition of entry to the OECD in 1995. International lending entered a "liberalized" domestic system and coincided with chaebol ambitions to attain global scale.

Underlying domestic conditions in Korea and Southeast Asian states also contributed to the crisis. In the former case, the economic dominance of a few chaebol has already been noted. Perhaps the single most important factor was the relaxation of firm state leadership as part of the democratization that occurred progressively after 1988, and particularly in the mid-1990s. Wade and Veneroso reach pessimistic conclusions regarding Korea's prospects (1998). By contrast, Matthews anticipates the emergence of a reworked state framework that is more attuned to Korea's expanded international economic role and its domestic democratic consolidation (1998). Others are more pessimistic about the embeddedness of its party system (Ahn, this volume). In Southeast Asia, lax control of financial markets, cronyism, and the eroding authority of the technocrats (in Indonesia and Thailand particularly), have already been noted.

In sum, the financial crisis and Japan's prolonged recession suggest a variety of issues for attention concerning government and market failure. The most prominent is perhaps the anarchic condition of the international financial system itself (Kapstein 1994).

The findings of this chapter can now be summarized – bearing in mind, however, that the complexity of the issues, the variations in economic (and political) dynamics, and the shortage of empirical data all point to a need for more evidence and analysis. The financial crisis of 1997 compounds these gaps and enhances the uncertainties.

The extent of pervasiveness of the developmental pattern described at the outset of this chapter is the first issue. This approach to economic governance exists in its most elaborated form in the states of East Asia. The states of Southeast Asia have been dirigiste, at least in some respects, but their practices depart significantly from the "ideal" developmental pattern in relation to both bureaucratic autonomy and embeddedness. These states have pursued an economic strategy of shared growth, but the results seem more uneven than those achieved in East Asia. Further, economic growth in Southeast Asian states was spawned by the regionalization of production and DFI was the catalyst, thus introducing a different context for economic governance from that of East Asia; moreover, overseas Chinese networks have dominated economic activity. Thus it seems difficult to discover a common pattern in the management of structural outcomes among these states: while Malaysia and Indonesia have endeavoured to influence the industrial structure and the formation of indigenous firms, Thailand and the Philippines have eschewed elaborate economic governance.

The political context for economic governance also varies between East and Southeast Asia. In both Korea and Taiwan, democratization and a move towards more consensual business-government relations is taking place. Meanwhile, the traditional pattern has been maintained in Singapore, though some pressures for change are beginning to emerge at the sectoral level. Thus, in all three states, as well as in the special case of Hong Kong, there is a trend towards more collaboration in economic governance, through democratization, through the elaboration of structures of business-government relations, through the need for strategies to accommodate labour, and through increasing reliance on information as a medium of exchange.

The political context for economic governance varies widely in Southeast Asia, with the Philippines and Thailand the most democratic, and Malaysia to an extent democratic while Indonesia remained authoritarian, at least until the downfall of Suharto. There is also some evidence of an active civil society, based on an urban middle class, in Thailand, Indonesia, and the Philippines, but only to a lesser extent in Malaysia (e.g., Laber 1997; Jesudasan 1995; Bell et al. 1995). In this latter case, at least so far, the established regime has mostly co-opted new groups, or groups which lack the weight to challenge the dominant order. All these states will be profoundly affected by the events of 1997 as middle-class expectations are curbed, elite rent seeking is curtailed, and unemployment expands.

Questions of social relationships lead to questions of politics; economic governance is obviously also dependent on politics as public servants can be helped or frustrated by the actions of politicians. We need, therefore, to bring together the findings relating to economic governance discussed in this chapter and those relating to politics examined in the previous chapter to see how far, in East and Southeast Asia, the links between politics and economics are likely to continue to result in growth and development, whatever constraints may be imposed on the states of the area by democratization. It is therefore to the character and to the consequences of the links between political behaviour and economic governance that the next chapter is devoted.

REFERENCES

Alagappa, Muthiah (ed.) (1995), *Political Legitimacy in Southeast Asia: The Quest for Moral Authority*, Stanford University Press, Stanford, Calif.

Anek Laothamatas (1992), *Business Associations and the New Political Economy of Thailand: From Bureaucratic Polity to Liberal Corporatism*, Westview Press, San Francisco.

———— (1996), "A Tale of Two Democracies," in R. H. Taylor (ed.), *The Politics of Elections in Southeast Asia*, Cambridge University Press, New York, pp. 184–200.

Aoki, Masohiko, Kim, Hyung-Ki, and Okuno-Fujiwara, Masahiro (1996), *The Role of Government in East Asian Economic Development*, Clarendon Press, Oxford.

Bell, Daniel, Brown, A. David, Jayasurya, Kanishka, and Jones, David Martin (1995), *Towards Illiberal Democracy in Pacific Asia*, Macmillan, London.

Berger, Suzanne and Dore, Ronald (eds.) (1996), *National Diversity and Global Capitalism*, Cornell University Press, Ithaca, N.Y.

Berger, Suzanne, and Lester, Richard (eds.) (1997), *Made by Hong Kong*, Oxford University Press, Hong Kong.

Bernard, Mitchell and Ravenhill, John (1995), "Beyond Product Cycles and Flying Geese," *World Politics* (January), pp. 171–209.

Bowie, Alisdair (1994), "The Dynamics of Business-Government Relations in Industrializing Nations," in Andrew MacIntyre (ed.), *Business and Government in Industrialising Asia*, Allen and Unwin, Sydney, pp. 167–95.

Callon, Scott (1995), *Divided Sun: MITI and the Breakdown of Japanese High-Tech Industrial Policy, 1975–1993,* Stanford University Press, Stanford, Calif.

Campos, Edgardo Jose and Root, Hilton L. (1996), *The Key to the Asian Miracle: Making Shared Growth Credible*, The Brookings Institution, Washington, D.C.

Cheng, Tun-Jen and Stephan Haggard (eds.) (1992), *Political Change in Taiwan*, Lynne Reiner Publishers, Boulder, Colo.

Clifford, Mark (1997), *Troubled Tiger*, rev. ed., Butterworth-Heinemann, Singapore.

Dore, Ronald (1996), "Convergence in Whose Interest?" in Suzanne Berger and Ronald Dore (eds.), *National Diversity and Global Capitalism*, Cornell University Press, Ithaca, N.Y.

Dunning, John H. (1993), *The Globalisation of Business*, Routledge, London.

East Asia Analytical Unit (1995), *Overseas Chinese Business Networks in Asia*, Department of Foreign Affairs and Trade, Canberra.

Enright, Michael, et al. (1996), *The Hong Kong Advantage*, Oxford University Press, Hong Kong.

Ernst, Dieter (1996), "Technology Management in the Korean Electronics Industry: Achievements and New Challenges," paper prepared for the Conference on Business-Government Relations in the Asian Region, National University of Singapore, March.

Evans, Peter (1992), "The State as Problem and Solution," in Stephan Haggard and Robert Kaufman (eds.), *The Politics of Economic Adjustment*, Princeton University Press, Princeton, N.J.

—— (1995), *Embedded Autonomy, States and Industrial Transformation*, Princeton University Press, Princeton, N.J.

Garrett, Geoffrey and Weingast, Barry (1993), "Ideas, Interests and Institutions: Constructing the European Community's Internal Market," in Judith Goldstein and Robert Keohane (eds.), *Ideas and Foreign Policy*, Cornell University Press, Ithaca, N.Y., pp. 203–5.

Gomez, Edmund Terence (1998), "Political Business in Malaysia: Cronyism, Change and Crisis," paper presented at the Workshop on East Asian Developmental Models in Crisis, Manchester Business School, June.

Gomez, Edmund Terence and Jomo K. S. (1997), *Malaysia's Political Economy: Politics, Patronage and Profits*, Cambridge University Press, Melbourne.

Hall, Peter and Taylor, Rosemary (1996), "Political Science and Three New Institutionalisms," *Political Studies* 44, pp. 936–57.

Hawes, Gary and Liu, Hong (1993), "Explaining the Dynamics of the Southeast Asian Political Economy: State, Society and the Search for Economic Growth," *World Politics* 45, pp. 629–56.

Hobday, Michael (1995), *Innovation in East Asia,* Edward Elgar, Aldershot.

Inoguchi, Takashi (1997), "Japanese Bureaucracy: Coping with New Challenges," in Purnendra Jain and Takashi Inoguchi (eds.), *Japanese Politics Today: Beyond Karaoke Democracy*, Macmillan, Melbourne, pp. 92–108.

Islam, Iyunatal (1994), "Between the State and the Market: The Case for Eclectic Neoclassical Political Economy," in Andrew MacIntyre (ed.), *Business and Government in Industrialising Asia*, Allen and Unwin, Sydney, pp. 91–113.

Jesudasan, James V. (1995), "Statist Democracy and the Limits to Civil Society in Malaysia," *Journal of Commonwealth and Comparative Politics* 33(3).

—— (1996), "The Syncretic State and the Structuring of Oppositional Politics in Malaysia," in G. Rodan (ed.), *Political Oppositions in Industrialising Asia*, Routledge, London.

Kapstein, Ethan (1994), *Governing the Global Economy*, Harvard University Press, Cambridge, Mass.

Kelm, Matthias (1995), *Economic Growth as an Evolutionary Process*, ESRC Centre for Business Research, University of Cambridge, Working Paper no. 17.

—— (1996), *Evolutionary and New Institutional Economics: Some Implications for Industrial Policy*, ESRC Centre for Business Research, University of Cambridge, Working Paper no. 46.

Khong, Cho-oon (1995), "Singapore: Political legitimacy through Managing Conformity," in Muthian Alagappa (ed.), *Political Legitimacy in Southeast Asia: The Quest for Moral Authority*, Stanford University Press, Stanford, Calif.

Kim, Hyung-Ki, Muramatsu, Michio, Pempel, T. J., and Yamamura, Kozo (eds.) (1995), *The Japanese Civil Service and Economic Development: Catalysts of Change*, Clarendon Press, Oxford.

Kong, Tat Yan (1995), "From Relative Autonomy to Consensual Development: The Case of South Korea," *Political Studies* 43(4), pp. 630–44.

Krugman, Paul (1994), "The Myth of Asia's Miracle," *Foreign Affairs* 73(6), pp. 62–78.

Laber, Jeri (1997), "Smouldering Indonesia," *New York Review of Books*, 9 January.

Lee, Yeon-ho (1997), "The Limits of Economic Globalisation in East Asian Developmental States," *Pacific Review* 10(3), pp. 366–90.

Lim, Suk-Jun (1996), "Politics of Industrialisation: Formation of Divergent Industrial Orders in Korea and Taiwan," paper presented at the Annual Meeting of the American Political Science Association, San Francisco, August–September.

MacIntyre, Andrew (1994a), "Business, Government, and Development," in Andrew MacIntyre (ed.), *Business and Government in Industrialising Asia*, Allen and Unwin, Sydney.

—— (1994b), "Power, Property, and Patrimonialism: Business and Government in Indonesia," in Andrew MacIntyre (ed.), *Business and Government in Industrialising Asia*, Allen and Unwin, Sydney, pp. 244–68.

McMillan, Charles (1996), *The Japanese Industrial System*, 3d ed., de Gruyter, New York.

Magaziner, Ira and Patinkin, Mark (1995), "Fast Heat: How Korea Won the Microwave War," in K. Ohmae (ed.), *The Evolving Global Economy*, Harvard Business Review Press, Cambridge, Mass.

Marsh, Ian (1995), *Beyond the Two Party System: Political Representation, Economic Competitiveness and Australian Politics*, Cambridge University Press, Melbourne.

Matthews, John (1997a), "A Silicon Valley of the East," *California Management Review* 39(4), pp. 26–54.

Matthews, John (1997b), "The Development and Upgrading of Manufacturing Industries in Taiwan: Industrial Development Bureau, Ministry of Economic Affairs," *Industry and Innovation* 4(2), pp. 277–303.

Matthews, John (1998), *Fashioning a New Korean Model out of the Crisis*, Japan Policy Research Institute Working Paper 46, Cardiff, Calif.

Mochtar, Pabottinga (1995), "Indonesia: Historicising the New Order's Legitimacy," in Muthiah Alagappa, *Political Legitimacy in Southeast Asia: The Quest for Moral Authority*, Stanford University Press, Stanford, Calif.

Moon, Chung-in, and Prasad, Rashemi (1994), "Beyond the Developmental State: Networks, Politics and Institutions," *Governance* 7(4), pp. 360–86.

Moore, Thomas. G. (1996), "Economic Globalization, Transnational Networks, and Late Development in the 1990s: External Influences on Economic and Political Change in Emerging East Asian NICs," paper prepared for the Annual Meeting of the American Political Science Association, San Francisco, August–September.

Murtha, Thomas P., and Lenway, Stefanie (1994), "Country Capabilities and the Strategic State," *Strategic Managewment Journal* 15, pp. 113–29.

North, Douglas (1992), *Institutions, Institutional Change and Economic Performance*, Cambridge University Press, Cambridge.

Okimoto, Daniel (1989), *Between MITI and the Market*, Stanford University Press, Stanford, Calif.

Radelet, Stephen and Sachs, Jeffrey (1997), "Asia's Reemergence," *Foreign Affairs* 76(6), pp. 44–59.

Redding, S. G. (1996), "The Distinct Nature of Chinese Capitalism," *Pacific Review* 9(3), pp. 426–40.

Rodrik, Dani (1995), "Getting Interventions Right," *Economic Policy* 20, pp. 53–108.

Sabel, Charles (1994), "Learning by Monitoring," in Lloyd Rodwin and Donald A. Schon (eds.), *Rethinking the Development Experience: Essays Provoked by the Work of Albert O. Hirschman*, The Brookings Institution, Washington, D.C., pp. 231–74.

Sako, M. (1997), *Wage Bargaining in Japan: Why Employers and Unions Value Industry-Level Co-ordination*, Discussion Paper 334, Centre for Economic Performance, London School of Economcs.

Schon, Donald (1971), *Beyond the Stable State*, Temple Smith, London.

Schwartz, Peter (1991), *The Art of the Long View*, Currency Doubleday, New York.

Shiau, Chyun-Jenq (1996), "Elections and the Changing State-Business Relationship," in Tien, Hung-mao (ed.), *Taiwan's Electoral Politics and Democratic Transition*, M. E. Sharpe, Armonk, N.Y.

Sicklen, Derek (1997), *An Overview of Overseas Investment and Trade Incentives*, Australian Economic Analysis Pty Ltd., Sydney.

Steinmo, Steven, et al. (1992), *Structuring Politics: Historical Institutionalism in Comparative Perspective*, Cambridge University Press, New York.

Stiglitz, Joseph E. (1996), "Some Lessons from the East Asian Miracle," *The World Bank Research Observer* 11(2), pp. 151–77.

Strange, Susan (1996), *The Retreat of the State*, Cambridge University Press, Cambridge.

Suchit Bungbongkarn (1992), "Elections and Democracy in Thailand," in R. H.

Taylor (ed.), *The Politics of Elections in Southeast Asia*, Cambridge University Press, pp. 184–200.

Thurow, Lester (1996), *The Future of Capitalism*, Allen & Unwin, Sydney.

—— (1998), "Asia: The Collapse and the Cure," *New York Review of Books*, 5 February, pp. 22–26.

Tilton, Mark L. (1996), *Restrained Trade: Cartels in Japan's Basic Industries,* Cornell University Press, Ithaca, N.Y.

Wade, Robert (1990), *Governing the Market: Economic Theory and the Role of the Market in East Asian Industrialization*, Princeton University Press, Princeton, N.J.

—— (1992), "East Asia's Economic Success: Conflicting Perspectives, Partial Insights and Shaky Evidence," *World Politics* 44.

—— (1998), "Gestalt Shift: From 'Miracle' to 'Cronyism' in the Asian Crisis," *Cambridge Journal of Economics* 22(6), pp. 693–706.

Wade, Robert and Veneroso, F. (1998), "The Asian Crisis: The High Debt Model versus the Wall Street–Treasury-IMF Complex," *New Left Review*, March–April.

Wang, Vincent Wei-cheng (1995), "Developing the Information Industry in Taiwan: Entrepreneurial State, Guerilla Capitalists and Accommodative Technologists," *Pacific Affairs*. pp. 551–57.

Weiss, Linda and Hobson, John (1995), *States and Economic Development: A Comparative and Historical Analysis*, Polity Press, Cambridge.

World Bank (1993), *The East Asian Miracle, Economic Growth and Public Policy*, Oxford University Press, New York.

4

Parties, bureaucracies, and the search for an equilibrium between democracy and economic development

Jean Blondel and Takashi Inoguchi

If there is to be a satisfactory relationship between democracy and economic development, the two key institutions which have been examined in the previous chapters, parties and bureaucracies, must be in harmony. Yet such a harmony is difficult to obtain; some might even suggest that it cannot be obtained. If parties are very strong, they are likely to wish to dominate the bureaucracy; if the bureaucracy is very strong, it is likely to try to reduce what it might consider to be the undue interference of the parties. The second of these situations characterizes authoritarian polities and it has characterized to a greater or lesser extent a number of states of East and Southeast Asia. If democracy is to progress in the region, parties must be strengthened and a genuinely pluralistic party system must emerge, as has already occurred in a number of countries. But a way has to be found to ensure also that such a development does not result in the bureaucracy being demoted and thus ceasing to exert a key role in the governance of the economy.

The aim must be to create a stable relationship in which each of the two sides has the authority and the power to play the part which it is best suited to fulfil. Parties must be able to ensure that the polity is pluralistic by providing the people with an adequate representation of their feelings and hopes; the bureaucracy must be able to steer the economy in such a way that it continues to develop rapidly. It is manifestly difficult to achieve both these goals simultaneously because societal conditions must be such that parties have strong roots in the community and because it is only natural that, once parties have begun to be influential, the strength and influence of one side should affect the strength and influence of the other. Having examined successively in the previous chapters the types of party characteristics and of party system arrangements, on the one hand, and, on the other, the kinds of bureaucratic structures which would appear to be best suited to achieve sound economic governance, we need now to look at the conditions under which a pluralistic party system and an active bureaucracy can coexist and thus make it possible for democracy to flourish while economic development is maintained.

Democratization has a number of implications and consequences for economic governance. It implies an active role for the political leadership: there may even be "national mobilization" based on what we referred to in chapter 2 as "programmatic" parties. In any case, democratization at least invites rivals for national office to campaign on equal terms, and this can be felt to be disruptive of the national consensus. Moreover, democratization licenses the formation of interests and these interests may start to create policy networks; indeed, as economic development proceeds, a more differentiated civil society can be expected to take shape, with a well-defined middle class and a distinct labour interest.

A "perfect" solution of the problems which arise in this way is unquestionably impossible to find, as such a solution would require that parties would be in control and yet that the bureaucracy would keep its area of complete autonomy. What one must look for is an acceptable arrangement, with each side being prepared (and obliged) to renounce a fraction of its potential power in order to allow the other side to achieve a large part at least of what it is essential that it should achieve. Given that we are looking for partial solutions of this kind, there is likely to be more than one optimal arrangement, the one best suited to a particular country being likely to be the one which best fits the specific societal conditions of that country.

There is, moreover, another aspect to the problem, for under certain conditions, a stable democratic political system based on strong parties can help the bureaucracy to maintain its influence. Economic development is unlikely to continue for very long in the face of an indifferent citizenry. The emergence of distinct interests both among segments of the middle class and between the middle class and labour will tend to undermine the position of the bureaucracy. It is in this respect that the party system can be of considerable value: it has even been suggested that consensus can be preserved if the party system adopts, for instance, a consociational structure, although other forms of party system may also help (Haggard and Kaufman 1992, 342). The form of the party system is thus a key feature in assessing the impact of democratization on economic governance.

The purpose of this chapter is therefore to investigate what types of relationships between parties and party systems, on the one hand, and the bureaucracy, on the other, can be expected to be practical. The best procedure is to look for guidance to contemporary examples across the world which might approximate the societal conditions of East and Southeast Asia. There is one example only, however, that of Japan, which meets truly closely the double requirement of political democracy and strong economic development steered by a powerful bureaucracy; yet some of the countries of East and Southeast Asia display societal characteristics which are likely to make it difficult for them to follow the Japanese path. It is therefore essential to examine also other examples – matching less neatly the required double goal, admittedly, but perhaps characterized by a socio-political structure more akin than that of Japan to those of these polities. Two types of examples are particularly relevant: one is constituted by presidential systems, primarily the United States; the other is provided by countries practising "consociationalism," notably the Low Countries of Northwestern Europe, Belgium and the Netherlands. Thus, after having analysed in the first section the general conditions under which different types of relationships between parties and bureaucracies can be expected to emerge, we will examine the ways in which these relationships may develop successfully by referring successively to the models of Japan, Belgium and the Netherlands, and the United States. This will make it possible to discover whether different governmental arrangements which have been adopted elsewhere can help, in the context of the countries of East and Southeast Asia, to provide a means of combining a lively party system with a strong bureaucracy.

Types of party-bureaucracy relationships and economic governance in a democratic context

Rather surprisingly, the problems posed by the relationship between party and bureaucracy have not so far been given the serious attention which they deserve. It is as if scholars had deliberately avoided the difficulty by parcelling out the problem, as there has been a curious compartmentalization between two types of studies. On the one hand, those who have been concerned with general analysis of political systems have focused on parties as key agents of representation in democracy. Consequently, they have maintained that the correct position for the bureaucracy is to be subordinated to the government, as the government is composed of the leadership group of the party or parties which have obtained a popular majority (Bagehot 1963, 116–18; Schumpeter 1979, 273–80; Huntington 1968, 397–432; Blondel 1978; Kamenka 1989; Shefter

1994). On the other hand, students of public administration have been concerned with management and governance as if these were exclusively matters for administrators: what they analyse are the mechanisms by which policies can be elaborated and implemented in a particular societal context, the main goal being to discover under what conditions a good "fit" will be achieved between a society and its administrators (see, e.g., Halligan and Turner 1995). Both these approaches are partially correct, but neither corresponds to the whole reality. The solution of the problem which the relationship between democratization and economic development poses lies in establishing a link between these two approaches in order to be able to see how, in East and Southeast Asia, for instance, the two sides can work together in harmony: these links have not so far been carefully investigated (Lane 1993, 47–89; Peters 1995).

This situation is surely in part due to the fact that, without being entirely novel, the problem came to arise particularly acutely in East and Southeast Asia. First, the rapidity of the economic success of the countries of the region has been unprecedented, except in the case of Japan. Second, such a rapid development occurred under the leadership of a bureaucracy which has both been unusually effective (by the standards of countries outside the West) and unusually proactive by world standards (except for Japan and perhaps, at some periods, France) (Ridley and Blondel 1969; Cerny and Schain 1980; Wright 1989, 236–55). Third, the extent of competitiveness and pluralism among the political parties in the countries of the region has been low by comparison with Western countries and with Japan. Either parties have simply been very weak and almost non-existent, or the government and the bureaucracy have had at their disposal a dominant party ready to mobilize the population and induce it to support the goals and the achievements of the bureaucracy.

Thus the key question which has to be answered with respect to the future of the political systems of the East and Southeast Asian countries consists in determining how far the bureaucracy will continue to be able to preside over economic development if the party system becomes fully pluralistic. Yet there is little experience to rely on to provide the guidelines for an answer, Japan and possibly France being the only countries whose evolution might be relevant in this context. Conclusions have therefore to be rather tentative, although the exploration has to be undertaken.

The starting point of such an exploration has to be the recognition that the introduction of a pluralistic system in a polity is bound to have at least some adverse effect on the role of the bureaucracy if the party system is to play a significant part in decision-making. On this basis, three questions have to be answered. First, how large will this effect be? Second, how rapidly will it occur? Third, how detrimental will it be to the ability

PARTIES

	STRONG	(II) "Responsible" party	(III) "Irresponsible" party: Bureaucratic state
BUREAUCRACY	**WEAK**	(I) Political machine	(IV) Regime of notables; corporate state; machine of incumbents

Figure 4.1 **Party and Bureaucratic Power I** (from Shefter 1994, 62)

of the bureaucracy to steer the economy of the countries concerned, in both the short and the long run?

In a rare attempt to analyse the (changing) relationship between parties and the state, in the context of the United States, M. Shefter examines what this relationship is likely to be depending on whether parties and/or bureaucracy are strong or weak. He thus develops a two-by-two matrix (figure 4.1) which enables him to distinguish between "responsible" parties, when both parties and bureaucracy are strong; "irresponsible" parties, when the bureaucracy is strong but the parties are weak; "machine" parties, when the parties are strong and the bureaucracy weak; and a variety of situations which are located in a single group and are labelled "regime of notables," "corporate state," and "machine of incumbents," when both parties and bureaucracy are weak (Shefter 1994, 62).

This matrix provides a means of examining generally what the relationship between (pluralistic) party systems and bureaucracies can be; however, it needs to be made a little more complex if it is to cover the reality of contemporary liberal democracies in general and in particular the democratization process taking place in East and Southeast Asia. This somewhat increased complexity can be obtained by introducing an "intermediate" category between the two extremes of "strong" and "weak" for both parties and bureaucracies (figure 4.2).

When such a threefold distinction is made, a strong (that is, truly proactive) bureaucracy can be defined as one in which there is, to adopt the expressions used in the previous chapter, "embeddedness" and "state steering." The intermediate category corresponds to cases in which there is embeddedness only, that is to say when the state penetrates the society and its decisions are implemented efficiently, but there is no state steering. Weak bureaucracies are those whose decisions are not implemented easily or efficiently.

In the same way, the strength of parties can be assessed by means of a threefold distinction. Strong parties are those which aim truly at implementing and endeavour in practice to implement a programme which

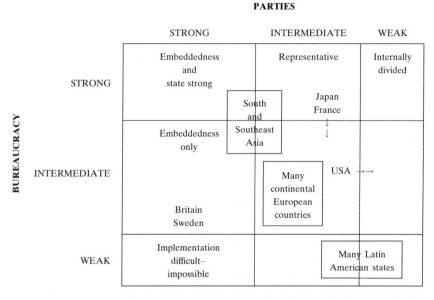

Figure 4.2 **Party and Bureaucratic Power II** (adapted from Shefter 1994, 62)

these parties have previously devised. The programme need not be radical – indeed it is often the case that radical programmes cannot be implemented – but a programme there must be, and it should be considered by both supporters and opponents to be the basis of the action of the government. Alongside such parties, which were referred to in chapter 2 as "programmatic," there are those which were referred to as "representative," and which do not really aim at implementing a programme or cannot do so as a result of having to participate in a coalition: whatever programme they may have adopted will be at best partially implemented. What characterizes these latter parties is more a desire to represent their electors and to make sure that they obtain benefits and suffer as little as possible from the policies which may have to be implemented as a result of the actions of other parties belonging to the ruling coalition. Finally, weak parties are those which are internally very divided, often on a geographical basis: not being cohesive, the help and benefits which they provide to their constituents are more the result of the action of individual representatives than of those of the party as such.

On the basis of these characterisations, liberal democratic countries can be located with relative ease. No country falls in two of the three cells corresponding to strong parties, as no country is found to have both strong parties and a strong bureaucracy; nor does any country have both strong parties and a weak bureaucracy. The first case is non-existent because of the manifest desire of strong parties to achieve their programmes and not to accept that the bureaucracy be fully in charge of steering the country's affairs, on the economic front or elsewhere; the second case is non-existent because a strong party cannot achieve its goals if the bureaucracy is so weak that it does not penetrate the society: parties which are truly strong need the support of the bureaucracy if they are to be effective. In general, Western countries do not have weak bureaucracies, while Latin American democracies are typically associated with weak bureaucracies which do not penetrate their societies well (Mainwaring in Mainwaring and Scully 1995, 388–97; Sloan 1984, 136–53).

The location of countries in figure 4.2 suggests the following conclusions. First, except for Japan, no liberal democracy has a truly strong bureaucracy: France had one in the past, but its strength declined appreciably in the last decades of the twentieth century (Frears 1981; Machin and Wright 1985; Wright 1989). Second, liberal democracies tend to have intermediate bureaucracies, that is to say bureaucracies characterized by a high degree of efficiency but not typically able or willing to do more than advise on how the polity should be steered; on the other hand, those countries vary appreciably in terms of the strength of their political parties. British and Swedish parties, for instance, are strong, while American parties have become weak, especially in the last decades of the twentieth century. The parties of most Continental countries are intermediate in strength: they are centralized and often have a large membership, but are more representative than programmatic, often because they cannot implement fully their programmes in the context of coalitions (Daalder 1987).

Since in liberal democracies, except in Japan, bureaucracies are intermediate in strength, it might seem to follow by analogy that the introduction of a pluralistic party system in East and Southeast Asia would result in the bureaucracy losing some of its current strength. Only Japan would appear to constitute a strong counter-example. The French evolution under the Fifth Republic suggests inevitability in the decline of the role of the bureaucracy when parties begin to be more effective; indeed, the strength of the Spanish bureaucracy was also markedly reduced by the fact that democratization occurred from the second half of the 1970s onward (Esping-Andersen 1992, 118–25).

The conclusion that bureaucracies tend to see their strength reduced as parties become stronger needs to be tempered for two reasons. First, what occurred in France took place over a long period: French parties had only a limited say in the decision-making process not only during the early years of the Fifth Republic, after 1958, but also between 1946 and 1958 during the Fourth Republic: throughout that time, the French economy was steered by the bureaucracy and this steering resulted in high levels of economic growth (Williams 1964). Thus it may be that, in the very long run, a decline in the role of the bureaucracy is likely to occur in a liberal democratic context. It may also be that economic growth will decline, but at least the French case and even more the Japanese case show that the process can be slow, indeed very slow; moreover, a variety of other factors, in particular international ones, can contribute to account for changes in the way the economy comes to be steered. Thus, European integration played a significant part in the French case; and we examined in chapter 1 the possible effect of the globalization of the world economy on the extent to which national economies can be steered at the national level.

Second, in the other Western democracies the bureaucracy was not normally placed in charge of steering the economy at the time when pluralistic party systems developed, typically because the prevailing ideology was opposed to the very idea that the state should be responsible for economic development. Thus bureaucratic agencies in these countries were typically assigned almost exclusively an implementation role and, at best, a role of advice, not of governance (Kellner and Crowther-Hunt 1980; Strauss 1961, 229–80). It is true that when the question of steering the economy did arise in the twentieth century in most if not all of these countries, it was also believed that the liberal democratic ideology entailed that politicians elected by the people should be those who had the authority to take the major decisions. But it is also the case that almost never were the governments of those countries confronted with a strong bureaucracy; nor was the idea of having such a strong bureaucracy, at least at the national level, ever seriously debated. In this respect, France is unique in Western Europe, largely because of the traditions of the French monarchy which, far from being superseded by the advent of the Republic (as was to be the case in Austria and in the Federal Republic of Germany), were reinforced by the rule of both Napoleon I and Napoleon III in the nineteenth century (Ridley and Blondel 1969, 28–31; Kamenka 1989, 97–101). Given that the idea of a strong bureaucracy was not on the agenda of these liberal democratic Western European countries, it is not permissible to conclude that a pluralistic party system necessarily implies the absence of a strong bureaucracy in the sense which was given to the term in this study. Meanwhile, the Japanese example shows that a strong bureaucracy can be combined with a liberal democratic system, while the French example suggests that it can at least take a long time for what was previously a strong bureaucracy to lose some of its capacity to steer the economy.

The fact that we simply cannot justifiably claim that the introduction of liberal democratic arrangements means the end of a strong bureaucracy suggests that we should examine, alongside the case of Japan, those of a number of liberal democracies; this will make it possible to analyse the conditions under which such a strong bureaucracy can coexist with a lively party system. If we are to undertake such a quest, however, there is little point in considering the cases of countries in which parties are strong in the sense we have given here to the term, such as Britain or Sweden, since a truly strong party system does not appear logically able to coexist with a strong bureaucracy: programmatic parties are not likely to accept that the bureaucracy should be involved directly in economic governance. Rather, examples drawn from among countries in which parties are weak or of intermediate strength should be examined. These parties can be associated with strong bureaucracies; indeed, they may be of great value to such bureaucracies, because these bureaucracies may be confronted with major societal pressures and even serious disturbances if there are no outlets for the population of these countries to manifest their discontent. Parties which are intermediate in strength and are thus representative only, and even parties which are weak and cater to local interests only through their elected representatives, can thus render strong bureaucracies more alert to the problems of their societies and can help, rather than hinder, the actions of these bureaucracies (Blondel 1978; Maisel and Cooper 1978; Katz and Mair 1994).

Moreover, given that some East and Southeast Asian countries are presidential or semi-presidential (Korea, Taiwan, and the Philippines, as well as, in a different constitutional context, Indonesia) and given that some countries are multicultural (Malaysia, Singapore, Indonesia, and the Philippines), it is most relevant to look at the cases of other presidential or semi-presidential systems and at multicultural consociational democracies in order to discover whether specific institutional or behavioural difficulties need to be faced if one wishes to see countries with these characteristics retain strong bureaucracies in a liberal democratic framework. Yet it is above all most relevant to consider the Japanese case which is, ostensibly at least, by far the closest to those of the democratizing countries of East and Southeast Asia. We shall therefore naturally turn first to an examination of the Japanese case; we shall then consider the cases of consociational parliamentary systems, specifically the Low Countries, and those of presidential systems, principally the United States, but also, to an extent, Latin American countries. It will be possible in this way to discover to what extent the experience of these types of government can constitute models at a time when East and Southeast Asian polities move towards pluralistic party systems but also wish to retain high-profile bureaucracies.

Japan: Liberal democracy and strong bureaucracy

In Martin Shefter's typology, Japan may be viewed as a system where strong bureaucracies and irresponsible parties live side by side. Indeed, bureaucracy enjoys much higher esteem than political parties in Japan: in both policy-making and implementation, the bureaucracy is widely recognized as a driving force. Three major historical turning points of Japanese political development over the past four centuries have given much more advantages to the bureaucracy than to parties.

The first turning point took place in the seventeenth century, when Tokugawa rule (1603–1858) was established and the early modern bureaucracy was set up in each of the 300-odd governing units called *han*. The bureaucracy was characterized by the following features. First, it consisted of disarmed warriors residing in castle towns and thus detached from land possession. These embryo bureaucrats were very small in number compared to the population; they were highly educated and helped to spread literacy among the population.

Second, the bureaucracy carried out the key major tasks of each governing unit except for defense, diplomacy, and external trade, which the Tokugawa wanted to keep as their prerogative. These tasks included taxation, crime control, flood control, and the promotion of indigenous industries and commerce. The bureaucracy was often too small for these tasks: this prompted it to delegate a substantial amount of business to large landlords and merchants. Warrior-bureaucrats retained their power over these non-warrior-bureaucrats as the highest social class of the regime.

Third, the ethos of the new bureaucracy was that of "honorific collectivism" as opposed to "honorific individualism," to use Keiko Ikegami's expression (1995). Their loyalty was not to the "lord of *han*" but to the organization headed by the lord, and to certain principles associated with it. The bureaucracy resembled some types of modern professional organizations in that it was not overly disturbed by an arbitrary, despotic, or incompetent lord.

The second turning point came in the mid-nineteenth century. The Meiji Restoration brought the emperor back to sovereign status, yet the policy apparatus to make the country rich and its army strong had to be created. The task went to bureaucracy. The trend of bureaucratization of the governing regime was further enhanced. Three hundred–odd bureaucracies at the *han* level were abolished, and a nationwide state bureaucracy recruited on a meritocratic basis was set up towards the end of the nineteenth century. Bureaucrats were to serve the country above partisan interests and work for the general interests of the nation. Although parliamentary democracy was also set up in a somewhat limited fashion toward the end of the nineteenth century, the policy apparatus remained firmly under the control of the bureaucracy. Parliamentarians in the Imperial Diet and local assemblies were drawn largely either from un-employed warriors or from overtaxed landlords: they were therefore regarded by the government as disgruntled upwardly mobile strata who could be co-opted. The Imperial Diet was a bastion of parliamentarians of this type until the 1910s when most were obliged to fit into a frame-work in which two major parties alternated in power. Meanwhile, policy-making and implementation rested firmly with the bureaucracy: the main task of parliamentarians was to take care of people's sentiments in their districts by participating in funerals, wedding ceremonies, business open-ing ceremonies, and festivals as well as by bringing in pork-barrel projects.

The third turning point came in the mid-twentieth century. After its crushing defeat by the United States in the Second World War, Japan was occupied by the U.S.-led Allied powers for seven years. The ancient regime was meant to be thoroughly destroyed in order that Japan be transformed into a peace-loving democratic country without military or industrial might. However, the exigencies of the Cold War led the United States to occupy Japan in an indirect way, i.e., through the Japanese bu-reaucracy. All political, social, and economic organizations were more or less tainted by wartime misconduct and thus eligible for political purge by the occupying powers: only the bureaucracy emerged more or less intact from the purge, though the Ministry of Internal Affairs was divided into a number of ministries such as Health and Welfare, Labour, Home Affairs, and Construction, and the war ministries were abolished. The Allies ruled Japan through the Japanese bureaucracy and the latter's power was im-mensely enhanced as counterbalancing institutions, including political parties, were almost all destroyed. Especially noteworthy is the fact that the Allies were at the origin of the dominance of economic ministries such as the Economic Planning Board (later the Economic Planning Agency), the Ministry of Finance, and the Ministry of International Trade and Industry. These were to become the foci of policy-making and implementing power in much of the latter half of the twentieth century.

Parliamentarians, now elected in a thoroughly liberal institutional manner, were again given their traditional role of taking care of con-stituencies rather than the function of designing broad policy lines or shaping policy itself. This policy role did increase significantly after the 1980s, admittedly, especially as a result of committee memberships; yet the change was one of degree only. Furthermore, even when newspaper headlines constantly proclaim scandals in the bureaucracy, the prestige of bureaucrats remains higher than that of politicians in the eyes of the public.

Given these three levels of bureaucratic strength over three centuries, it is only natural that in Japan the bureaucracy should reign supreme, even if its prestige and power have somewhat declined by comparison with that of parliamentarians and of political parties. In any case, one should not conclude that the bureaucracy is overwhelmingly strong and political parties extremely weak. First, an egalitarian trend is at work in which social background also plays a part: as their educational levels were high, bureaucrats of ex–warrior family origin were disproportionately numerous until the 1920s, forming half of the total intake, although the recruitment was meritocratic. After the Second World War, any reference to social background became politically incorrect and therefore no systematic evidence exists as to class origin. More importantly, the egalitarian trend means that bureaucrats are increasingly regarded as being on a par with ordinary citizens. A streak of anti-authoritarianism has been increasingly obvious in Japanese society after the Second World War: for instance, in the mid-1980s, respondents who gave a favourable response to the view that "greater respect should be accorded to authority" were about one-tenth in Japan of the percentage in the United States or United Kingdom.

Second, globalization now permeates the Japanese body politic, undermining the basis of political institutions. It may not subvert overnight the whole system of the territorial sovereign nation state, as Jean Marie Guehenno contends, but it weakens and undermines the society steadily. In tandem with the loosening of the nation state's grip on the population, democracy is threatened, as Guehenno argues. Globalization first divides competitive firms from non-competitive firms, competitive sectors from non-competitive sectors, competitive regions from non-competitive regions. Competitive actors start to behave as if government-imposed rules and frameworks were barriers while non-competitive actors increasingly seek government action. The former tend to pay a disproportionate portion of government tax revenue while the latter normally do not shoulder any tax burden at all. Yet, in political terms, the latter have the votes. For instance, in the 1996 Metropolitan Assembly elections, only those in their sixties and older voted in overwhelmingly high proportions while voters from other age groups abstained at a disturbingly high rate. Aged people are highly dependent on public money. Also, those parliamentarians who represent sparsely populated areas are markedly more numerous than those representing metropolitan districts. Only a few dozen business firms in the automobile, electronic, and machine industries contribute to the trade surplus while thousands of other businesses do not. Although Japanese society is highly adaptable, globalization does undermine closely organized relationships among actors and institutions. The closely organized relationships between government agencies and business sectors, between business firms and banking sectors, big business firms and subcontractors, and between management and labour are being forced to change.

Third, with civil society becoming stronger, the power of its representatives, the parliamentarians, is enhanced. However historically structurally handicapped it may be vis-à-vis bureaucrats, business is increasingly self-confident: its power is far less dependent on government subsidies, credit rationing, preferential treatment in public works, or official development assistance than in the past. The number of non-governmental organizations (NGOs) has steadily risen, thus falsifying the observation, which is often made, that in Japanese society there are only two categories: government organizations (GOs) and non-governmental individuals (NGIs). A recent manifestation of this rise is the seeming success of the administrative reform efforts of Prime Minister Ryutaro Hashimoto. In the past, efforts of this kind but on a smaller scale had died a premature death, largely because of the bureaucrats' diehard resistance; but Prime Minister Hashimoto was able to bring the recommendations of the Administrative Reform Council for approval to the governing parties and to the National Diet.

As a consequence, first, the top echelon of governmental agencies is increasingly politicized: top-ranking bureaucrats at the higher level are increasingly under the influence of the prime minister and other leading party politicians. Second, some sections of the governmental agencies are becoming guardians-cum-agents of business sectors. In the past the bureaucracy had definitely the role of guardian, but it is now sometimes an agent and a colony of some business sectors, such as agriculture, financial services, transportation, or telecommunications. Governmental agencies therefore face increasing difficulties when they claim to represent the general interest of the nation. Third, the social prestige of bureaucrats has steadily declined: those economic ministries which enjoyed high prestige are at their nadir whilst "order"-orientated ministries are regaining some of the prestige they enjoyed before 1945.

Despite all of these counter-trends, the basic configuration of a strong bureaucracy and of weak political parties has not been changed fundamentally, at least by comparison with other countries. The bureaucracy has been the key element shaping Japanese society for the last three to four centuries. It monitors the society and its various segments. It identifies policy needs, designs policy frameworks, and shapes policy itself from the bill drafting phase onward. It then implements and assesses policy. The bureaucratic sector may be based on meritocratic recruitment, but school ties are important. Japanese bureaucracy may not be "a government of strangers"; yet there are school networks at the top. Equally important is the relative isolation of the bureaucracy from other sectors in terms of recruitment. Bureaucrats can descend from heaven after retirement but virtually no one was recruited from outside the bureaucratic sector as far as the top echelon is concerned. This is in sharp contrast with France, which is also a society dominated by the bureaucracy: ENA graduates go to the bureaucracy, to business and to politics; they change their profession in a far more flexible manner.

Japanese political parties have a number of special features. Except for the Communists, they are not strongly programmatic parties. The basis of their popular support is not primarily socio-economic; party identification is not as strong as in the United States. On the other hand, personal linkages play a decisive role in campaigning: to reach the hearts of con-stituents and to bring pork to their districts are major tasks of parlia-mentarians, in which political party headquarters may not have much to say.

Moreover, the party system has distinctive features. First, the largest party has been the governing party of the Centre-Right which has cap-tured a vast contingent of voters. Second, opposition parties are divided and much smaller than the governing party. They rely heavily on some special sectors or on some wind blowing against the government because of its misconduct or of that of well-known individual parliamentarians. Third, within the governing party, factions play a strong part: they com-pete while also co-operating to sustain the government. They may not be states within the state, but they cannot be disregarded where candidate selection, cabinet composition, and party positions are concerned.

Two elements may induce East and Southeast Asian nations to emulate the Japanese model based on a strong bureaucracy, one predominant party, and a few relatively small opposition parties. First, like Japan from the 1930s to the 1960s, many countries of the region industrialized rapidly from the 1960s to the 1980s. Japan's state-led industrialization strength-ened the power of the bureaucracy and especially that of the economic ministries: countries which are similarly motivated will try to emulate Japan's approach. From the 1960s and 1970s to the 1980s "developmental authoritarianism" was the key expression in the region, leading to what might be labelled top-down emulation. It is questionable how successful this was: indeed, there is some doubt as to whether, even at the height of developmental authoritarianism, the bureaucracy in most countries had the political muscle which Japanese economic ministries enjoyed in the 1950s and 1960s. Second, the spread of Japan's vast manufacturing net-works throughout East and Southeast Asia means that emulation from the bottom up is also at work as a result of the adoption of Japanese-style factory management, *keiretsu*, and business-government practices. Of course, Japan's manufacturing preponderance is far from absolute; its institutional influence is far from hegemonic. Yet so long as Asia is in Japan's embrace in manufacturing sectors, the economic base is bound to have some influence on the political framework. The combination of a strong bureaucracy and of one dominant governing party may therefore be the preferred framework in many East and Southeast Asian states. But this combination may be ephemeral even when developmental authoritarianism prevails: once democratization begins to take place, the bureaucracy comes to be increasingly under the influence of the politicians and the single dominant party often evaporates overnight. Thus the Japanese model of a strong bureaucracy in a liberal democratic context is not likely to fit easily other polities of the region; nor are these countries likely to adopt the Japanese model of one dominant governing party and a number of small opposition parties.

The consociational parliamentary model and the maintenance of a strong bureaucracy

Since the Japanese model may not suit very well at least some of the countries of East and Southeast Asia for a variety of socio-cultural and political reasons, it is worth at least considering some alternatives. In fact, the political arrangements of the Low Countries may be regarded as providing a valuable model. Admittedly, neither Belgium nor the Netherlands, and especially not Belgium, has a truly strong public bureaucracy, although the bureaucracy of these countries is efficient and penetrates well into the society; but the parallel with some East and Southeast Asian countries is striking, as the social structure of Malaysia, Singapore, and – though in a different way – Indonesia and the Philippines is closer to that of Belgium and the Netherlands than to that of Japan. This is because the complex ethnic or religious divisions which characterize these countries need to be given their full weight in the political order if these polities are to remain stable and to continue to progress in a harmonious and peaceful manner.

The social cleavages or "pillars" which characterize the multicultural polities of East and Southeast Asia are admittedly different from those of the Low Countries. In Belgium and the Netherlands, the main cleavage was traditionally the religious one, to which a class cleavage was gradually added; in Belgium, the linguistic cleavage grew increasingly in importance until it became paramount in the last decades of the twentieth century (Daalder 1987; Lijphart 1977; Lijphart 1984). In Malaysia and Singapore, on the other hand, the principal cleavage is ethnic, though a religious division is associated with this; in Indonesia and in the Philippines, and to an extent in Malaysia as well, the basic cleavage occurs along geographical lines, while in continental Malaysia, by and large, and naturally in Singapore, the different "pillars" are found in the same areas.

In Belgium and the Netherlands, some of the cleavages occur also along geographical lines: this is particularly the case in Belgium, where the linguistic boundary runs approximately east-west, with Dutch being spoken in the north of the country and French in the south; a geographical division also occurs to an extent in the Netherlands as the south of the country is Catholic while the north is Protestant.

Thus the contrast is sharp between Japan, where there is a profound cultural homogeneity, and the Low Countries, where means had gradually to be found to accommodate social cleavages in order to maintain political order and ensure peaceful progress (Lijphart 1977; Lijphart 1984). Similarly, in East and Southeast Asia, the contrast is also sharp between Japan (and also Korea) and Malaysia and in a different way Singapore, which have had to accommodate deep-seated ethnic-cum-religious cleavages in order to avoid serious social problems. Moreover, whether Indonesia and the Philippines can long avoid being structured on the basis of principles of social and political accommodation seems somewhat doubtful, despite the fact that in both countries, and in particular in the latter, presidentialism, as opposed to the cabinet system, would appear to make it more difficult for the principle of accommodation to be introduced.

The principle of accommodation led to the development of consociationalism on the political plane, as we noted in chapter 2. This principle has been in force not only in Belgium and the Netherlands, but also in Switzerland since at least the middle of the nineteenth century and in Austria since World War II (Daalder 1987). Belgium and the Netherlands constitute the best basis for a comparison with East and Southeast Asia, however: in Switzerland, consociationalism is so deep and affects the whole political system to such an extent that it can scarcely be imitated (except, somewhat surprisingly perhaps, but very logically, at the level of the European Union) (Blondel 1998); in Austria, on the contrary, consociationalism has been based almost exclusively on the class cleavage and it was adopted to prevent a repetition of the violent conflicts of the 1920s and 1930s, but its impact has gradually been reduced (Gerlich in Daalder 1987, 61–106).

Consociationalism means setting aside the majority principle, at least with respect to certain key issues which are deemed to be so fundamental for the well-being of the society that they need to be handled by means of arrangements leading to compromises between the political representatives of the major groups in the country. Thus consociationalism prevails whether a particular group is in the majority or not. This principle has had two fundamental consequences for the structure of politics in Belgium and the Netherlands. The first consequence is that the alternation of parties in power plays a limited part and that accommodation extends beyond those parties which happen to be represented in the government at a given point in time, to affect others which were before and are likely to be again later part of the ruling coalition. In the Netherlands, the adoption of the principle has undoubtedly been helped by the fact that no single party has ever come close to obtaining a majority in parliament; in Belgium, only once in the 1950s did a party (the Christian Democrats) achieve such a result. Thus, both countries are governed by coalitions which vary only to a limited extent, as, with rare exceptions, one of the parties, the Christian Democrats, is the pivot of the majority while the other parties come in and out of the government but are never considered to be very far from it. Given that each party in government at a given point in time knows that the parties which are out of power are likely to join the ruling coalition in the future, it is manifestly not in their interest to pursue policies to which the parties which are in such a temporary opposition deeply object. Thus, by osmosis, the consociational principle extends, to a degree, to most of the parties and at least to the parties which embody the major social cleavages in the country, a development which has led to the idea that these parties may constitute a kind of "cartel," as was noted in chapter 2 (Katz and Mair 1995, 5–28).

The second consequence of the consociational principle is that parties are neither truly strong nor truly weak. They are not as strong as British or Swedish parties; they are not as weak as American parties because they have emerged from the broad social cleavages which are their *raison d'être*. Admittedly, these cleavages have declined markedly in the Netherlands; but, in Belgium, the "pillars" on which the society is based have remained strong. Even in the Netherlands, the traditional strength of these "pillars" is such that parties have remained highly centralized and the local influence which individual politicians may exercise is channelled through and on behalf of the parties. On the other hand, as each party knows that it has to operate in the context of a coalition and, more generally, that compromises have to be made on key issues, the nature of party expectations has come to be markedly reduced: since parties do not believe that they can implement their goals on their own, they are not strong in the sense of being programmatic, as defined in this study, even if they issue programmes at election time. Given that these organizations all know that they have to work with others to build coalitions, the programmes which they propose are more in the nature of opening gambits than of genuine proposals. The real aim of these parties is thus to represent their electors and in particular to represent what they regard as the interests of the social groups from which they have emerged.

Such a state of affairs would clearly seem to be advantageous for the

establishment of a good working relationship between parties and bureaucracy. As parties have relatively limited goals and have intermediate
strength only, the bureaucracy is not prevented from being strong.
Moreover, as there cannot be more than limited alternation in power
among the parties, there can be continuity of governmental action, and
efforts made by the bureaucracy to move the economy in a particular direction are unlikely to be impeded; in particular, an election result will
not lead to the coming to power of a party or of a presidential team
whose views and aims are wholly different from those of the outgoing
government.

Yet, despite these ostensible advantages from which the bureaucracy
might benefit in a consociational system, the experience of Belgium and
of the Netherlands does not suggest, in particular in the Belgian case, that
the part played by the bureaucracy will necessarily be large in practice.
Two types of serious limitations to the role of the bureaucracy have indeed characterized the Low Countries. First, the claim has often been
made, seemingly on the basis of substantial evidence, that the consociational system, far from leading to the bureaucracy being on top, results in
the political parties using the bureaucracy in order to bring favours to
party members and supporters. Such a development has not occurred
significantly in the Netherlands, but it has occurred in Belgium on a very
large scale (as well as in Austria) (Blondel and Cotta 1996, 72–75, 103–
8). This practice might even be described as constituting a form of compensation for the fact that the parties cannot fully satisfy their supporters
in terms of programme implementation: the compromises which are
struck between the top leadership groups of the coalition parties might be
less easily accepted by the rank and file if the system was not "oiled" by
means of favours distributed to supporters. These supporters also know
that they must remain loyal to their party, even though that party may
not implement the policies which they would wish to see adopted, as
otherwise, the purely personal benefits which they have enjoyed in the
past may cease to come their way.

The second problem which the bureaucracy has faced in the Low
Countries has originated from the way in which compromises are arrived
at the governmental level. As there have to be compromises, the policy-
making process is more likely to be characterized by meandering than
by clear-cut decisions based on well-defined goals. This is likely to be true
at the time governments are formed; it is also likely to be true during the
lifetime of governments when unforeseen circumstances arise and one of
the parties in the coalition (or even a party outside the coalition) insists
on different arrangements being worked out in order to take into account
the new developments. While these complex and often difficult negotia-

tions take place, the bureaucracy's goals with respect to the economy may be set aside or modified in order to achieve the accommodation which is required to maintain political peace.

It is therefore understandable that despite the advantages from which it ostensibly benefits in terms of governmental continuity, the bureaucracy may also find its power markedly reduced where consociationalism prevails. However, the fact that the bureaucracy has not been able to assert its strength in the Low Countries does not entail that it will not remain strong in those multicultural polities of East and Southeast Asia where it might be appropriate to adopt consociational arrangements: to come to a realistic conclusion in this respect, two profound differences between the political evolution of the Low Countries and that of the polities of East and Southeast Asia have to be taken into account.

First, the colonization of the bureaucracy by the political parties has not been universal in Western European consociational countries, as we saw: it has occurred on a major scale in Belgium but not in the Netherlands. The reasons for this sharp contrast are numerous and range probably from differences in political culture to differences in the relationship between the executive and the legislature in the two countries. What should also be remembered is that patronage does play a large part as well in some non-consociational Western European countries but not in all (Blondel and Cotta 1996). What the contrast between Belgium and the Netherlands does show is that the distribution of favours via the parties is not an integral part of consociationalism. Moreover, although this may be regarded as distasteful, favours extracted from the public bureaucracy play a large part in many of the polities of East and Southeast Asia, whether these are consociational or not: while it would clearly be wrong to promote a type of governmental arrangement likely to develop on an even greater scale the distribution of favours from the public sector to party supporters, it has to be noted that these practices exist and that they will be uprooted only gradually. Moreover, as favours are being extracted from the public sector in a context in which the bureaucracy also promotes rapid economic development, it follows that the two elements are not incompatible, however unhappy we may be to have to arrive at such a conclusion. As the experience of the Low Countries shows that favours are not intrinsically linked to a consociational system, it must therefore be concluded that the introduction of consociationalism should not be ruled out on the grounds that it might result in a decline in the strength of the bureaucracy because favours are distributed from the public sector to party supporters.

Second, the patterns of behaviour of the leadership groups of the coalition parties in consociational systems would seem likely to have a definite impact on the part which the bureaucracy plays in ensuring that the progress of the economy is regular. However, with respect to the expansion of the role of the bureaucracy, there is a sharp contrast between the current situation in East and Southeast Asia and the situation which has characterized Belgium and the Netherlands since liberal democracy was introduced in those countries. In Belgium and the Netherlands, the development of the party system and the implementation of the accommodation principle antedated markedly the development of bureaucracy, though in the Netherlands, the bureaucracy did retain the somewhat autonomous status which it had acquired earlier under the constitutional monarchy even when the executive came to be controlled by the political parties at the beginning of the twentieth century. This separation may, indeed, have accounted in part for the fact that the Dutch bureaucracy was never colonized by the political parties as it was to be in Belgium. Yet, in neither country was the bureaucracy given the task of steering the economy or indeed of the general governance of the country. The role of the bureaucracy was always conceived as lower-key, and it continued to be lower-key even when the political parties came to be in charge of the government in the twentieth century. In a situation such as that of East and Southeast Asia where, on the contrary, the emphasis on economic development has been dominant, it is not very likely, to say the least, that any political party which would belong to a consociational arrangement would challenge the ideology of economic development and the right of the bureaucracy to take a firm lead in this respect.

In East and Southeast Asia, the bureaucracy would therefore be able to benefit to the full from the development of consociationalism. These benefits are above all constituted by the fact that the political parties can provide the representative base which is needed for the political system to function regularly and without major upheavals. In this way the parties are able to reduce the tensions which might arise among key groups in the society and ensure that these conflicts do not impinge significantly on the direction which the bureaucracy wishes to give to the economy. The capacity of the parties to achieve these results is already noticeable in what must be regarded as the somewhat limited consociational formula prevailing in Malaysia: were such a arrangement made truly consociational by being wholly pluralistic at the level of party campaigning and electoral practices, the effect would be to give full legitimacy both to the links between the coalition parties and to the relationship between these parties and the bureaucracy. What could thus occur in Malaysia could manifestly also occur in the other East and Southeast Asian polities in which the complexity of the ethnic and/or religious social structure suggests that there is a need for a consociational arrangement.

Presidentialism on the United States and Latin American models and the maintenance of a strong bureaucracy

While the Japanese model may appeal to a number of polities in East and Southeast Asia and while the consociational model may serve the needs of those polities which are multicultural, there are also countries in the area in which presidential or semi-presidential rule has prevailed for decades, Korea and the Philippines in particular. These are not likely to want to move or, if they attempted to do so, to move easily and quickly, towards a parliamentary system either of the Japanese or of the Belgian and Dutch variety. There is therefore a case for seeing whether a full-fledged pluralistic form of presidentialism is compatible with a strong influence of the bureaucracy in steering the economy. One must therefore examine the way in which parties and bureaucracy relate in those presidential systems which have had a long experience of pluralistic rule, in particular in the United States.

At first sight, such an examination does not seem reassuring for the future role of the bureaucracies in East and Southeast Asia. The United States is the Western country which has probably the weakest political parties; it is also probably the country in which the bureaucracy, while efficient, has been least able and even least inclined to act on its own initiative. Both parties and bureaucracy have come to be highly divided internally. The level of decentralization of the two main American parties is such that it has often been suggested that there are in reality one hundred parties – two per state, rather than two in the country as a whole; it is perhaps even questionable whether there is, or at least whether there is any longer, a genuine party system in the United States (Ware 1987, 118; Peele, Bailey, and Cain 1992, 63–82). The bureaucracy is divided among federal, state, and local authorities; but it is further divided as a result of the existence of a large number of regulatory and semi-autonomous agencies (Peele, Bailey, and Cain 1992, 165–89). Thus, not surprisingly, parties must be described as weak; the bureaucracy may be regarded as occupying an intermediate position between strength and weakness because of its efficiency, but it is not proactive.

The problems posed by both parties and bureaucracy in the United States are partly the consequence of the institutional structure. As we noted in chapter 2, presidentialism has been widely criticized especially on two main grounds, although the distinction is not always made between characteristics which are specific to the United States and stem from the nature of American society and characteristics which appear to result from presidentialism itself. The first ground is that it divides parties internally rather than unites them because of internal competition among presidential candidates of these parties, and the second is the fixed duration and the non- or limited reeligibility of the presidential incumbents (Linz 1990; Shugart and Carey 1992, 273–87).

The first criticism, according to which presidentialism divides parties internally, stems from the fact that as the survival of the executive does not depend on the loyalty of the members of the legislature in the way it does in parliamentary systems, these elected representatives seem likely to give priority to maintaining their popularity in their districts rather than to supporting the executive. This conclusion may not be an inevitable consequence of presidential systems, however. In some Latin American countries, for instance Argentina and Venezuela, parties are centralized and disciplined: this suggests that other factors are likely to be at play and/or that the decentralization of parties may be due, in part at least, to specific characteristics of American society (Coppedge 1994; McGuire in Mainwaring and Scully 1995, 200–248).

Presidentialism is also criticized because of the fixed duration of the mandate of the chief executive, which results in lack of flexibility; this fixed duration may also be rather short, especially if it is coupled with the widely adopted rule according to which incumbents may not stand again (typical in Latin America, especially before the 1990s) or can stand again once only (in the United States). The fixed terms and the non- (or limited) reeligibility rules result in repeated changes at the top of the executive: this is allegedly detrimental to policy continuity and, therefore, to the ability of the bureaucracy to steer the society and in particular the economy. Thus, even if the same party wins successive elections, changes at the top of the administration have an effect which may not be markedly different from the effect which results from a different party coming to power.

This state of affairs is particularly detrimental to the bureaucracy since presidents, once elected, are able (indeed expected) to choose their immediate subordinates at will: they are not – especially in the United States currently, though less so in Latin America and indeed in the United States in the nineteenth century – constrained to appoint their cabinets from among members of the leadership of their parties. As a matter of fact, presidents often have to reward those who have helped them during the election campaign by giving them positions in the government. Two consequences follow, both of which have an impact on the role of the bureaucracy. First, the members of the executive are likely to want to pursue their own policies and disregard the bureaucracy as much as possible: one side effect may well be a marked loss of morale among some of the top public servants. Second, the government is not truly a team, as its members are appointed for reasons which have more to do with the personal circumstances of the individuals concerned than with the work they might previously have done for the good of the party (Heclo 1977, 84–112). These characteristics, too, are more marked in U.S. administrations than in Latin American executives: some of these are indeed based on party coalitions in which the members of the cabinet are selected by the leadership of the parties concerned (Coppedge 1994; McGuire in Mainwaring and Scully 1995, 200–248).

A number of characteristics of the presidential system and in particular of the U.S. presidential system are thus likely to have a negative effect on the role of the bureaucracy. But another aspect, which we also noted in chapter 2, works at least to an extent in favour of the bureaucracy: both as it developed in the United States and as it developed elsewhere, the presidential system has one strongly positive value, which is to ensure the stability of the executive in countries in which parties tend to be "naturally" internally divided, for instance on a geographical basis; or in which the party system is highly fragmented, because it is not based on a small number of deeply felt and therefore strong social cleavages. When either or both of these cases obtain, the parliamentary system tends to lead to unstable governments while the presidential system brings about at least a substantial degree of executive stability.

Given the weakness of parliamentary executives where the party system is highly fragmented and in particular highly localized, the role of the bureaucracy is likely to be impaired. Admittedly, in France, immediately after World War II and during the dozen years of the Fourth Republic before De Gaulle installed a form of semi-presidentialism in 1958, the bureaucracy seemed paradoxically to have benefited from the weaknesses of the parliamentary system: as a result of the absence of governmental leadership, the bureaucracy exercised for a while considerable influence, in particular over the economy. The circumstances were exceptional, however. The bureaucracy's role was boosted by the imperatives of postwar reconstruction and modernisation, and it is doubtful whether it would have been maintained its great strength for very much longer had not De Gaulle protected it in turn against the pressure of the politicians, but in the very different institutional context of the Fifth Republic. Above all, the system of the Fourth Republic collapsed in 1958 at least in part because the instability of the parliamentary executive had shown the system to be ineffective, had therefore fostered popular discontent, and had led to demands for a complete overhaul of political arrangements. Thus the strength of the bureaucracy in conditions of parliamentary instability was temporary; as a matter of fact, it came to be better established during the first decades of the Fifth Republic, in the 1960s and 1970s, until the party system became more programmatic as a result of the increased popularity of the Socialist Party from the late 1970s (Frears 1981; Machin and Wright 1985; Wright 1989).

Thus, in countries in which broad social cleavages are weak or almost non-existent, the presidential system provides an opportunity to create, somewhat artificially to be sure, a relatively stable executive. The liberal democratic form of government is likely to acquire greater legitimacy as a result: this is indirectly advantageous to the bureaucracy as it is then in a better position to resist demands made by local politicians and to maintain a degree of autonomy vis-à-vis elected representatives. Both because of the nature of the pressures which tend to be exercised by legislators and because the institutional framework of government is likely to be regarded by the population as more legitimate than a weak and unstable parliamentary executive, the presidential system may help a strong bureaucracy to continue to exercise its influence in countries where the party system remains rather inchoate.

Yet the strength of the bureaucracy may also be undermined in part because the stability of the presidents and of their administration is only relative and in part because of the autonomy of the presidents in the selection of their cabinets: these characteristics may make it difficult for public servants to maintain a consistent line of action and even to preserve their collective identity. Presidential governments are sometimes inclined to engage in forms of populism, in which the bureaucracy is a target for criticism: such a mode of behaviour has been noticeable in the United States in a number of instances when crusades aimed at cleaning up the bureaucracy were started. The ostensible purpose of these crusades may be to ensure that appointments are made on the basis of merit rather than as a result of patronage and that subsequent career prospects of public servants be more regular and based on equity. But the likely result is to provide a further reason for the politicians to intervene in the workings of the bureaucracy and even to reduce its *esprit de corps* by instilling the view, for instance, that the bureaucracy must be more "democratic" and take popular demands more into account (Shefter in Maisel and Cooper 1978, 211–66).

These developments, coupled with the vertical division of powers in the United States among federal, state, and local authorities, have ensured that the U.S. bureaucracy is not strong in the sense which has been given to this expression throughout this chapter. Yet the fact that the U.S. bureaucracy is not truly strong should not be attributed exclusively to the effect of the presidential system on the character of bureaucracies. The origins of the U.S. polity are vastly different from those of Latin American polities; they are also vastly different from those of the Philippine or Korean polities, despite the fact that a widespread American influence was exercised in these two countries, and in particular in the Philippines. The aspect of the political system which these two countries have in common with the United States is constituted by the fact that parties are highly regionalized or even localized, and that there are no strong national cleavages helping to cement the allegiance of citizens to these parties. On the other hand, while in the United States the electoral structure and the liberal democratic processes preceded and in effect created the bureaucracy, in Korea and the Philippines the bureaucratic structure antedated the introduction of an elected executive, even if one takes into account the reorganization which took place in the Philippines under American rule before World War II and in Korea immediately after that war when the country gained its independence. It is important to note that in Korea as well as in Taiwan, Japanese influence predominated previously and had led to the setting up of a strong bureaucracy, while Spanish rule in the Philippines also had a manifestly bureaucratic character.

It follows that in Korea in particular, and to a lesser extent in the Philippines, the reality is that of a kind of presidential system in which two forces compete within the executive, the presidency and the bureaucracy. The power relationships characterizing these two countries are thus in sharp contrast with the power relationships which characterize the United States. It seems therefore highly improbable that the strength of the bureaucracy will be quickly eroded, or at least quickly eroded to a significant extent, in either Korea or the Philippines. The president and the cabinet are confronted in both countries with a cohesive and highly motivated bureaucracy, and the opportunity which a rather transient president may have to succeed in shaking – supposing that the president even wishes to shake – the prerogatives of such a bureaucracy is very limited and probably non-existent in practice.

Indeed, a further reason militates in favour of the maintenance of a strong bureaucracy, especially in Korea, but also, and perhaps by way of imitation, in the Philippines. In the United States, the basic ideology has always been the pursuit of the happiness of the citizens, a pursuit which is expected to be achieved by individual effort and through the exercise of personal freedom; but the prevailing ideology on which a state such as Korea has been based has been the goal of economic development achieved by means of a collective and cohesive effort. Following the success, not merely of Japan, but of Korea itself and of the other "Tigers," a similar ideology has come increasingly to be adopted in other East and Southeast Asian countries, for instance in the Philippines. It is widely believed – whether with truth or not is beside the point, at any rate so far – that such a rapid economic development could not have taken place without the presence of a strong bureaucracy at the helm. Given this belief, presidents and their cabinets are, to say the least, extremely unlikely to want to upset pre-existing arrangements; on the contrary, they are most likely to want to strengthen them. They will therefore tend to support the bureaucracy – and draw some prestige out of this support – rather than reduce its power and establish their own strength at the expense of and against the bureaucracy.

Thus the presidential system does not prevent the bureaucracy from being strong despite the fact that, in the American case – though essentially as a result of the historical conditions in which the political characteristics of that country emerged – the bureaucracy has not been dominant although it has been efficient. To the extent that in some of the East and Southeast Asian countries, the party system displays American features of marked decentralization and high localism rather that what can be regarded as European characteristics of centralization based on broad national cleavages, the presidential system appears to be the most appropriate formula to adopt. Given its traditional strength in East and Southeast Asia, the bureaucracy is not likely to be prevented by the existence of a presidential structure from steering the economy in the manner which made it possible for these countries to achieve the "miraculous" successes which characterized them in the last decades of the twentieth century.

The examination of the three models constituted by Japan, by consociationalism in Belgium and the Netherlands, and by the United States and other presidential systems, suggests that, if a number of conditions are respected, East and Southeast Asian polities can continue to see their economies steered by a strong bureaucracy while adopting a truly pluralistic political system in which a number of political parties play a significant part. One of the key conditions to be respected is that political parties should not be fully programmatic; but this is not likely to occur, as the party systems of East and Southeast Asian countries have so far been based either on dominant, near single-party systems closely tied to the government and the bureaucracy, or on a number of rather small and nationally divided or localized parties in which a multitude of leaders predominate.

Prima facie, the Japanese model is the one most likely to enable the bureaucracy to retain its power while parties gradually acquire greater strength where they were very weak, or more autonomy where they depend on the government; but the Japanese model may not be easily adopted by multicultural polities, and/or by those in which there has been a prolonged tradition of presidential rule. The consociational model of the Low Countries and the presidential system on the American pattern therefore have relevance for the area.

It remains to be seen whether or not the evolution of the polities of East and Southeast Asia indicates that in practice, these countries will move, and indeed are already moving, along the paths which would appear to be best suited to them, given their socio-political characteristics. The aim of the second part of this volume is to provide at least the beginning of an answer to this question by a close analysis of current developments in each of the countries concerned.

REFERENCES

Bagehot, W. (1963), *The English Constitution*, Fontana, Glasgow.

Bartolini, S. and Mair, P. (1994), *Party Politics in Contemporary Europe*, Cass, London.

Blondel, J. (1978), *Political Parties*, Wildwood, London.

——— (1989), *Switzerland: A Model for the European Union*, Institute of European Affairs, Dublin.

Blondel, J. and Cotta, M. (eds.) (1996), *Party and Government*, Macmillan, Basingstoke.

Cerny, P. and Schain, M. (eds.) 1980, *French Politics and Public Policy*, Methuen, London.

Coppedge, M. (1994), *Strong Parties and Lame Ducks: Presidential Patriarchy and Factionalism in Venezuela*, Stanford University Press, Stanford, Calif.

Daalder, H. (ed.) (1987), *Party Systems in Denmark, Austria, Switzerland, The Netherlands, and Belgium*, Pinter, London.

Esping-Andersen, G. (1992), "Budget and Democracy: Towards a Welfare State in Spain and Portugal, 1960–1986," in I. Budge and D. McKay (eds.), *Developing Democracy*, Sage, Los Angeles.

Frears, J. (1981), *France in the Giscard Presidency*, Allen and Unwin, London.

Haggard, S. and Kaufman, R. (eds.) (1992), *The Politics of Economic Adjustment*, Princeton University Press, Princeton, N.J.

Halligan, J. and Turner, M. (eds.), *Profiles of Government Administration in Asia*, Australian Government Publishing Service, Canberra.

Heclo, H. (1997), *A Government of Strangers*, Brookings Institution, Washington, D.C.

Huntington, S. P. (1968), *Poitical Order in Changing Societies*, Yale University Press, New Haven, Conn.

Ikegami, Keiko (1995), *The Taming of the Samurai: Honorific Individualism and the Making of Modern Japan*, Princeton University Press, Princeton, N.J.

Kamenka, E. (1989), *Bureaucracies*, Blackwell, Oxford.

Katz, R. S. and Mair, P. (1994), *How Parties Organise*, Sage, Los Angeles.

——— (1995), "Changing Models of Party Organisation and Party Democracy: The Emergence of the Cartel Party," *Party Politics* 1, pp. 5–28.

Kellner, P. and Ld Crowther-Hunt (1980), *The Civil Servants*, Macdonald, London.

Lane, J. E. (1993), *The Public Sector*, Sage, Los Angeles.

Lijphart, A. (1977), *The Politics of Accommodation*, University of California Press, Berkeley, Calif.

——— (1984), *Democracies*, Yale University Press, New Haven, Conn.

Linz, J. (1990), "The Perils of Presidentialism," *Journal of Democracy* 1(1), pp. 59–69.

Machin, H. and Wright, V. (eds.) (1985), *Economic Policy and Politics under the Mitterrand Presidency 1981–1984*, Pinter, London.

Mainwaring, S. and Scully, T. R. (eds.) (1995), *Party Systems in Latin America*, Stanford University Press, Stanford, Calif.

Maisel, L. and Cooper, T. (eds.) (1978), *Political Parties*, Sage, Los Angeles.

Peele, G., Bailey, C. J., and Cain, B. (eds.) (1992), *Developments in American Politics*, Macmillan, Basingstoke.

Peters, B. G. (1995), *The Politics of Bureaucracy*, Longman, White Plains, N.Y.

Ridley, F. and Blondel, J. (1969), *Public Administration in France*, Routledge, London.

Schumpeter, J. (1979), *Capitalism, Socialism, and Democracy*, Allen and Unwin, London.

Shefter, M. (1994), *Political Parties and the State*, Princeton University Press, Princeton, N.J.

Shugart, M. S. and Carey, J. M. (1992), *Presidents and Assemblies*, Cambridge University Press, New York.

Sloan, J. W. (1984), *Public Policy in Latin America*, University of Pittsburgh Press, Pittsburgh.

Strauss, E. (1961), *The Ruling Servants*, Allen and Unwin, London.

Ware, A. (ed.) (1987), *Political Parties*, Blackwell, Oxford.

Williams, P. (1964), *Crisis and Compromise*, McKay, New York.

Wright, V. (1989), *The Government and Politics of France*, Unwin, London.

Country studies

5

Taiwan

Hsin-Huang Michael Hsiao and Cheng Hsiao-shih

Introduction

Before the government of the Republic of China (ROC) was defeated by the Chinese Communists and took refuge in Taiwan in 1949, the ruling party, the Kuomintang (KMT, or Nationalist Party), was already torn apart by factional conflicts and plagued by rampant corruption. Its army was disintegrated and humiliated by the debacle in the Civil War. Furthermore, the émigré regime was strongly resented by the native Taiwanese for the brutal and bloody massacre triggered by the February 28 Incident in 1947.

In economic respects, the prospect for development was dismal as well. The war-ridden island was mountainous and heavily populated. Its natural resources were scarce. Ninety-nine per cent of its oil supply depended on imports, for instance. In the early 1950s, the government even had to set aside more than 50 per cent of its national budget for defence spending per annum to cope with the armed threat from the People's Republic of China (PRC).

And yet, Taiwan survived and throve, even though it was cut off from crucial diplomatic ties from the early 1970s. By the late 1970s, it had been widely recognized as a "miracle" by the world. Its economy had grown rapidly and continuously; the society had been transformed from one of agriculture to one of industry, with a fairly equal income distribution among different social classes. This phenomenal economic and social success was made possible despite the KMT's long-lasting authoritarian rule. These simple and basic facts pose some intriguing theoretical questions. To what extent and in what ways, if at all, has the KMT party-state contributed to Taiwan's socio-economic development? Was the KMT's authoritarian rule merely coincident with or a necessary condition for Taiwan's admirable socio-economic development? These are the critical questions that this chapter is intended to tackle.

We will begin by examining the developmental trend under authoritarianism between the 1950s and 1986. Taiwan's social and economic development since the democratization process was formally staged in 1987 will then be assessed. The impact of democratization and the consequently emerging party politics on post-democratization economic governance will also be analyzed.

Socio-economic developments in the authoritarian era 1950–1986

Overall development patterns

Taiwan's economy has been growing continuously since the early 1950s. The gross national product (GNP) rose from US$1.674 billion in 1952 to US$77.296 billion in 1986. During this period of time, the annual growth rate of GNP was 9.0 per cent on average. Per capita GNP rose from US$196 in 1952 to US$3,993 in 1986 (see table 5.1).

In terms of its production structure, Taiwan's economy had been transformed from an agricultural system to an industrial system. As clearly shown in figures 5.1 and 5.2, the role of agriculture in the Taiwan economy began to be taken over by the industry and service sectors after the mid-1960s. Foreign trade, the lifeline of Taiwan's economy, initially exhibited the same track of industrialization, but from 1966, raw and processed agricultural products were outweighed as a proportion of exports by industrial products. In 1952, 52.4 per cent of the total population worked in the agricultural sector, but the percentage dropped to 22.1 by 1986 (CEPD 1997, 64).

In terms of ownership, state enterprises played a pivotal role in Taiwan's industrialization during the 1950s and 1960s. In 1952, state enterprises accounted for 57 per cent of total industrial production and 43 per cent of domestic capital formation, and employed 17 per cent of Taiwan's civilian employees. The center of gravity gradually shifted to private enterprises in the 1970s. By the early 1980s, state enterprises contributed less than 20 per cent of total industrial production (Hsiao 1995, 81; CEPD 1997, 82). This does not mean that state enterprises' influence on industry

Table 5.1 **Taiwan economic indicators, 1952–1996**

	Economic growth rate at 1991 prices (per cent)	GNP (US$ million at current prices)	GDP (US$ million at current prices)	Per capita GNP (US$)
1952	12.00	1,674	1,675	196
1955	8.10	1,928	1,928	203
1960	6.30	1,717	1,718	154
1965	11.10	2,811	2,816	217
1968	9.20	4,236	4,248	304
1969	9.00	4,915	4,921	345
1970	11.40	5,660	5,670	389
1971	12.90	6,589	6,592	443
1972	13.30	7,906	7,904	522
1973	12.80	10,727	10,730	695
1974	1.20	14,458	14,463	920
1975	4.90	15,429	15,517	964
1976	13.90	18,429	18,624	1,132
1977	1.02	21,681	21,816	1,301
1978	13.60	26,773	26,836	1,577
1979	8.20	33,229	33,218	1,920
1980	7.30	41,360	41,418	2,344
1981	6.20	47,955	48,218	2,669
1982	3.60	48,550	48,586	2,653
1983	8.40	52,503	52,421	2,823
1984	10.60	59,780	59,139	3,167
1985	5.00	63,097	62,062	3,297
1986	11.60	77,299	75,434	3,993
1987	12.70	103,641	101,570	5,298
1988	7.80	126,233	123,146	6,379
1989	8.20	152,565	149,141	7,626
1990	5.40	164,076	160,173	8,111
1991	7.60	183,736	179,370	8,982
1992	6.80	216,254	212,150	10,470
1993	6.30	226,243	222,604	10,852
1994	6.50	243,934	240,986	11,597
1995	6.00	262,978	260,175	12,396
1996	5.70	275,144	273,050	12,872

Source: CEPD 1997, 1.

declined correspondingly, however. Strategic sectors, such as petroleum, electricity, gas, water, steel, railways, shipbuilding, post and telecommunications, tobacco and spirits, and banking and finance, were still monopolized by the state.

In addition to the direct control of state enterprises, the KMT owned wholly or partly around 50 companies, mostly through two powerful and

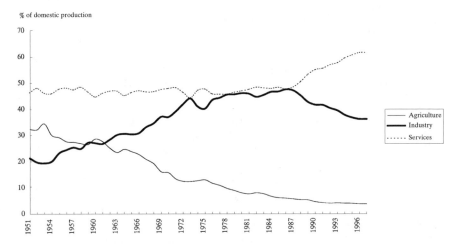

Figure 5.1 **The changing pattern of Taiwan's economic structure, 1951–1996** (Sources: Soong Kuang-yu 1993; CEPD 1996, 2)

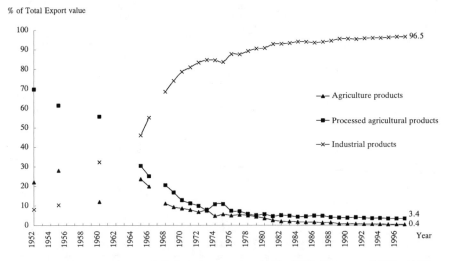

Figure 5.2 **Composition of Taiwan's exports, 1952–1996** (Source: CEPD 1997, 192; data for 1953–54, 1956–59, and 1961–64 are not available)

privileged party-owned investment firms. These companies were active in communications, petrochemicals, steel, electronics, and finance and securities. This bestowed on the KMT a strong hand to intervene in economic activities.

Another important business category is big private enterprises. In 1988, Taiwan's top 100 "business groups," conglomerates composed of indi-

Table 5.2 **Numbers of medium and small enterprises in Taiwan and their percentage of all enterprises, 1982–1994**

	All enterprises	Medium and small enterprises	Per cent
1982	711,326	701,839	98.67
1983	706,526	696,438	98.57
1984	731,610	719,440	98.37
1985	727,230	716,224	98.49
1986	751,273	737,350	98.15
1987	761,553	743,274	97.60
1988	791,592	773,511	97.72
1989	798,865	778,042	97.39
1990	818,061	794,834	97.16
1991	850,679	825,556	97.05
1992	900,801	871,726	96.77
1993	934,588	901,768	96.49
1994	969,094	932,852	96.26

Source: MSEA 1995, 356–57.

vidual 700 to 800 firms, accounted for 34 per cent of the total GNP, yet they employed only 4.6 per cent of the labour force (Hsiao 1995, 83). These groups have heavily concentrated their investments and business operations in capital- and technology-intensive industries.

A special feature characterizing Taiwan's production structure is the large number of small and medium enterprises, namely those with turnover under US$1.5 million and total assets below US$4.8 million. In 1961, there were 178,916 such enterprises, or 99.6 per cent of all registered enterprises (Hsiao 1995, 83–84). In 1986, 98.2 per cent of 751,273 registered enterprises fell in this category. They contributed 66.4 per cent of the total value of exports (MSEA 1995, 356, 396; see also table 5.2).

The small and medium enterprises display several salient characteristics. First, most of them, or around 60 per cent of the total, are in the commercial sector (see table 5.3). Second, in sharp contrast to big enterprises, the small and medium enterprises are export-oriented and rely on the former for raw materials. There exists a dichotomous or dual structure in Taiwan's production system, with the big enterprises producing goods for internal needs and the small and medium enterprises producing goods for export. Third, most of these enterprises have less than 50 employees. According to surveys from 1966 to 1986, 80 per cent of all manufacturing units in Taiwan employed fewer than 20 persons, and 70 per cent fewer than 10 (Hsiao 1995, 83). Fourth, most of these enterprises, or nearly 60 per cent of the total, operate with independent capital: that is, most managers are also owners (GIO 1996, 835). Fifth, most enterprises are family-centered: family ties are the base for employment and financial

Table 5.3 **Medium and small enterprises in Taiwan, by economic sector, 1982–1994** (per cent)

	Agriculture, fishing, mining	Manufacturing	Housing, building, and constructing	Commercial	Transportation and communication	Social and private services	Other
1982	2.11	17.32	2.64	61.79	4.08	12.05	0.01
1983	2.49	17.35	2.69	61.53	4.30	11.63	0.01
1984	3.13	16.82	2.57	61.49	4.89	11.10	0.01
1985	0.74	16.63	2.61	62.21	5.51	12.30	0.01
1986	0.75	17.59	2.96	60.89	6.00	11.79	0.01
1987	0.59	19.52	2.97	59.51	6.01	11.39	0.02
1988	0.58	19.76	2.97	58.87	6.19	11.62	0.02
1989	0.59	20.03	3.10	59.30	4.77	12.19	0.02
1990	0.57	19.53	3.33	59.77	4.51	12.27	0.02
1991	0.55	18.66	3.83	60.20	4.24	12.49	0.03
1992	0.53	17.90	4.38	59.96	3.83	13.38	0.03
1993	0.51	17.16	5.33	59.57	3.53	13.86	0.04
1994	0.91	16.45	6.06	58.76	3.45	14.33	0.04

Source: MSEA 1995, 356–57.

Table 5.4 **Distribution of personal income in Taiwan, by household, 1964–1995** (per cent)

	Lowest fifth	Second fifth	Third fifth	Fourth fifth	Highest fifth	Ratio of highest fifth's income to lowest fifth's
1964	7.7	12.6	16.6	22.0	41.1	5.3
1966	7.9	12.4	16.2	22.0	41.5	5.3
1968	7.8	12.2	16.3	22.3	41.4	5.3
1970	8.4	13.3	17.1	22.5	38.7	4.6
1972	8.6	13.2	17.1	22.5	38.6	4.5
1974	8.8	13.5	17.0	22.1	38.6	4.4
1976	8.9	13.6	17.5	22.7	37.3	4.2
1978	8.9	13.7	17.5	22.7	37.2	4.2
1979	8.6	13.7	17.5	22.7	37.5	4.4
1981	8.8	13.8	17.6	22.8	37.0	4.2
1982	8.7	13.8	17.6	22.7	37.3	4.3
1983	8.6	13.6	17.5	22.7	37.6	4.4
1984	8.5	13.7	17.6	22.8	37.4	4.4
1985	8.4	13.6	17.5	22.9	37.6	4.5
1986	8.3	13.5	17.4	22.7	38.2	4.6
1987	8.1	13.5	17.5	22.8	38.0	4.7
1988	7.9	13.4	17.6	22.9	38.3	4.9
1989	7.7	13.5	17.7	23.1	38.0	4.9
1990	7.5	13.2	17.5	23.2	38.6	5.2
1991	7.8	13.3	17.4	23.0	38.6	5.0
1992	7.4	13.2	17.5	23.2	38.7	5.2
1993	7.1	13.1	17.7	23.4	38.7	5.4
1994	7.3	13.0	17.4	23.2	39.2	5.4
1995	7.3	13.0	17.4	23.4	39.0	5.3

Source: Kuo et al., 1981, 34–35; CEPD 1997, 61–62.

support. And finally, compared to big businesses, the small and medium enterprises are less protected and supported by the government.

One other most cherished achievement is that Taiwan has been able to maintain relatively equal income distribution in the course of rapid economic growth. Simon Kuznets and many other economists suggested in the 1950s and 1960s that as income increases from low levels in a developing society, its distribution must first worsen before it can improve (Kuo et al. 1981, 1). Taiwan's experience in this regard is the opposite. As table 5.4 indicates, the disparity of income distribution decreased in the 1950s and remained fairly stable for three decades. In addition to land reform, the existence of a large number of small firms with significant capital decentralization has been one of the major structural reasons underlying Taiwan's relatively equal income distribution (Hsiao 1992d, 21).

What was the nature of the KMT regime during this period? What kind of role did it play in socio-economic development? And, specifically, what strategies and policies did it adopt for such development?

The KMT had been a Leninist political party with an anti-Communist ideology. Immediately after moving to Taiwan, Chiang Kai-shek put into effect a party reform program to create a party-state. Almost all institutions, such as the government, the military, the judicial departments, and the schools, and social forces, such as workers, farmers, intellectuals, women, and youth, were penetrated and controlled by the Party (Kung 1995). The Party's ideology became the national ideology, and candidates in all official examinations were required to be tested in it. As all these practices were unconstitutional, the KMT suspended the Constitution in 1948 by the Temporary Provisions Effective during the Period of Communist Rebellion, a supplement to the constitution promulgated in the same year, and a declaration of martial law in 1950. Before martial law was lifted in 1987, Taiwan was in fact an authoritarian party-state, in which civil rights were suppressed and no political opposition was allowed (Cheng 1992; Cheng 1989).

Nevertheless, unlike other Leninist party-states, the KMT regime was not totalitarian. It did not try to control socio-economic activities in their entirety, despite its unquestionable dominance in this domain. In this regard, the KMT's ideology should be taken into account, especially the Principle of Social Welfare. This principle is basically a developmental and capitalist doctrine, although it does contain strong socialist elements, such as land reform and state control of certain enterprises. In general, however, the adoption of a free economic system that paid due respect to private ownership and market mechanisms set the keynote for Taiwan's later economic development.

The lessons that the KMT learned from the defeat on the Chinese mainland also partly account for certain important policies it pursued in the 1950s, such as land reform and control of inflation and prices. Failure to implement land reform on the mainland was considered by the KMT to be a vital factor in the success of the Communists' peasant revolution. Furthermore, the galloping inflation in the late 1940s made the KMT extremely sensitive to the problem of price controls.

We now turn to the strategies implemented by the KMT government in the course of Taiwan's industrialization. Generally, Taiwan's industrialization policy can be divided into four phases: (1) the import substitution phase of the 1950s; (2) the export-oriented industrialization phase of the 1960s; (3) the second phase of import substitution during the 1970s; and (4) the liberalization and globalization phase since the early 1980s.

Import substitution industrialization (ISI) in the 1950s

Like many newly independent states after World War II, Taiwan inherited a colonial economy and a war-battered society, and faced the problems of food shortage, population pressure, inflation, budget deficits, and shortage of foreign reserves. One of the KMT's most important policies to cope with these difficulties was land reform, carried out from 1949 to 1953. As mentioned earlier, the loss of the mainland prompted the KMT to implement this policy in Taiwan. Nevertheless, the KMT elite's lack of vested interests in Taiwan's land and ties with landlords was a decisive factor contributing to the success of this reform.

No less important were the measures taken to stabilize prices. During the period of the Civil War (1946–49), prices rose initially at an annual rate of about 500 per cent, which then soared to about 3,000 per cent in the first half of 1949. In June 1949, monetary reform and other stabilization policies, such as preferential interest savings deposits, were implemented. By the end of 1951, inflation was effectively controlled. Between 1952 and 1960, the annual increase in prices was brought down to 8.8 per cent (Kuo et al. 1981, 64–66).

As landlords were compelled to sell their excess land, they were compensated to the extent of 70 per cent of the land price in land bonds and 30 per cent in stock of four state-owned enterprises. By this measure, not only was inflation prevented, but also the landlords were forced to shift their capital into industry, thereby becoming the first generation of indigenous capitalists (Hsiao 1995, 78). With encouragement and support from the government as it pursued its ISI strategy, a dynamic export manufacturing sector thus emerged and would soon outweigh the textile and food processing sectors that dominated Taiwan's industry in the 1950s. The primary goals of ISI were to meet domestic economic needs and to build local industrial capabilities. In addition to the emerging Taiwanese landlords turned capitalists, the state-owned enterprises, the mainlander-owned industries, and the local entrepreneurs who quickly responded to the state's industrial initiatives were the main beneficiaries of ISI.

Finally, U.S. aid also played an important role in economic development at this stage. Before 1961, almost no private foreign capital flowed into Taiwan. Nearly half of the investment was financed by the United States (Kuo et al. 1981, 29). The total amount of U.S. aid from 1951 to 1968 was US$1.547 billion (CEPD 1997, 225).

Export-oriented industrialization (EOI) in the 1960s

Partly pushed forward by domestic market constraints and external U.S. pressure (resulting from recession and a worsening balance of payments in the U.S. economy) and partly induced by the expanding world market, Taiwan's government made a strategic shift from ISI to EOI. The primary objective of EOI was to promote exports by developing labor-intensive industries. In retrospect, export expansion was indeed a decisive factor for the take-off of the Taiwan economy. In terms of percentage of GDP, industrial sectors started to outweigh agricultural sectors in 1963 (see figure 5.1).

Economic policies favoring export expansion were devised in the late 1950s and implemented in the early 1960s. In the Third Four-Year Plan, an optimistic growth target of 8 per cent was set for the period 1961–64. To achieve this goal, various measures were taken to reform the structure of industry. Most significant of all was the Nineteen-Point Financial Reform. Included in the reform package were devaluing of the currency to make exports more competitive, relaxing control over foreign trade, allowing the entry of foreign direct investment to set up export manufacturing enterprises, and initiating a single exchange rate along with eliminating import restrictions. Pursuant to these reform measures, the Statute for Encouragement of Investment was enacted to offer greater tax reductions to stimulate private investment and exports. A typical case was the establishment of the Kaohsiung Export Processing Zone within which no duties were imposed on imports (Hsiao 1995, 78–79; Kuo et al. 1981, 73–77).

In terms of structural change, the EOI strategy dramatically expanded the small and medium businesses and created a "dichotomous" or "dual market structure." That is, most rising small and medium businesses were export-oriented, while the domestic market was dominated by big business groups and state-owned enterprises. This dualization process can be traced to the ISI stage. Under the government's protectionist policy and political maneuvers, the domestic market had been monopolized or oligopolized by the big private and state-owned enterprises by the end of 1950s. The newly emerging small and medium businesses could only turn to the expanding world market. On the other hand, they were pulled in this direction, especially to the United States, by the demand for labor-intensive and low-tech products, such as textiles, garments, and shoes, from the industrialized market.

The second phase of ISI in the 1970s

In the early 1970s, faced with the loss of its seat in the United Nations, the devaluation of the U.S. dollar, and the oil crisis, Taiwan experienced a serious setback in economic performance. The diplomatic setback led to a legitimacy crisis for the KMT regime, and the drop in business confidence and the outflow of capital brought about a temporary halt to export dynamism. Prices, which had been relatively stable for two decades, abruptly rose by 22.9 per cent in 1973 and 40.6 per cent in 1974 (CEPD 1997, 1). To deal with these difficulties, some stabilization measures, such as a high interest rate policy, a one-shot adjustment of oil prices, and tax reduction, were implemented. More importantly, the government pursued a second phase of ISI strategy to restructure the economy by developing energy-intensive and capital-intensive industries and staging large-scale infrastructure projects, known as the "Great Ten Constructions."

In the course of this phase, state enterprises increased their significance as leaders of domestic investment. Big private businesses also received a great boost from the state and formed "business groups," the Taiwanese version of conglomerates. Small and medium businesses, on the other hand, also survived the world energy crisis and recession and were re-energized for further growth and development from the late 1970s.

Liberalization and globalization in the 1980s

Under pressure from major foreign trade partners, especially the United States, to improve the trade balance, liberalization was accelerated in the 1980s. The nominal rate of protection decreased significantly in this period, and the average tariff rate was dramatically brought down. Financial deregulation was another point of emphasis in government policy. After a decade of preparation, the Banking Law was amended in 1989. All controls on both deposit and lending interest rates were removed, and foreign bank branches were permitted to accept long-term saving deposits. The establishment of new private banks was also allowed. Furthermore, a significant step in the liberalization of capital movements was taken in 1987. Foreign exchange controls were largely relaxed to allow direct transfers of capital by the non-bank private sector.

All these efforts were supported by the Statute for Upgrading Industries of December 1990 (Howe 1996, 1184–85). After a decade of trial and error, the success of these efforts was demonstrated by the high competitiveness of Taiwan's information technology industry, which yielded a total production value of US$21.3 billion, and made Taiwan the world's third largest computer hardware supplier in 1995 (GIO 1997, 162).

Based on the above analysis, we may conclude that the state played a pivotal role in Taiwan's socio-economic development during the period of the KMT's authoritarian rule. The KMT regime was clearly a "strong state," dominated by a Leninist-style political party with a basically capitalist ideology. The state was predominant and interventionist in the socio-economic arena, and yet it was development-oriented and non-market-suppressive; moreover, it adopted effective strategies and policies to promote socio-economic development. In spite of the KMT's pro-longed authoritarian rule, therefore, Taiwan's society and economy throve. The KMT's role should not be overstated, however. By recognizing it, we do not mean to suggest that authoritarian rule is a necessary condition for socio-economic development. Obviously, Taiwan's regime was an exception among the numerous authoritarian regimes that failed to promote development. Furthermore, the argument for the necessity of authoritarian rule is also disproved by the fact that Taiwan's more recent socio-economic development is associated with democratization.

Democratization and the changing political economy

Overall democratization trends

The lifting of martial law in July 1987 was a landmark of democratization for Taiwan. Civil rights such as the freedom of speech and publication and the freedom of assembly and association, which had been suspended for 38 years, were restored. With the rise of party politics and a series of constitutional reforms, the authoritarian political system of Taiwan was transformed into a democracy.

Between the lifting of martial law in July 1987 and the death of Chiang Ching-kuo in January 1988, Taiwan's politics experienced a democratic opening. With the National Security Law and the Civic Organization Law, enacted in 1987 and 1989 respectively, however, the KMT did manage to limit the scope of liberalization. The democratic transition since the late 1980s has featured several important events, including Lee Teng-hui's election as KMT chairman in July 1988; his reelection to the presidency in March 1990; the Council of Grand Justice's ruling in June 1990 ending the tenure of long-term parliamentarians as of December 1991 and the resulting elections to the three reorganized representative bodies in 1991 and 1992; and the first opposition victories ever in the December 1994 elections for the mayors of Taipei and Kaohsiung and the governor of Taiwan Province. During this period, several significant democratic institutional reforms were launched. In particular, the anti-democratic Temporary Provisions were finally repealed, the "Period of National Mobilization for Suppression of the Communist Rebellion" was ended in May 1990, and a constitutional amendment was approved in May 1992. All of these marked a break from undemocratic extraconstitutional political structures and a restoration of constitutional rights for the nation. Though the constitutional amendment was far from being either complete or satisfactory, with revisions restricted primarily to procedural rather than substantive issues, the state was slowly taking steps toward democratic reinstitutionalization in order to address continuing pressures from the oppositions.

Students, university professors, liberal journalists, and legal professionals had all joined together in the pro-democracy movement, and these alliances reinforced their demands for constitutional reform, freedom of speech, structural changes in the parliamentary body, a clear definition of the power of the executive, a guarantee of civilian democratic government without military interference, and support for the development of party politics. In other words, under the leadership of intellectuals and professionals from the new middle class, Taiwan's civil society has indeed taken the establishment of democracy as its primary goal for the 1990s. The direct elections for the two mayoral positions and the provincial governorship signified a major step toward completing the transition to procedural democracy. Political elites and the three major political parties then all engaged in intensive political negotiations over the Presidential Election and Recall Bill in the Legislative Yuan. On 20 July 1995, the important 107-clause bill was finally approved; it officially declared that a presidential election would be held on 23 March 1996.

The March 1996 presidential election was seen by many in the middle class not only as an opportunity to exercise their right as citizens to elect their own president for the first time in Taiwan's history, but also as a significant break with the past. Many of them believed that as long as the 1996 presidential election was carried out in a peaceful and democratic manner, regardless of its outcome, Taiwan was bound to begin a phase of democratic consolidation. Despite China's threatening missile tests in the midst of the electoral campaign, the Taiwanese people courageously participated in their first direct, democratic presidential election.

Constitutional structure and electoral system

As mentioned earlier, the 1947 Constitution had not been fully implemented before 1987, due to the restrictions of the Temporary Provisions and martial law. After these obstacles were removed, the Constitution was revamped to create a workable democratic order. Three rounds of constitutional amendments took place in 1991, 1994, and 1997 respectively. The amendments of the first round were designed to reflect the fact that Taiwan and the Chinese mainland are governed by two separate political entities. They also provided the legal basis for the election of the completely new National Assembly and Legislative Yuan. The amendments of the second round laid the groundwork for the popular election of the president and the vice-president of the Republic and transformed the Control Yuan (an oversight body) from a parliamentary body to a quasi-judicial organ.

Lastly, the amendments of the third round restructured the relationships among the president, the Executive Yuan, and the Legislative Yuan. The Legislative Yuan has the power to pass a no-confidence vote against the premier (i.e., the president of the Executive Yuan), while the president of the Republic has the power to dissolve the Legislative Yuan. On the other hand, the premier is to be directly appointed by the president of the Republic, and the consent of the Legislative Yuan is no longer needed. Furthermore, under this latest revision, the Control Yuan is deprived of its power to impeach the president of the Republic, and the provincial government is to be streamlined and the popular elections of the governor and members of the provincial council are suspended. Despite some remaining flaws, the revised Constitution has provided a commonly acceptable ground for constructing a democratic order. The restructuring process has been peaceful and has taken place at low social cost.

Perfecting the electoral system is another important dimension of the democratic transition in Taiwan. In fact, the democratization process is in part driven by the local elections that have been continuously and regularly held since the early 1950s. Local elections provided a democratic seed and brought the ethnic Taiwanese into the political system. In the 1970s, direct elections were partly extended to the national level, i.e., the supplementary elections for the National Assembly and the Legislative Yuan. The electoral space was completely opened up during the 1990s by the legislative election of 1992, the gubernatorial election of 1994, and the presidential election of 1996. The laws pertaining to election and recall had been overhauled several times in the late 1980s. The campaign rules were significantly relaxed and the mass media became totally free. Although the elections have still been heavily polluted by bribery, fairness has no longer been a major problem.

Founded in 1980, the Central Election Commission is responsible for holding and supervising national and local elections. To guarantee its impartiality, a law rules that commissioners from any single political party shall not constitute more than two-fifths of the whole commission. For the election of members of both the national and local representative bodies, a peculiar electoral system, dubbed the single non-transferable vote (SNTV), is employed. Normally, several representatives are elected from a single constituency which is demarcated essentially by existing administrative boundaries. In a given constituency, each voter casts only one vote, and the several leading candidates get elected. As some scholars have pointed out, this system creates intraparty competition and reduces the utility of party labels (Tien and Cheng 1997, 14). Since the National Assembly election of 1991 and the Legislative Yuan election of 1992, a number of seats have been reserved for a national constituency and the overseas Chinese communities. These seats are allocated by proportional representation (PR). In general, both the SNTV and the PR systems benefit the smaller parties, for as long as they win a certain number of votes, they are able to secure at least a few seats. But in elections for administrative offices, the situation is quite different. Normally, only the two largest parties emerge victorious in these single-seat contests, and third parties are very much at a disadvantage (GIO 1998, 108–9).

Emerging confrontational party politics

As of August 1997, 84 political parties have officially registered with the Ministry of the Interior (GIO 1998, 109). Among them, only four, the KMT, the Democratic Progressive Party (DPP), the New Party (NP) and the Taiwan Independence Party (TAIP) are politically active and electorally influential, however. Generally speaking, the KMT is still dominant in this newly emerging party system. It has been able to win over 50 per cent of the electoral vote in various national and local elections. The DPP has been the largest opposition party ever since its official establishment in September 1986 when martial law was still in effect. It normally gains around 35 per cent of the total votes in elections. The NP, a splinter group of the KMT, became the third largest political party in 1993. It has received around 10 per cent of the electoral votes in recent elections (see tables 5.5, 5.6, and 5.7). The TAIP, a splinter group of the DPP, came onto the political scene in December 1996. It has not yet been tested in large and significant elections.

The major difference characterizing these parties is political, although ethnic cleavage and public policies are also involved. "To be or not to be independent" has long been the most controversial political issue in Taiwan politics, in the face of the unification pressure from China ever since the late 1970s. This issue was forbidden to be discussed during the authoritarian period, but as democratization started, it soon became the single most important basis for party formation, realignment, and conflict. In the 1980s, it was hotly contested between the KMT and the DPP. In the early 1990s, it triggered severe intraparty conflicts within the KMT and finally led to a minor split and the establishment of the NP. On the other hand, in December 1996, dissatisfied with a softening of the DPP's stance of pursuing Taiwan independence, a group of DPP members decided to organize its own party, the TAIP. On the independence-unification political spectrum, the NP is at the far right, followed by the KMT and the DPP, with the TAIP at the far left. This means that there is a trend of convergence between the ruling KMT and the largest opposition party, the DPP. While the KMT is claiming to look for "conditional" unification with China in the far future and the DPP is claiming to search

Table 5.5 **Distribution of the popular vote and seats in Taiwan elections, 1991–1996**

	KMT	DPP	New Party	Independent
1991 National Assembly Election				
Popular vote (per cent)	71.17	23.94	n.a.	4.89
Seats	254	66	n.a.	5
Seats (per cent)	78.2	20.3	n.a.	1.5
1992 Legislative Yuan Election				
Popular vote (per cent)	52.51	30.79	n.a.	16.70[1]
Seats	101	51	n.a.	9
Seats (per cent)	62.7	31.7	n.a.	5.6
1995 Legislative Yuan Election				
Popular vote (per cent)	46.06	33.17	12.95	7.82
Seats	85[2]	54	21	4
Seats (per cent)	51.8	32.9	12.8	2.4
1996 National Assembly Election				
Popular vote (per cent)	49.68	29.85	13.67	6.80
Seats	183	99	46	6
Seats (per cent)	54.8	29.6	13.8	1.8

Source: Tien and Chu 1996, 1158.

[1] Includes votes for a large number of KMT candidates who entered the race without party endorsement, and candidates from small parties such as the Socialist Democrats.

[2] Two months later, the KMT expelled one member for his defection in the election for speaker.

Table 5.6 **Distribution of the popular vote in the 1994 Taiwan elections** (per cent)

	KMT	DPP	New Party	Independent
Executive offices				
Taiwan area aggregate	52.05	39.42	7.70	0.83
Governor of Taiwan	56.22	38.72	4.31	0.75
Mayor of Taipei	25.89	43.67	30.17	0.28
Mayor of Kaohsiung	54.46	39.29	3.45	2.80
Representative offices				
Taiwan area aggregate	49.16	31.71	6.09	13.04
Provincial assembly	51.03	32.54	3.74	12.69
Taipei city council	39.48	30.41	20.83	9.28
Kaohsiung city council	46.28	24.85	4.82	24.06

Source: Tien and Chu 1996, 1161.

Table 5.7 **Distribution of the popular vote in the 1996 Taiwan presidential election**
(per cent)

	KMT Lee-Lien	DPP Peng-Hsieh	New Party Lin-Hau[1]	Independent Cheng-Wang
Overall	54.00	21.13	14.90	9.98
Taipei City	38.90	24.34	24.87	11.89
Taiwan Province	56.76	20.13	13.42	9.68
Kaohsiung City	50.62	27.32	12.77	9.29
Kinmen-Matsu	41.31	1.59	30.64	26.45

Source: Tien and Chu 1996, 1162.
[1] Lin-Hau was not the New Party's own ticket, but an independent ticket that it endorsed.

for "conditional" independence soon, both parties share the same positions in maintaining the status quo and actively promoting Taiwan's international status.

In terms of ethnic composition, most DPP and TAIP key members and their core supporters are Taiwanese (that is, those who emigrated to Taiwan from the southeast coast of the Chinese mainland before 1949). In sharp contrast, most NP members are mainlanders (that is, those who came to Taiwan after the Civil War) and their descendants. The KMT claims to have two million members, about 80 per cent of them Taiwanese, while the mainlanders account for less than 20 per cent. This means that the émigré KMT has been indigenized in terms of the composition of its social base.

Indigenization or Taiwanization of the KMT was initiated by President Chiang Ching-kuo and completed by President Lee Teng-hui. As Chiang became a powerful political figure in the 1970s, he began to recruit Taiwanese technocrats and local politicians to some important positions in the party and the government. Nevertheless, by January 1988 when Chiang died, political power in the KMT and the state remained predominantly in the hands of mainlanders. The completion of the KMT's Taiwanization came several years after President Lee's succession. Since Lee is a native Taiwanese and did not have a tangible power base of his own, he was challenged on all sides by powerful old guard mainlanders in the government, the party, and the military. After a series of power struggles within the party, Lee successfully forced some of his obstinate opponents out of power, and marginalized some of those who refused to leave. Through this process, the KMT was also transformed from an authoritarian party with a revolutionary heritage to a more or less democratic party with a strong indigenous character. Among other factors, such as the legitimacy that the KMT gained from its previous performance in socio-economic development, indigenization is decisive in contributing to the survival of the KMT regime even under the strong pressure of democratization in Taiwan.

As noted earlier, the KMT and the DPP have been moving toward convergence in recent years. The KMT's indigenization has also contributed substantially to this. It helped to reduce the antagonism between the two parties and to foster a healthier environment for party politics. To consolidate his power under the KMT and to pursue further democratic reinstitutionalization, President Lee took many effective measures to gain the support of DPP political figures. Political dissidents were released from jails, and exiles were allowed to come home. The stringent Article 100 of the Criminal Code on treason and sedition was abolished so that people would no longer be fearful about advocating Taiwan independence. The deep resentment caused by the February 28 Incident was also alleviated through both symbolic and material means. More importantly, President Lee has adopted many important policies that were first advocated by the DPP, notably the separation of the military from the KMT, the effort to rejoin the United Nations, the direct popular election of the president by the people, and "welfare state" programmes such as universal health insurance, subsidized housing, and state-financed welfare provisions for the elderly.

This cultivated a widespread pro-Lee sentiment among the DPP members known as the "Lee Teng-hui Complex," which DPP leaders find it hard to deal with. On the other hand, the strong anti-Lee sentiments of the NP supporters were subsiding, especially after China launched several rounds of military exercises to protest Lee's unofficial visit to the United States and to dissuade Taiwan's people from voting for Lee in the first direct presidential election in March 1996. Facing the same difficulties in losing political leverage, somewhat ironically, the two ideologically antagonistic parties searched for reconciliation and alliance in mid-1996. Their common appeal was the assault on the KMT's practice of vote-buying and its connection with organized crime, legacies of clientelism in KMT-affiliated local political factions. Nevertheless, the fragile coalition soon broke apart.

All this does not mean that the current system of one-party dominance will last. It only means that the KMT's indigenization has exerted a profound impact on both the KMT itself and party politics in Taiwan. In the process, the KMT has also shown greater flexibility and adaptability than before, another important factor contributing to its continuing dominance.

Rising economic governance issues under democratization

The Taiwan-China economic nexus and its political ramifications

In the years following the lifting of martial law, Taiwan's investment environment deteriorated rapidly. As the KMT government no longer enjoyed arbitrary power, there appeared strong and militant environmental, labor, and consumer movements, which had long been suppressed under authoritarian rule. Social crimes and speculation in money and land were rampant, while entrepreneurs were in dire need of labor and land. Many small and medium businesses were thus forced to shift their investment abroad, especially to Southeast Asian countries. As table 5.8 shows, external investment in these countries grew rapidly and reached a peak in 1991.

This wave of investment was then surpassed by investment in China. In 1987, President Chiang Ching-kuo decided to allow mainlanders who had returned to the mainland to visit their relatives in Taiwan. This opened a new page in the interaction between the two sides of the Taiwan Straits after 48 years of separation. Mutual trade and investment through Hong Kong have increased dramatically since then. According to an official estimate, mutual trade increased over tenfold from 1987 to 1994, or from US$1.5 billion to US$17.9 billion (GIO 1996, 1409–10). China has become the second largest trade partner of Taiwan behind the United States. A worry thus looms large for Taiwan: trade dependence on China is sharply rising. Approximately 10.5 per cent of Taiwan's 1995 trade was with China, 4.4 per cent more than in the previous year. Export dependency stood at 17.4 per cent and import dependency at 3 per cent (GIO 1997, 159).

Private Taiwanese investment in China also surged. According to Taiwan's official statistics, investment in China from 1991 to 1996 totalled US$6.87 billion (see table 5.8). The actual figure was much higher, because many businessmen did not comply with the requirement of the government to register and thereby to get permission for their investments. This is reflected in China's official estimate, according to which total investment from Taiwan had reached over US$27 billion by 1995 (GIO 1996, 1410).

As figure 5.3 shows, the first peak of Taiwanese investment in China came in 1993; during that year the amount reached US$3.17 billion, or 65.6 per cent of total external investment in the same year, according to Taiwan's official record. (The Chinese official figure for the corresponding year was US$9.97 billion.) Alarmed by the increasing dependency of Taiwan's economy on China, the KMT government formulated a so-called "Southward Investment Policy" in late 1993 to promote invest-

Table 5.8 Taiwan's outward investment in the PRC and the Southeast Asian countries, 1987–1996

	Total outward invest- ment	Invest- ment in the South- east Asian countries	Per cent of total	Invest- ment in the PRC[1]	Per cent of total	Individual countries					
						Singapore	Philippines	Indonesia	Thailand	Malaysia	Vietnam[2]
1987	102,751	28,874	28.10			14,087	2,640	950	5,366	5,831	
1988	218,736	69,300	31.68			16,571	36,212	1,923	11,886	2,708	
1989	930,986	347,926	37.37			71,053	66,312	311	51,604	158,646	
1990	1,552,206	592,740	38.19			72,980	123,607	61,871	149,397	184,885	
1991	1,830,188	781,047	42.68	174,158	9.52	73,811	1,315	160,341	86,430	442,011	17,139
1992	1,134,251	487,952	43.02	246,992	21.78	187,616	1,219	39,930	83,293	155,727	20,167
1993	4,829,346	427,173	8.85	3,168,411	65.61	63,003	6,536	25,531	109,165	64,542	158,396
1994	2,578,973	471,671	18.29	962,209	37.31	174,672	9,600	20,571	57,323	101,127	108,378
1995	2,449,591	369,473	15.08	1,092,713	44.61	75,024	35,724	32,067	51,210	67,302	108,146
1996	3,394,645	593,251	17.48	1,229,241	36.21	170,961	74,252	82,612	71,413	93,534	100,479

Source: IC-MOEA 1997, 2–3, 41–42.
[1] Data on investment in the PRC before 1991 are not available.
[2] Data on investment in Vietnam before 1991 are not available.

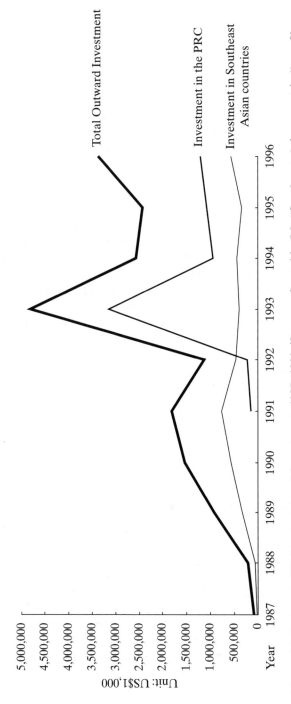

Figure 5.3 **Patterns of Taiwan's outward investment, 1987–1990** (Sources: See table 5.8. "Southeast Asian countries" are Singapore, the Philippines, Indonesia, Thailand, Malaysia, and Vietnam; data for Vietnam 1987–90 and the PRC before 1991 are not available)

ment in Southeast Asian countries, which had been slackening since 1991, and to discourage the too rapid expansion of investment in China. To implement this policy, government officials from President Lee downward intensively visited Southeast Asian countries in early 1994. They were accompanied by a large group of top decision makers in state-owned and KMT-owned enterprises and by leading private businessmen.

The rationale underlying this policy is both economic and political. Its first objective is to make Taiwan an international communications and transportation node, or so-called the "Asia-Pacific Regional Operations Center," taking the place of Hong Kong after its return to China in 1997. The second objective is to promote diplomatic relations with Southeast Asian countries through economic means. Third and most importantly, this policy is intended to divert investment from China, and thereby to reduce the political and economic risks of overdependence (Chen 1994; Ku 1994). Taiwan's anxiety over the unstable relations between the two sides of the Straits deepened after mid-1995, as China launched several rounds of military exercises near Taiwan in the autumn of 1995 and the spring of 1996. On this account, soon after his reelection President Lee publicly called for a slowdown in investment in China and successfully persuaded some of the leaders of large private business groups, notably Wang Yong-ching, president of the Formosa Plastics Corporation, to suspend their investment projects. In return for Wang's co-operation, in October 1997 President Lee bestowed on him a medal of honor and promised to improve the domestic investment environment and promote the efficiency of the bureaucracy. On the other hand, the government is tightening its control of investment in China by seriously implementing the Act on the Relations of People across the Taiwan Straits. Those who invest in China beyond the official maximum amount of money without registration are liable to serious punishment. In September 1997, over 8,500 applications were filed for retrospective registration, involving a total of over US\$3.6 billion.

The policy of promoting investment in Southeast Asian countries and discouraging investment in China seems to be working to some extent, as figure 5.3 suggests. Nevertheless, its effectiveness remains uncertain. Challenges to this policy from the leaders of large business groups continue to grow. In addition to Wang Yong-ching, Chang Rong-fa, president of Evergreen Marine Corporation, also openly criticized this policy in October 1997. This suggests that the government no longer has the power over large private businesses that it enjoyed in the authoritarian era. And the issue of investment in China will continue to stir up debates concerning the priority of economic development and national security. It might also change the relations between large private business groups and political parties. Generally speaking, the DPP supports the KMT's policy, while the NP has been critical. The position of the two parties on this issue is a reflection of their conflicting political platforms concerning the future of political relations between Taiwan and China.

A stable social base and politicized media

Relative social equality and impressive economic prosperity in Taiwan clearly provided a favorable environment for the healthy functioning of party politics. Based on a survey of ten countries, Stephan Haggard and Robert R. Kaufman (1997) have argued that democratic transitions are conditioned by the legacy of economic performance of authoritarian regimes. Democratization under conditions of economic crisis and social inequality tends to polarize society, fragment the party system, and induce the appearance of militant social movements and anti-market political parties. On the other hand, under favorable socio-economic conditions the incumbent party tends to be less vulnerable to splitting and to enjoy greater leverage in bargaining over the terms of democratic transitions, i.e., the formal constitutional rules and the informal understandings that govern political competition in the new democratic system. The case of Taiwan obviously falls in the latter category. Favorable socio-economic conditions made the ruling KMT more confident in taking reform measures on the one hand, and circumscribed the confrontational and mobilizational strategies that the opposition might employ on the other. The same favorable conditions account for the gradual waning of various civil protests and social movements that appeared in the beginning of democratization, and the relatively weak association between these movements and the opposition parties. The prolonged alliance of the anti-nuclear movement with the DPP is the exception rather than the rule.

In terms of general socio-economic development in the democratization period, Taiwan's economy continued to grow after 1987, although the growth rate was slower than in the previous two decades (see table 5.1). Also, the disparity of income distribution increased a little (See table 5.4). However, these changes are rather moderate and could have been the result of various factors. Thus, at the present, it is hard to clearly assess the KMT government's performance under democratization in comparison with the previous authoritarian period. With regard to economic policies, the KMT government has continued to pursue the directions of liberalization and globalization. Upgrading industry has remained a primary goal. In social welfare, as mentioned earlier, the KMT has absorbed some of the proposals of the opposition parties and social movements by taking measures to care for the elderly and the disabled. Most significantly, the National Health Insurance program was officially implemented in March 1995.

It is also quite important to point out that the liberalized media sector under Taiwan's democratization process has been also becoming more and more "politicized," taking polarized positions on various controversial political issues that divide the parties. Moreover, the controversy over independence vs. unification vis-à-vis China among the political parties and the general public has further politicized the media: it is easy to classify Taiwan's major newspapers and TV stations as pro–Lee Teng-hui or anti–Lee Teng-hui, pro–Taiwan independence or pro–unification with China. This is not so much a result of the continuing ethnic cleavage or individual journalists' political orientation as a reflection of the re-alignments of political and economic interests among the media, political parties, and the state. The political cleavages within the media have been facilitated and reinforced by confrontational party politics and the growing political tension between Taiwan and China, two inevitable consequences of Taiwan's democracy-building process.

The controversy over the nuclear power policy

Conflicts over the issue of nuclear power between the new middle-class liberal intellectuals and concerned environmental groups on the one hand, and the Taiwan Power Company on the other, intensified after 1986. At first, the anti-nuclear voices mainly came from academic and social movement circles. But from 1988 onward, residents in the area of the proposed site of a fourth nuclear power plant on the northern coast of Taiwan began actively participating in the anti-nuclear movement. Since then, Taiwan's environmental movement against nuclear power has become a social movement in which intellectuals from the new middle class, civil society organizations, and local residents have joined forces. The main force behind the anti-nuclear movement has been the TEPU (Taiwan Environmental Protection Union) which since the mid-1980s has devoted almost all its organizational resources to combatting the proposed nuclear power plant. The TEPU was established by volunteers from among university professors and students. It also established a local chapter at the proposed site in order to sustain the mobilization of local residents. As the years have gone by, the anti-nuclear movement has turned into a nationwide No Nukes movement to take on the KMT state's energy development policy and the pro-growth ideology behind it.

The Taipei County Government, controlled by the opposition DPP, even organized a countywide referendum on the fourth nuclear power plant plan in 1995, but the result of the referendum was not validated due to insufficient turnout. The Taipei city government, also controlled by the DPP, also held a referendum on the nuclear power issue in conjunction with the presidential election of 23 March 1996. The result revealed that 52 per cent of the Taipei voters cast "No" votes on the issue. Obviously, the anti-nuclear movement has developed a clear coalition with a major opposition political party. The DPP has even written the anti-nuclear position into its charter by opposing any further construction of nuclear power facilities on the island. The NP is also inclined to oppose the use of nuclear power for Taiwan's future energy needs. The most recently formed Green Party (GP), though insignificant in its political influence, has even adopted total rejection of nuclear power. Thus, the dispute over nuclear power has developed into a political conflict between the pro-nuclear KMT and the anti-nuclear DPP, NP, and GP. Recently, the anti-nuclear movement also adopted a more confrontational approach, of the kind commonly used by anti-pollution activists, in staging protests against the Taiwan Power Company and the state. The nature conservation movement has also allied itself with the anti-nuclear movement, as both are concerned with the protection of Taiwan's nature and ecology, and both have targeted the KMT state and its pro-growth and anti-environment ideology.

Taiwan's anti-nuclear movement, and a sharp cleavage among elites, with KMT and opposition politicians, technological bureaucrats and environmentally inclined academics on opposite sides, have successfully put obstacles in the way of the KMT state's nuclear energy policy. Due to the widespread opposition, proposals for the new power plant have been deferred three times, and the Legislative Yuan has even twice frozen the government budget for the plant. More importantly, considering the steady growth of domestic electricity consumption, which increased on average by 8.4 per cent a year from 1981 to 1994, the trend in the proportion of electricity generated from nuclear power plants fluctuated significantly from a 30 per cent increase in 1983–84 to a 7 per cent decline in 1987–88 and 1988–89. The percentage of electricity produced by nuclear energy actually dropped from 52 per cent in 1985 to 30 per cent in 1994. Thus, the rise of the anti-nuclear movement in the mid-1980s has postponed the expansion of nuclear power and served to lower Taiwan's dependence on nuclear energy.

Finally, the anti-nuclear movement, in alliance with the opposition parties, is still struggling to postpone, if not to stop altogether, the construction of the fourth nuclear power plant. The KMT still controls more than half of the seats in the Legislative Yuan and it won the votes in the legislative body to approve the first-year budget for the proposed plant in 1995. The opposition DPP and NP legislators have declared that they will continue the battle against the future nuclear power plant's annual funding. In other words, the field of the conflicts over future nuclear power generation has now moved from civil society to the political realm.

Conclusion

To summarize, after a decade of democratization, the authoritarian party-state has been transformed into a liberal multi-party system. Since the democratic transition took place under relatively favorable socio-economic conditions, the KMT has been able to remain in power, though the opposition parties have gained significant popular support. Party formation and realignment are based on political rather than socio-economic cleavages. National identity is the most important issue in the competition of political parties. Relations with China have been and will continue to be a critical factor in influencing confrontations in party politics and controversies over economic policies. In the path toward democratic consolidation, the government is going to play a less dominant role in the economy, and the ruling KMT no longer has the absolute power to control the economic sector that it did in the authoritarian era. Nevertheless, the government is still effective in governing and regulating economic activities, and the continuing consensus on the framework of the developmental state is reflected in the platforms of the different parties. On major economic policies (except for nuclear power) radical difference between the KMT and the DPP do not exist.

The impact of the financial crisis of 1997 on Taiwan has not been as serious as on other countries of East and Southeast Asia. The government's various financial policies and measures in response to the crisis have been rather cautious, and have not become a political issue with the opposition parties. The economic bureaucracy is considered to be strong and capable of dealing with the sudden external shock. However, it is inevitable that the government will face greater pressures and challenges from both opposition parties, politicians, capitalists, and various conflicting forces in civil society.

REFERENCES

CEPD (Council For Economic Planning and Development, Taiwan, Executive Yuan) (1996, 1997), *Taiwan Statistical Data Book*, CEPD, Taipei.
Chen, Hung-yu (1994), "Southward Policy and Regional Economic Integration," *Journal of Sunology* 8(3), pp. 1–37.
Chen, Wen-Chun (ed.) (1996), *Political Democratization in Taiwan* (in Chinese), National Sun Yat-sen University, Kaohsiung.

Cheng, Hsiao-shih (1992), "The State and the Military: A Framework for Analyzing Civil-Military Relations in Taiwan (1950–1987)" (in Chinese), *Journal of Social Sciences and Philosophy* 5, pp. 129–72.

Cheng, Tun-jen (1989), "Democratizing the Quasi-Leninist Regime in Taiwan," *World Politics* 41, pp. 461–99.

Copper, John F. (1996), *Taiwan: Nation-State or Province?* Westview Press, Boulder, Colo.

Dessus, Sebastien, Hsu Chia-tong, and Hsu Mao-Hsuan (1996), *Chinese Taipei: The Origins of the Economic "Miracle"* (in Chinese), Institute of Economics, Academia Sinica, Taipei.

GIO (Government Information Office, Taiwan, Executive Yuan) (1996, 1997, 1998), *The Republic of China Yearbook*, GIO, Taipei.

Haggard, Stephan, and Robert R. Kaufman (1997), "The Economy of Democratic Transitions," *Comparative Politics* 29 (April), pp. 263–83.

Howe, Christopher (1996), "The Taiwan Economy: The Transition to Maturity and the Political Economy of Its Changing International Status," *China Quarterly*, pp. 1171–95.

Hsiao, Hsin-Huang Michael (1992a), "The Business-Making Process of Taiwan's Small to Medium and Big Businessmen" (in Chinese), *Journal of Chinese Sociology* 16, pp. 139–68.

——— (1992b), "Explaining the Taiwan Development Model: Lessons to be Learnt," in D. Kim et al. (eds.), *The Role of the Market and State: Economic and Social Reforms in East Asia and East-Central Europe*, Institute of East and West Studies, Yonsei University, Seoul, pp. 127–47.

——— (1992c), "The Rise of Social Movements and Civil Protests," in T. J. Cheng et al. (eds.), *Political Change in Taiwan*, Lynn Rienner, Boulder, Colo., pp. 57–72.

——— (1992d), "The Taiwan Experience," *Development and Democracy* 2, pp. 18–32.

——— (1995), "The State and Business Relations in Taiwan," *Journal of Far Eastern Business* 1, pp. 76–97.

——— (1998), "Normative Conflicts in Contemporary Taiwan," in Peter Berger (ed.), *The Limits of Social Cohesion: Conflict and Mediation in Pluralist Societies*, Westview Press, Boulder, Colo., pp. 320–51.

Hsiao, Hsin-Huang Michael and Koo, Hagen (1998), "The Middle Classes and Democratization," in Larry Diamond et al. (eds.), *Consolidating the Third Wave Democracies: Themes and Perspectives*, Johns Hopkins University Press, Baltimore, pp. 312–33.

Hsiao, Hsin-Huang Michael and So, Alvin (1996), "The Taiwan-Mainland Economic Nexus: Sociopolitical Origins, State-Society Impacts, and Future Prospects," *Bulletin of Concerned Asia Scholars*, 28(1), pp. 3–12.

IC-MOEA (Investment Commission, Ministry of Economic Affairs) (1997), *Statistics on Outward Investment and Indirect Mainland Investment*, IC, MOEA, Taipei.

Klein, Lawrence R. and Yu, Chuan-Tao (eds.) (1994), *Economic Development of ROC and the Pacific Rim in the 1990s and Beyond.* World Scientific Publishing Co., Singapore.

Ku, Samuel C. Y. (1994), "The Political Economy of Taiwan's 'Southward Policy,'" *Journal of Sunology* 8(3), pp. 39–65.

Kung, I-Chun (1995), "The Penetration Capacity of an Immigrant State: The Formation and Consolidation of the Social Base of the KMT Regime, 1950–1969," Ph.D. diss., National Taiwan University.

Kuo, S. W. Y. (1994), "Key Factors for High Growth with Equity – The Taiwan Experience, 1952–1990," in Klein and Yu 1994, pp. 1–17.

Kuo, S. W. Y., Ranis, Gustav, and Fei, John C. H. (1981), *The Taiwan Success Story*, Westview Press, Boulder, Colo.

MSEA (Medium and Small Enterprise Administration, Taiwan, Ministry of Economic Affairs) (1995), *The White Paper for Medium and Small Enterprises 1995*, MSEA, Taipei.

Shyu, Huoyan (1992), "Party Realignment in the Democratic Transition of Taiwan: A Study of Changes in Democratic Values and Party Preferences" (in Chinese), *Journal of Social Sciences and Philosophy* 5, pp. 213–63.

Simon, Denis Fred and Kau, Michael Y. M. (eds.) (1992), *Taiwan: Beyond the Economic Miracle*, M. E. Sharpe, New York.

Soong, Kuang-yu (1993), *Taiwan Experience: Historical Economy* (in Chinese), Tong-Ta Publishers, Taipei.

Tien, Hung-mao (1989), *The Great Transition: Political and Social Change in the Republic of China*. Stanford University Press, Stanford, Calif.

―――― (1996), *Taiwan's Electoral Politics and Democratic Transition*, M. E. Sharpe, New York.

Tien, Hung-mao and Cheng, Tun-jen (1997), "Crafting Democratic Institutions in Taiwan," *China Journal* 37, pp. 1–27.

Tien, Hung-mao and Chu, Yun-han (1996), "Building Democracy in Taiwan," *China Quarterly*, pp. 1141–70.

6

South Korea

Ahn Chung-si and Jaung Hoon

Introduction

South Korea was one of the poorest countries in Asia up to the early 1960s, with little endowment in resources and few prospects for development. From the late 1960s, however, it underwent an economic and social transformation of immense proportions: for the following quarter of a century its economic growth was to be among the fastest in the world. With a rapidly growing economy, it has been hailed by many as a model for the so-called Third World and a prime example of the "Asian miracle." In social terms as well, a once overwhelmingly agrarian society has been transformed into a nation of city dwellers with strong middle-class aspirations: the number of Koreans living in cities jumped from 28 per cent in 1960 to about 75 per cent at the end of the twentieth century, a proportion similar to those of the United States, Japan, or France.

Meanwhile, in political terms, until the mid-1980s at least, moves towards democracy lagged far behind the rapid economic and social changes; since 1987, however, the country made a decisive turn away from military authoritarianism and South Koreans have been praised for their success in achieving both economic prosperity and political democracy. Although, by comparison with other nations, elements of uncertainty and major obstacles remain, the pace of change has come to be regular and positive. Many therefore believe that a reversion to authoritarianism is out of the question and that factors working for a continuous process of democratic consolidation are likely to prevail.

After a brief historical survey of the main factors accounting for the way politics and the economy developed, this paper considers the shape and characteristics of the party system and its contribution to democratization. It then looks at the character of economic governance in the country and examines the changes which occurred in this respect in the 1990s. Finally, it attempts to assess what the impact of democratization may have been on economic governance.

The historical legacy

Before democratization

Twentieth-century Korea has been marked by political turbulence as the country struggled to survive and to adapt its traditional institutions to the demands of a modern political order. The modernization process began to have an impact at the end of the nineteenth century, but it was only at the beginning of the twentieth century that Korea started to move away from the social order which had prevailed under the old Choson dynasty. As a result, traditional Korea had a very weak political structure as a basis on which to deal with foreign encroachments. Japan took advantage of this weakness, first by forcing the "hermit" kingdom to open its doors to the Western world, and from 1910 by ruling the country in a colonial manner for 35 years. Korea was liberated in 1945, when Japan surrendered to the Allied powers, but, almost as soon as that occurred, it was divided and a vicious internal war broke out.

After starting as separate governments, South and North Korea followed two fundamentally different paths towards nation building and development. While the North began to build a Soviet-backed totalitarian regime, in the South, efforts were made to transplant Western-style liberal democracy with capitalism as its developmental aim. The constitution of South Korea did emphasise liberalism and a free-market economy, but the reality was far from favourable to these goals. The country was then one of the poorest in the world: it lacked a sizeable middle class to ensure political stability. The Korean War of 1950–53 added the dislocating social effects of intense economic destruction and unprecedented internal migration. Fierce military and ideological confrontation persisted between the two Koreas after the end of the war and the armistice, hampering political stability and economic development in the South.

South Korea was at that time economically poorer than North Korea. The country had to depend heavily on the United States not only for its national security, but also for its financial survival. The government had to face the challenge of economic reconstruction and of development under constant threats from the North. The civilian rulers of the 1950s did not rise to that challenge, however; they failed to steer the economy out of its age-old poverty. This led to a military coup in May 1961, staged by General Park Chung Hee, who was to lay the foundation of the "Korean miracle" by adopting an export-led economic growth strategy.

The miracle was a mixed blessing, however. The South did overtake the North economically by the early 1980s; rapid economic development also promoted a Korean sense of identity and national pride and accelerated the development of a strong civil society better able to sustain democratic political institutions. Yet these changes had uneven and ambivalent effects on the culture and society of South Korea. Social mobility increased, but social cohesiveness and moral standards among individuals and groups were steadily eroded. In spite of the rapid modernization process, the majority of the Korean people continued to feel unable to exercise control over the society: self-criticism and pessimism coexisted with a dynamic, highly mobilized, and materialistic society strongly motivated to seek higher standards in quality of life and economic performance.

Thus, until the mid-1980s, South Korea's political dilemma was essentially characterized by the fact that political change lagged well behind economic development. Society was controlled by a top political elite and by governmental institutions which were, on the whole, highly efficient and successful, but authoritarian, coercive, and largely illegitimate. Features of radicalism – such as the prevalence of an extremist political rhetoric and violent political actions – were common. Opposition politicians and other advocates of democracy tenaciously fought for participation and social justice; student demonstrations regularly clashed with the police; labour disputes were rampant. Thus the society appeared brittle and chaotic to outside observers: only in 1987 did South Korea enter an era of significant political transformation and adopt democratic patterns of behaviour.

The country has lived under six republics since 1948, each having its distinctive constitutional arrangements. A peaceful transfer of power took place for the first time in October 1987 with the advent of the Sixth Republic. Since then, Korean politics has been characterized by a search for a political structure aimed at replacing authoritarian, military-influenced politics. President Kim Young Sam, who took office in February 1993, was South Korea's first civilian president in three decades. The election of President Kim Dae Jung, the opposition candidate, in December 1997, marked a new development, in which a peaceful and regular transfer of government took place from one ruling party to another.

Political life in South Korea has long been centred on the presidency and on the central administrative branch of the government, while the

National Assembly has not been strong and has remained subordinated to the presidency. Politicians at the local level have tended to be weak and dependent on central control and administrative guidance. Cabinet members, including the prime minister, have been chosen by the president, usually from outside the National Assembly. They act principally as administrative heads, having rarely been allowed to build their own independent political power base. They have also usually been in office for short periods: the average tenure of Korea's cabinet ministers since 1947 has been between one year and eighteen months.

An issue that continues to bedevil South Korean society on its road to becoming a democratic polity has been the primacy of regionalism. Many Koreans maintain a strong sense of attachment to a particular locality even though their families may have lived elsewhere for generations. There are several reasons for this high level of regionalism. One is Confucianism, which has long dominated many aspects of Korean life and emphasizes family, community, school, and regional ties as the bases of individual identity and of social action. Even despite industrialization, the minds, values, and behavioural orientations of many Koreans continue to be affected by and dependent on the regions, and this affects both their collective identity and their political choices, especially when regional identity is stressed by their leaders.

Problems of economic development and of socio-economic discrimination since the 1960s further increased regional consciousness and regional cleavages. As a latecomer country aiming at industrializing rapidly, Korea adopted a strategy of uneven development, which resulted in strong geographical differences in economic growth and an unequal distribution of social benefits in the various parts of the country. This led to intense regional conflicts, which had not abated by the late 1990s.

These conflicts have been politically mobilized by politicians who have maintained charismatic leadership over their regions. To the extent that it reflects the high levels of personalization associated with the "three Kims," regionalism may be less strong when a generational change of leadership occurs; already the election of Kim Dae Jung in 1997 may reduce geographically based conflicts, for instance between Kyungsang and Cholla provinces. However, as long as regionalism is associated with economic and social discrimination, it will remain prominent in many aspects of Korea's rapidly changing society even after democracy becomes consolidated.

Economic growth and the delayed transition to democracy

Before 1987, economic development in South Korea was based on an authoritarian approach which was fostered by the military leaders who

Table 6.1 **Growth of South Korean GDP and merchandise trade, compared with middle-income oil-importing economies, 1960–1970 and 1970–1980**

	South Korea	Middle-income oil-importing economies
	GDP (average annual growth rate, per cent)	
1960–1970	8.6	5.8
1970–1980	9.5	5.6
	Merchandise trade (average annual growth rate of exports, per cent)	
1960–1970	34.1	7.1
1970–1980	23.0	4.1

Source: *World Development Report 1982*, quoted in Hart-Landsberg 1993, 27, 31.

had led the country for over two decades. The regime's goals were implemented by a highly efficient bureaucracy in which corruption was limited; there was little interference from the civil society, so that the state was autonomous. "Miraculous" economic successes justified developmental authoritarianism. The main economic programme had been defined by Park Chung Hee in 1961, as he launched an ambitious plan for rapid industrialization to compensate for his weak political legitimacy. While the strategy and priority of the industrialization programme went through different stages from the 1960s to the 1980s, the basic pattern of that programme as well as the macroeconomic strategy remained unchanged for the subsequent three decades.

The results were astounding. Following the beginning of the First Five-Year Economic Development Plan in 1962, Korea's GNP expanded by 8.6 per cent a year in the 1960s and 9.5 per cent a year in the 1970s, despite the world recession of the period, and by over 8 per cent again in the 1980s; it grew from US$2.3 billion in 1962 to US$451.7 billion in 1995, making Korea the world's eleventh largest economy. As table 6.1 shows, the contrast between the Korean "miracle" and the performance of the middle-income oil-importing economies is sharp: among these, the average annual growth rate was only 5.8 per cent in the 1960s and 5.6 per cent in the 1970s. The annual export growth rate showed an even greater contrast: among middle-income oil-importing economies it was 7.1 per cent and 4.1 per cent during the 1960s and 1970s respectively, while in Korea it was 34.1 and 23 per cent for the same periods.

These economic developments led to rapid social change. The proportion of white-collar workers increased from 4.8 per cent in 1965 to 17.1 per cent in 1985, while the working class increased between 1965 and 1983 from 32.1 per cent to 49.5 per cent (Economic Planning Board

1984). Surveys indicated that more than 70 per cent of South Koreans identified themselves as middle-class.

In the process, society became more pluralistic but also more contentious. There were rising popular demands for political participation and social equality, which made the continuation of authoritarian rule increasingly costly. None the less, although the middle class and the working class wanted more democracy, the authoritarian regime was maintained for some years, thus rendering the structure of the state seriously "unbalanced." The polity was, in fact, in severe political crisis as a result of its economic development. There were mounting popular distrust of political institutions and increasing regional conflicts over the distribution of wealth and the sharing of key power positions. Anti-regime movements and civil disobedience reached a peak at the end of June 1987; the two most prominent opposition politicians, Kim Dae Jung and Kim Young Sam, mobilized the masses in close collaboration with street demonstrators. The situation seemed to be leading to a bloody civil war. At that point, however, the ruling coalition lost its cool, and split between softliners and hardliners. This provided the opportunity for a democratic transition to occur, as President Chun came to accept the major demands of the opposition.

It did take a long time for socio-economic development in Korea to bring about democracy, seemingly because of the existence of a "bureaucratic-authoritarian" structure which, as we shall see later in this chapter, was able to control economic developments (O'Donnell 1973). Meanwhile, as the size and complexity of the economy increased, the private sector and other social groups became more vocal about the negative aspects of the state-centred development policy: these criticisms produced pressures for more liberalization. Yet the political opening only occurred with the dramatic people's uprising in 1987 which finally led the then presidential candidate Roh Tae Woo, through his "29 June Declaration," to initiate the transition to democracy.

Transition via negotiation and compromise

South Korea's process of democratization was one of "transplacement," in Huntington's terms, not a "replacement" in which "democratization results from the opposition gaining strength and the government losing strength until the government collapses or is overthrown" (Huntington 1991, 142). The government and the ruling party not only survived but also continued to play a predominant role: this "transplacement" was possible because a balance of power existed between contending political forces and elite groups, and both sides saw the value of negotiation in initiating a change of regime.

In contrast to Latin America or Eastern Europe, the transition to democracy in Korea took place in the middle of economic success and not at a moment of crisis. Moreover, economic development does set the stage for democratization and thus shapes the structural contours of any transition process. In addition, the economic context within which democratic transitions take place largely determines the mode of transition processes and the outcomes of democratization. But the very process of democratization cannot be automatically deduced from the structural parameters of economic development and from the concomitant societal change.

As recent literature on democratic transition stresses, it is the transition process itself that makes a crucial difference to the kind of democracy that is likely to emerge and survive. Movements for democratization are often initiated under the impact of a momentary popular upsurge. The "opening" space for democratic transition usually begins with a split between hardliners and softliners within the polity. The transition to democracy is then often completed by an implicit or explicit political pact among different civilian political actors. The character of the transition in Korea, the fact that it was not only peaceful, but that it took place without any break in the institutional structures of the regime, played an important part.

The importance of economic development should not be overlooked, however. There cannot be a comprehensive right of the working class to organize and form associations with other subordinate classes without the growth of the "civil society": it is economic development that fosters the growth of that civil society, through which both the middle and working classes improve their ability and skills to organize, communicate their interests, and participate in alliances (Ruschemeyer et al. 1992). This development counterbalances the power of a strong state and opens and enlarges, perhaps in a more stable way than otherwise, a political space for negotiated pacts for democratization among opposing actors.

The economic performance of the preceding authoritarian regime thus did set the terms and affect the mode of the transition. Economic dynamism, leading to popular demands for democratization, facilitated a relatively smooth passage by means of negotiation and compromise, while, on the other hand, economic failure would have been likely to make the process extremely rocky, led to confrontation, and resulted in either imposition from above or transformation from below. Thus, in Korea, economic development brought about changes in the state-society relationship, which, in effect, empowered the civil society to gain autonomy vis-à-vis the state. Successful economic development built the pro-democratic forces that eventually pushed the existing regime towards more democracy. Progress in the economic sphere gave the society the energy, so to speak, to achieve success and to move to a new era of political openness, although such a social transformation does not of course guarantee political consolidation and institutionalization.

Thus economic progress helped the transition to be smooth and the smoothness of the transition helped political progress to take place. Yet despite these developments, the cultural and historical legacy of authoritarian rule and in particular of the prevailing regional cleavages continues to shape the country's political life. The Constitution, having undergone nine revisions between 1948 and 1987, still does not provide a basis for liberal democracy to take shape fully. Power is more evenly spread between different branches of the government, to be sure, both the legislature and the judiciary having gained in strength at the expense of the executive; but the handling of major issues of economic policy, security, and international relations has remained essentially in the hands of the executive and the bureaucracy. Old-style elite political networks function in much the same manner as before 1987. A rubber-stamp legislature, an imperial president, a presidential power cult, a politics of "pushing through" instead of persuasion and compromise, and artificial reshuffling of parties after elections are familiar phenomena in Korea. The rules of the electoral game have been made more regular, but the underlying basis of party politics has not markedly changed.

Democratization, party politics, and the party system

The nature of party politics is perhaps what poses the most serious challenge to Korean democracy. During the authoritarian period, the party system was based on a dominant party, which had close relationships with the bureaucracy. Post-transition Korea has led to a move from the one-dominant-with-one-opposition-party system toward a multi-party system. But all political parties suffer from lack of institutionalization and Korea has a long way to go before it achieves a viable, pluralistic party system. Parties have very limited influence in economic governance, which has long been dictated mainly by the state. In addition, standards of political behaviour and the quality and background of the elected officials have also remained more or less unchanged.

External constraints on party system development: Presidentialism and the electoral system

The Constitution and presidentialism

To begin with, a number of external constraints have limited the development of a healthy party system. First, the constitutional structure and specifically the presidential form of government seem be a hindrance. It has often been noted that the presidential form of government is associated with weak and less disciplined political parties (Sartori 1994, 176–77; Mainwaring 1993). In the United States in particular, the most and indeed almost the only successful case of presidentialism, parties are relatively weak; in Latin America, the situation is more mixed, but while parties are sometimes strong, regimes have typically been unstable, at least up to the mid-1980s.

In Korea, presidentialism has led to the president monopolizing the state's power, and to the marginalization of other political institutions such as parties and Congress. Parties tend to be excluded from key decision-making processes and are often regarded as subordinate, insignificant actors; this has in turn rendered their institutionalization difficult. The concept of "delegative democracy," a term used to characterize new democracies, with special reference to Latin America, by Guillermo O'Donnell, may help in this connection (O'Donnell 1994). While representative democracy in advanced democratic countries tends to operate on the basis of well-established institutions and with a high degree of institutional accountability, delegative democracy tends to rely on individuals. Once elected democratically, presidents behave as if they were the sole embodiment of the nation, standing above both parties and organized interests. The "delegative" president seeks support directly from voters, whose judgement of the chief executive's policies is not "restricted" by institutional checks and balances. The role of political parties is clearly markedly impaired by the mighty power of the presidency.

Specifically, the typically negative attitudes of South Korean presidents to parties and party politics have undermined the role of these organizations, not just in relation to decision-making but in relation to policy implementation as well. As the formation of the policy agenda and the aggregation of social demands is performed by presidential aides in the Blue House and through bureaucratic channels, parties have little room or incentive to develop their structure to fulfil those functions. For instance, in the major conflict relating to the new labour laws in December 1996, the governing New Korea Party (NKP) was reported to have abruptly changed its position on a key aspect of the law as a result of pressure from the president's office, even to the extent of violating the National Parliament Law (*Chosun Daily*, 22 December 1996). The governing party had no mechanisms by which it could explain its position to voters.

The electoral system

The rules and practices of the electoral system also restrict the development of parties. The Constitution gives the people the right of free expression and the right to form political associations freely, but party laws and electoral regulations vastly limit these rights. For instance, the formation of new parties and in particular of parties organized by industrial workers is overtly discouraged, as industrial workers are not allowed to form any political organizations, including parties; labour unions are also prohibited from donating political funds to political organizations. The linkage between people and parties is thereby distorted since the demands of industrial workers are scarcely articulated. There is a paradox here: Korean politics has become increasingly contentious and confrontational as industrialization has developed, but the cleavage between workers and employers cannot easily be translated into party conflict because of legal constraints. Furthermore, despite constitutional freedom, the existing parties use various tactics to discourage new parties from coming into existence. As a result, even after a long period of democratic transition, the country's party system continues to be dominated essentially by conservative parties, many of which have been re-named or re-formed since 1987 without having appreciably altered their old ways of doing politics under the authoritarian system (Jaung 1996).

The mechanics of voting have introduced further obstacles to party system development, as since 1988 elections have mainly been conducted on the first-past-the-post system with single-member constituencies: only 46 of the 299 seats in the National Assembly (15 per cent) are filled by a kind of proportional representation formula. This has resulted, as in other countries using the same system, in a substantial "bonus" for the largest party. Thus at the 1996 election, the governing NKP received 34 per cent of the votes but obtained 47 per cent of the seats; the second party, the National Congress for New Politics (NCNP), obtained a proportional share, 26 per cent of the seats for 25.3 per cent of the votes; but the third and fourth parties, the United Liberal Democrats (ULD) and the Democratic Party (DP), were at a disadvantage: the ULD obtained 16.5 per cent of the votes but only 10 per cent of the seats while the DP received 3 per cent of the seats for 10.9 per cent of the votes. The "bonus" in seats for the governing NKP was thus 13 per cent, while the "deficit" for the ULD and the DP was 5.5. and 4.9 per cent respectively. However, the NCNP and the ULD did succeed in obtaining a sizeable number of seats because of their strength in the Honam and Chungchong areas (see table 6.2).

Moreover, the first-past-the-post system, in Korea as in other countries which have adopted this system, makes it difficult for new parties to succeed, fundamentally because such parties experience problems in building grassroots organizations which can mobilize substantial numbers of electors. The dominant parties tend therefore to be traditional and rather conservative, while those which have different sets of goals, and espe-

Table 6.2 **Results of the South Korean general election, 1996**

	NKP	NCNP	DP	ULD	Independent
Percentage of vote (a)	34.4	25.3	10.9	16.5	13.0
Percentage (number) of seats from Districts (b)	47 (121)	26 (66)	3 (9)	16 (41)	6 (6)
Percentage (number) of seats from PR list	39 (18)	28 (13)	13 (6)	19 (9)	
Percentage (number) of total seats	46 (139)	26 (79)	5 (15)	16 (50)	5 (16)
Distortion effect: (b) − (a)	13	0.7	−7.9	0	

Source: Compiled from National Election Commission 1996.
For explanations of party acronyms, see the text of this chapter and the List of Acronyms, p. ix.

cially those which do not have a strong regional base, are markedly penalized.

Finally, the rise of media politics provides challenges as well as opportunities for the development of the party system in democratic Korea. In most advanced democracies, the mass media have played an increasing role in electoral and party politics in recent years. A similar phenomenon is just beginning in Korean democracy. This was evident in the 1997 presidential election. The three major candidates had several television debates which were watched by millions of voters. The candidates also relied heavily on political advertising via television and radio. As the new election laws prohibit outdoor mass rallies, the mass media became critical to electoral success.

There is abundant evidence for the increasing significance of media politics in Korean democracy. For instance, a significant portion of survey respondents indicated that television debates would influence their voting choice. Within political parties, more power and campaign funds than before were allocated to those who managed media campaigns.

The increasing influence of the media is likely to affect the future of political parties and electoral politics in democratic Korea in several ways. First, it will strengthen the influence of party leaders. As election campaigns rely more upon media than upon party organizations, the relative significance of party organizations, including local and provincial organizations, will not increase. Instead, media-centred campaigns will reinforce the role of presidential candidates because these emphasize the personal attraction of the candidate rather than the policy positions of parties. In other words, the rise of media politics may hamper the decentralization of politics which is required for the development of parties. Second, more reliance upon media campaigns will increase the demand for campaign funds. While Korean politicians and citizens have been struggling since the democratic transition to control the demand and supply of political funds and to introduce more transparency in this area, media politics may work against such reform.

Party and party system characteristics

These external constraints account only in part for the fact that Korean parties are scarcely institutionalized, which is primarily due to three fundamental aspects of their structure. The first and most obvious of these aspects is volatility: splits and mergers have been legion (an overview is provided in figure 6.1). Second, Korean parties are dominated by popular leaders who treat them as their own property. Third, and perhaps above all, parties are so regionally based that it is questionable whether they can be described as forming truly a national system.

Ever since the republic was installed after World War II, Korean ruling parties have been primarily set up to provide organizational support for the national leader, the president, and for the inner group gathered around him. In such a context, the key requirement for participation in politics at the highest level of power has been to place personal loyalty above institutional loyalty when the two have been in conflict. It is therefore not surprising that the parties of the three dominant presidents of the authoritarian period of Korean politics, Syngman Rhee's Liberal Party, Park Chung Hee's Democratic Republican Party, and Chun Doo Hwan's Democratic Justice Party (DJP) should have risen and fallen with their leaders.

The political parties

A malleable governmental party

In the space of less than a decade, between 1987 and 1995, the governmental party changed its name and its composition three times. It started as the Democratic Justice Party in 1987, became the Democratic Liberal Party (DLP) in 1990, and was transformed into the New Korea Party in 1995. The DJP had originally been formed as an institutional framework to buttress the rule of Chun Doo Hwan and his power group. At the end of Chun's rule in 1987, adjustments were made to ensure that Roh Tae

Woo would be accepted as Chun's successor, so that President Roh "inherited" the party. However, the DJP failed to win a majority of seats at the 1988 general election; moreover, ex-President Chun was found guilty of wrongdoing and abuse of his presidential powers. To give the impression that the party had been rejuvenated and cleaned up, it was renamed "Democratic Liberal"; but there was more to this move than a change of name, since President Roh succeeded in attracting to his party both Kim Young Sam's Reunification Democratic Party (RDP) and Kim Jong Pil's New Democratic Republican Party (NDRP). Almost immediately after the DLP was set up, however between 1990 and 1992, the leaders of the major factions which had been brought together to form the party became presidential contenders. Kim Young Sam finally emerged as the presidential candidate and won the election in 1992, but not long after his inauguration, in order to bring the party more in tune with his personal image, he changed its name from "Democratic Liberal Party" to "New Korea Party." Eventually the NKP merged with the small Democratic Party in the course of the 1997 presidential election and changed its name yet again, to the Grand National Party.

The opposition parties

After the 1996 National Assembly election, Korea had three main opposition parties. One was the National Congress for New Politics, founded in 1995 by Kim Dae Jung: it obtained 79 seats. A second, the United Liberal Democrats, which obtained 50 seats, was the result of the fact that Kim Jong Pil's National Democratic Republican Party, having joined the DLP in 1990, defected from it five years later and adopted a new name. The third party was the Democratic Party, which had been founded in 1990 by Kim Dae Jung by merging a number of small parties, including what was left of the PPD, and had succeeded in gaining 77 seats at the 1993 election, but only obtained 15 seats in 1996 after its leader defected from it and set up the NCNP.

There is little to distinguish these parties from each other in terms of ideology; as a matter of fact, their role as opposition parties has not been very significant either. Typically, South Korean opposition parties participate marginally in the political process, their main role being to accommodate ever-shifting coalitions of personality-based factions. Allegiance to faction leaders is more important than is allegiance to the party as an institution: institutional loyalty is weak. Consequently, the structure of opposition parties, like that of the ruling party, tends to be authoritarian, matters being settled in a highly centralized manner in Seoul, while grass-roots organisations play little part in decision-making. The opposition parties have seldom attempted to enlist systematically the support of labour unions, consumers, environmental bodies, or other sectoral pressure groups.

1987 Election	1988 Election	1992 Election	1996 Election	1997 Election

```
DJP -----------------⎫
                      ⎪                                        NPP
                      ⎪                                        (1997)
RDP ---------------- ⎬  DLP -------------------- NKP ----------- GNP
                      ⎪  (Jan. 1990)              (1996)        (1997)
NDRP--------------- ⎭                      ULD ------------------
                                           (1995)
PPD ------------------------------- DP ------------ DP -------------
                                                    (1996)
                                                    NCNP ------------------
                                                    (1996)

Hangyore -------- X
Peoples ----------- X

              RNP (1992) -- X
```

Figure 6.1 **The evolution of the South Korean party system after democratization, 1987–1997** (Source: compiled from *Chosun Daily*. "X" indicates dissolution of a party; for explanations of party acronyms, see the text of this chapter and the List of Acronyms, p. ix)

Splits and mergers, regionalism, and the personalization of leadership

The three characteristics of Korean parties, volatility, personalization, and regionalization, are intrinsically linked. Regionalism stems from but also reinforces peronalized leadership, while the idiosyncrasies of leaders account for major splits and mergers. Thus regional identity is stronger than other affiliations, whether party membership, religion, or social class; it accounts in large part for the outcomes of both national and local elections. It is also a crucial element in the determination of major policy issues: politicians appeal to electors on a regional basis rather than on the basis of national programmes, goals, and visions. So long as personalization and regionalism reinforce each other, a stable national party system can hardly be expected to emerge.

The problem of party institutionalization

According to Huntington, the level of institutionalization of political organizations can be measured by their adaptability, complexity, autonomy, and coherence (Huntington 1968, 12–22). "Adaptability" refers to the capability of a party to adjust successfully to changes in its environment: evidence for this feature can typically be based on the age of an organization. "Complexity" means both the multiplication of hierarchical and functional subunits and the differentiation of these. "Autonomy" involves the extent to which political organizations exist independently of other social groupings. "Coherence" relates to the extent to which the party is united in terms of the functions of the organization and of the procedures for resolving disputes within it.

In developed Western democracies, parties tend to score relatively highly in terms of the four characteristics: in particular, their organization and ideology remain stable for lengthy periods, while being able to adapt to changing environments. In Korea, on the contrary, parties have scarcely become institutionalized during the 1980s and 1990s. They have all been unstable, as figure 6.1 shows: every significant party has experienced a merger, has split, or has disappeared. Thus, as we saw, the DJP merged with the RDP and the NDRP in January 1990, but the DLP experienced a split after only six years, the dominant faction of the DLP having purged Kim Jong Pil's faction to avoid an intense power struggle within the party. Opposition parties underwent similar mergers, split, or disappeared. None of the four major parties participating in the 1987 founding election after the democratic transition maintained its identity for more than six years. Korea's party system is thus clearly unable to adapt to changing environments.

Nor are Korean parties complex organizations. They may appear to have subunits, but these exist only on paper: national, provincial, and local levels play a very limited part in decisions on campaign strategy and fund-raising. These decisions are taken by top-level party leaders and their immediate entourages. Thus, in spite of democratization, Korean political parties suffer from the same kind of volatility as that which characterizes many parties in authoritarian regimes: the parties have experienced delayed development, which stems largely from the fact that they are kept in tutelage by popular leaders whose bases are essentially regional.

The primacy of regionalism over other social cleavages

To become consolidated, parties need deep social roots and have to be internally united (Randall 1995; Evans and Whitefield 1993). These two elements are related in that when parties have a social base, they are likely to have numerous, disciplined, and loyal supporters. Hence the importance given by Lipset and Rokkan to the social base of parties, a feature that has come to be viewed as critical both in the West and in those non-Western countries, such as Korea, which became democratic in the late twentieth century (Lipset and Rokkan 1967, 67).

As was noted earlier, nearly all Korean parties have one, and only one, social base, regionalism. This is the one social base, however, which is least likely to lead to a stable party system. The fact that regionalism predominates makes it naturally rather easy for regionally based politicians to build a strong personalized support; this in turn prevents the parties from developing lively internal structures and from becoming as a result disciplined and stable. What emerges, on the contrary, is volatile bodies plagued by factionalism. Korean parties display these characteristics: consequently, their institutionalization has been delayed and they have known many splits and mergers.

Moreover, paradoxically perhaps, the more liberal political environment which emerged after 1987 enabled certain features of regionalism to prevail even more. Given that all the major parties have a core regional base; that they draw support heavily from their regions; and that they were set up by or are markedly dependent on regionally strong personal leaders, differences among the regions have come to be a key element in the popular appeal of these leaders. At the same time, voters appear to reward the leaders for their emphasis on sectional geographical platforms. As a result, electoral support in all major parties has increasingly been dependent on the regional factor, rather than on social class or religion, for instance: regionalism is the key mobilizing element on which politicians base their appeal and to which the voters respond. Thus Kim Dae Jung has been strong in the Cholla provinces and areas in Seoul where many people migrated from these provinces; the people of the Chungchong provinces primarily backed Kim Jong Pil; Kim Young Sam's main power base has been Pusan and South Kyungsang Province; and the disunity of opposition politicians along regional lines between the Kyungsang and Cholla provinces enabled Roh Tae Woo to win the presidency in 1987. A similar pattern existed in the 1988 National Assembly election, as can be seen from table 6.3.

Interestingly, the strength of this regional factor has not decreased with the progress of democratization: the regional concentration of the vote continues to be remarkable. Thus the DJP obtained 66.8 per cent of the votes in Roh Tae Woo's home province of Kyungbuk; and the RDP, whose candidate was originally from Kyungnam Province, obtained 52.8 per cent of the vote in the region in the 1987 election. The concentration is even more marked in the case of the Party for Peace and Democracy (PPD), as it drew 86.2 per cent of the vote in two Honam provinces where its candidate, Kim Dae Jung, was born. The intensity of regional voting even increased at the 1992 presidential election: Kim Young Sam obtained 52.8 per cent of the vote in his home region in 1987, but in 1992 he obtained 72.1 per cent; in the Honam region, Kim Dae Jung obtained 90.9 per cent of the votes. The dominance of the regional cleavage was equally marked at the National Assembly election of 1992 and the election of 1996 showed almost no change at all in this respect.

Regionalism and voting alignments have also been intimately linked in local elections. In the June 1991 election which re-established provincial assemblies after a 30-year suspension, Kim Dae Jung's then New Democratic Party gained 83 per cent of the seats in Kwangju, 92 per cent in South Cholla, and 98 per cent in North Cholla; but it did not win a single seat in the two metropolitan communities of Pusan and Taegu or in the five provinces of Kangwon, North Kyungsang, Chaeju, and North and South Chungchong (Ahn and Back 1995). Local elections were held again in June 1995 for the municipal and provincial assemblies and for heads of local governments: the Cholla provinces were won by Kim Dae Jung's Democratic Party, the Chungchong provinces were taken by Kim Jong Pil's United Liberal Democratic Party, and Seoul was divided because of its mixed regional composition.

With regionalism being the social base for the parties, national institutionalization has not even begun to occur. Leaders can use their regional support in whatever way they wish: when political leaders form or dissolve coalitions as a result of changed circumstances, their parties merge or split. When a popular leader launches a new party for reasons best known to himself, his region swiftly changes its support toward the new party.

This pattern both leads to and is reinforced by the weak internal structure of parties. Party organizations are dominated by the top leaders; these are typically wholly responsible for managing the affairs and finances of the party, as well as for elaborating political tactics, nominating candidates for elections, and running electoral campaigns. So long as regional cleavages remain the social basis for electoral mobilization, and so long as personalized leadership with a monolithic regional identification dominates the party system, there will be little party institutionalization. The internal conditions for a stable party system can therefore be said to be absent in South Korea at the end of the twentieth century.

Democratization and economic performance

Whether democracy helps or hinders economic performance has become a prominent issue in newly democratizing countries: as a matter of fact, the evidence on this question is largely inconclusive and contradictory. Some contend that the newly introduced democratic regimes of Asia and Latin America have affected the economy negatively; others claim that democracies have achieved a better and more efficient economic performance than authoritarian states. (Sagong 1993; Cheng 1995; Maravall 1994; Pei 1994; Geddes 1994).

Economic performance and the bureaucratic state

The success of the South Korean economy has owed a great deal to the "strong state," with its ability to formulate "proper policies" and to

Table 6.3 **South Korean presidential election results by region, 1987–1997** (per cent)

	Seoul/Kyunggi	Chungchong	Kangwon	Honam	Kyungbuk	Kyungnam	National total
1987[1]							
DJP (Roh Tae Woo)	33.7	32.2	57.9	9.6	66.8	35.9	36.6
RDP (Kim Young Sam)	28.2	19.5	25.5	1.2	26.1	52.8	28.0
PPD (Kim Dae Jung)	28.0	11.6	8.6	86.2	2.4	6.8	27.0
NDRP (Kim Jong Pil)	8.1	33.7	5.3	0.5	2.3	2.6	8.1
1992[1]							
DLP (Kim Young Sam)	36.0	36.2	40.8	4.2	61.6	72.1	42.0
DP (Kim Dae Jung)	34.8	27.3	15.2	90.9	8.7	10.8	33.8
NRP (Jeong Ju Young)	19.8	23.8	33.5	2.3	17.0	8.8	16.3
Others	9.4	12.7	10.5	2.6	12.7	8.3	7.9

1997[2]

Region	Provinces/metropolitan cities	Share of votes by candidate			Turnout rate
		Lee Hoi Chang	Kim Dae Jung	Rhee In Je	
Chungchong	Taejon	29.2	45.0	24.1	78.6
	North Chungchong	30.8	37.4	29.4	79.3
	South Chungchong	23.5	48.3	26.1	77.0
Cholla	Kwangju	1.7	97.3	0.7	89.9
	North Cholla	4.5	92.3	2.1	85.5
	South Cholla	3.2	94.6	1.4	87.3

North Kyungsang	Taegu	72.7	12.5	13.1	78.9
	North Kyungsang	61.9	13.7	21.8	79.2
South Kyungsang	Pusan	53.3	15.3	29.8	78.9
	Ulsan	51.4	15.4	26.7	81.1
	South Kyungsang	55.1	11.0	31.3	80.3
Others	Seoul	40.9	44.9	12.8	80.5
	Kyunggi	35.5	39.3	23.6	80.6
	Inchon	36.4	38.5	23.0	80.0
	Kangwon	43.2	23.8	30.9	78.5
	Cheju	36.6	40.6	20.5	77.1
Total		38.7	40.3	19.2	80.7

Source: National Election Management Commission 1987, 1992, 1997.
[1] For explanations of party acronyms, see the text of this chapter and the List of Acronyms, p. ix.
[2] The presentation of data for 1997 reflects the changes made by the National Election Management Commission in the organization of election data for 1997 as against previous elections.

channel both public and private resources effectively for dynamic industrial growth. The state oversaw labour relations and the flow of human, capital, and natural resources; it could mobilize investment funds through forced savings via taxes and inflation, foreign borrowing, and financial intermediation, and then channel these funds selectively to a number of projects. The state created public enterprises and manipulated provisions of loans and incentives to the private sector as well. In brief, it played a dominant role in almost all aspects of economic life in South Korea (Jones and Sagong 1980; Deyo 1987; Amsden 1989; Choi 1989; Woo 1991; Haggard and Moon 1993; Ahn 1994). Yet the very success of the strong state planted the seeds of its undoing. As the economy grew in size and complexity, the effectiveness of state intervention decreased. Increased industrialization and increased market dependency led to further interference in both economy and society to a point where this interference became impossibly costly and counter-productive.

The process of industrialization enhances the power and influence of society and of civic organizations relative to that of the state and public organizations, while limiting the state's ability to influence society and thus eroding its freedom of intervention. The state has therefore to adjust its methods and its manner of acting on society. This occurred in Korea when economic growth and industrialization created the social and political preconditions for democracy. With deepening industrialization, pro-democratic forces were strengthened and acquired increasing political influence, although this did not guarantee their success.

As has been argued for Latin America, and as has indeed occurred in the newly industrializing countries of East and Southeast Asia, authoritarianism appears to be necessary or even inevitable for a capitalist developing economy to bring about the changes in its production structure which are necessary for its industrial deepening. Studies of East Asian newly industrializing countries (NICs) also tend to argue that the "soft" authoritarianism of the "capitalist developmental states" has a certain advantage over purely socialist or capitalist policies in providing efficiency in economic resource mobilization, especially during the early stages of industrialization. In effect, these theories end up saying that Korean society needed (or condoned) lack of democracy in order to achieve rapid economic development (Amsden 1989). Perhaps, however, Korea's rapid economic development was made possible not only because of the authoritarian "strong state," but also because of other factors; likewise, Korea's non-democratic past is due more to specific factors in Korean politics than to the urge for economic development, such as its unique strategic position in the capitalist world system as well as the absence of a countervailing elite based on an institutionalized party system.

The economy during the transition period

To examine the Korean case more closely, let us begin by considering the macroeconomic performance of Korea between 1987 and 1995. As table 6.4 shows, that performance has been mixed during the transition period. There was an economic downturn during the early period under Roh Tae Woo; the economy then appeared to recover under Kim Young Sam, albeit with weaknesses in some sectors.

Prior to the democratic transition, the performance of the Korean economy was good: in 1987, for instance, the last year of the Chun Doo Hwan regime, the economy grew by an impressive 12.3 per cent; the current account balance was US$9.9 billion in surplus; inflation was 3 per cent and unemployment 3.1 per cent. In the early democratic period, on the other hand, the economy began to slow down. The growth in GNP fell from 12.3 per cent in 1987 to 6.9 per cent in 1989 and to 5.0 per cent in 1992; the current account plummeted to US$5.1 billion in 1989 and was in deficit both in 1991 (US$8.7 billion) and in 1992 (US$4.5 billion); inflation rose to 5.7 per cent in 1989 and to 9.3 per cent in 1991. Thus, by several indicators, the Korean economy seemed to have been paying a price for the transition.

However, that economy began to revive with the Kim Young Sam government. The GNP grew by 5.8 per cent in 1993, by 8.2 per cent in 1994, and by 8.7 per cent in 1995. Inflation was reduced to 4.8 per cent in 1993 and 4.5 per cent in 1995, while unemployment was kept at 2.8 per cent in 1993 and 2.0 per cent in 1995. The balance of payments continued to deteriorate, however, except in 1993 when there was a small surplus of US$380 million; the deficit returned in 1994, when it was US$4.6 billion; it increased to US$8.8 billion in 1995 and to US$20.1 billion in 1996. By late 1997, when the economy suffered a serious financial crisis, it seemed that the ostensibly sound performance of the economy during the Kim Young-Sam government may have been in part due to these vast deficits.

On the basis of these figures it is therefore not permissible to pass a clear judgement on the impact of democratization on economic performance. When the economy began to show signs of recovery in the early years of Kim Young Sam's presidency, some felt that the Korean economy might have been paying the price of the democratic transition (Cheng 1995; Ahn 1996) There were indeed a number of positive, if not rosy, signs; as a matter of fact, Korea's economy had the highest growth rates among the new democracies even during the most difficult period of transition under President Roh Tae Woo (1987–92). By 1995, per capita income exceeded US$10,000; in December 1991, South Korea became a member of the ILO and in the course of the democratization process, both labour and management had started to overcome their conflicts: the

Table 6.4 **South Korea's economic performance, 1987–1995**

	1987	1988	1989	1990	1991	1992	1993	1994	1995
Growth rate of GNP[1]	12.3	12.0	6.9	9.6	9.1	5.0	5.8	8.2	8.7
GNP[2]	133	179	220	251	292	305	330	376	451
GNP per capita[3]	3,218	4,295	5,210	5,883	6,757	7,007	7,513	8,483	10,076
Current account[4]	9.9	14.2	5.1	−2.2	−8.7	−4.5	0.38	−4.5	−8.8
Consumer prices[5]	3.0	7.1	5.7	8.6	9.3	6.2	4.8	6.2	4.5
Unemployment rate	3.1	2.5	2.6	2.4	2.3	2.4	2.8	2.4	2.0
Gross savings[6]	37.3	39.3	36.2	35.9	36.1	34.9	35.2	35.4	36.2
Gross domestic investment[7]	30.0	31.1	33.8	37.1	39.1	36.8	35.2	36.2	37.5

Source: Compiled from National Statistics Office, *Major Statistics of Korean Economy* (Seoul, 1996), quoted from Moon and Kim 1996, 15.

[1] Annual per cent change at 1990 constant prices.
[2] In current US$ billions.
[3] In current US$.
[4] In US$ billions, BOP basis.
[5] Annual per cent change at 1990 constant prices.
[6] Percentage of GNP.
[7] Percentage of GNP.

number of disputes was significantly reduced from its 1993 level; finally, the country joined the OECD at the end of 1996.

However, the prospects for sustained growth and for economic maturity came to be further in question as the economy was hit by another downturn in 1996 and by the explosive events of 1997. The growth rate of the GDP was reduced to 6.4 per cent in 1996; the current account deficit swelled. The Hanbo Steel scandal led to massive economic turbulence in early 1997, only to be followed by a series of bankruptcies of scores of ranking business firms including a few leading chaebols. By late 1997, as a result of mounting external debts, South Korea was close to national insolvency, and had to rely on the financial support of the International Monetary Fund.

Given these ups and downs, there is apparently no clear association between democracy and economic performance in Korea. The concept of political democracy is too broad to be closely related in a general manner to economic performance. It might therefore be better to look for a more limited concept that will enable us explore the association between the two variables.

We noted earlier that while democratization has proceeded speedily and successfully, the institutionalization of the party system has been deficient: it may therefore be that economic mismanagement has been caused by the gap between the democratization of the polity and the weakness of the party system. In countries where pluralistic parties compete on the basis of policy platforms, economic governance is more likely to become transparent, democratic, and performance-oriented. As Maravall argues, "to achieve successful economic reform, democratic governments need to listen, to negotiate, and to persuade" (Maravall 1994, 23). Moreover, a democratic regime can more easily gain the popular trust required for long-term planning and for economic reforms. The legitimacy of democratic regimes also provides leaders with strong political mandates enabling them to launch effective economic reforms. Thus a case can be made for the view that when a new democracy has a stable and institutionalized party system, it can also be economically efficient as well as less vulnerable to economic crises.

The changing Korean strong state

The changing role and capacity of the state in economic governance may be a further intervening variable linking democracy and economic performance. In the course of the democratization process, the Korean state, which had been the dominant actor in economic decision-making, underwent significant changes. Democratic transition caused a moderate decline, though not a serious undermining, of a number of elements of the strong developmental state: it is no longer fully insulated and autono-mous since private business and the civil sector in general have gained strength. This has had an effect on the consistency and coherence of the bureaucracy in the elaboration and implementation of economic policy-making, as well as on the adaptability of the state to changing external political and economic environments.

First, as a result of liberalization and democratization, the autonomy of the state began to be eroded. In a post-authoritarian situation, business and labour had greater political freedom to make their own voices and demands felt; social criticism and political protest against state domi-nance gained strength. For example, when business organizations, whose influence had grown substantially in the course of the process of eco-nomic liberalization, pushed the government to introduce new laws to allow flexibility in the labour market in December 1996, unions and workers began to protest vehemently, with the effect that the laws had to be postponed. As elections became more democratic and more regularly held, and as the political legitimacy and survival of the government came to rest increasingly on electoral support, the autonomy and insularity of the state declined even further. The political atmosphere made it impos-sible for the state to stop wage increases, for instance; as a result, nominal wage rates substantially exceeded increases in labour productivity. This in turn had major consequences for South Korea's competitive edge in the world market.

Second, the weakening of the strong state also brought about ineffi-ciency and inconsistency in the government's economic policy. Both the Roh Tae Woo and the Kim Young Sam governments performed erratic twists in economic management. The Roh government, on its inaugura-tion, attempted to introduce new economic reform programmes which included a reduction of the concentration of the economic power of the chaebols and amendments to labour laws: because of the contradictory character of these policies, the package of reforms led to an economic recession. To offset this recession, Roh's government abruptly returned to expansionary, pro-business policies which further increased inflation (Moon and Kim 1996, 10). Subsequently, when real estate and stock market speculation became wild, the government switched back to an al-ternative set of policies in order to diminish the effect of this speculation.

Kim Young Sam's government was also characterized by abrupt and frequent changes of direction between reform policies and conserva-tive policies. On the inauguration of the president, the government announced ambitious plans to alter financial transactions and to cam-paign against corruption. Allegedly in order to enhance economic justice, in 1993 President Kim banned the use of false and borrowed names in all financial transactions, the main objective being to block the flow of illegal or unethical political donations that smacked of corruption. In addition, the government announced that all real-estate titles had to be registered under the real name of the owner (Ahn 1996, 253). These measures had unintended results, however: they led, for instance, to sharp increases in consumption, and in imports of luxury goods. Confronted with these negative consequences as well as with mounting difficulties in the world market, the government returned to conservative policies: in 1994, instead of emphasizing reform, the government began to stress the need to recover international competitiveness with the catchphrase of *segyehwa* or "globalization."

It was in such a context that the government attempted to enforce, in December 1996, a new law primarily aimed at allowing flexibility in the labour market and at providing businesses with more favourable conditions in which to compete in world markets. The law was sent prematurely to the National Assembly, however, without enough efforts having been made to consult with opposition parties and labour organizations. Despite very strong opposition, the government and the ruling party nonetheless endeavoured to see to it that the law was passed, with only the members of the ruling party secretly gathering and voting without debate. This led both to political turmoil and to economic chaos. Fierce protests came not only from labour organizations, but from many sectors of the new middle class (*Economist*, 18 January 1997, 27). Rapid changes in economic policy thus plagued the governments of democratizing Korea. Erratic and frequent twists in direction have hurt the credibility of the government, and this may well in turn have had severe consequences for overall economic performance.

Finally, democratization tends to cause a decline in the state's ability to adapt in a timely manner to the external economic environment. The Korean economy had previously adjusted successfully to changes in the world market with timely, effective, and consistent economic measures. In the context of the late 1990s, the bureaucracy became more vulnerable to the interests of business groups and to the pressure exercised by other private or civic organizations, this being another aspect of the reduction of the insularity of the state. The result has been a weakening of the bureaucracy's power of policy co-ordination and generally of its power to adapt to the changing world economy.

Since 1996, the Korean economy has begun to suffer from a number of factors in world markets. It was particularly affected by the decline of the Japanese yen and by high wages: exports of key items such as semiconductors sharply dropped. To meet these challenges, the economy needed quick policy changes, but with the decline of the strong developmental state, the government and economic bureaucrats were no longer able to undertake such changes: the Korean economy was no longer being efficiently governed by a developmental state run by tough bureaucrats. Moreover, as part of Korea's accession to the OECD in 1996, financial controls by the central authorities on the banking system had been attenuated and even in part eliminated. Other key players in the Korean economy – notably business and labour – were markedly more powerful than in the past. A new relationship among these players and between them and the state had therefore to be established: until this occurs, the Korean economy is likely to continue to fluctuate in accordance with the conditions dictated by external actors and by the global environment in general.

Conclusion

As South Korea enters the twenty-first century, it is confronted with the twin needs of having to consolidate its democracy and revitalize its economy. The democratization process of 1987–96 helped the country to move, seemingly irreversibly, from an authoritarian to a democratic polity. Since this move has taken place, the nation has been committed simultaneously to political and economic restructuring. In the Schumpeterian sense of the term at least, South Korea has become a democracy: it has a democratic constitution which allows for freedom of political expression and freedom of association; it has a free press, several parties, regular elections, and open competition for power among major political forces; above all, since 1987, changes of government have been peaceful and regular.

Yet the legacy of authoritarian elite rule, regional cleavages, and the lack of institutionalization of political parties has blocked Korea's path towards a mature democracy. As we saw, parties have made less progress than other institutions. Party organizations are not true mediating agents between social demands and the government. They are not stable or durable, all major parties having undergone mergers and splits since 1987. Their autonomy as organizations has been undermined by the dominance of personal party leaders entrenched in rigidly circumscribed regional strongholds. The proper role of the parties as parties has been usurped by these leaders instead of being performed in accordance with settled procedures. Presidential politics has also prevented parties from being key actors, while the first-past-the-post electoral system tends to favour large existing parties and makes it difficult for new social forces to find a place in political life: all significant parties have been criticized for being in effect conservative parties, and thus for further distorting the links between party and society (Jaung 1996).

As a new kind of presidency emerges under former opposition leader

Kim Dae Jung, South Korea's democracy faces a number of political challenges. First, government performance and policy effectiveness need to be improved in order to meet citizens' expectations. Second, reform drives and democratization programmes have to be better co-ordinated in order to improve the quality of life of the people at large. Third, the values, goals, and norms of democracy need to be firmly rooted in the cultural orientation and the behaviour patterns of the population. Fourth, the future of South Korean democracy largely depends on whether it develops a social and economic base enabling it to achieve a peaceful unification of the two Koreas and thus to give the North Korean people the opportunity to live under democratic rule (Ahn 1997).

Economically, South Korea faces the task of moving successfully from being an exporter largely of cheap manufactures to being able to succeed against more aggressive and sophisticated competitors in the global market of high-technology and knowledge-intensive industries. State-centred economic governance continues in some respects. Indeed, part of the IMF package entails restoring the state's supervision in some fields, such as financial supervision; moreover, the Economic Planning Board, which had been weakened and subsumed in the Finance Department in 1994–95, is to be resurrected as an Office of Management and the Budget; furthermore, the state's prominent role in R & D and new product development as well as in encouraging small and medium-sized enterprises and exports is to remain. There may be more emphasis on collaboration than on hierarchy and direction, but the state's role has not been abandoned.

However, in other aspects, state governance is substantially reduced. As was shown by the harsh resistance of labour organizations and the strikes and political turmoil which followed the abortive attempt by the government to enact the new labour law in late 1996, there are serious doubts about the power of the state to be able to repress labour: in order to create a flexible labour market or to lower wage costs, the government needs therefore to listen, co-operate, negotiate, and persuade. The time has passed when state bureaucrats could deal with workers by using heavy-handed methods.

Meanwhile, on the international plane, the country is moving away from being a client of the United States to becoming an independent, middle-ranking actor functioning as a key player in the region's and even in the world's political and economic order. From a nation divided by ideology and bitter war, it has set itself the goal to achieve national re-unification through reconciliation and peaceful processes.

By the time Kim Dae Jung was elected president in 1997, Korean society had come to the painful realization that the national economy had reached a crucial juncture. In the past, low labour costs had fuelled dynamic growth through export-led expansion. At the end of the twentieth century, on the other hand, industries need to be upgraded to achieve high-tech production if their international competitiveness is to be maintained. Excessive wage increases, high capital costs, and exaggerated bureaucratic red tape, not to mention institutionalized corruption, have weakened the international competitiveness of the economy; prospects are even worse as external economic circumstances deteriorate. Meanwhile, mounting demands have also been made to cut down the power of the chaebols, the mainly family-run conglomerates which served South Korea well as engines of growth in the 1970s and 1980s, but which have since then lost their competitive edge in overseas export markets.

At the time of his election, President Kim promised to reinvigorate the economy by trimming government and reducing the red tape which stifles efficiency. He also committed himself to striking a balance between labour and management and to introducing measures to support small and medium-sized enterprises. His administration also had to reshape the heavily indebted financial institutions in order to enable them to conform to the requirements of the IMF rescue package, while giving banks and financial institutions greater autonomy. The choices which President Kim Dae Jung had to make were very hard: they required considerable skill to enable him to implement the necessary political and economic agenda, while maintaining coherence in economic and social policies.

REFERENCES

Ahn, Chung-Si (1993), "Democratisation and Political Reform in South Korea: Development, Culture, Leadership and Institutional Change," *Asian Journal of Political Science* 1(2), pp. 93–109.

——— (1994), "The State, Society and Democratisation in South Korea: The Impact of Deepening Industrialisation," in Stuart S. Nagel (ed.), *Asian Development and Public Policy*, St. Martin's Press, New York, pp. 32–43.

——— (1996), "Economic Dimensions of Democratisation in South Korea," in Anek Laothamatas (ed.), *Democratisation in Southeast and East Asia*, Institute of Southeast Asian Studies, Singapore, pp. 237–58.

——— (1997), "Democratization and Quality of Life in Korea," *Korean Social Science Review* 19(1), pp. 7–21.

Ahn, Chung-Si and Back, Jong-Gook (1995), "Democracy and Local Governance: Korean National Report of Local Elite Survey," *Social Science and Policy Research* 17(2), pp. 217–47.

Amsden, Alice H. (1989), *Asia's Next Giant: South Korea and Late Industrialisation*, Oxford University Press, New York.

Blondel, Jean (1996), "Democratisation, Parties, Party Systems, and Economic Growth in East and Southeast Asia," unpublished manuscript.

Cheng, Tun-jen (1995), "Democratic Transition and Economic Development: The Case of the Republic of Korea," paper presented at a conference on 50 Years of Korean Independence, 50 Years of Korean Politics, organized by the Korean Political Science Association, Seoul, 20–21 July, 1995.

Choi, Jang-Jip (1989), *Labour and the Authoritarian State: Labour Unions in South Korean Manufacturing Industries, 1961–1980*, Korea University Press, Seoul.

Deyo, Frederic C. (ed.) (1987), *The Political Economy of the New Asian Industrialism*, Cornell University Press, Ithaca, N.Y.

Economic Planning Board (1994), *Social Indicators of Korea*, Economic Planning Board, Seoul.

Evans, Geoffrey and Whitefield, Stephen (1993), "Identifying the Bases of Party Competition in Eastern Europe," *British Journal of Political Science* 23, 521–48.

Geddes, Barbara (1994), "Challenging the Conventional Wisdom," *Journal of Democracy* 5(4), pp. 104–18.

Haggard, Stephan and Moon, Chung-In (1983), "Liberal, Dependent or Mercantile? The South Korean State in the International System," in John Ruggie (ed.), *Antinomies of Interdependence*, Columbia University Press, New York.

Haggard, Stephan and Moon, Chung-In (1993), "The State, Politics, and Economic Development in Postwar South Korea," in Hagen Koo (ed.), *State and Society in Contemporary Korea*, Cornell University Press, Ithaca, N.Y.

Hart-Landsberg, Martin (1993), *The Rush to Development: Economic Change and Political Struggle in South Korea*, Monthly Review Press, New York.

Huntington, Samuel P. (1968), *Political Order in Changing Societies*, Yale University Press, New Haven, Conn.

—— (1991), *The Third Wave: Democratization in the Late Twentieth Century*, University of Oklahoma Press, Norman.

Im, Hyug Baeg (1996), "Korean Democratic Consolidation in Comparative Perspective," paper presented at an international conference on Democratic Consolidation in South Korea, Korea University, Seoul, 19–20 June.

Jaung, Hoon (1996), "Democratic Transition and The Emerging Party System in South Korea: The Rise of A Conservatives-Dominant Party System," unpublished manuscript.

Jones, Leroy and Sakong, Il (1980), *Government, Business, and Entrepreneurship in Economic Development: The Korean Case*, Harvard University Press, Cambridge, Mass.

Koo, Hagen (1993), "The State, Minjung, and the Working Class in South Korea," in Hagen Koo (ed.), *State and Society in Contemporary Korea*, Cornell University Press, Ithaca, N.Y.

Lipset, Seymour, and Rokkan, Stein (1967), *Party Systems and Voter Alignment*, Free Press, New York.

Mainwaring, Scott (1993), "Presidentialism, Multipartism, and Democracy: The Difficult Combination," *Comparative Political Studies* 26, 198–228.

Maravall, Jose Maria (1994), "The Myth of the Authoritarian Advantage," *Journal of Democracy* 5(4), pp. 17–31.

Moon, Chung-In, and Kim, Song-min (1996), "Democracy and Economic Performance in South Korea," paper presented at an international conference on Consolidating Democracy in South Korea, Korea University, Seoul, 19–20 June.

Moore, Barrington, Jr. (1966), *Social Origins of Dictatorship and Democracy*, Beacon Press, Boston.

National Election Management Commission (1987, 1992, 1997), *The Presidential Election Data*, Seoul.

——— (1996), *The 1996 General Election*, Seoul.

O'Donnell, Guillermo (1973), *Modernization and Bureaucratic Authoritarianism*, Institute of International Studies, Berkeley, Calif.

——— (1994), "Delegative Democracy," *Journal of Democracy* 5.

Pei, Minxin (1994), "The Puzzle of East Asian Exceptionalism," *Journal of Democracy* 5(4), pp. 90–103.

Przeworsky, Adam (1992), *Democracy and the Market: Political and Economic Reforms in Eastern Europe and Latin America*, Cambridge University Press, New York.

Randall, Vicky (1995), "Parties and Democratisation in the Third World," paper presented at an international conference on Party Politics in the Year 2000, Manchester University, U.K., 13–14 January.

Ruschemeyer, Dietrich, Stephens, Evelyn H., and Stephens, John D. (1992), *Capitalist Development and Democracy*, University of Chicago Press, Chicago.

Sagong, Il (1993), *Korea in the World Economy*, Institute for International Economics, Washington, D.C.

Sartori, Giovanni (1994), *Comparative Constitutional Engineering*, Macmillan, London.

Stepan, Alfred (1986), "Paths toward Redemocratization: Theoretical and Comparative Considerations," in Guillermo O'Donnell, Philippe C. Schmitter, and Laurence Whitehead (eds.), *Transitions from Authoritarian Rule: Comparative Perspectives*, Johns Hopkins University Press, Baltimore, pp. 64–84.

Woo, Jung-en (1991), *Race to the Swift: State and Finance in Korean Industrialization*, Columbia University Press, New York.

7

The Philippines

Renato S. Velasco

In ousting a dictatorship in 1986, the Philippines was an important part of the democratic wave that swept the world in the 1970s and 1980s. During these decades many authoritarian regimes in Asia, Eastern Europe, Latin America, and Africa fell from power, and more liberal and democratic political systems took their place. After years of dictatorial rule, these polities experienced the return of civilian rule, free elections, and political parties, a democratic awakening which resulted in much optimism and even euphoria. Francis Fukuyama described this historical phase as the "end of history." He argued that the eventful triumph of democracy over authoritarianism signals the universalization of Western liberal democracy as the final form of human government.[1]

Other analysts, however, adopted a more cautious attitude toward the restoration of democratic regimes. Relating it to past political trends, Samuel Huntington described the recent episode as "third-wave democratization." On the basis of this concept, he put forward two arguments: first, this democratic awakening is simply a continuation of two previous movements (the first wave in 1828–1926 and the second wave in 1943–62); second, each of the two earlier waves was followed by a return to non-democratic regimes (the first reversal in 1922–42, the second in 1958–75). The implication is that the current third wave of democratization will also lead to a reversal.[2]

Transitions to democracy do not necessarily lead to democratic consolidation or deepening: there are indeed serious threats to new and old

167

democracies. One of these threats is economic slowdown or stagnation which hampers the capacity of the state to deliver services and to introduce reforms while undermining public confidence in democratic politics. The downfall of several authoritarian regimes has been attributed to bad economic mismanagement. The legitimacy of newly restored democracies is therefore tied to their ability to restore and sustain economic growth.

Another threat comes from messianic and egoistic leaders who perpetuate a personality-based leadership, thus impairing the development of democratic procedures, structures, and institutions. Moreover, social dislocation leads to alienation and breeds anti-regime violence. Finally, the military has yet to accept fully or adjust to its diminished role in post-authoritarian politics.

Thus the question is whether the restored democracies of the 1980s and 1990s have a better chance at consolidation and survival into the future than their predecessors had 30 or 50 years ago. This in turn depends largely on the nature of the political parties within the democracies. While strong parties may not be necessary to establish democratic regimes, they are necessary for the long-term consolidation of these regimes. As Diamond and Linz noted:

an important element in the institutional resilience of democracy has been the strength of the party system and the high degree of institutionalization and popular loyalty achieved by the major parties. All of our cases call attention to the institutional strength or weakness of parties as a determinant of success or failure with democracy, and each of them grapples with the problem of institutionalization in terms that inevitably recall Samuel Huntington's classic formula: coherence, complexity, autonomy and adaptability.[3]

Political parties are the products as well as the creators of democracy. Their activities promote the formation of an organized opposition which is essential for democracy. Through their operation, the people become involved and educated politically. Modern democracy is unthinkable without parties.

Parties also contribute to economic growth, which in turn enhances the durability of democratic regimes. The most developed economies are also those with the longest history of and most institutionalized party systems. Political and party leaderships which steered economic development in Western Europe, America, and Japan brought about the affluence of these countries. Parties and politicians, together with the bureaucracy, established the appropriate legal and policy infrastructure that made sustained and rapid growth possible.

How far do these characteristics apply to Philippine political parties? Do they promote democratization as well as economic growth? What are their basic organizational features? What is the impact of the constitutional structure and the electoral system on their nature, orientation, and operations? How do they relate to the bureaucracy in economic policy-making? To what extent does the bureaucracy define economic policies and outcomes, and what are the modes of co-operation and conflict between the parties and the bureaucracy? What are the outcomes of this co-operation in terms of policies and growth?

To address these questions, this chapter first discusses the historical context of party politics and of economic policy-making and democratization. It then examines the constitutional set-up, electoral system, and mass media, and looks at their impact on the political parties. The programmes and platforms of the parties are analysed in the context of the setting up of a "growth coalition" and its impact on democratization and economic governance. Finally, the paper surveys the background, capability and role of the bureaucracy in economic policy-making, and the modes of co-operation and tension between parties and bureaucrats as well as the outcomes of economic policy-making resulting from interactions between politicians and bureaucrats.

Historical background

A middle-income country with a population of 70 million, the Philippines has one of the longest records of democratic governance in Asia. It has been extensively exposed to liberalism. It was Asia's oldest republic (1898); it is the only Christian country in Asia; it was a working democracy between 1946 and 1972; and, after a dictatorial interlude between 1972 and 1986, the dictatorship was ousted by a non-violent "people power" revolt in 1986.

During a long resistance against 300 years of Spanish colonialism, the country was strongly influenced by the libertarian ideals of the French and American revolutions. At the height of the revolt in 1898, Filipino revolutionaries drafted a republican constitution based on civil liberties, a representative assembly, and the separation of church and state. The Philippine-American War of 1899–1902 ended that republic, which was replaced by American occupation up to 1946 when independence was declared.

Post-war democratic politics, 1946–1972

Post-war politics was based on a separation of powers system with checks and balances on the U.S. model. The American-inspired 1935 Constitution had provided for universal suffrage. Its provisions for civil rights and secular representative democracy complemented the liberal concepts of the 1898 Constitution.

Between 1946 and 1972 political life was based on two parties, the Nationalista Party (NP) and the Liberal Party (LP). Minor parties occasionally challenged this two-party dominance but they were hampered by the built-in strength (historical, financial, and even legal) of the two main parties. Elections were popular among Filipinos. The elite consensus was thereby strengthened, resulting in political system stability and predictability. Although there was fraud and violence, most political leaders and citizens put their faith in the democratic process. The Philippines is thus one of the few Asian countries in which the turnover of leadership has tended to be peaceful. Between 1946 and 1972, there were three transfers of power from the elected government of one party to the elected government of another.

Martial law politics, 1972–1986

This record of democratic politics was broken in 1972 when President Ferdinand Marcos declared martial law. He exploited the dissatisfaction which had emerged as a result of the oligarchical character of the leadership of the two parties and used martial law to extend his term. Constitutional provisions on civil liberties were suspended, Congress was abolished, and opposition leaders and critics were arrested and imprisoned. Relying on the military, Marcos promulgated a new Constitution and established a regime which he described as one of "constitutional authoritarianism." A single-party system was established, based on the Kilusang Bagong Lipunan (KBL – New Society Movement) with *barangays* or neighborhood groups as grassroots organizations. The hegemony of the KBL was unchallenged for over a decade.

The regime promised stability and growth on the basis of developmentalism: these promises proved empty. The external shocks of the oil and debt crises in the 1970s and 1980s exposed the internal weaknesses of the regime: protectionism, monopolies, and debt-powered growth. As a matter of fact, the huge foreign debt burden combined with capital flight and the fall in export revenues led to negative growth in the early 1980s. Politically, the authoritarian power structure and the lack of a regular succession mechanism alienated many groups and caused anxiety among investors. The rapid growth of a Muslim-based rebellion and of a Communist-led New People's Army (NPA), and the assassination of the noted opposition leader Senator Benigno "Ninoy" Aquino caused widespread alarm, including within the U.S. government which had extended economic and military assistance to the regime because of its strategic interests in the country. There came to be a strong united opposition against the regime which included the Catholic Church, business groups, and disgruntled military leaders. In February 1986, the "people power" revolt deposed Marcos, and Corazon Aquino, the widow of the slain senator, became president.

The restoration of democratic politics, 1986–present

The fall of Marcos brought about the restoration of representative institutions and procedures in the post-1986 political system. A new constitution, ratified by over three-quarters (78 per cent) of the voters in 1987, laid down the democratic framework. Congress was re-established. Despite its dominance, the Catholic Church never decided electoral outcomes: thus former Defense Secretary Fidel Ramos, a Protestant, was elected president in 1992. In May 1998, Vice-President Joseph Estrada was also elected president despite the strong opposition of the Catholic Church. The media are regarded as among the freest in Asia. Human rights and civil liberties are enshrined in the Constitution, and interest groups advocating various policies abound. Over 15,000 people's organizations (POs) and non-government organizations (NGOs) form part of an extensive civil society. An independent Supreme Court serves as the final arbiter on points of law above the network of civil and criminal courts.

The post-1986 democratic system – especially since 1992 – saw the restoration of political stability and was concomitant with a remarkable economic turnaround which put the country back into the growth race alongside other Southeast Asian nations. Peace talks with military and Muslim rebel groups took place as a result of which these groups came to be integrated into regular political life; talks with the Communists proved more difficult, but they progressed despite a number of suspensions.

Established monopolies and cartels in the telecommunications, banking, shipping, coconut, and other strategic industries were dismantled. To liberalization and privatization measures were added moves towards decentralization, as a result of the enactment of a Local Government Code in 1991. This led to greater private and local initiatives, which in turn resulted in more investments. Economic dynamism as reflected in the growth in GNP, the expansion of exports, the increase of foreign exchange reserves, and a fairly low rate of inflation, made some begin to see the Philippines as an emerging "tiger" economy.

The constitutional structure and electoral system

The structure of the state and electoral system are defined in the 1987 Constitution and the Omnibus Election Code (OEC). The 1987 Constitution restored the pre-1972 presidential system but replaced the two-party system by "a free and open party system" which encouraged the setting up of a multi-party system and led to the emergence of a number of parties in post-1986 elections. The introduction of a party list system for the election of some representatives in Congress further resulted to the strengthening of the multi-party system.[4]

The framers of the 1987 Constitution preferred a multi-party system as they wished to avoid the return of the oligarchical tendencies of the pre-1972 two-party system under which electoral contests tended to be confined to a few wealthy political families. This prevented the emergence of really democratic politics. Under a multi-party system, it was believed, elective positions would be open to a large number of political groups.

According to the Constitution, the three branches of government, executive, legislature, and judiciary, are equal, as in the United States. Presidents are popularly elected for a fixed single term of six years. They have considerable power: this enables them to attract large numbers of representatives and to be supported by a majority in Congress, even if this was not the case before the election. The pre-1972 adage, that it is the Filipino president who creates his party and not the party which creates the president, is still applicable today.[5]

Congress is bicameral. The 24 members of the Senate are elected nationally for a maximum of two consecutive terms of six years each. 200 of the 250 members of the House of Representatives are elected by legislative districts, based on population size except for some very small ones, for a maximum of three consecutive terms of three years each. The first-past-the-post system applies in these cases; but the other 50 members of the House are elected from party lists on a proportional basis. For these seats, the lists are closed and election depends on the candidate's placement on the party slate. The limitation on tenure is prescribed by the Constitution to discourage the revival of pre-1972 political dynasties and promote a more equal access to representatives of other parties.

Elections are regulated by the 1987 Constitution and the OEC; amendments to this code were incorporated in electoral reform laws following the 1987 and 1992 elections. The provisions of the Constitution in this respect are that there shall be no literacy, property, or other discriminatory qualifications restricting the right to vote.

The task of enforcing election laws rests with the Commission on Election (COMELEC). Members of this body are appointed by the president with the consent of Congress. It exercises exclusive jurisdiction over the qualifications of candidates, the accreditation of parties and citizens' election groups, and canvassing. It sets the dates of opening of campaigns (60 days for the president, and 45 days for House members and local officials); ensures that candidates are provided free, equal, and publicly financed media exposure; regulates campaign expenses (a maximum of P10.00 (or US$.25) per voter); and acts against terrorism, voter harassment, and electioneering by government officials and employees.

While there are laws to induce fairness and counter the so-called "three Gs" (guns, goons, and gold) which used to characterize Philippine elections, enforcement remains poor. Compliance or non-compliance with the rules has been largely dependent on COMELEC. There were problems at both the 1987 and 1992 elections but these were overlooked because of the authority of the COMELEC leadership. Fraud at the 1995 elections and repeated administrative lapses subsequently have eroded that authority, and COMELEC has been criticized as inefficient and subservient to the power wielders.[6]

Some features of the electoral system affect the integrity of the democratic process and the growth of parties. One of these is the traditional and cumbersome method of having to write the names of preferred candidates on the ballot; another is the fact that the count is done manually. This leads to delays and to fraud. There would be savings if the system were modernized, since the whole procedure would take place more quickly. Instead of having to extend over three to five days, the whole process of counting would take only a day or two at the maximum.

Another difficulty stems from the fact that national and local elections are held simultaneously. This constitutes a substantial advantage for voters, although they may also find evaluating and writing the names of about 20 or more candidates burdensome. The system is certainly disadvantageous for COMELEC, since this body has to supervise the election of over 40,000 public officials in 77 provinces, 68 cities, and 1,550 municipalities. Moreover, parties are adversely affected, as simultaneous elections weaken party links between national and local candidates. Before 1972, when local and national elections took place at different times, local leaders could devote their full energy to supporting candidates for national office and vice versa: this they cannot do any longer, as they have to fight their own electoral battles during the same period.

A further problem is constituted by the limited amount of state financial support given to parties and candidates during elections. Political advertising is banned and this provides incumbents, media personalities, and well-known candidates a marked advantage; state subsidies would also strengthen parties as they would lessen the dependence of these parties on wealthy individuals.

The elimination of party representatives in the Board of Election Canvassers (BOC) has also weakened party strength. Before 1972, when party representatives were BOC members, parties could exercise more influence since they could protect the votes of their party betters and supervise the fairness of the electoral process: since 1987, on the other hand, many candidates feel they do not need the support of a party to make sure that the count is done honestly: citizens and church-based electoral watch groups such as the National Movement for Free Elections (NAMFREL) and the People's Pastoral Council for Responsible Voting (PPCRV) have promoted popular participation, but the role of parties has diminished in the process.

Perhaps the most important feature of the system, however, is the fact that the first-past-the-post system is in force for the election of the president and vice-president. This means that a candidate may be elected with a small minority only, if there is, as has been the case since 1987, a large number of relatively strong candidates. Thus Fidel Ramos was elected with only 24 per cent of the votes in 1992, and in the 1998 elections, Joseph Estrada was elected with 38 per cent of the votes. Not surprisingly, there have been repeated calls for the return of the two-party system.

The mass media in Philippine politics

The media play an important role in the democratization of Philippine politics. They have rendered policy-making more transparent by providing ways and means for the public to know more about governmental activities and policies. Freed from political control since the ouster of the dictatorship, the mass media were revitalized and came to shape public opinion and thus become an important locus of power. They are a mechanism for popular feedback as well as an effective instrument for building consensus on national policies. The strong influence of the Philippine media is discernible in their ever widening reach and variety. Their active role in the creation of a more demanding and discriminating public has come to be documented.[7]

Twenty-four daily newspapers (9 broadsheets and 14 tabloids) are published in the National Capital Region. Outside Manila, there are at least one local and one provincial paper in each of the 12 regional centres of the country. Radio and television have a wider and larger reach. It was estimated in 1993 that 82 per cent of households owned a radio set, 54 per cent owned a television set, and close to one million were cable TV subscribers.

The media have become as a result an effective vehicle for information and interest articulation. They have tended to replace parties and politicians as links between government and people. Few approach parties or politicians for their daily concerns; most go to popular media personalities or public affairs programmes such as the popular *Hoy Gising!* ("Hey! Wake Up!"). TV and radio public affairs programmes get instant attention and provide quick solutions to personal problems. Radio and

TV announcers have come to acquire an aura of omnipotence: even on cases of limited importance, they often awake a Cabinet member, legislator, or public official at five o'clock in the morning and expect not only to be spoken to but also to be thanked.[8]

As in the United States, the media exercise a strong influence on public policy: this was manifested in the case of Flor Contemplacion, a Filipino household worker in Singapore charged with murder and sentenced to death by the Singaporean authorities. The coverage of the case was such that the Ramos government had to make strong efforts to save the overseas worker. Bowing to public outcry, it recalled the Filipino ambassador to express its displeasure with Singapore's refusal to stay the execution of Contemplacion. The Foreign Affairs Secretary, Roberto Romulo, and the Labor Secretary, Nieves Confessor, were forced to resign as the media had claimed that they had been negligent in protecting Filipino overseas workers.

Media or public relations experts have in effect taken over many of the functions of party organizers. In Congress, public relations teams in the offices of several senators and representatives are often provided with more personnel and resources than other sections or departments. Elective officials, especially those aspiring to higher positions, consider the media as the fastest and most effective mechanism to communicate with their constituents and to display their images to the electorate.[9]

Not surprisingly, parties endeavor to recruit media personalities in order to cash in on their built-in popularity and exploit the personality-oriented culture of Filipino voters. Some of these celebrities have indeed obtained important national and local positions: at the 1992 elections, for instance, the second highest position in government, the vice-presidency, was won by a former movie actor, Joseph Estrada, while two other media personalities topped the senatorial race, the popular comedian Vicente Sotto, and the movie star Ramon Revilla. This feat was repeated in the 1998 elections with the election of Joseph Estrada to the presidency and the victories of media personalities Loren Legarda and Rene Cayetano in the senatorial race.

The major political parties

There are three main parties in the Philippines: Lakas ng Tao–National Union of Christian Democrats – (Lakas-NUCD, usually known simply as Lakas); Laban ng Makabayang Masang Pilipino (LAMMP – Struggle of the Nationalist Filipino Masses); and the Liberal Party (LP).

Two of these, Lakas and the LAMMP, were established only in 1992 and 1997 respectively: hence their low level of institutionalization (see table 7.1)[10] Their mass membership is low and their organizational structure limited. As before 1972, the parties are loose coalitions of provincial and regional political clans and families mainly put together to contest elections. They are parties of notables whose main support is drawn from the politically active elite, and hence they are highly decentralized. Intraparty democracy is weak or non-existent. Rank-and-file members are seldom consulted or involved in policy-making: the most important policies are formulated by a national executive committee or national directorate composed of a few party leaders and personalities. Although their highest policy-making body is deemed to be the national party congress, the role of that body is largely ceremonial: it consists in reaffirming the decisions of the national executive committee or directorate.

Being dependent on and controlled by bosses, the parties tend to be set up mainly to serve the ambitions of a few people, and in particular of presidential candidates. These leaders control party positions and activities, both as founders, in the case of two of the three parties, and as major recruiters and financiers. Hence the view that in the Philippines there are no real parties, only politicians: for the parties are primarily instruments for mutual aid for the capture, retention, and exploitation of public offices.[11]

The social base of the parties is naturally determined by the geographical or ethnic origin of the top leaders. This support often stems from the fact that a prominent politician's family has dispensed favours locally – financial or in kind. This obviously occurs mostly in remote and poor rural areas where the lack of alternatives reinforces the role of bosses, patrons, and overlords.

The three parties are essentially concerned with vote-maximizing, and their platforms therefore have a catch-all character. They claim to subscribe to liberal democracy and seldom articulate class, sector, or geographically specific interests. As vehicles for seekers of elective offices, they espouse popular principles to please as many voters as possible and antagonize the least number, or if possible none at all. Linkages with organized religious and ideological groups are often transient, tactical, and opportunistic.

There is therefore little programmatic diversity and political differentiation among the main parties. To an extent, this is due to the fact that the party elites recognize that the newly restored representative institutions are fragile and need nurturing before being subjected to major conflicts over policy positions. Three political events played a key part in the development of such a low-conflict approach: the 1986 "people power" revolt which rejected authoritarianism and restored democracy; the 1987 ratification of the new Constitution which laid down the liberal foundations of post-1986 democracy; and the 1987 and 1992 elections

Table 7.1 **Basic indicators of party institutionalization in the Philippines**

Party[1]	Adaptability		Complexity		Autonomy		
	Age (years)	Leaders' generation	Personality orientation	Organization	Power of bosses	Party type	Ideology
Lakas-NUCD	6	pre-1972	strong	chapters	strong	catch-all	liberal
LDP	10	post-1986	strong	national	strong	catch-all	liberal
NPC	6	pre-1972	strong	national	strong	catch-all	liberal
LP	51	pre-1972	strong	national	strong	catch-all	liberal

Source: Renato S. Velasco, "Democratization, Growth and the Institutionalization of Filipino Political Parties," paper presented at the Philippine Political Science Association National Conference, Quezon City, 8 May 1997.
[1] For explanations of party acronyms, see the text of this chapter and the List of Acronyms, p. ix.

which reaffirmed public support for political forces espousing the ideals of the 1986 revolt. Thus, the platforms of the main parties point to a consensus on major issues, notably with respect to the promotion of democracy and economic growth, the superiority of liberalization over protectionism, and the leading role of the private sector in the economy.

Lakas

Lakas came to be the largest party after the election of Fidel Ramos to the presidency in 1992. (For the comparative strengths of the main parties, see table 7.2.) It was established in 1992 by a handful of former Laban ng Demokratikong Pilipino (LDP – Struggle of Democratic Filipinos) members to be Ramos's vehicle for the presidential election, as Ramos was then partyless, having resigned from the LDP when that party did not nominate him for president.

In accordance with the adage about the president creating parties and not vice versa, Lakas was quickly transformed from a minor party to the majority party as many followers of defeated presidential candidates left their parties to join Lakas. Thus, its small membership in Congress and local authorities before 1992 increased dramatically, first after Ramos's victory at the 1992 election, and again after a Lakas-led electoral sweep at the 1995 midterm elections. After four years of the Ramos presidency, Lakas came to control the majority of seats in the House and held most provincial governorships and city mayoralties.

The political base of Lakas is in two large and strategic provinces which are the strongholds of its top leaders. One is Pangasinan, the home province of Ramos and former speaker of the House Jose De Venencia. This is one of the 10 biggest provinces, with over a million voters or over half the electorate of Northeast Luzon. Cebu is the other power base, being the stronghold of Emilio Osmena, Ramos's defeated vice-presidential running mate: it is another large province with more than a million voters in the southern region of Eastern Visayas, which has produced two of the past ten presidents of the country. The province is considered to be second only to Metro Manila, the National Capital Region, in terms of economic and political strength.

Lakas has strong links with big business because its leaders were in power under Ramos and because of its pro-business policies. Apart from frequent business conferences and joint government-business workshops which bring Lakas and business leaders together, these close links are underscored by the fact that many leaders of big business groups were also top Lakas campaigners and financiers during the 1992 presidential elections: among these are Peter Garrucho of the Management Association of the Philippines, Roberto Romulo and Roberto Del Rosario, Jr., of

Table 7.2 **Party affiliations of members of Congress and governors in the Philippines, 1992, 1995, and 1997**[1]

	1992			1995			1997		
	Senate	House	Governor	Senate	House	Governor	Senate	House	Governor
Lakas-NUCD	2	8	22	2	118	56	4	134	58
LDP	3	130	26	19	32	7	9	21	6
NPC	0	10	16	2	26	8	2	20	7
LP	10	30	5	1	12	3	2	10	3
KBL		4	3		3	2		3	1
PRP	0	0	0	0	0	0	1	0	0
NP	1	6	0	0	2	0	0	1	0
Others/Independent	9	22	2		13	3	5	16	2

Sources: Commission on Elections 1992, 1995; *Congresswatch Report*, Makati Business Club, December 1996; Lakas, LDP, NPC, and LP rosters of members, 1995; *Today, Manila Times, Philippine Daily Inquirer*, 21 and 31 May 1995; *Philippine Daily Inquirer*, 4 April 1997.
[1] For explanations of party acronyms, see the text of this chapter and the List of Acronyms, p. ix.

the Makati Business Club, and Jose Concepcion of the Federation of Filipino Industries.

The Laban ng Makabayang Masang Pilipino

The LAMMP is a coalition of two major and one minor opposition parties, namely the Laban ng Demokratikong Pilipino, the Nationalist People's Coalition (NPC), and the Partido ng Masang Pilipino (PMP – Party of the Filipino Masses). It was set up in October 1997 to consolidate the opposition and increase its electoral chances against Lakas. The LAMMP is led by Senator Edgardo Angara, former head of the LDP, and the secretary-general is Senator Orlando Mercado, former president of the PMP.[12]

The victory of its presidential candidate, Joseph Estrada, in the May 1998 elections has made the LAMMP the new ruling coalition, with many members of Lakas-NUCD and other parties defecting to its camp. There were talks and preparations with a view to transforming the coalition into a formal merger to be called Labian ng Masang Pilipino (LAMP— Struggle of the Filipino Masses) with Angara, Estrada's defeated running mate, as president and Estrada himself as chairman.[13]

The Laban ng Demokratikong

Before the LAMP merger, the LDP was the largest opposition party. It was the ruling party during the Aquino administration, having been set up in 1988 by prominent anti-Marcos politicians led by the then Senate President Neptali Gonzales, House Speaker Ramon Mitra, and Congressman Jose Cojuangco, purportedly to organize legislative and political support for the Aquino administration. Despite repeated efforts to recruit her into the party, Aquino refused to join. This proved to be a major factor in the decline of the party, especially when Aquino endorsed the candidacy of Ramos and diverted the administration's resources and bureaucratic machinery to Lakas. The LDP lost much of its political credibility soon afterwards when its presidential candidate, Speaker Mitra, lost the 1992 election and many LDP members resigned to join the president's party.

The organizational problems of Laban were made worse by factionalism. The strife was between the so-called "pro-coalition" ("pros"), headed by Senator Gonzales, who wanted to continue the alliance with Lakas, and the "anti-coalition" ("antis"), led by Senator Angara, who wanted to break away from the coalition and fight Lakas.

This division was the result of a complete U-turn as the Gonzales-led pros had at first opposed the coalition with Lakas while the Angara-led antis were the ones who engineered it. Eventually, infighting within the

LDP reached such proportions that it lost the Senate presidency in 1996. Despite an LDP majority in the Senate, the NPC president, Senator Ernesto Maceda, defeated Gonzales as Angara, the LDP president, allied with him and other Lakas senators.

The party was further demoralized by a situation in which its own president had contributed to the defeat of an LDP Senate president by a non-LDP leader. Not long afterwards, many of the party's noted and longtime leaders resigned from it, among them Senators Gonzales, Alberto Romulo, Gloria Macapagal-Arroyo, and Orlando Mercado, House Deputy Speaker and Laban Secretary-General Hernando Perez, and Laban's founding secretary-general, Rep. Jose Cojuangco, Jr. In October 1997, the Angara-led LDP faction allied with the NPC and PMP to form the LAMMP.

The Nationalist People's Coalition

The NPC was the second biggest opposition party before its coalition with LDP and PMP. It was akin to Lakas in having been formed in 1992 primarily to support the presidential campaign of its candidate, Eduardo Cojuangco, Jr., a wealthy Marcos crony and cousin of President Aquino. Conjuangco lost the presidency but the party won some seats in the Senate, the House of Representatives, and local governments. Its strength was further reduced after the Lakas-led coalition victory in the 1995 mid-term elections.

Cojuangco resigned the leadership which went to Senator Ernesto Maceda, and Maceda's shrewd manoeuvres proved successful in building up the NPC's role in party politics despite its weak base. He won the Senate presidency by aligning with the Angara faction and the PMP, the minuscule party of then Vice President Joseph Estrada. He consolidated the alliance by forming it into LAMMP, but resigned from LAMMP when Angara was chosen over him as Estrada's vice-presidential running mate in the May 1998 elections. He then ran for mayor of Manila and lost; and on 11 June 1998 the NPC dissolved itself as a party. Its members are expected to join LAMP which is set to replace Lakas as the ruling party.

The geographic strongholds of LAMMP are identical with the zones of influence of its top leaders. Except for Negros, the home province of the NPC's founder, Cojuangco, the LAMMP bases are mostly in medium-sized and small provinces with small voting strength and little economic power. What seems to be the compensating factor is the fact that these provincial bases are scattered in strategic parts of the country. These include the Ilocano provinces (Maceda), Aurora in Southern Tagalog (Angara), as well as the bailiwicks of close allies of Angara such as Bohol in Eastern Visayas (Senator Ernesto Herrera), Camarines Sur in Southern Luzon (Governor Luis Villafuerte), Albay in Southern Luzon (Rep. Edcel Lagman), and Agusan in Mindanao (Governor Democrito Plaza).

The LAMMP is said to have links with business groups, notably the corporate clients of Angara's law firm, known as the ACCRA Law Office. Another base of support is provided by the Filipino Chinese who supported Vice-President Estrada's anti-kidnapping campaigns when he chaired the Presidential Anti-Crime Commission. The support given by these business groups to LAMMP has been indirect due to the coalition's oppositionist stance and the fact that the business community tends to benefit from the economic policies of the Lakas-led administration. LAMMP also receives support from the Trade Union Council of the Philippines, an influential federation of organized labour, whose secretary-general is Senator Herrera.

The Liberal Party

The third main party is the Liberal Party, the only remaining pre-1972 party. During the Aquino administration, this party controlled the Senate and exercised influence in the House. Like the LDP, it suffered a major setback in the presidential and congressional elections in 1992. On the whole, the party has tended to hold left-of-center views and it has been credited with being responsible for the rejection of the Philippines-America Co-operation Treaty which led to the withdrawal of the U.S. military bases in the country.

Although it has only a few members in the Senate and the House, they hold important leadership positions in Congress, such as chairman of the Senate Committee on Ways and Means, House senior deputy speaker, and House assistant majority floor leader. As a coalition partner of Lakas, the LP has been given more positions and access to government resources by the ruling party.

The strongholds of the LP are also in medium-sized and small provinces. These include Samar (Rep. Raul Daza), Marikina (Rep. Romeo Candazo), Batanes (Rep. Florencio Abad), Capiz (Rep. Manuel Roxas II), and Bataan (Rep. Felicito Payumo). The party has no direct support from or close links with big business although some of its leaders, notably Roxas and Daza, are known to have extensive business interests. It is also linked to a number of cause-oriented groups.

Party policies, ideologies, platforms, and views

All three main parties subscribe to the fundamental liberal principles of free enterprise, limited government, and civil rights and liberties. This corresponds to the consensus of post-1986 political elites on basic policy issues. There is broad acceptance of peaceful and democratic means of acquiring and remaining in power. On a few policy nuances, there are differing opinions, but elections are regarded as being the main way to resolve these differences. Furthermore, there is a de facto consensus on major economic issues and in particular on the importance of economic growth, which is viewed as the key to the solution of many socio-economic problems, as well as on the leading role of the private sector in the economy, and on the fact that globalization of the economy has to be accepted.

Lakas describes itself as *maka-Diyos* (pro-God), *makabayan* (pro-country or nationalist), *makatao* (pro-people) and *maka-kalikasan* ("Green," or pro–environment). It pledges itself to work for a strong and stable republic, the enhancement of representative government, people empowerment, establishment of a market economy, protection of the environment, and progressive development of the rule of law. After winning the presidency in 1992, Lakas rallied around President Fidel Ramos's vision of "Philippines 2000." This goal has two basic objectives: to make the country's economy globally competitive by the year 2000 through liberalization, privatization, and deregulation; and to promote people empowerment.

The LAMMP has adopted the *FLAMES* program, which stands for *F*ood security and environmental protection, *L*ivelihood and jobs, *A*nti–graft and corruption, *M*ass transportation and traffic management, *E*ducation and health reform, and *S*afety and public order. These are the same areas in which Lakas as the government party can boast of achievements.

Prior to its dissolution and absorption into the LAMMP, the LDP, in both its 1988 and 1995 platforms, sought to "promote the rule of law, national political stability, self-reliant economy, and improvement of the standard of living of the people." It pledges itself to work "for the development of a national philosophy and the growth of a socially progressive citizenry."

In the same vein, the other component of the LAMMP, the NPC, parallels LDP's call for a national philosophy to "rekindle Filipino patriotism and self-esteem." It also reiterates its commitment to the goals of "recognizing private initiatives and individual freedom, protection of private property, deregulation, and adherence to the rule of law."

The LP has the most detailed program. Unlike its counterparts which simply present general statements, the LP has developed positions on specific issues such as opposition to nuclear weapons, the reduction of the foreign debt, and genuine land reform. Despite these differences, however, the LP's basic standpoints on the "rule of law, respect for property rights and limited state intervention" are similar to those of the other main parties. In its 1995 revised party program, it reiterated its support for a free-market economy and downplayed nationalist protectionism.

The main parties tend to support similar standpoints for a number of reasons. First, the social background of post-1986 party leaders differs from that of the pre-1972 leaders. The latter constituted a narrow elite, which was closely associated with the landed oligarchy whose rent-seeking interests were anchored on state patronage and intervention. With a broader economic base and diverse career backgrounds, the post-1986 party elites are more disposed towards free enterprise and limited government.

Second, the new elite has in common the fact that its members all experienced the Marcos dictatorship and were allies during the 1986 "people power" revolution. They are more aware, if not convinced, of the virtues of democratic politics because of the negative consequences of authoritarianism and other modes of political extremism. Their support for liberalization stems from their awareness of the flaws and costs of economic protectionism before 1972 and its more parasitic form of crony capitalism during the Marcos regime. They favor elections and other peaceful and democratic modes of change after having witnessed repeated public rejection of military coups and other violent means to settle conflicts.

Finally, the professional and material interests of party elites have grown during the post-1986 democratic regime. If the status quo has been generally good for their careers, why change it?

There are drawbacks resulting from the similarity of standpoints and platforms, however. First, only mainstream policy positions and interests are accommodated. Alternative programs, especially those from marginal groups, are seldom articulated. Second, party loyalty and ideology have little weight. Erratic personal styles and ambitions rather than firmer policy positions become the driving force of most parties. This explains the frequent changes of party by leading politicians, a practice that is rare in more developed democracies. Pre-1972 "political butterflies" who were thought to have ceased to exist in the "new politics" of the post-1986 political era have made a comeback. Lakas chairman and former president Ramos was an LDP leader before he set up Lakas; likewise, LAMMP chairman and president Joseph Estrada was an LP leader prior to his LAMMP affiliation.

Party policies and economic governance

Despite these drawbacks, the fact that parties have broadly similar views has a positive impact in the transitional phase of redemocratization when decisive policy-making is critical. Notably, it has spared the fledgling representative bodies from the debilitating impact of "elite fragmentation" and "demosclerosis"[14] which results from excessive policy disputes and leads to gridlock and institutional combat among the branches of government. Policy consensus, even if short-lived, has allowed the major parties to forgo short-term interests and work together for structural reforms to firm up the foundations of democratic politics.

The initial building blocks of this "growth consensus" were laid down immediately after 1986. The LDP, then in power, dismantled the Marcosian structures of cronyism and political centralization and enacted a number of liberalization and decentralization measures. Although the party lost the presidential elections in 1992, it retained a majority in the Senate. Instead of adopting the traditional role of an opposition party as a "fiscalizer" (an English word used in Filipino slang to mean "watchdog"), it drafted a common reform agenda with the Lakas-led executive branch. A number of legislative-executive economic summits were subsequently held; these were later expanded into "People's Summits" in which private-sector and civil society groups were actively involved.

The co-operation between Congress and the president was institutionalized through the establishment of the Legislative-Executive Development Advisory Council (LEDAC). This body, in which the president, members of the Cabinet, and leaders of Congress including those from the opposition, meet weekly, determines priority social and economic measures and facilitates policy-making. It exposes the president to views other than those articulated in Cabinet meetings. Leaders of Congress are also given more opportunities to study administration measures and to make clear to the executive their points of agreement and disagreement. Since LEDAC meets weekly, both monitoring and follow-up of previous commitments are possible. Moreover, the impact of LEDAC has been strengthened by the attention to detail and the micromanagement style of President Ramos, which results in the fast-tracking of such important but contentious issues as the safety nets against the effects of the GATT Law, the expanded value-added tax, the financial restructuring of the Central Bank, the Export Development Act, the anti-dumping law, and comprehensive tax reform. Obviously satisfied by LEDAC's valuable role in policy-making, an LP leader and LEDAC member described it as "the most efficacious vehicle in untangling gridlock and resolving conflicts between the Executive and Legislative branches."[15]

The collaboration between president and Congress reached its peak with the formal setting up of a coalition between Lakas and the LDP parties in 1995. For the first time in Philippine history, an alliance was formed on the basis of growth-oriented reforms and not merely for practical electoral objectives. This "growth coalition" outlined in its "Compact for Change" the common beliefs of the parties and the major reforms they would undertake. The coalition agreement underscored the "need for co-operation, not needless partisan strife; the need for unity, not discord." It identified the main elements of the common legislative program of Lakas and the LDP, which included: tax and fiscal reform; streamlining the bureaucracy; the dismantling of monopolies and cartels; the promotion of competitiveness and exports; the modernization of agriculture; and increased public investments for social reform.

Lakas also forged a separate coalition with the LP and with a small party, the Philippine Democratic Party (PDP), with a common legislative agenda. In April 1995, the Lakas-LDP/Lakas-LP /Lakas-PDP coalition fielded a common slate in the senatorial elections. Some described it as reflecting "maturity of Philippine politics" and the "birth of coalition politics," although others dubbed it a clear "surrender or co-optation of the opposition" (*Philippine Daily Inquirer*, 13 February 1995). The competing personal ambitions of President Ramos and Senator Angara stood in the way of the Lakas-LDP coalition and it broke up in November 1996.

The Lakas-led coalition made it possible to avoid deadlock and paralysis in policy-making. It was able to deal with the question of the "rentier" economy and to adopt a more open approach, and to lay out a more open and level playing field, in many strategic sectors. These legislative-executive measures include: deregulation of foreign exchange transactions; the liberalization of access to the Philippines for foreign banks; the extension of land lease tenure by foreigners to 75 years; the dismantling of monopolies and cartels in telecommunications, land, sea, and air transport as well as in the coconut and sugar industries; the privatization of large state-owned enterprises such as Philippine Airlines, the Philippine National Bank, and the Metropolitan Waterworks and Sewerage System; the entry of more investments through the removal of forty-year-old tariff barriers; the expansion of growth centres through the creation of special economic zones across the country; incentives for private-sector involvement in power, infrastructure, and other capital-intensive projects through the Build-Operate-Transfer law; making the Central Bank independent of the government; the acceptance of liberalization as the overall framework of growth through the early ratification of the GATT; the improvement of the tax base and tax collection through the expanded value-added tax and the comprehensive tax reform law; and the promotion of export-oriented enterprises as a result of the Export Development Act.

The macroeconomic reforms responsible for the country's economic turnaround have apparently helped to foster a good public image of the major parties. Despite the fact that their institutionalized features are weak and much criticized, and that they have strong personalistic tendencies, the main parties, and especially those which formed part of the growth coalition (Lakas, the LDP, the LP, and the PDP) have been assessed markedly more positively than most of their critics had anticipated (see table 7.3)

As was pointed out earlier, the post-1986 state elites, especially since 1992, have had a different social background from and therefore weaker ties with the old oligarchy and the landed families. This relative autonomy from dominant classes, as well as from dominated social groups, increased the state's capacity to play a strategic role in forming the growth coalition and in leading the members of that coalition to undertake profound structural reforms.[16]

The traditional landed elites, as well as the labour unions, depended on protectionism and state patronage for their privileges: they therefore tended to block efforts designed to liberalize the economy. For decades they frustrated industrialization and growth policies. This was altered by the 1986 revolution as new political forces came to the fore; with the 1992 presidential elections, these forces became dominant and old elites were marginalized. The ability of the political system to transform, or at least expand, the social base of its elites, among other factors, has led to a positive public evaluation of the country's democratic polity. As table 7.4 shows, satisfaction ratings of Filipinos vis-à-vis their political system have been high – higher, indeed, than those of the citizens of such developed democracies as Belgium, Italy, France, and the United Kingdom.

At the root of the electoral defeat of the old oligarchy were important changes in the economic structure which in turn led to the erosion of the oligarchy's influence. The traditional export crops which used to sustain its hegemony became less significant as the economic share of new sectors like garments, electronics, and the service industries expanded. The share of export crops in total exports dropped from 54 per cent in 1980 to 23 per cent in 1988, while during the same period, the share of new sectors rose from 46 per cent to 77 per cent. Between 1980 and 1995, the demographic profile and class composition of the country were also markedly altered: the urban population rose from 36 to 48 per cent of the population, while the rural population dropped from 74 per cent to 52 per cent. There has also been a significant expansion of overseas Filipino workers (OFWs), of the urban lower middle class and service workers.[17] Meanwhile, an increasing number of Filipinos receive secondary and tertiary education.

Globalization and information technology, which have made possible instant movement of capital and a 24-hour stock market, have led to growth in many sectors and integrated these sectors to the global econ-

Table 7.3 **Net trust ratings of Filipino political parties, July 1991–June 1997**[1]
(percentage difference between those saying that they trust and those saying that they distrust each party)

	July 1991	April 1992	August 1994	December 1994	June 1995	June 1997	Average
Lakas	1	23	23	23	20	38	25.4
LDP	5	11	10	13	5	29	11.5
PDP						28	16.5
PMP	−5	3	6	11	0	24	6.5
LP	7		2	3	−7	20	5.8
NPC		−1	−4	−3	−2	19	1.8
KAMPI						19	9.0
NP	3	−2		−2		17	4.0
PRP	−5	16		1		17	4.8
KBL		−10	−1		−2	16	3.3
PNB	2			4			2.0

Source: *Social Weather Stations*, June 1997.
[1] For explanations of party acronyms, see the text of this chapter and the List of Acronyms, p. ix.

Table 7.4 **Satisfaction with democracy: The Philippines compared with European countries, 1993**

	Very/fairly satisfied	Not very/not at all satisfied
Belgium	49	46
Denmark	81	18
France	41	56
Greece	34	65
Italy	12	88
Luxembourg	72	24
Netherlands	68	30
Philippines	**58**	**42**
Portugal	54	43
Spain	41	55
UK	49	46

Source: *Social Weather Stations*, 1993; *Eurobarometer*, 1993, pp. 1–4.

omy and the international communications network. More than four million OFWs, former OFWs, and their families have gained better incomes; they have also acquired insights into other models of growth and governance and this has made them less dependent on local patrons and more assertive of their rights.

Parties, the bureaucracy, and economic governance

The history of the short-lived yet productive Lakas-led coalition demonstrates the positive role played by parties in economic policy-making. Although parties are not the originators of economic reforms nor its key implementers, the Lakas coalition's growth-enhancing measures would not have been possible without party politics.

Unlike President Aquino who did not join any political party, her successor played a leading role as Lakas party chairman. He is generally regarded as having transformed it from a small and insignificant organization into a strong support for the administration.

Through Lakas, Ramos gained control of the House of Representatives and won the co-operation of the LDP-controlled Senate, before making his political coalition with LDP. This unprecedented collaboration between the executive and legislative branches of government facilitated decision-making. Budgets were passed without much delay and important government projects were implemented without encountering, as in the past, the obstruction of noisy legislators. The kind of elite fragmentation and bickering which characterized the Aquino administration was replaced by effective party and coalition politics under President Ramos.[18]

Before the Lakas-LDP coalition, executive-legislative relations were confrontational. Economic bureaucrats from the Department of Finance, Central Bank, Department of Trade and Industry, and National Economic Development Authority often saw themselves confronted with hostile legislators who openly challenged and undermined their policies, in particular with respect to debt management, as under populist pressure, Congress repeatedly attempted to limit the service of the debt and amend the law on automatic appropriation for debt service. The contents and procedures of negotiations with the International Monetary Fund and with creditors were scrutinized and economic managers were subjected to repeated grilling and even to ridicule in public hearings.

Budgets of uncooperative Cabinet members were also reviewed thoroughly and those who remained recalcitrant had their appropriations cut down in order to make them more amenable towards Congress: this occurred for instance with the budget of the Economic Intelligence Bureau of Gen. Jose Almonte which was reduced to P1.00 ($.03) during the Aquino administration. Moreover, the confirmations of several presidential appointees such Central Bank Governor Jose Fernandez, Finance Secretary Roberto Del Rosario, Trade Secretary Rizalino Navarro, Transportation Secretary Pablo Garcia, Foreign Affairs Under-Secretary Rodolfo Severino, Tourism Secretary Pedro Pilapil, and Health Secretary Hilarion Ramiro were either held in abeyance or rejected.

The bureaucrats were not always on the defensive. Given their technical expertise, longer tenure, and access to more resources and data, they were not exactly helpless, nor merely the innocent victims of the intransigence of Congress. While Congress seemed often to have won the battle in the media, the bureaucrats tended to obtain most of what they wanted in the end: they made Congress pass many of their economic reform measures into law, thus turning them into binding and stable policies. To this extent, the originators and implementers of the post-1986 economic reforms were the bureaucrats, not the parties or politicians.

Indeed, bureaucrats have often regarded legislators as short-sighted, intellectually weak, and parochial. When asked in Congress why he only sent a summary and not all the documents relating to debt negotiations, the then Central Bank Governor Jose Fernandez said the documents were just too complicated to be understood by the lawmakers. In his memoirs, former Education Secretary Isidro Carino cited his frustration with legislators whom he claimed to be obsessed with their parochial and petty interests and indifferent to broad national goals. During a public hearing of the Senate Committee on Defense, Armed Forces Chief of

Staff Arnulfo Acedera refused to stop talking after he had been asked to. When asked the reason for his defiance, he said: "I do not yield to a Pepsodent salesman" – obviously referring to the committee chairman, Senator Orlando Mercado, a former media personality who had advertised toothpaste products.

Thus bureaucrats usually withhold data and information, especially on economic and finance matters, because they consider them to be too technical and complicated for the lawmakers: cases of irrelevant questions and demands for unrelated documents by legislators sometimes justify this charge. Bureaucrats also use the expectation of foreign loans or the IMF seal of housekeeping as a leverage to compel Congress to pass the economic measures they propose.[19] Congress is often forced to approve the economic proposals of the administration as these are usually tied to the release of the much-needed loans or of required tax revenues. Congress may have the power of the purse, but this power is useless if the purse is empty.[20]

Bureaucrats also undermine the implementation of policies passed by Congress, if they consider these to be contrary to the priorities of the administration. This has been the case with the way the Department of Budget Management (DBM) releases funds for projects, especially those which have a pork-barrel character, such as the Countrywide Development Fund (CDF). Lakas members, especially those close to President Ramos or DBM officials, often see their CDF projects released early while those in the opposition parties like NPC and Laban receive their appropriations late. But the early release of funds by the bureaucracy does not only take place in order to placate certain politicians: it is also used to induce Congress to pass the pet bills of the administration.

Finally, bureaucrats try to appease or control Congress by means of monitoring and co-option. The Presidential Legislative Liaison Office regularly scans legislative activities. The PLLO is composed of Legislative Liaison Officers from various line departments who are assigned to monitor, co-ordinate, and assist their respective counterparts on the standing committees of Congress. In this way, the bureaucracy is regularly apprised of the activities of Congress and can exert influence on the policies initiated by legislators.

The power of the bureaucracy is further boosted by the co-option of politicians. Leading members of Congress from various parties are appointed to the Cabinet: thus, President Aquino appointed to her Cabinet Senator Raul Manglapus as foreign affairs secretary and Reps. Oscar Orbos and Florencio Abad as executive secretary and agrarian reform secretary, respectively. The same technique was adopted by President Ramos who appointed to the executive branch Senator Teofisto Guingona as justice secretary, and Reps. Salvador Escudero as agriculture secretary, Robert Barbers as local government secretary, and Edilberto Amante as executive secretary.

A bloated and politicized bureaucracy

A tug of war between lawmakers and bureaucrats characterizes economic policy-making and governance. Although the rights and duties of civil servants are defined by the Constitution, their independence and professionalism are undermined by the pressures of electoral politics. Two institutional arrangements are particularly responsible for the subordination of bureaucracy to political influence and for its permeability to vested interests.

The first results from the presidential power to appoint not only cabinet members but many high-ranking and middle-level officials in various departments and agencies. Senior career officials are bypassed, and requirements for entry into the civil service (such as possession of a college degree or passing the civil service examinations) are waived to reward with important government positions those who helped in the election campaign. Apart from unnecessarily increasing the size of the bureaucracy, this presidential discretion (which has its parallels among among Cabinet members and elected local government representatives) results at a minimum in a substantial loss in administrative efficiency as these appointees adjust to their new jobs. The fact that some them are later reassigned or dismissed from office further slows down government operations. The problem is often worsened by the strong tendency of presidents to create new offices for their pet projects: this results in a corresponding expansion of the bureaucracy, the loss of power by functional agencies, and overall incoherence in policy direction. Some unfinished yet critical programs are also terminated or replaced by different projects when a new administration arrives. This tendency to launch presidential schemes explains the series of much-vaunted but largely unfinished reorganization plans launched by Filipino presidents since 1946, with the notable exception of Presidents Diosdado Macapagal and Fidel Ramos.[21]

Second, the democratic system of checks and balances between the executive and legislature is often used to harass bureaucrats. In the context of an institutional set-up which obliges every department and agency to present and defend its annual appropriations before Congress, a culture of quid pro quo politics has emerged. Bureaucrats often give in to requests of legislators and include them in the agency's programmes to ensure the passage of their budget. This impedes systematic planning and leads to inefficient resource allocation. Scarce state resources are wasted or misused and this situation has led to several cases of corruption in pork-barrel funds.[22]

A few good bureaucrats

The finance and economic agencies, specifically the Central Bank, the Department of Finance, the Department of Trade and Industry, and the National Economic Development Authority, appear to be exceptions in the otherwise the bloated, expensive, and inefficient bureaucracy. These agencies are least affected by electoral politics and maintain a critical core of competent officials who are strongly inclined towards export-oriented growth and economic liberalization. Their free-market orientation and rapport with business groups and creditors have provided a good foundation for increased state capacity and for a remarkable economic dynamism since the late 1980s.

These financial and economic civil servants first gained prominence during the Marcos regime. Known as "the technocrats," they constituted the most productive of the so-called "three pillars of the regime," the other two being the military and the cronies of the president. They were recruited by Marcos in order to inject efficiency and add prestige to his regime. Their apolitical and corporatist background and dislike of the policy paralysis and irrationalities of pre-1972 democratic politics made them attractive to Marcos.

With graduate degrees from noted American schools and as former bankers, professional managers, academics, or consultants of the World Bank, the IMF, and multinational companies, these technocrats were critical of protectionism and adhered to free-market principles as the best formula for economic growth. They had extensive training and experience in research and were quite adept in management and economic planning. They were familiar with the language of global trade and international finance and they also knew the key players. These characteristics and credentials rendered them useful to the regime, especially in securing much-needed foreign loans. Their technical expertise combined with the support they enjoyed from foreign creditors helped them to be somewhat insulated from political pressures. They brought greater rationality to government and improved the state's administrative apparatus by introducing sophisticated modern management techniques, notably development planning and statistical analysis for effective policy and programme monitoring and evaluation. The World Bank itself recognized the competence of these civil servants when it described the Philippines as a model of economic development and made it one of its largest aid recipients.[23] The combination of this generous external assistance and bureaucratic competence resulted in impressive growth rates in the seventies, but these successes were undermined by cronyism and eventually completely nullified as a result of corruption and plunder. Many analysts believe that had Marcos restrained his greed and provided the civilian technocrats with more powers and more autonomy, the country could have counted as an NIC by the mid-1980s.[24]

The 1986 revolution did not reduce the influence of economic and finance bureaucrats, who were maintained in their posts, except for a few high-profile Marcos appointees. Their expertise made them difficult to replace, unlike those in other agencies. Perhaps more importantly in a situation in which the government was short of cash, these bureaucrats had links with foreign and local creditors. This played an obvious part in the decision of President Aquino to reappoint Central Bank Governor Jose Fernandez, a top Marcos appointee, despite strong opposition from her close advisers. The heads of economic agencies were replaced by Aquino's appointees but the under-secretaries, bureau directors, and division chiefs were retained. Former top Marcos technocrats like ex–prime minister and finance minister Cesar Virata were brought back through the back door as consultants of the economic and financial agencies.[25]

The post-1986 top economic bureaucrats are an example of new wine in old bottles. Their politics and leadership styles may be at variance from those of their predecessors but they hardly differ in economic outlook and orientation. They all share the common belief in the growth paradigm of liberalization, privatization, and deregulation, a characteristic which accounts for the basic similarities between the economic policies of the Aquino and Ramos administrations. This also explains why Finance Secretary Jaime Ongpin strongly interceded for the reappointment of Fernandez to the Central Bank, where he was Ongpin's close collaborator in the debt negotiations and economic policy-making. Although with weaker academic and professional credentials than those of Marcos technocrats, the post-1986 civil servants also belong to an old boys network of professional managers, academics, and consultants with links to the IMF, the World Bank, and multinational corporations.[26]

Economic policy-making and economic growth

When the growth coalition was put in place, the economic technocrats were protected against political pressures and were better able than before to formulate and implement market-oriented reforms. These liberalization measures opened up the economy, led to greater investments, and brought back the country on the growth path that characterized East and Southeast Asia at the time. The gains resulting from post-1986 economic policy-making are shown in table 7.5.

Except for 1992, the growth rate hovered between 4 and 7 per cent

Table 7.5 **Macroeconomic indicators at the end of the Marcos regime and during the Aquino and Ramos administrations, 1985–1996**

	1985	1986	1988	1990	1992	1994	1996
GNP growth rate[1]	−6.96	3.64	7.21	4.78	1.55	5.3	6.9
GDP growth rate[1]	−7.31	3.42	6.75	3.04	.34	4.4	5.7
Balance of payments[2]	−.80	−1.20	−.59	−.93	−1.49	−1.80	−3.92
Balance of trade[2]	−.50	−.20	−1.08	−4.02	−4.69	−7.85	−11.4
Exports[2]	4.6	4.80	7.10	8.2	9.8	13.5	20.5
Imports[2]	5.1	5.00	8.10	12.2	14.5	21.3	31.9
Investment[2]	−.32	10.06	14.69	15.83	7.83	8.63	20.3
Inflation rate[1]	23.4	−0.4	8.9	14.2	8.9	9.0	8.4
Unemployment rate[1]	17	14.0	9.6	8.4	9.8	9.5	9.2
Poverty incidence[1]	44.2	n.a.	40.2	n.a.	37.0	35.5	n.a.

Source: National Economic Development Authority *Economic Indicators*, January 1998; Central Bank of the Philippines, *Statistical Bulletin*, October 1997.
  [1] Figures are percentages.
  [2] US$ billion.

during 1986–96. This growth rate is rendered even more significant because it was export- and investment-led and was accompanied by a single-digit inflation rate, increased employment, and a reduction of poverty incidence. The only negative indicator was the balance of trade which showed a deficit increasing from US$1.08 billion in 1988 to US$11.4 billion in 1996. However, a large part of the import bill was due to capital expenditures such as machinery, raw materials, chemicals, and power plants. These could be expected to result in higher efficiency and greater productivity. Meanwhile, exports also grew from US$8.2 billion in 1990 to US$13.5 billion in 1994 and US$20.5 billion in 1996. Indeed, the Philippines had the highest growth rate of exports among the Asian countries between 1993 and 1996. During this period, the country's exports exceeded those of such Asian export leaders as Taiwan, South Korea, and Thailand. If it sustains this growth rate in exports, the trade gap could be wiped out by the year 2000.

The export performance is in part the result of improved investor confidence, as is shown by the fact that investment steadily increased from US$15.83 billion in 1990 to US$20.3 billion in 1996. There is also a good balance between portfolio and foreign direct investment inflows: this minimizes the potential for a sudden economic downturn if an abrupt flow reversal occurs. The share of net portfolio investments declined from

53 per cent in 1995 to 45 per cent in 1996, an indication that an increasing amount of investments is being channelled into longer-term, more productive projects.

The currency crisis and the "tiger cub" economy

In the context of the 1997 financial turmoil in East and Southeast Asia, the Philippines seem to be in a better position than other countries of the region which succumbed to the crisis. Some indicators suggest, indeed, that the economic performance of the country is on firmer foundations than in the past. First, previous growth records were mainly induced by external factors such as U.S. quotas, a boom in export crops in the 1950s and 1960s, and low-interest foreign loans in the 1970s: they did not result from substantial changes in the Philippine political economy. On the other hand, the growth of the 1990s was preceded by bold reforms and structural adjustments. These have resulted in more competition and in greater efficiency in the liberalized sectors and rendered the economy more resilient.

These reforms are also more stable than previous measures. They became law in a democratic context and enjoyed the support of a broad coalition of political and social forces. This combined with the benefits which they produced to render them firmly grounded. They will remain in force as it would be difficult and unpopular for any political party or group to revise or abolish them in the near future.

The sustainable character of Philippine economic dynamism is enhanced by its broad geographical base: all regions, including poor and remote ones, have experienced real growth in gross regional domestic product. Region 1 which includes the Cordillera Autonomous Region in Northeastern Luzon, and Region 5 or the Bicol region in Southern Luzon, had growth rates of over 7 per cent and 2.9 per cent respectively between 1993 and 1995.[27] Previously, economic expansion took place in Metro Manila only: post-1986 growth led to the emergence of robust growth in the special economic zones in Subic in Zambales and Clark in Pampanga, and in industrial and manufacturing parks in Cavite-Laguna-Batangas-Quezon in the Luzon mainland, Cebu and Iloilo growth centres in the Visayas, and in the Cagayan de Oro, General Santos, and Davao growth areas in Mindanao.

These achievements have provided good protection against the regional currency crisis of the late 1990s. The turmoil did cause an economic slowdown, but the Philippines is expected to come out of it relatively well. First, the country experienced a series of boom-and-bust cycles in the 1970s and 1980s and this experience is valuable. As the former "sick man of Asia," it learned to be modest; its public also learned to discover both the short-term costs and the long-term benefits of fiscal discipline and austerity measures. Being a latecomer can also be an advantage. It is possible to learn from both the negative and the positive experiences of early starters. This is the case, for instance, with the ceilings imposed by the Central Bank on bank loans in real estate and property development, as well as with its close monitoring of exposures in car loans and credit cards: these measures have been effective in checking bankruptcies from property glut and bad loans.

Investors and analysts have noted the strengths of the Philippine economy. While it has the smallest foreign reserves among the ASEAN countries, it has had the least currency depreciation. Not only has it not asked for a financial rescue package from the IMF and the World Bank, but it has completed an exit agreement with the IMF. Exports have increased and the depreciation of the Philippine peso is expected to make the country's exports cheaper and more competititive. The World Bank hailed the country's adjustment measures while Credit Lyonnais Securities Asia, one of world's largest brokers, said: "The Philippines is ahead of the game. By no means is it going to suffer as badly as Thailand and Indonesia."[28]

Finally, the country's macroeconomic fundamentals are supplemented with good political fundamentals. The country's democratic politics promotes growth by providing fairness and predictability in the system through the rule of law, transparency in decision-making, and other democratic principles and procedures. In two important respects, democracy, for all its oft-cited flaws, is superior to authoritarianism in attaining growth and stability: first, democracy has built-in feedback mechanisms in the form of competitive elections and freedom of expression for self-regeneration and reform; and second, democracy requires public consent and consensus in governance, which are critical for long-term stability and better policy formulation and implementation.

Conclusion

A number of points can be made about the relationship between political parties and the bureaucracy with respect to economic growth in the Philippines.

First, the political parties in the Philippines do not play a leading role in economic policy-making. Their low level of institutionalization restricts their ability to be agents of policy aggregation and social mobilization. They are essentially parties of notables whose main support is drawn from the political elites. Most of them were set up primarily to serve the presidential ambitions of their founders, who in turn direct and control most of their policies and activities. Their social bases are limited to the ethnic groupings and political bailiwicks of party founders and bosses. The ruling party has extensive linkages with big business; other parties have closer ties with labour federations and civil society organizations. To be sure, these weak organizational features are due in part to the fact that the parties are new; but they are also due to the constraints of the electoral system. In addition, the personalistic leadership of the parties and the rival force of the mass media erode their ability to play a part in interest articulation and aggregation and to be a link between the government and the citizenry.

Second, the similarity of party programmes, for instance on liberalization, the market economy, and democracy, results from the fact that the social background of their leaders is similar and that these leaders have all experienced the dangers resulting from protectionism, cronyism, and authoritarianism. Although criticized as leading to an "issueless" and personalistic politics, this similarity in policy views has proved valuable in the context of the still fragile foundations of growth and democratization. The basic policy consensus hastened the setting up of a growth coalition among the main parties which in turn improved policy-making, and succeeded in resolving several conflicts between the legislative and executive branches. Structural reforms were undertaken by the alliance, which resulted in a reduction of the rentier economy, as well as in greater competition and promotion of growth in many sectors and in many parts of the country. Through the coalition, the parties – despite their low degree of institutionalization – perform a direct and positive role in growth promotion: thus they have fulfilled at least some of the functions which are theirs in a democratic context.

A series of factors rendered the growth coalition possible. The post-1986 leadership had weaker ties with the traditional oligarchy, especially since 1992: thus it could enjoy relative autonomy from both the dominant and the dominated social groups. The political leadership could count on an economic administrative apparatus able to increase the state's capacity for structural reforms. Meanwhile, changes in the political economy were eroding the power base of the old landed elites: the importance of export crops declined while that of manufacturing and service industries markedly increased. Globalization and information technology induced growth in many sectors and integrated these sectors into the world economy and communications network. The rural population declined and the number of city dwellers expanded: this meant a larger middle class with better incomes, a higher level of education, and more access to information. Being more politically sophisticated, the new middle class is dissatisfied with the old system of governing and has given its support to alternatives to oligarchical politics.

Third, the institutional context must be improved to strengthen parties and party politics. Electoral reforms such as the modernization of the electoral process, restoration of party representation in the board of canvassers, and uncoupling of national and local elections are among the measures which can strengthen parties and the party system. Above all, perhaps, as in developed democracies, the public financing of parties should be introduced: it would render them more professional and reduce their dependence on patrons and financiers. Resource dependency has been the major reason for the maintenance of a state of affairs in which the presidents create the party when it should be the other way around.

Fourth, much of the bureaucracy is bloated and inefficient, this being largely the consequence of electoral politics. The rapid turnover of top and middle-level bureaucrats caused by periodic changes of administration leads to a loss in work momentum, poor institutional memory, and policy incoherence. However, the finance and economics sections of the bureaucracy constitute notable exceptions; they have a core of competent career officials with a strong orientation towards liberalization and market reform. Many are graduates of leading American universities and had extensive training in administration during the Marcos regime. They belong to a small network of highly paid professional managers, noted academics, and former consultants of the IMF, the World Bank, and multinational corporations. The technical nature of the expertise of these civil servants helps them to avoid being affected by electoral politics. Notwithstanding the regime change in 1986, they retained their foothold in the bureaucracy. Only a few high-profile Marcos appointees have been replaced. Their main characteristic is to believe strongly in the growth paradigm of economic liberation, privatization, and decentralization.

Shielded from politics thanks to the growth coalition, the economic and financial bureaucrats have been able to design and better implement long-delayed market-oriented reforms. Admittedly, economic policies and outcomes, especially in a democratic polity such as the Philippines, are far from being wholly determined by the actions of a small number of decision makers, however competent they may be. But this competence counts in combination with the international contacts of these decision makers: in the economic field at least, they play a larger part than parties and politicians.

Both growth and democratization will in all probability continue. Parties have begun to show an ability to overcome their parochial interests and to harness their efforts in order to strengthen the fragile foundations of the newly restored democracy. Admittedly, the difficulties resulting from the 1997 financial and currency crisis have tended to break the policy consensus among the main parties; but this may have a positive effect.

As the opposition parties are likely to adopt critical positions, policy differentiation will increase and a more issue-oriented type of politics may emerge, giving rise to a wider range of alternatives. Meanwhile, on the economic front, the growth which the country enjoyed in the 1990s has been healthier. It has been based on structural reforms which have increased competition and improved efficiency in many sectors: the expansion has also taken place broadly across the country.

In the Philippines, economics and politics have gone hand in hand in the 1990s. Democracy has promoted growth and has proved superior to authoritarianism. Although the country has had to travel a rocky road, it has so far surmounted all difficulties. The great challenge is to sustain both political vibrancy and growth momentum. There are encouraging signs that the Philippines can meet this challenge successfully.

Notes

1. Francis Fukuyama, "The End of History," *The National Interest* Winter 1989–90; 18: pp. 12–35.
2. Samuel P. Huntington, *The Third Wave: Democratization in the Late Twentieth Century* (Norman: University of Oklahoma Press, 1991).
3. Larry Diamond, John Linz, and Seymour M. Lipset (eds.), *Democracy in Developing Countries: Latin America*, Vol. IV (Boulder, Colo.: Lynne Rienner, 1989), pp. 20–21.
4. 1987 Philippine Constitution, Art. XII, Sec. C.
5. For a historical account of the powers and role of the Filipino presidents in government and politics, see Alex B. Brillantes and Bienvenida M. Amarles-Ilago, *1898–1992: The Philippine Presidency* (Quezon City: CPA, University of the Philippines, 1994). The critical role played by U.S. presidents in the rise and fall of major American parties is discussed in Martin P. Wattenberg, *The Decline of American Political Parties, 1952–1994* (Cambridge, Mass.: Harvard University Press, 1996) esp. pp. 73–124.
6. *Philippine Daily Inquirer,* 11 October 1997.
7. Dennis Arroyo and Gerardo Sandoval, "Do The Mass Media Really Affect Public Opinion?" *Social Weather Bulletin* May 1993, pp. 3–4. See also "Media in the Present Crisis," *Kasarinlan* First Quarter 1990; 7: pp. 90–99.
8. Randy David, "Media Education Challenges in the 1990s," in *Media Expo '91* (Manila: Metro Times, 1991), p. 13.
9. The author, as former chief of staff of House Assistant Majority Leader Manuel Roxas II and consultant to Senate President Edgardo Angara and Senator Gloria Macapagal-Arroyo, has personally seen the clout wielded by public relations teams in many offices of legislators in both houses of Congress.
10. A high degree of institutionalization achieved by major parties is considered to be an important element in the institutional resilience of democracy. Samuel Huntington devised a formula which identifies coherence, complexity, autonomy, and adaptability as indicators of party institutionalization. See Samuel P. Huntington, *Political Order in Changing Societies* (New Haven, Conn.: Yale University Press, 1968), pp. 10–32.
11. Carl H. Lande, *Leaders, Factions and Parties* (New Haven, Conn.: Yale University Press, 1965), p. 69.

12. Manuel F. Almario, "Birth of A New Opposition Party," *Philippine Graphic*, 3 November 1997, pp. 12–15.
13. *Today*, 18 June 1998.
14. For cases of elite fragmentation during the Aquino administration, see Rigoberto Tiglao, "Dilemmas of Economic Policy-Making in a 'People Power State,'" in David Timberman (ed.), *The Politics of Economic Reform in Southeast Asia* (Makati: Asian Institute of Management, 1992), pp. 91–116. For a related account, see Jonathan Rauch, *Demosclerosis: The Silent Killer of American Government* (New York: Times Books, 1994).
15. Felicito C. Payumo, "Year End Review and Prospects: A View from Congress," *Kasarinlan*, Fourth Quarter 1994; 10(3): p. 26.
16. P. Evans, "Predatory, Developmental and Other Apparatuses: A Comparative Political Economy Perspective on the Third World State," *Sociological Forum* 1989; 4(4): pp. 559–62, and Jose T. Almonte, "The Politics of Development in the Philippines," *Kasarinlan* Fourth Quarter 1993 and First Quarter, 1994; 9(2–3): pp. 107–17.
17. Figures cited in Filologo Pante and Erlinda Medalla, *Philippine Industrial Sector: Policies, Programs and Performances*, (Makati City: PIDS, July 1990), p. 17, and *World Bank Development Report, 1993*, pp. 378–84.
18. Tiglao, "Dilemmas of Economic Policy-Making," pp. 91–116. See also Charles Lindsey, "The Political Economy of International Economic Policy Reform in the Philippines," in Andrew J. MacIntyre and Kanishka Jayasuriya (eds.), *The Dynamics of Economic Policy Reform in Southeast Asia and the Southwest Pacific* (Singapore: Oxford University Press, 1992), pp. 74–93.
19. Foreign loans were first used to introduce/compel radical reforms in trade and monetary agencies by economic bureaucrats during the Marcos regime. See Robin Broad, *Unequal Alliance, 1979–1986: the World Bank, the International Monetary Fund, and the Philippines* (Quezon City: Ateneo Press, 1988), pp. 128–38.
20. Renato S. Velasco, "A Debt Perestroika for the Philippines," *Foreign Relations Journal* December 1990; 4(4): pp. 1–53.
21. Brillantes and Ilago, *The Philippine Presidency*, pp. 90–95.
22. The pork-barrel funds are of two types. First, there is the Countrywide Development Fund, which is a fixed amount of P18 million for each senator and P14 million for every House member. A legislator can use his or her fund for any kind of project from scholarships and the construction of basketball courts to the building of public markets. The second type is the Congressional Initiative Allocation, which is inserted by a legislator in a particular department as the implementing agency of a pet project. Depending on his or her leadership position in Congress, relationship with bureaucrats, and general creativity, the allocation of a legislator can range from P500,000 to P2 billion. For scandals in the CDF involving House members see *Philippine Daily Inquirer*, 12–15 September 1996.
23. Ibid.
24. The major reasons for the failure of the Philippines to become an NIC are discussed in Manuel Montes, "Overcoming Phillippine Underdevelopment," *Third World Quarterly* July 1989; 2(3): pp. 107–19, and Renato S. Velasco, "Lessons from the NICs for the Philippines," *Contemporary Southeast Asia* September 1990; 12(2): 134–50.
25. Ledevina Carino, "Bureaucracy for A Democracy: The Struggle of the Philippine Political Leadership and the Civil Service in the Post-Marcos Period," *Philippine Journal of Public Administration* July 1989; 33(3): pp. 12–18. See also Olivia Caoili, *The Philippine Congress: Executive-Legislative Relations and the Restoration of Democracy* (Center for Integrative and Development Studies, University of the Philippines, 1993).

26. These post-1986 economic bureaucrats include: former World Bank senior officer and Development Bank of the Philippines president Roberto Ocampo, Department of Finance secretary; lawyer and long-time Central Bank deputy governor Gabriel Singson; former professional manager and businessman Cesar Bautista, Department of Trade and Industry secretary; University of the Philippines economics professor and Harvard Ph.D. Cielito Habito, National Economic Development Authority director-general. See Aiichiro Ishii et al, *National Development Policies and the Business Sector in the Philippines* (Tokyo: Institute of Developing Economies, 1988), esp. pp. 206–58.

27. "Highlights of Trends in Gross Regional Domestic Product, 1993–1995," *Regional Development Digest* July 1996; 1(3), pp. 1–3.

28. *Today*, 7 November 1997 and 3 April 1998.

8

Thailand

Dan King

Introduction

Thailand has been blamed for starting off the meltdown of Asian markets and currencies in mid-1997, an assessment which may be partly true since the 2 July 1997 devaluation of the baht began a chain reaction throughout the region. The central bank, the Bank of Thailand, has since come under intense scrutiny and heavy criticism for having depleted its foreign reserves and lent just over Bt 1 trillion to ailing banks and finance companies, more than the entire national budget for fiscal year 1997.

Yet only a year or two previously, the general view of Thailand's bureaucracy responsible for economic policymaking was quite different: Thailand was said to benefit from experienced technocrats at the key ministries and agencies, including the Bank of Thailand, and these technocrats were credited with keeping Thailand's own version of the Asian economic miracle on track. Indeed, meddling on the part of elected politicians was the danger that had to be guarded against, as, otherwise, the politicians and their pork-barrel politics might affect adversely the country's rate of economic growth which was so admired around the world. Most members of the political elite would have agreed that it was better to let the technocrats do their work unencumbered by political considerations. It is sufficient to remember that in 1996 the World Bank declared Thailand the top growth country in the world for the decade of 1985–94, ahead of China or South Korea.

What happened? From a prime example of semi-strong government–led economics to international pariah, Thailand's fall by the end of 1997 was as meteoric as its previous climb into the ranks of the near-NICS. Meanwhile, as Thailand's economy fell, the country's pursuit of political democracy accelerated with peaceful transitions of power by electoral means in 1995 and 1996, as well as with the discussion and adoption of the Constitution in September 1997. Thus, in late 1997, having to face both a new constitution and the IMF's aid package requirements, Thailand's political leaders and technocrats were confronted with a new set of rules for both economy and politics.

Political and economic development

After a brief historical survey, this essay will focus first on the nature of democratization in Thailand and in particular on the character of the parties. It will then examine economic governance and the relationship between the parties and the party system and the bureaucracy. It will finally consider the prospects for the future of the relationship between parties and bureaucracy and between democratization and economic development.

Since the fall of the absolute monarchy in 1932, Thailand's pursuit of political democracy has been at best uneven. Prior to World War II, neither the Constitution nor Parliament succeeded in resolving the competition between the military and the bureaucracy: to seize power, political leaders declared new rules of the political game and penalized opponents. From 1945 to 1973, there were only a few short periods of democratic reform interspersed among long-lasting military-led governments which suppressed political participation and manipulated electoral processes.

A crucial change occurred between October 1973 and October 1976, however, when democratic and antidemocratic forces engaged in forceful competition (Morell and Chai-Anan 1981). After student demonstrations had been crushed by a massive show of force on 14 October 1973, young King Bhumiphol Adulyadej dismissed the prime minister, who fled the country together with other government leaders. What followed was a period during which the student movement flourished, public discussion of political and social liberalization expanded, and the Communist Party developed rapidly. In 1975, after the military factions had regrouped and observed the dominoes of Vietnam, Laos, and Cambodia fall, right-wing elements and students clashed more frequently and with greater acrimony. A coup took place in October 1976, which was characterised by massive violence and acts of torture against students at the hands of right-wing groups and of the security forces: these events remain a stain on Thailand's collective conscience.

A new constitution was proclaimed in 1978 by the military-led government with the aim of introducing a limited form of democracy. Elections were held in 1979, parties which had survived the 1970s re-emerged, and parliamentary democracy was re-introduced (Girling 1981). Under the tutelage of Prime Minister General Prem Tinasulanond, former army commander-in-chief, Thai democracy, however limited, became more stable: it was not interrupted by coups d'état. Prem presided over several successive cabinets and three parliamentary elections (1983, 1986, and 1988), and attracted the respect of the elites, the press, and the Royal Family. Being tired of the manoeuvrings of Cabinet politics, however, Prem announced his retirement after the 1988 elections: he had been eight years in power, without having led a political party or competed for election. He was succeeded by Chatichai Choonhawan, head of the then largest party in Parliament, who built a coalition government and thus became Thailand's first elected prime minister in 12 years.

Meanwhile, since the 1950s Thailand's leaders had focused on industrialization, with a good record of overall success. Except in the aftermath of the oil crises of the 1970s and the recession of the early 1980s, Thailand's economy grew rapidly. The growth rates for agriculture averaged 4.4 per cent for the period 1970–80, and 3.8 per cent for the period 1980–93. Manufacturing growth rates were most impressive, reaching 9.7 per cent in the 1970s and 11.0 per cent between 1980 and 1993. The proportion of Thais living in poverty fell from 57 per cent in 1962 to just 13.7 per cent in 1992, although the population rose during the same period from 29 million to 57.3 million (World Bank 1996). During Chatichai's administration growth rose to new records and was regarded as sustainable: the NESDB's National Five Year Plan for 1997–2001 was based on the assumption of 8 per cent growth per annum.

However, under Chatichai allegations of corruption against members of the Cabinet became widespread; as in the 1950s, 1960s, or 1970s, coalition partners battled amongst themselves for payoffs and power, while disaffected military factions demanded changes in the Cabinet. This eventually led to a coup which toppled the Chatichai government in February 1991. This type of instability derived from the weakness of Thai political parties is key to a well-accepted view of Thai politics: the "vicious cycle" outlined by Chai-Anan Samudavanija (1982).

Periods of Thai democracy, Chai-Anan has argued, have been short-lived because of the failure of elected governments and the political institutions that supported them. In each cycle, a new constitution was written, political parties were legalized, open debate was allowed, elections were held, and a cabinet was formed. After a short time, that cabinet was widely regarded as corrupt and unable to manage the affairs of the nation; the military eventually intervened to end the democratic experiment in the interests of political stability. Usually, political parties were banned and civil liberties restricted in the retrenchment that followed. In this view of Thai politics, the parties themselves sowed the seeds of their own destruction because of their inherent weaknesses (Chai-Anan 1982, 1–5).

Between February 1991 and September 1992, the coup leaders, headed by General Suchinda Kraprayoon, sought to bring back old-style politics. The 1978 Constitution was replaced by a more authoritarian one; promotions in the military and the police were manipulated to ensure support for the coup leaders and their followers; a new political party was created which was expressly designed to buttress General Suchinda in the prime ministerial office. Meanwhile, former Cabinet members had their assets frozen until they could prove themselves innocent of the charge of having become unusually wealthy. These moves were challenged, however, as pro-democracy groups became active in opposing the revised Constitution and mobilized the public against the return to a managed form of democracy led by a general turned prime minister. After the March 1992 elections and Suchinda's subsequent appointment to the post of prime minister, a coalition composed of political parties, pro-democracy activist groups, and students started to demonstrate against the prime minister. These demonstrations were joined by middle-class citizens, workers, and managers who formed what came to be known as the "mobile phone mobs."

The movement against the prime minister reached its peak on 17–20 May 1992 when government forces struck and a bloody crackdown ensued. The repression was halted by the king on May 20: Suchinda was forced to resign, the jailed demonstration leaders were released, and new elections were scheduled for September 1992. The alignment at that election was between those parties which had and those which had not supported the Suchinda government, two camps which the press dubbed "devils" and "angels" (King 1992, Surin 1992). The angels won a slim majority and formed a coalition government which lasted from September 1992 to July 1995 under the leadership of Chuan Leekphai.

Chuan was replaced in July 1995 by opposition leader Banharn Silapaarcha, who remained prime minister for just a year and four months up to the November 1996 election. At that election, Banharn was replaced by retired General Chavalit Yongchaiyuth, who in turn resigned in November 1997, having lost the support of his coalition; Chuan Leekphai become once more head of the government. Thus electoral democracy had prevailed in Thailand throughout the 1980s and 1990s, except for one year in 1991–92; in general, governmental crises had been the result of electoral upsets or had been handled in a constitutional manner by means of reshuffles.

The economic downturn of 1996 and the crisis of 1997

While Thailand's democracy was becoming institutionalized, the economy was sliding gradually into recession. When the Banharn government came to office, Thailand's economy was already experiencing a slowdown: growth was 8.6 per cent in 1995, but 6.4 per cent in 1996, and then turned into recession in 1997. Exports in 1996 experienced negative growth of 0.2 per cent as Thailand's fundamental competitiveness in world markets was coming into question. Banharn's government was composed of mostly businessmen turned politicians and lacked roots in the politically influential capital. Characterized by the press as a collection of greedy country bumpkins, the Banharn government ignored the economic warning signs and did little to stop Thailand's economic decline.

General Chavalit and his New Aspiration Party edged out the Chuan-led Democrat Party in the November 1996 election. Having formed a government, he installed a new team of economic policy makers, but despite repeated warnings from the IMF, Thailand's new leaders did little to guard against the growing mountain of bad debt piling up in the financial system. Instead, they stuck stubbornly to the managed foreign exchange system which effectively pegged the baht to the U.S. dollar. When that peg was broken, the baht weakened sharply and Thailand's economy, which had appeared so strong, rapidly fell into recession. Faced with major criticisms over Thailand's economic woes as well as allegations of corruption against several Cabinet ministers, Chavalit had to face a no-confidence motion in November 1997. In exchange for coalition support in the no-confidence vote, Chavalit resigned immediately afterward so that others could form the next government.

As Chavalit left office without dissolving the House and organizing new elections, both the existing government coalition and the opposition parties were able to engage in a political free-for-all in their attempts to form a new coalition. For several days in November 1997 it was not clear which group of parties would form the next government. Two separate coalitions even held news conferences within hours of each other to declare that a new government majority would be formed. The Social Action Party and the Prachakorn Thai Party were initially claimed to support both camps.

Eventually, the Social Action Party sided with the Democrat-led coalition, and in a rather bizarre twist, most of the Prachakorn Thai Party MPs, not including their party leader, pledged their support to the coalition. Chuan Leekphai became prime minister for the second time on 8 November 1997. Although initially the strength of this coalition government was questionable, a transition has occurred successfully and the prime minister even began speaking of scheduling the next elections for as late as 2000 or 2001.

Thai democratization and party system development

Against the backdrop of a historic economic downturn, questions have naturally been raised about the Thai government's ability to handle the crisis. Such questions would have previously been put to the bureaucrats as, then, parties and parliament would not have been considered relevant. By the late 1990s, however, the functioning of Thai democracy had improved: there had not been a coup since 1991, even if the interplay between parties, coalition partners, and even prime ministers and their governments had not been smooth. The question of whether Thailand's political elite could make the necessary adjustments to the new reality had therefore become meaningful.

Yet, however positively Thai democracy can be regarded, the parties still have to be described as weak in view of their limited organizational structures, their disunity, and their lack of clear ideologies (Chai-Anan 1989; Neher 1987; Somsakdi 1987; Suchit 1990). The Thai political system had been modeled on Westminster, at least since the 1978 Constitution re-introduced a parliamentary system with a fully elected House of Representatives and an appointed Senate. Parliamentary elections were to be held at least every four years, although the prime minister could dissolve the House at any time. The electoral system was based on provinces, each of which was in turn divided into single-member, two-member, or three-member constituencies. As the population of the provinces grew, constituencies were given more seats and/or more constituencies were created. The number of seats in the House thus increased from 301 in the 1979 election to 357 in 1988 and 395 in 1996. Although the Constitution was revised in 1991 and again in 1992, the electoral framework remained broadly the same, whereas the 1997 Constitution was to introduce major changes.

Parties are regulated by the Political Party Law of 1981 which is currently being modified to comply with the provisions of the 1997 Constitution. Until the changes fully take place, the current law requires parties to register with the Interior Ministry, to submit copies of their regulations and a list of their leadership, and to seek ministry approval to register new branches. The aim had been to create mass-based parties by requiring that each party must have at least 5,000 members dispersed throughout the nation. In addition, to be eligible to compete in elections, parties had to submit a number of candidates equal to half of the available House seats.

The legal requirements and constraints regarding party registration and electoral competition constitute significant barriers to new party formation. Thai parties have been forced into a quasi-mass-based party organizational structure, at least formally, and this has curtailed the multiplication of parties. However, despite the legal requirements, few parties have actually succeeded in establishing (or even attempted to establish) mass organizations which would possess a complex organizational structure, a network of party branches, and a significant number of members. Although the Palang Dharma Party attempted to build up a mass-based party, it failed; only the Democrat Party (the oldest continuous Thai party) can make a credible claim to a network of party branches.

The weakness of Thai parties stems largely from the character of the relationship between these parties and their candidates. Candidates must belong to a party (since 1983), but the parties must nominate a sufficient number of candidates in each election or risk court-ordered dissolution. Since voters do not punish candidates who switch parties, and there are many parties, candidates who are expected to run strong campaigns are in high demand and, as a result, if they leave a party, another will readily accept them. By "strong campaigns" I mean ones in which candidates earned a number of votes equal to or greater than 50 per cent of the vote total of the winning candidate, or, on average, approximately 20 per cent of the total field of candidates (King 1996).

The media play a major role in Thai elections. They typically take a horse-race approach to reporting, focusing on whichever potential prime minister appears to be on top. Television and the press are free; the press in particular frequently reports allegations of vote buying and other types of election law violations as well as the more interesting or entertaining campaign techniques. Newspapers often announce their support for a potential prime minister late in the election contest. As parties have been allowed to advertise on television since 1995 only, election expenditure has typically been devoted to advertising via posters and banners, renting fleets of pickup trucks to enable candidates to tour constituencies, and to direct contacts with networks of vote buyers. Vote buying is without argument for many candidates the largest single expense.

Thai parties have also been regarded as weak because they lack substantive policy stands, let alone an ideology. There are no clear left-wing or right-wing parties, with the exception of the illegal Communist Party; labour, Green, or royalist parties have yet to surface. It has been argued that the basis of party formation in Thailand is constituted by the political

Table 8.1 **Thai parliamentary election statistics, 1979–1996**

	1979	1983	1986	1988	March 1992	September 1992	1995	1996
Parties contesting	36[1]	16	16	16	15	12	12	13
Parties winning seats	15	11[2]	15	15	11	11	11	11
Candidates	1,626	1,876	3,813	3,606	2,851	2,417	2,372	2,310
Seats	301	324	347	357	360	360	391	393
Bangkok voter turnout[3]	19.0	32.5	37.3	38.0	42.6	47.4	49.8	49.0
Overall voter turnout[3]	43.9	50.8	61.4	63.6	59.2	62.0	61.6	62.0

Source: Manoot 1986, 1998; Election Reports, Department of Local Administration, Interior Ministry 1992a, 1992b, 1995, 1996.
[1] Parties were not formally allowed to exist until after the promulgation of the Political Party Act in 1981, but parties did exist informally. In addition to groups that called themselves "parties," there were 28 other groups that submitted candidates.
[2] After the elections of 1983, independents were not allowed to hold seats in parliament, so that all independents were forced to join parties. The figure of parties that won seats does not include parties that gained seats only after the general elections due to party switching.
[3] Figures are percentages.

ambitions of individuals or of factions. Indeed, whether in the 1950s or the 1980s, party policy content has been essentially local in character: each candidate or MP is primarily concerned with such parochial concerns as a new village school, a new road, or donations to the local temple (Kanok 1987; Phillips 1958). According to Kramol, even in the politically charged atmosphere of the 1973–76 period, there was a "lack of clear ideological direction and commitment on the part of most noncommunist elites" (Kramol 1982, 34). As all non-Communist parties pledged their support to the democratic parliamentary system and to the troika of official Thai political values – Nation, King, and Religion – there were no clear distinctions among parties: "non-communist party members could switch parties without feeling that they [had] abandoned or deviated from their ideology" (Kramol 1982, 34). Since Thai parties were focused on electoral victories, party policy was relegated to the more concrete offers of favours that voters appreciated. As Suchit argues:

Parties' policies and performances were not a determinant of voting behavior, particularly in the provinces. Thus, in their election campaigns, a number of prominent politicians concentrated on their individual policies, achievements, and patrons, and rarely emphasized the party's performance. They had to set up their own election campaigns and campaign organizations, financing and recruiting their own campaign staff.... their election success depended on their own efforts rather than [those of] the party. (Suchit 1990, 261)

The major Thai parties and their link with society

There have been five major parties in Thailand in the 1980s and 1990s. These are the Democrat Party, the New Aspirations Party (NAP), the Chart Thai or Thai Nation Party (CTP), the Social Action Party (SAP), and the Chart Pattana or National Development Party (CPP). There are also a number of small parties.

The Democrat Party

Although it was only Thailand's second largest party at the time, the Democrat Party led the coalition government formed by Chuan Leekphai at the end of 1997. It is Thailand's oldest party, its roots dating back to 1945. With solid bases of support in the southern region and in Bangkok, it is probably the party best aligned with the capital's elite public opinion. Known somewhat derisively as a "party of professors," its leadership includes a number of Ph.D.'s and respected bankers and diplomats, as well as lawyers and former academics. The party also has a rural wing consisting of MPs who have often been accused of vote buying and various other types of corruption. With over 150 registered branches and over 300,000 members in 1996, the Democrats may be Thailand's most extensively organized party, but little systematic effort has been made to recruit or register new party members (McCargo 1997). Although the financial markets and business leaders have praised the party's approach to solving Thailand's economic woes, questions have been raised about the future of the party after the next few years of painful economic policy choices that certainly must be made.

The New Aspiration Party

The NAP, led by General Chavalit, was formed in 1991–92 after Chavalit retired from active military service in the army's highest positions. Chavalit's new party was being organized just as the 1991 coup occurred; it was initially thought to benefit from the coup since many military leaders had been close to Chavalit. Chavalit did oppose the takeover, however, and the coup leaders were instead supported by the Samakhitham Party, which was formed with their help. Chavalit continued to develop the NAP in opposition. From a core of ex-military and academic party founders, Chavalit's party grew in strength to win 72 seals in the March 1992 election. In the September 1992 campaign, in spite of being dubbed an "angelic party," the NAP shrank to 51 MPs but was able to join the government coalition. The party eventually defected to the opposition over a dispute concerning decentralization policy, and grew in the 1995 and 1996 elections to 125 MPs, thus being able to form the core of the post–1996 election government and in particular to give Chavalit the opportunity to fulfill his long-held dream of becoming prime minister.

Chavalit's administration survived one year only; it fell four months after the devaluation of the baht in July 1997, having been widely criticized for foot dragging with respect to the implementation of important economic reforms and ineptitude in responding to the economic crisis. Although many business leaders supported Chavalit while Bangkok voters did not, neither the NAP, nor indeed any other Thai party, can easily be linked to particular social groups or social cleavages. On a regional basis, the NAP has included a southern and a northeastern wing. In 1996, the party won 22 seats in the central region and 20 in the north, but had its greatest success in the northeast with 78 seats.

The Chart Thai Party

The CTP is led by a quintessential rural businessman turned politician, Banharn Silapa-archa. Banharn's conglomerate of business interests in construction and industrial chemicals provided sufficient funds for him to bankroll several CTP campaigns as its secretary-general and eventually as its leader. Formed in the mid-1970s by a group of retired military officers turned businessmen, the CTP has fluctuated from 108 MPs in 1983 to 77 in 1992. It has served in most coalition governments throughout the 1980s and 1990s even though it was dubbed a "devil party" due its participation in the Suchinda government. It is sometimes referred to as a businessman's party, but the expression is more appropriate for the party's founders and subsequent leaders than for its supporters. The CTP has usually garnered support from at least two or three major regions, not including Bangkok; it is strongest in the central region. After Banharn's short-lived government in 1995–96, the CTP shrank to 39 MPs in the 1996 elections.

The Social Action Party

The SAP was also organized in the mid-1970s. It ceased to be a large party in the mid-1980s, typically winning 20–30 seats in a broad cross-section of geographic regions, mostly in rural constituencies. The party's main campaign plank has been its support for the agricultural sector and rural development, admittedly a policy approach shared by many other parties.

The Chart Pattana Party

The CPP was formed in the wake of the May 1992 violence and the resignation of Prime Minister Suchinda. The core of that government was the Samakhitham Party which had, prior to the March 1992 election, proclaimed its support for Suchinda. Defectors from that party, along with former CTP party leader Chatichai Choonhawan, formed the CPP. The CPP has grown to a mid-size party by winning 52 seats in the 1996 parliamentary elections. Its main strength has been in the north and northeast, although it has won seats in other regions as well. When Chatichai was at the helm, the party's key election approach was support for an eventual Chatichai bid for the post of prime minister on the grounds of his expertise in economic policy and his skills in international diplomacy. After joining the Chavalit government in 1996, Chatichai accepted only a minor economic advisory role and the CPP's Cabinet members did not distinguish themselves in economic policy-making or in diplomacy. With Chatichai's death in May 1998, the party leadership has been passed to his son-in-law Korn Dabaransi and a younger generation of leaders.

It is difficult to say whether the CPP or other Thai parties represent specific business interests in telecommunications, construction, or finance, for instance, or particular social groups such as manual workers, labour movement leaders, or farmers. Even the CPP, despite its claims to expertise in managing economic policy, did not differ substantially from other Thai parties in the policies which its leaders proposed during the election campaigns of 1995 or 1996. Yet although the links are not obvious, some connection does exist between Thai parties and their supporters. What is more in question is whether these linkages are long-lasting, exclusive, or even significant in terms of electoral success.

Any linkages which exist are clearly not exclusive, however. Major business groups are known to make contributions to a variety of leading parties and to develop reciprocal relationships that outlast particular governments or coalitions. It is difficult, if not impossible, to identify a farmers' party since all parties express support for, and curry favor with, the 60 per cent of the population engaged in agriculture. Nor is there a clear conservative, elite-centered party since nearly every party is conservative in terms of political ideology and support of existing institutions and modes of political interaction. Nor can a labour party or a Green party be easily identified. This does not mean that Thai parties have no linkages with society, but that the linkages are overlapping, conditional, perhaps based more directly on promises of electoral support, and probably organized and managed as much by candidates as by party leaders.

The spread of democracy and the development of the party system

In the course of the second half of the twentieth century, there has been greater support in Thailand for democratic ideals and a greater understanding of the complexities that result from attempts to govern in accordance with democratic precepts than at any other time in Thai political history. Surveys indicate that support for democratic ideals is rather widespread and strong, as against earlier findings that found that few Thais understood the concept or even the Thai-language word for democracy (LoGerfo 1995; Wilson 1962). Support for parties is typically tempered by suspicion. Few would argue that democracy could function without parties or that parties are unnecessary, but their history of fractiousness and of electoral spending violations has resulted in parties having a bad reputation. The actions of the 1991 coup leaders indicate that they understood the need for parties: parties were not banned, and a party was set up as a political vehicle for post-coup consolidation. But their actions also clearly indicate a common attitude among political elites, according to which parties can be easily manipulated, and easily established or dissolved depending on agreement or discord among powerful politicians. The relatively ease with which Thai parties can be established and the fractious nature of Thai politicians has further contributed to a roll-over effect in which each occurrence of parliamentary elections sees at least one or two parties dissolve and one or two new parties emerge.

Another widely accepted point is that the prime minister should be the head of the largest party based on its number of MPs in the House. This was not the case in the 1980s when Prem was the perennial favorite for prime minister despite the fact that he never held a party post or stood for election. The idea of elections as competitions between possible prime ministers and the link between support for a party's candidates and support for its party leader as prime minister are emphasized in election campaigns. It is widely understood that one must lead a big party to become prime minister and therefore that parties support their candidates at election time even if they do not entirely control or finance those candidates.

The September 1997 Constitution: New rules for the political game

The new Constitution was approved by Parliament in late September 1997 and came into force immediately after it was agreed to by king and published in the royal gazette at the beginning of October 1997. The rules of the political game became in many ways significantly different: there are increased guarantees of individual rights, an elected Senate, a new Election Commission to supervise elections, separation of the elected Parliament and the Cabinet (MPs or senators are no longer allowed to simultaneously hold a Cabinet post and a seat in Parliament), a new electoral system based on a combination of single-member districts and a party-list system, and new requirements for candidates.

Increased guarantees for individual rights

The constitutional guarantees are increased for such individual rights as the freedom of speech and the freedom to associate while a new Human Rights Commission is being set up. These provisions may over time increase political participation, but the 1997 Constitution also introduces compulsory voting. A right to recall MPs is also given to citizens for the first time, by means of a petition which, if signed by 50,000 electors, can initiate the procedure. Meanwhile, petition signers can initiate a recall motion against an elected MP. Entirely new sections in the Constitution cover the duties of citizens and the duties of the state toward citizens.

Among the more positive rights, the Constitution guarantees twelve years of basic education. Since 1995, successive governments have made such a pledge but the reality lagged far behind and most educators felt that the system of state schools had difficulty in providing even nine years of basic education. The proportion of the Thai work force having received secondary education has remained static at 33 per cent for some years (World Bank 1996).

An elected Senate

The new Constitution has also established an elected Senate to replace the appointed chamber which was in part modelled on the British House of Lords and included military officers on active duty, top-level bureaucrats, leading businessmen, university professors, and labour leaders. In contrast, the new Senate has 200 members elected for six years from single-member districts based on the country's 76 provinces. Senators can no longer serve concurrently as military officers or as any other type of civil servant. The powers of the Senate remain broadly the same: that body can reject or delay ordinary legislation and consider measures designed to implement the provisions of the new Constitution, but no longer has the right to vote on no-confidence motions.

A new Election Commission

The Department of Local Administration in the Ministry of the Interior traditionally administered national and local elections. Under the provisions of the 1997 Constitution, this role passes to an Election Commission. The length of the campaign remains fixed at 45 days. The government is required by the Constitution to ensure that electoral contests are fought fairly by arranging for free radio and television time for the parties, publicizing the election, arranging appropriate access to locations for candidates to campaign, and enabling the Election Commission to carry out its duties. The commission also becomes the official registrar of the parties.

Voting becomes compulsory and the penalty for not voting could include the loss of the right to vote in subsequent elections. A number of concrete provisions are also specified in the Constitution: ballots must be counted at one location in each electoral district and no longer at each polling station; voters are allowed to cast a "none of the above" vote, thereby fulfilling their obligation to vote but being nonetheless able to reject the available candidates. This opportunity was already given from the March 1992 election onwards, and 2 per cent of votes were cast in this way in the 1995 and 1996 elections.

The new ballot-counting arrangements are designed to reduce vote buying which is considered to constitute the bulk of campaign spending and is estimated in the billions of baht. Counting the ballots at each polling station (there were over 62,000 polling stations used in the last election, or approximately one polling station for every 250 votes cast) allowed candidates to check whether their network of canvassers down to the sub-village level had been effective. By removing the opportunity to do such checking, the constitution drafters hoped to make vote buying less attractive: it will be more difficult to check not only that votes bought were actually cast, but also which canvassers were effective and which might have simply kept the money for themselves. Other anti–vote buying measures include the use of larger single-member districts which will make it more expensive for candidates to pay off a majority of voters.

Even more significant than these measures is the provision for the separation of Parliament and the Cabinet. Under the new Constitution, MPs or senators must give up their seats on accepting a Cabinet post. It has been frequently argued that since holding a Cabinet office is a highly prized opportunity for corruption, a significant number of politicians run for election to Parliament in the hope of being offered a Cabinet post. As the benefits to be reaped by a Cabinet minister are limited only by imagination and skill, it appears highly rational to invest in a House seat by buying votes in order to secure a return on one's investment through corrupt activity. In order to avoid a cascade of by-elections, it is assumed that the parties will select Cabinet members from among party-list MPs and not from those elected in single-member districts.

New requirements for parliamentary candidates

Some new requirements for candidates and MPs relate to the future of Thai political parties. Formerly, MPs expelled by their party automatically lost their seat and a by-election was held; under the new Constitution, such MPs have been given the right to retain their seats if they join another political party within 30 days. This provision may tend to weaken party discipline. For example, in 1993 an MP from the Social Action Party was expelled for frequently criticizing the coalition government to which his party belonged and refusing to heed the party's order to cease making comments to the press. Although this member was reelected on the Chart Thai Party ticket, the party to which he previously belonged was at least able to obtain a degree of discipline from its MPs. Parliamentary candidates will also be required to have at least a bachelor's degree from an accredited institution of higher education. This provision sparked considerable discussion since college attendance is still relatively rare in Thailand. In practice, the proportion of MPs holding at least a bachelor's degree has increased from 52 per cent in 1979 to 73 per cent in 1996.

New requirements for political parties

Even before a new political party law is enacted, two changes have been introduced by the new Constitution. First, a party can be established by as few as 15 persons instead of 5,000 as previously; second, parties which nominate candidates for parliament but fail to win seats are no longer automatically disbanded. These provisions could lead to a proliferation of parties and in particular to more small parties competing in parliamentary elections.

In contrast, the new provisions relating to single-member districts and the existence of party-list voting with a 5 per cent threshold clause should reduce the number of parties elected in the House. Overall, therefore, the new Constitution is likely to have a series of rather contradictory effects on parties and on electoral practices.

Economic policy management and the party system

The economy is hotly debated during electoral campaigns in Thailand, yet parties do not differ appreciably in terms of the broad economic policy lines which they support. Discussions on the subject are not ideological, but concrete and detailed. All parties agree about a generally capitalist approach to economic development with a measure of government intervention on the Japanese model. They do disagree over what priority to give infrastructure projects, for instance whether subways or overhead rails are preferable, or whether four-lane or six-lane regional transportation links are necessary. There have been debates as to whether the government's rubber price support policy was as successful as had been claimed, or whether the price of rubber increased simply in response to world market forces, but no party argues that the rubber support program should be phased out. Instead of debating over ideology, parties take turns to respond to local needs and present different shopping lists of infrastructure projects, investment incentives, or industrial liberalization measures. Thailand's decline into economic crisis has focused political debate more directly on economic policy and economic policy-making. Successive governments have tried to portray Thailand's economic difficulties as an occasion for national unity since the currency and capital markets usually react negatively to political debate about the IMF-led US$17.2 billion economic rescue package.

A few years before the 1997 crisis occurred, MPs had already started to serve in key economic posts. Previously, finance or commerce ministers might be selected from among respected non-parliamentarians and were often non-partisan. Subsequently, MPs gradually came to hold positions such as those of economic ministers and deputy ministers so long as their experience and background seemed adequate in the eyes of the business community.

Under the military-led governments of the late 1970s and early 1980s, parties appeared ready to leave the administration of the economy to experts and to popular prime ministers such as Prem. After the oil crisis of 1978–79, Prem's government instituted austerity measures, brought inflation under control, and devalued the baht in 1984. Both these austerity measures and the currency realignment are usually regarded as having given Thailand a solid macroeconomic base by the time Chatichai became prime minister in 1988 and the Thai economy grew at its most rapid annual rates. It was then commonly pointed out that Prem had relied heavily on technocrats and that they had been able to administer national affairs quite autonomously. Thailand was thus called by some a "premocracy" (Likhit 1988; Neher 1988; Yos 1989).

As in many other countries, Thailand's central bank, the Bank of Thailand, is formally independent although the finance minister has the power to name the bank's governor. A long-standing tradition has placed the Bank of Thailand, the Ministry of Finance, the Bureau of the Budget, and government economic and planning committees above political interference. Parliament has historically had few powers and fewer resources to influence the details of the government's budget or to challenge economic policy-making. Thailand's Westminster-type parliamentary system resulted in Cabinet government, and therefore, no government would purposely endow Parliament with powers that might subsequently be used to challenge or defeat the government.

Beyond the current structural characteristics which bolster the role of bureaucrats in economic policy-making, the history of the Thai bureaucracy's influence and power can be traced back to the formation of the Thai state and to the apparatus developed under King Mongkut and King Chulalongkorn from the mid-1800s. The state bureaucracy has been considered the choice career track for prestige-conscious elites who preferred honorific positions to better-paid opportunities in private business. In the Thai language, civil servants are known as *khaa ratchakarn* or "servants to the monarchy." Until the fall of the absolute monarchy in

1932, state business was considered to be the king's business, and an aura of honor and prestige has remained.

Cabinet ministers as political appointees have gradually sought to control, or at least influence, the state bureaucracy. Yet, until the mid-1970s, most Cabinet members were selected either from the bureaucracy or from the military. The military-led and military-dominated governments from 1932 to the mid-1970s were strongly associated with the bureaucracy (Riggs 1996). The Prem cabinets from 1980–88 included significant representation from the bureaucratic and military elites, not the least of which was Prem himself. The Chatichai government (1988–91) constitutes perhaps the most significant attempt by elected politicians to control the affairs of the state (Robertson 1996).

In terms of "embeddedness" as defined by Evans (1992), or the capacity of the state to penetrate society, Thailand does indeed exhibit the characteristics required at the basic level. The state is able to create the conditions necessary for a market economy: law and order prevail, an infrastructure is provided, the administration is competent. Corruption does exist, as does clientelism, but not to the extent of unduly undermining economic activity.

Evans (1992) identifies at least three elements in what he terms "elaborated embeddedness": the forums available for interaction between the state and business; the sources of influence available to the state; and the capacity of business to participate in these exchanges. The first criterion refers to the institutional arrangements through which interaction between government and business takes place. In Thailand since the mid-1980s, business groups have been increasingly organized into business associations, and these associations are increasingly functioning with effectiveness in negotiating with the state (Anek 1988). The second element refers to the resources available to the state to influence behaviour in these exchanges. The Thai state has the taxation and legal regulatory powers needed to force compliance to some degree by means of laws frequently designed to direct economic activity. Thus the Bank of Thailand began in 1995 to discourage lending to the property sector, first by classifying that sector as "unproductive" and subsequently by requiring higher levels of provisioning against risk assets. Through the state's Board of Investment which doles out over half of the privileges at its disposal to domestic investors, and its Exim Bank, among other institutions, the state can arrange capital to be made available, allocate funds, or grant subsidies. However, the Thai state does lack the third element which Evans associates with elaborated embeddedness, namely sophisticated sources of information (aside from information on state contracts or concessions) and a broad array of deliberative councils.

Power flows between the bureaucracy and the parties

The following examples illustrate the changes that have occurred in the Thai bureaucracy, in its status and reputation, and in its effectiveness and relative insulation in administering economic affairs in Thailand. First, Dr. Amnuay Viravan, who can be considered a quintessential Thai technocrat, served most of his professional life in a variety of positions in both government and private-sector banking. He became finance minister in the first Chuan administration (1992–95) under the New Aspirations Party's quota of Cabinet seats. Despite high marks from the business community for his experience and expertise, Amnuay came under pressure from NAP MPs who preferred to see elected MPs fill the party's quota of Cabinet posts. Amnuay was forced to abandon his previously valued neutrality and join the political fray by resigning from the Cabinet and setting up his own political party, the Nam Thai (Thai Leadership) Party.

The Nam Thai Party self-consciously portrayed itself as a party of technocrats who could, because of their superior training and experience, serve in public office for the common good of the nation. However, although a number of respected bureaucrats and academics joined Amnuay's party, in order to grow quickly, the party was faced with the same dilemma other Thai parties face, namely to accept rural politicians who could deliver House seats or to be true to its founding principles and only endorse candidates who met the party's high standards. Unfortunately for Amnuay, the Nam Thai Party won only 18 seats, half of them rural, while it failed to win a single seat in Bangkok. Amnuay's view that voters would support highly educated and experienced technocrats was dashed by electoral competition realities, namely the lack of grassroots support networks, as well as the shortness of time to prepare for the next election. Amnuay joined the Cabinet but later abandoned his party to join the NAP. He was reelected in 1996 and led Gen. Chavalit's economic "Dream Team." However, Thailand's economic slowdown and the political ambitions of coalition partners resulted in Prime Minister Chavalit overruling an important economic policy line advocated by Amnuay who subsequently decided to resign.

The Chuan government's (1997–) finance minister, Dr. Tarrin Nimmanhaeminda, and its commerce minister, Dr. Supachai Panichpakdi, have similar backgrounds to Amnuay. Both belonged to the top levels of management in Thailand's banking system before accepting cabinet posts in the first Chuan government (1992–95) as unelected non-partisan outsiders with strong technocrat qualifications. Both men subsequently abandoned their non-partisan status, joined the Democrat Party, and won seats in Bangkok. They both thus made the transition from unelected, neutral technocrats to elected politicians.

Aside from the transformation of the Thai bureaucracy from technocrat-led to elected politician–led, perhaps the most important factor that has changed the power flows between the elected politicians and the bureaucrats has been the actions of the Bank of Thailand itself. As the nation's central bank, it is supposed to operate independently from the government, administer the nation's monetary supply, and regulate the banking and finance sectors. Before 1995, it was regarded as the best example of Thailand's technocracy working for the good of the nation, but the actions of the bank in relation to the Bangkok Bank of Commerce (BBC) dented this shining armor. The BBC's financial health began to deteriorate prior to 1995. Through venality or simple neglect by the Bank of Thailand, the BBC had to be rescued to stave off bankruptcy. In the investigation which ensued, BBC officials were accused of granting loans without adequate collateral, including to influential politicians, lending large amounts to the bank's top management through a maze of holding companies, and falsifying documents. In view of the Bt 75 billion price tag (then approximately US$3 billion) to clean up the BBC mess, the reputation of the central bank as a bastion of expert technocrats was markedly impaired.

Following on the heels of the BBC fiasco, from late 1996 to August 1997, the Bank of Thailand provided Bt 430 billion in liquidity loans to a total of 58 finance companies. This information was not made public until the IMF package was almost approved in August 1997. Generally, a firm would only borrow from the central bank if it was having liquidity problems to the point of insolvency. Despite the fact that most of these firms were teetering on the brink of bankruptcy, the bank continued to extend its loans to them until it had lent an astonishing U$12.3 billion, equivalent to nearly half of the government's fiscal budget. To complicate matters, the bank and the Ministry of Finance suspended operations at 16 finance companies in June 1997, and then at another 42 firms in August 1997. After allowing these firms to submit rehabilitation plans, the bank eventually closed 56 of the 58 firms in December 1997 and later went into the process of liquidating their assets. In March 1998, the bank admitted to having lent over Bt 1 trillion to banks and finance companies since 1996.

In addition to the BBC fiasco and the financial sector rescue costs, the Bank of Thailand also came under intense criticism for its failed defense of the baht. From the devaluation of the baht in November 1984 to July 1997, the bank administered a de facto fixed exchange system which pegged the baht to a basket of currencies. Although the exact specification of the basket was a closely guarded secret, it was widely known that the U.S. dollar, the yen, and the mark constituted the core elements, the

U.S. Dollar accounting for approximately 80 per cent of the overall weightings. As a result, the baht floated within a very narrow range and it came under pressure in late 1996 as the currency weakened from Bt 24.5/US$1.00 to Bt 25.5/US$1.00.

Speculative attacks against the Thai currency heightened in February and March 1997 as the baht weakened to above Bt 26/US$1.00. The attacks intensified in May and June 1997. In response to these attacks, to preserve the value of the baht, the Bank of Thailand spent a total of US$23.8 billion in forward currency contracts, or nearly three-quarters of its entire reserves which at the end of May 1997 stood at US$33.3 billion. The news of these forward contracts was not released to the public until August 1997 after the IMF package had been signed and the bank was pressed for greater transparency. The attempt to save the baht was doubly unsuccessful: not only was the baht floated on 2 July 1997, but since the bank's reserves were so depleted, no defense of the currency could be attempted, so that the baht weakened to Bt 45/US$1.00 by the end of 1997.

Within the course of just two years, the Bank of Thailand and Ministry of Finance came under nearly constant attack over the BBC collapse and rescue, the liquidity loans to finance companies, the messy closure of 56 finance companies, and the costly and unsuccessful defense of the baht. With six finance ministers and four central bank governors involved in the process over just three years, the reputation of Thai technocrats has been seriously affected.

Globalization and its impact on Thailand's economy

Apart from domestic economic and political events that reshaped the power relationship between Thailand's elected politicians and its bureaucracy, globalization of the Thai economy has produced new forces and new challenges. The impact of globalization can be traced back to the government's decision in the mid-1980s to adopt an export-led growth strategy. Although heightened export activity brought with it more rapid economic growth, Thailand was also subject to the fluctuations of the international trade markets as its production base was forced to respond to international market demand and to foreign competition. Under the WTO agreement of which Thailand is a member, most of Thailand's protected industries have had to be liberalized progressively. Given the severe economic problems experienced in 1996–97, and the widely held expectation that the Thai economy will not turn around until 1999–2000, the extent of the commitment of Thai policy makers to the WTO liberalization plans is in question, as these plans were agreed upon when the Thai economy was robust and ready to adapt to international competition.

One aspect of globalization that has come under scrutiny is that of international finance and capital flows. Under pressure from the international community and leading world powers, Thailand began liberalizing its finance sector in 1993–94. Specifically, the formation of onshore/offshore lending facilities increased access to international financial markets. Due to high local interest rates and increased access to international funding sources from 1992 to 1996, Thailand's privately held external debt increased dramatically, to US$73.7 billion by the end of 1996. Although foreign capital helped fuel 8 per cent economic growth in 1993–95, the burden of this debt after the baht devaluation has proved crushing to Thai corporations. As the baht weakened by over 45 per cent against the U.S. dollar at the end of 1997, Thai government representatives were sent to ask Japanese, American, and other international bankers to roll over short-term debt which represents about two-thirds of the total debt. Furthermore, along with international capital comes increased monitoring by international rating agencies such as Moody's Investment Service, Standard & Poors, and the Japan Bond Rating Agency. Announcements of ratings downgrades by Moody's in particular have on each occasion resulted in slumps in the Thai stock market and increased funding costs for those Thai corporations that could still borrow from abroad.

A final aspect of globalization is the multinational aid package of US$17.2 billion organized by the IMF and agreed to in August 1997. From that point onward, Thailand's economic policy makers became bound by certain guidelines and goals and were subjected to advice from the IMF, World Bank, and other multilateral and bilateral organizations on everything from financial sector reform to capital market development to the privatization of state enterprises. In some important ways, the IMF agreement that rescued Thailand narrowed the parameters under which Thai policy makers could operate and still maintain the confidence of the international currency and financial markets. By accepting the multinational aid package, Thailand's bureaucrats effectively admitted that the problems were beyond their capacity. Although it is commonly the case that other nations tie their aid to the IMF's support for Thailand, this situation also sends a signal that Thai political leaders are only to be trusted in so far as they can be trusted by the IMF.

These developments have reduced policy choices for bureaucrats and elected political leaders. Thus government spending has come under close scrutiny. Spendthrift projects and even some deals that could have been kept under wraps have come under greater public scrutiny. The spectre of losing IMF confidence is too great to risk for a juicy contract for one's political allies. Opposing sides can now use the loss of IMF confidence as a potent weapon in their political battles, although on the other hand, opposing sides also criticize each other for giving in too readily or too slavishly to IMF demands.

While Thai politicians have always been sensitive to international sentiment and to the reactions of the international capital markets to local political manoeuvring, this sensitivity has increased dramatically since August 1997. The opposition might have previously criticized the government over economic policy, but when the Thai economy kept growing at 8 per cent or more per year, the criticisms did not carry much weight. Since 1997, a government mistake, or the use by the opposition of obstructionist tactics, can result in a quick and sharp weakening of the baht and in turn lead to higher inflation, higher interest rates, and heavier corporate debt burdens.

The battle at present is over the assessment of blame. Throughout 1997 and into the beginning of 1998, Thai bureaucrats, especially those at the central bank, were quoted frequently in the local press offering their explanations for the Thai economic crisis: the effects of a regional economic downturn, interference by elected politicians in economic policy-making, and the excesses of Thai private corporations. The elected politicians have similarly sought to lay the blame at the feet of the bureaucrats. In the widely distributed findings of the report of the Nukul Committee which was established to investigate the workings of the Bank of Thailand, the central bank's officers and procedures were harshly criticized.

Conclusion: Party development, democratization, and economic governance in Thailand

Thailand has a century-long history of a strong bureaucracy acting with a wide measure of autonomy. In the 1990s, however, democratic processes have become more firmly entrenched. Under Thailand's style of cabinet government, elected ministers (or a few non-elected ministers selected by the political parties) have directed the workings of the bureaucracy to the same extent as in many other countries: ministers may set overall policy directions or goals, and may exercise some control over budgeting, but policy implementation is more problematic. Disciplinary controls are typically limited: ministers may be allowed to promote or reassign top ministry officials, but may not control the assignments of lower-level officials. One factor which has inhibited the development of more extensive control of the bureaucracy by elected politicians is the short life of most Thai cabinets. As a result of frequent elections and cabinet reshuffles, from 1979 to 1998 no coalition government has survived unchanged for over two years. Given that ministers cannot build up networks of loyal and compliant allies among the permanent bureaucrats within a few weeks or months, the short duration of a minister's tenure strongly constrains cabinet ministers and prevents parties from extending their control over the bureaucracy. Moreover, coalitions have led to a type of cabinet structure in which no single party exclusively controls a particular ministry: ministers of one party typically work with deputy ministers selected from among the coalition's other parties.

Under the 1997 Constitution, the separation of the Cabinet from Parliament could divorce the government from the demands of local politics. As cabinet members are drawn from the House and are elected from small constituencies, they often represent concerns specific to their constituencies or to the regions in which their parties are strong electorally. Under the new rules, cabinet ministers are likely to be selected from each coalition partner's party-list candidates, these being in turn selected from a single national constituency. Ministers will therefore tend to reflect party policies rather than local concerns.

The 1996–97 economic downturn in Thailand is partially a reflection of similar problems in the Southeast Asian region, yet there is sufficient evidence to conclude that Thailand's bureaucrats ignored important warning signs, made poor judgements, and leveraged the nation's international reserves to a precarious position. The US$17.2 billion aid package granted by the IMF is a clear signal that the economy was mismanaged and that significant changes should be implemented. As a result of a series of errors and mishaps, Thai bureaucrats lost ground to the political parties and to elected leaders. However, Thailand's parties have historically been weak, and only in the mid-1990s has the party system been strengthened and the legitimacy of elections as the proper mechanism for government change been improved. Weak parties with little significant programmatic content may not be able to take full advantage of this historic opportunity. Although the new Constitution provides certain checks on the powerful bureaucracy, many of these guarantees and mechanisms are designed for citizens, and not parties, to exercise.

The end of the twentieth century is a highly dramatic and significant period both for Thai economic policy-making due to the pan-Asian economic crisis, and also for Thai political development based on the requirements of the new Constitution. While Thailand's economy contracts in a significant recession of an estimated negative 4 to 5 per cent in 1998 according to government estimates, unemployment is expected to rise significantly as domestic businesses cut back on labour costs and foreign investors slow projects. Income levels are expected to remain flat or fall as business after business implements salary cuts and the baht weakens against international currencies.

Thailand's experience with more stable government and the institutionalization and legitimization of parliamentary and electoral politics coincided with strong economic growth from 1980 to 1996. When Thailand's economy began to slow in 1996, there were calls for political change and many commentators bemoaned the lack of technical skills on the part of the Banharn government (1995–96). Banharn's short-lived administration gave way to Chavalit's administration which included more qualified ministers with technocratic backgrounds. However, as the economy slowed even further and the baht was floated on the international currency market, there were calls for Chavalit to step aside for one of the respected and non-partisan ex–prime ministers Prem (1980–88) or Anand (1991–92). Another option raised was the idea of a "national government" in which the government coalition would secure an overwhelming majority in the House to provide additional stability.

Although debated in public forums and in the press, both ideas were rejected by political leaders. The formation of the Chuan government in November 1997 to replace the outgoing Chavalit government was applauded by the markets due to the inclusion of several respected technocrats turned politicians. What is still unclear is what will happen when the economy really bottoms out in the months or years ahead and Thais are faced with street demonstrations, in part as a result of the inability of the government to solve the economic problems, given that these problems might be beyond what a single country's government can accomplish. It could very well be the case that the real test of democracy and economic governance is just beginning.

REFERENCES

Anek Laothamatas (1988), "Business and Politics in Thailand: New Patterns of Influence," *Asian Survey* 27(4), pp. 451–70.

Chai-Anan Samudavanija (1982), *The Thai Young Turks*, Institute of Southeast Asian Studies, Singapore.

——— (1989), "Thailand: A Stable Semi-Democracy," in Larry Diamond, Juan J. Linz, and Seymour Martin Lipset (eds.), *Democracy in Developing Countries*, vol. 3, *Asia*, Lynne Rienner, Boulder, Colorado.

Dahl, Robert (1971), *Polyarchy: Participation and Opposition*, Yale University Press, New Haven, Conn.

——— (1989), *Democracy and Its Critics*, Yale University Press, New Haven, Conn.

Diamond, Larry, Linz Juan, and Lipset Seymour Martin (1989), preface to Larry Diamond, Juan Linz, and Seymour Martin Lipset (eds.), *Democracy in Developing Countries*, vol. 3, *Asia*, Lynne Rienner, Boulder, Colo.

Election Division, Department of Local Administration, Interior Ministry (1992a), *Report on the Election to the House of Representatives* (in Thai), 22 March 1992.

—— (1992b), *Report on the Election to the House of Representatives* (in Thai), 13 September 1992.

—— (1995), *Report on the Election to the House of Representatives* (in Thai), 2 July 1995.

—— (1996), *Report on the Election to the House of Representatives* (in Thai), 17 November 1996.

Evans, Peter (1992), "The State as Problem and Solution," in Stephan Haggard and Robert Kaufman (eds.), *The Politics of Economic Adjustment*, Princeton University Press, Princeton, N.J.

Girling, John L. S. (1981), *Thailand: Society and Politics*, Cornell University Press, Ithaca, N.Y.

Kanok Wongtrangan (1987), *Kanmuang nai ratsapha* [Politics in the Parliament], Chulalongkorn University Press, Bangkok.

King, Daniel E. (1992), "The Thai Parliamentary Elections of 1992: Return to Democracy in an Atypical Year," *Asian Survey* 32(12), pp. 1109–23.

—— (1996), "New Political Parties in Thailand: A Case Study of the Palang Dharma Party and the New Aspiration Party," Ph.D. diss., University of Wisconsin at Madison.

King, Daniel E. and LoGerfo, Jim. (1996), "Thailand: Toward Democratic Stability." *Journal of Democracy* 7(1), pp. 102–17.

Kramol Tongdhamachart (1982), *Toward a Theory of Political Parties in Thai Perspective*, Institute of Southeast Asian Studies, Singapore.

Likhit Dhiravegin (1988), "Demi-democracy and the Market Economy: The Case of Thailand," *Southeast Asian Journal of Social Science* 16(1), pp. 1–25.

McCargo, Duncan (1997), "Thailand's Political Parties: Real, Authentic and Actual," in Kevin Hewison (ed.), *Political Change in Thailand: Democracy and Participation*, Routledge, New York.

Manoot Wathanakomen (1986), *Khomuun phuenthan phakkanmuang nai pachuban le kanluaktang* [Baseline data on present Thai political parties and the 1979–86 elections], Social Science Association of Thailand, Bangkok.

—— (1988), *Khomuun phuenthan phakkanmuang nai pachuban le phakkanmuang kab kanluaktang pii 2531* [Baseline data on present Thai political parties and political parties in the 1988 election], Social Science Association of Thailand, Bangkok.

Morell, David and Chai-Anan Samudavanija (1981), *Political Conflict in Thailand: Reform, Reaction, Revolution*, Oelgeschlager, Gunn & Hain, Cambridge, Mass.

Neher, Clark D. (1987), *Politics in Southeast Asia*, Schenkman Books, Rochester, Vt.

—— (1988), "Thailand in 1987: Semi-Successful Semi-Democracy," *Asian Survey* 28(2), pp. 192–201.

Phillips, Herbert P. (1958), "The Election Ritual in a Thai Village," *Journal of Social Issues* 14(4), pp. 36–50.

Riggs, Fred (1996), *Thailand: The Modernization of a Bureaucratic Polity*, East-West Center Press, Honolulu.

Robertson, Philips S., Jr. (1996), "The Rise of the Rural Network Politician," *Asian Survey* 36(9), pp. 924–41.

Somsakdi Xuto (ed.) (1987), *Government and Politics of Thailand*, Oxford University Press, Singapore.

Suchit Bunbongkarn (1990), "The Role of Major Political Forces in the Thai Political Process," in Clark D. Neher and Wiwat Mungkandi (eds.), *U.S.–Thailand Relations in a New International Era*, Institute of East Asian Studies, University of California, Berkeley.

Surin Maisrikrod (1992), *Thailand's Two General Elections in 1992: Democracy Sustained*, Institute of Southeast Asian Studies, Singapore.

Wilson, David A. (1962), *Politics in Thailand*, Cornell University Press, Ithaca, N.Y.

Yos Santasombat (1989), "The End of Premocracy in Thailand," *Southeast Asian Affairs, 1989*, pp. 317–35.

9

Malaysia

Edmund Terence Gomez and Jomo Kwame Sundaram

Malaysia was established as an independent, federal state in 1957. From the late eighteenth century until this latter date, Malaya had been a British colonial possession. The major social legacy of colonial rule was the creation of a multi-ethnic society. Chinese and Indians were both encouraged to immigrate to work in tin mining and rubber plantations, the industries that were the twin pillars of the colonial economy. Malay involvement in the emerging capitalist economy was not encouraged. Malay economic exclusion and numerical predominance were thus established as the grounding characteristic of the new state of Malaysia.

This chapter reviews the formal context and development of politics and the impact of the political system on the economy. First, requirements and circumstances surrounding the electoral system are reviewed. Second, the structure, organization, and membership base of Malaysia's major parties are summarized. The third section explores economic governance and the chapter concludes with a review of the political outlook.

Elections and the electoral system

Electoral and voting rules

Parliamentary and state elections are held regularly. These are run on a first-past-the-post basis in single-member constituencies. There is no public electoral funding. Voting is not compulsory, and all Malaysians above the age of 21 are eligible to vote.

Since the first federal election in 1955, parliamentary elections have been conducted as constitutionally required. The conduct of elections is regulated by various acts and the Constitution provides for an independent Election Commission, whose members are appointed by the king. Electoral participation by eligible citizens has been consistently high. In the federal elections held between 1959 and 1990, voter turnout ranged between 70.0 and 78.9 per cent, while the turnout in state elections during the same period ranged between 71.7 and 78.9 per cent (NSTP Research and Information Services 1994).

Elections are competitive in that a number of parties compete in the electoral process – any party registered with the Registrar of Societies is eligible to contest an election. By subjecting the choice of government to the electoral process at regular intervals under such conditions, the governing Barisan Nasional (BN – National Front) coalition has been able to legitimize its right to rule, especially since the BN has been voted out of office on a few occasions in state-level elections.

Electoral divisions

Although the Election Commission is responsible for reviewing the division of parliamentary and state constituencies, the electorates in these constituencies have always been disproportionately smaller in predominantly Bumiputera rural areas compared to the mainly Chinese-majority urban constituencies; such electoral boundaries favour the governing coalition, the BN, particularly its largest member, the United Malay National Organisation (UMNO), whose main support is from rural Malays. This has been a key factor behind the BN's consistent victories in federal-level elections (Crouch 1996b).

In the 1960s, Bumiputera-majority constituencies constituted 57 per cent of all parliamentary seats; by the 1980s, this had risen to 65 per cent. The overrepresentation of Sabah and Sarawak Bumiputeras has also enhanced Bumiputera dominance in Parliament. In 1990, although only 16.5 per cent of the population resided in Sabah and Sarawak, the 48 constituencies in these two states constituted 27 per cent of the seats in Parliament; Bumiputeras in the Borneo states, particularly Sarawak, have tended to support the BN.

This has meant that any party in the peninsula which could command the support of most Bumiputeras would be able to control the federal government, and if it collaborated with Bumiputera parties of some influence in Sabah and Sarawak, it would be able to command a comfortable majority in Parliament (Crouch 1996b).

By 1994, UMNO had secured a strong base in Sabah in Muslim Bumi-putera-majority constituencies (that is, those with a majority of Malays and other indigenous peoples), while its relationship with the Parti Pesaka Bumiputera Bersatu (PBB – United Bumiputera Party), Sarawak's long-standing ruling party, was particularly strong. Such gerrymandering has meant that even if the opposition garnered strong electoral support in terms of the total number of votes cast, the number of seats it would secure in Parliament would be much less. In the 1990 general election, although the opposition obtained 48 per cent of the total votes cast, it secured only 29 per cent of the 180 parliamentary seats. In the 1995 polls, the opposition secured 35 per cent of the vote, but only 15 per cent of parliamentarians.

Media

UMNO has a majority stake in Utusan Melayu Bhd which publishes the influential Malay newspapers, *Utusan Malaysia, Mingguan Malaysia*, and *Utusan Melayu*. Businessmen closely associated with UMNO deputy president Anwar Ibrahim have controlling interest in TV3 and The New Straits Times Press Bhd, which publishes the English newspapers, the *New Straits Times* and *Business Times*, and the Malay newspaper, *Berita Harian*. An investment arm of the Malaysian Chinese Associates (MCA), Huaren Holdings Sdn Bhd, has a controlling interest in Star Publications Bhd, which publishes the popular English tabloid, *The Star*, while *The Sun*, another English tabloid, is controlled by Vincent Tan Chee Yioun, who has strong ties with the UMNO elite. Most of the Tamil press is controlled by leaders of the Malaysian Indian Congress (MIC), while some leading Chinese newspapers, including the *Nanyang Siang Pau*, are controlled by the Hong Leong Group, which has business ties with UMNO-linked companies. *Sin Chew Jit Poh*, the country's best-selling Chinese newspaper, is controlled by a Sarawak-based tycoon who was also a BN senator (Gomez 1994).

Given the ownership of the mainstream media, it is not surprising that opposition members have repeatedly complained that they are unable to get their manifestos publicized during campaign periods, while their statements are usually taken out of context when carried by the press. The opposition has also claimed on numerous occasions that press reports of their activities have been blatantly false. Major newspapers are, however, used to carrying full-page – usually colored – advertise-ments of the BN's manifestos and accomplishments, while the views of government leaders are given wide and favourable coverage (Sankaran and Hamdan 1988; Khong 1991; Gomez 1996a).

Campaigns

The manner in which campaigns are conducted heavily favours the BN. The major influencing factors have been commonly termed the "3Ms" – money, media, and machinery. There have been complaints about the BN's excessive use of funds, abuse of its control of Malaysia's leading newspapers as well as television and radio networks, and misuse of government machinery (Chandra 1982; Sakaran and Hamdan 1988; Khong 1991; Gomez 1996a).

Other factors which benefit the party in power include the shortness of the election campaigns, a ban on open rallies, and the application of state funds. The Election Commission decides the length of the campaign period and ensures that it is kept very short – normally just over a week – ostensibly in the interests of maintaining ethnic harmony. Open rallies have been banned since the 1978 general election. Yet, BN leaders blatantly campaign at huge rallies while ostensibly officiating at government functions. Finally, through their control of federal funds, BN leaders often promise new development projects, threaten financial cuts, or distribute state largesse just before and during the campaign period.

Compared to the opposition parties, the BN's campaign machinery, especially that of UMNO, is efficiently and effectively run during elections. The effectiveness of the BN's machinery is partly attributable to its easy access to funds. Since public rallies are banned, door-to-door canvassing is the most common form of campaigning, which requires much manpower; most BN campaign workers are well remunerated, while the opposition relies heavily on unpaid voluntary help. Since the number of campaign posters and vehicles used during the campaign period is not specifically limited by law, this tends to benefit parties with greater access to funds, invariably the BN parties.

The most common allegation made during elections is that funds are used to buy constituency support. Before the 1990 poll, the BN was reportedly prepared to spend an average of RM 1 million in each parliamentary constituency (*Far Eastern Economic Review*, 5 July 1990). Vote buying was still rampant during the 1995 general election. There were numerous allegations by the opposition that votes were secured through the distribution of funds and gifts in Kelantan, Terengganu, and Kedah, and in some urban constituencies in Perak and Kuala Lumpur. In Kelantan, the opposition alleged that there were candidates who spent almost RM 5 million to secure support, with voters paid between RM 500 and RM 1,000 each (Gomez 1996a). Although all candidates are required to file the total funds used during the campaign with the Election Commission following the election, they are not required to divulge the sources of their funds.

Given UMNO's vastly superior membership base and extensive party machinery, during elections most BN parties depend on UMNO to run an effective campaign to secure electoral support. The MCA, MIC, and the Gerakan Rakyat Malaysia (Gerakan – Malaysian People's Movement) tend to perform unsatisfactorily in non–Bumiputera-majority constituencies, thus increasing their reliance on UMNO to muster Bumiputera votes.

In the 1986 and 1990 general elections, even the leaders of the MCA, Gerakan, and MIC acknowledged that their electoral victory was due primarily to the Malay support that UMNO had managed to secure for them. Moreover, the MCA and Gerakan's influence in the east coast of the peninsula is not extensive while their influence in Sabah (and Sarawak) is negligible despite efforts to establish a base in the state.

Election outcomes

All the ten federal-level elections that have been held since 1955 have been won by the UMNO-led Alliance or BN coalitions. On all occasions, except in 1969, a two-thirds majority was secured in Parliament (table 9.1).

Political parties in Malaysia

The ruling coalition

Launched in 1973, the BN was a re-organization of the Alliance following the latter's dire performance in the 1969 general election. At this time, most opposition parties – including the main Malay opposition party, Parti Islam SeMalaysia (PAS – Pan-Malaysian Islamic Party), the People's Progressive Party (PPP), and the Gerakan – were brought into the BN. This followed the racial strife of May 1969.

The BN's enlarged system of consociationalism was an effective means to consolidate electoral support on the basis of both ethnicity and class. The objectives of the UMNO, MCA, and MIC are based on ethnic ideologies. This has enabled these parties to represent their leaders as ethnic patrons (Brown 1994, 206–57). By the 1990s, UMNO's main bastions of support were still the peninsula's rural Malays and Sabah's rural Muslim Bumiputeras (the party does not have a presence in Sarawak). The MCA helps the BN marshal Chinese business and middle-class support, while the MIC has been more successful in mobilizing broader Indian support. The nominally multiracial, but largely Chinese Gerakan has been able to complement the MCA in attracting Chinese support, especially from the middle classes.

Table 9.1 **Malaysian Federal Parliament election results, 1955–1995[1]**

	1955	1959	1964	1969	1974	1978	1982	1986	1990	1995
Alliance	51	74	89	74						
BN[2]					135	130	132	148	127	162
PAS[3]	1	13	9	12		5	5	1	7	7
DAP				13	9	16	9	24	20	9
Socialist Front		8		2						
PPP[4]		4		2						
P. Negara		1								
P. Malaya		1								
UDP			1							
PAP			1							
Gerakan[4]				8						
USNO				13						
SCA				3						
SNAP[4]				9	9					
SUPP[4]				5						
Pesaka										
Semangat									8	6
Pekemas					1					
PBS									14	8
Independent		3		1		2	8	4	4	
TOTAL	52	104	104	144	154	154	154	177	180	192

Source: *New Straits Times*, 23 April 1995.

[1] For explanations of party acronyms, see the text of this chapter and the List of Acronyms, p. ix.

[2] The Alliance was enlarged and renamed the BN from 1973.

[3] PAS was part of the BN for the 1974 general election.

[4] These parties joined the BN after the 1969 election except for SNAP which joined after the 1974 election.

UMNO's BN initiative has meant that the Chinese support enjoyed by the Gerakan has diminished the MCA's influence, while the incorporation of the PAS, whose influence was primarily in the predominantly Malay states in the north of the peninsula, enhanced Malay electoral support. UMNO's refusal to allow PAS to increase the number of seats it won in 1969 in the subsequent general election of 1974 further strengthened UMNO hegemony in the coalition, though PAS eventually returned to the opposition in 1978. In 1996, the constituent number of parties in the BN stood at 14.

Although the BN is the governing coalition, it cannot be construed as an actively functioning party. Even the BN's Supreme Council meetings, comprising leaders of all component parties, are held infrequently, usually before a federal or state election. Discussions on policy matters between members of the BN are kept to the minimum, while major decisions are made by a select group of leaders, mainly from UMNO, before being passed down for endorsement, usually at cabinet level. This has been confirmed by leaders of BN parties: according to Koh Tsu Koon of the Gerakan, "the basic problem is that there is not enough consultation among the Barisan parties" (*Malaysian Business*, 1 December 1987). Michael Yeoh from the MCA has stated, "Let us revive the BN Supreme Council, make it a more credible, truly consultative body. Now it is only revived every time there is a general election, to discuss the allocation of seats" (*Malaysian Business*, 1 December 1987). This suggests that the role of the BN's Supreme Council as the main governing body is merely perfunctory although it is presented as the medium through which consultations are held to maintain ethnic coexistence.

Since the leaders of most of the main BN parties are represented in the Cabinet, this forum is promoted as the main avenue through which inter-ethnic consultations are regularly held and differing viewpoints expressed. In view of UMNO's hegemony in the executive and the fact that the choice of Cabinet ministers is the sole prerogative of the prime minister, and given the heavy reliance of most component parties on UMNO to secure their victories in elections, interparty consultations are not conducted on an equal footing.

UMNO

UMNO's hegemony is attributable to its size, its national presence, and its extremely efficient party machinery. UMNO has approximately 2.765 million members, spread out among 17,355 branches in all parliamentary constituencies in the peninsula and Sabah (*New Straits Times*, 6 September 1997; table 9.2). UMNO's party structure is organized hierarchically, with the branches forming the base, followed by the divisions, the State Liaison Committees and the Supreme Council. In UMNO's system of

Table 9.2 **UMNO membership breakdown by state, 1997**

State	Total membership
Johore	388,828
Sabah	362,494
Selangor	308,015
Kelantan	285,631
Perak	252,055
Kedah	229,336
Pahang	192,116
Terengganu	169,400
Negeri Sembila	119,045
Penang	114,765
Federal Territory	103,169
Malacca	86,579
Perlis	43,174

Source: *New Straits Times*, 6 September 1997.

election, delegates are chosen from branches to attend divisional meetings where nominations are made for Supreme Council posts. Delegates to UMNO's general assembly are chosen from among delegates attending the divisional meetings.

Under the party's constitution, nominees for the posts of UMNO president and deputy president are awarded ten bonus votes for each divisional nomination they receive; these bonus votes are added to the number of votes that the candidates receive during the election at the general assembly. The provision for the bonus votes was designed to consolidate the position of the top two leaders in the party since the chairmen of the State Liaison Committee are usually the *Mentri Besar* (chief ministers) of the respective states, who are appointed by the party president in his capacity as prime minister. The party's national headquarters, a sprawling edifice in the heart of Kuala Lumpur, serves as the centre where the party's operations are monitored; UMNO also has a state headquarters in each major city in the peninsula.

Patronage

Patronage politics has long been the primary means through which a strong grass-roots base is created in the party. The distribution of economic favours also contributed to growing ties between business and politics. The development of this phenomenon, popularly referred to as "money politics," has also involved distributing cash and gifts and offering expenses-paid trips to members in return for votes (Gomez 1990, 1991a, 1994).

Though the party was dominated mainly by rural teachers since UMNO's formation, businessmen began to gain control of its branches and divisions by the 1980s. In 1981, teachers still made up 41 per cent of delegates to UMNO's annual General Assembly; this dropped to 32 per cent in 1984, and declined further to 19 per cent in 1987. By 1987, businessmen constituted 25 per cent of delegates, while elected representatives made up 19 per cent. By 1995, almost 20 per cent of UMNO's 165 division chairmen were millionaire businessmen-cum-politicians (*Wawancara*, December 1995).

As businessmen entered mainstream politics in the 1980s, money politics became rampant in the contests for positions in UMNO's Supreme Council and in the election of branch and division leaders. In the 1984 UMNO elections, the total money spent to secure support was allegedly well in excess of RM 20 million (Milne 1986). Within a decade, during the 1993 UMNO election, the money spent during the campaign had increased by more than tenfold, to an estimated RM 200–300 million. In 1985, one politician was willing to spend as much as RM 600,000 in his bid to become division chairman. In a bid for a similar post in 1995, one candidate allegedly spent RM 6 million (Gomez 1994).

Political patronage has become the key to wealth. This is clear from the business interests of Prime Minister Mahathir Mohamad's sons, and from those of supporters of his UMNO rival Anwar Ibrahim, as well as from widespread ownership of corporate stock by business protégés of former Finance Minister Daim Zainuddin, currently Government Economic Advisor and UMNO treasurer. For example, Daim protégés include: Tajudin Ramli, a director of Malaysian Airline System, Malaysian Helicopter Services, and two other companies; Wan Azmi W. Hamzah, a director of R J Reynolds Land and General; Halim Saad, director of six companies; and Samsudin Abu Hassan, director of two companies. Business protégés of Mahatir include his sons, Mirzan, Mokhzani and Mukhriz, who have each been nominated to four boards and Mohd Noor Yusoh, a director of three companies including TV3. Finally, at least nine have benefited from Anwar's patronage including Mohd Sarit Yusoh, Ishak Ismail, Ahmad Zahid Hamidi, Ibrahim Ahd, and Kamaruddin Jaffar. Anwar associates were all beneficiaries of the takeover of the New Straits Times Group and TV3.

1987 factional crisis

Persistent factionalism within UMNO is closely tied to the party's hegemonic position and its control of state resources. In 1987, an UMNO faction, led by the then trade and industry minister, Razaleigh Hamzah, alleged that Mahathir had formed a kitchen cabinet which had centralized decision-making powers, with most government contracts and business opportunities distributed to members of this inner circle; these allegations justified his decision to contest the party presidency. In the election, Mahathir narrowly clinched victory, securing merely 51 per cent of the votes of the delegates to the UMNO general assembly (Shamsul 1988). This proved to be a defining moment in Malaysian politics as it precipitated a series of authoritarian measures by Mahathir as he moved to consolidate his position. Within the next year, more than 100 government critics were detained under the Internal Security Act (ISA), which allows for long-term detention without trial; some newspapers had their licences revoked; members of the judiciary, including the lord president, were removed from office through questionable means; and UMNO was declared an illegal party in a ruse to establish a new UMNO firmly under Mahathir's control (see CARPA 1988; Lee 1995).

UMNO's illegal status stemmed from a High Court ruling in February 1988 on a suit filed by Razaleigh's faction challenging the results of the 1987 UMNO election on the grounds that delegates from 30 unregistered branches were present at the party's General Assembly. The court ruled that the presence of the unregistered branches made UMNO an illegal society under the Societies Act. Mahathir immediately formed a new party, UMNO Baru (New UMNO), which provided him with the opportunity to deny his critics membership in the new party. Razaleigh and his loyalists formed the Parti Melayu Semangat 46 (Semangat – Spirit of '46 Malay Party) and crossed over to the opposition.

1993 deputy presidential election

The use of patronage to develop a strong coterie of politically aligned businessmen and a large grass-roots base, the abuse of money in party elections, and the growing influence of businessmen in politics were all obvious during the 1993 UMNO election, when Anwar Ibrahim ousted Ghafar Baba as deputy president. Anwar's faction, calling themselves the "Vision Team," captured most key party posts by arguing that with rapid economic development and the growth of a Malay middle class, UMNO itself had to change. They called on members to embody their modern vision; for them, the era of the "New Malay" had arrived.

Though their conceptualization of the New Malay remained nebulous, it implied that the pursuit of wealth was a social virtue, enhancing the already increasingly materialistic outlook of UMNO members; greed became good. However, there was growing discontent within UMNO over the fact that the gains made by individual members from their political affiliations had been spread very unevenly. Mahathir was eventually forced to denounce this new culture, calling it the "culture of greed," which was dividing the party against itself (*New Straits Times*, 20 October 1994).

After the 1993 UMNO election, very pronounced pro- and anti-Anwar factions emerged. While the pro-Anwar faction mainly comprised a younger group of politicians eager to displace senior politicians, the anti-Anwar factions were generally led by more senior politicians wary of Anwar's meteoric rise in the party. Anwar, who had only been recruited into UMNO in 1982, had been a prominent critic of the BN and the long-time president of the nongovernmental organization, Angkatan Belia Islam Malaysia (ABIM – Malaysian Islamic Youth Movement).

Anwar's supposed recruitment of old ABIM colleagues into his UMNO inner circle had led to growing anxieties, even from within his own "Vision Team." Its rapid disintegration confirmed widespread speculation that its basis was political. Its demise has led to the emergence in UMNO of several overlapping factions.

Mahathir consolidation

Although Mahathir was not challenged for the presidency during the 1993 UMNO election, it was widely believed that Anwar was emerging as the most powerful politician in the country, subtly laying siege to the prime minister. It was believed that Mahathir, unlike Anwar, had not spent enough time cultivating the grass roots, leaving a vacuum that had been filled by the energetic Anwar and his ambitious younger men. From 1993, however, Mahathir moved decisively to consolidate his presidency.

Before the 1995 general election, Mahathir despatched some Anwar allies in the Federal Cabinet to the state level, or vice versa, and sent some of his own loyalists to contest state constituencies, which would enable them to be appointed as *Mentri Besar* later. A number of Anwar's associates were sidelined – including some from ABIM who had hoped to be fielded instead of other UMNO members. In the post-election Cabinet, Anwar's rivals were promoted to senior portfolios while his allies were restricted to uninfluential ministries or to the backbenches.

Mahathir also brought about changes within UMNO to protect his position, even proposing changes to the party constitution. Mahathir proposed that the bonus votes provision be reviewed and that a code of ethics to curb money politics be drawn up. This code was designed to be used against those who threatened Mahathir's position. Half a year before the 1996 UMNO election, a new rule was introduced, requiring candidates wishing to contest party posts to declare their intentions well in advance, thus blocking a possible late challenge. As the elections approached, even campaigning was banned. Mahathir justified this as "the party's way of ensuring fairness to all because there are some candidates who can afford to campaign while others cannot.... Banning campaigning is to level out the opportunity for all" (*Far Eastern Economic Review*, 25 April 1996).

This series of actions in UMNO and in the Cabinet reinforced Mahathir's political dominance, making it extremely difficult for anyone to topple him from within UMNO. The competition among factions was fought out at lower party echelons, in the contests for the vice-presidencies, for control of the youth and women's wings, and at divisional and branch levels. Though UMNO may be badly factionalized, it appears to be held together by Mahathir's seemingly unassailable grip on the apex.

During the 1996 UMNO election, although results of elections at division and branch levels suggested that members aligned to Anwar had secured grass-roots control, none of the three directly elected vice-presidents were seen as particularly close to Anwar. However, the leadership of the UMNO youth and women's wings was secured by those in Anwar's camp. The overall impression that emerged from the results of the elections was the evenly divided strengths within the party.

Other BN members

Although the MCA, MIC, and Gerakan have rather similar organizational structures, their respective party machineries, although active, are much less effective than that of UMNO, due primarily to their much smaller membership base and financial power. The MCA has approximately 715,000 members in 2,917 branches, in all states except Sarawak. The MIC has almost 350,000 members in 2,500 branches in only the peninsula. The Gerakan has about 250,000 members in 1,259 branches (*New Straits Times*, 8 April 1996, 1 August 1996).

The leading Sarawak-based BN component party, the PBB, is a Bumiputera-based party led by Abdul Taib Mahmud, Sarawak's long-standing chief minister and a former Federal Cabinet member. PBB is the dominant party in the Barisan Tiga (Tripartite Front), also comprising two other Sarawak-based BN members – the Chinese-based Sarawak United People's Party (SUPP) and the Iban-based Sarawak National Party (SNAP). Though a BN member, the Parti Bangsa Dayak Sarawak (PBDS – Sarawak Dayak People's Party), a Dayak-based breakaway from the SNAP, had the unique position of remaining an opposition party at state level. The PBDS subsequently sought and gained admission into the state ruling coalition after faring badly in the 1991 state elections. None of these parties has any influence outside Sarawak.

In Sabah, the turnover of parties from the BN has been high. The former BN component members which once led the Sabah state government but are now in the opposition include the United Sabah National Organization (USNO) (1963–76) and the Parti Bersatu Sabah (PBS – United Sabah Party) (1985–94); the Bersatu Rakyat (Berjaya—United People), which ruled Sabah from 1976 to 1985, is nearly defunct, though technically still a BN member. Among the current Sabah-based BN members are the Dusun-based Angkatan Keadilan Rakyat (AKAR – People's Justice Movement) and the Chinese-based Liberal Democratic Party (LDP), both minor parties with little influence. In 1994, several newly formed Sabahan parties were accepted into the BN – the Chinese-based Sabah Progressive Party (SAPP) and the Kadazan-based Parti Bersatu Rakyat Sabah (PBRS – or United Sabah People's Party) and the Parti Demokratik Sabah (PDS – Sabah Democratic Party). All these parties are led by former PBS leaders, most of whom defected in 1994 when it became clear that the PBS was losing control of the state government.

The opposition

The two main opposition parties are the Democratic Action Party (DAP) and the PAS. There are two smaller opposition parties, the PBS and the Parti Rakyat Malaysia (PRM – Malaysian People's Party).

Democratic Action Party

The DAP was constituted from the rump of Singapore's ruling People's Action Party after the separation of the republic in 1965. Espousing the PAP's commitment to the creation of a democratic, socialist Malaysia, the DAP asserts the principle of racial equality more than social and economic justice. The DAP stresses the need for a level playing field for all ethnic communities in politics, business, and education. Not unexpectedly, the DAP does not have much Malay support. Even though its membership is open to all Malaysians and it has a multiracial leadership, the DAP is seen as a "Chinese" party, a view that is buttressed by the commonly held perception that it primarily raises Chinese concerns. By consistently exposing corruption in government and promoting transparency and accountability, the party has managed to garner sizeable urban, non-Malay middle-class support.

The DAP emphasizes the need for greater democratization, arguing that the true spirit of democracy in a multi-ethnic society is expressed through racial equality, mutual respect, and tolerance. A strident and consistent critic of authoritarian rule, the DAP objects to the BN contention that majority rule and restrictions on freedom of the press, assembly, and expression are essential to maintain ethnic harmony and promote economic growth. On the contrary, the DAP claims that Malaysian history bears reliable witness to the fact that majority rule has contributed to the denial of basic human rights and the creation of greater social injustices; the party has also argued that concentration of power has contributed to significant inequality in the distribution of wealth (see Lim 1978).

Parti Islam SeMalaysia (Pan-Malayan Islamic Party)

The Islamic party, PAS, a breakaway UMNO faction formed in 1951, is the main opposition party with the capacity to undermine UMNO's influence among rural Malays. Following a leadership change in 1982, the PAS began adopting a more Islamic stance. Current leaders are primarily Islamic-educated *ulama* (religious teachers), and the party's influence is limited to the northern Malay heartland states of Kelantan, Terengganu, Kedah, and Perlis. The PAS first secured a majority in the Kelantan legislature in 1959 and governed the state until 1978. PAS also gained control of Terengganu after the 1959 general election, but ceded control of the state in 1961 following defections from the party to UMNO. During the 1990 general election, the PAS swept back to power in Kelantan with the aid of the newly established Malay party, Semangat, led by the Kelantan prince, Razaleigh Hamzah, the former finance minister and a long-standing UMNO vice president. The PAS retained control of Kelantan in the 1995 general election, and obtained a marginal increase in support in Terengganu and Kedah. But because of its continued stress on its desire to establish an Islamic state, its influence on the west coast of the peninsula, and in Sarawak and Sabah, is scant even among Muslim Bumiputeras, which restricts its ability to achieve power at the federal level.

Among opposition parties, the PAS has the largest membership base with about 436,840 members in 3,377 branches (*New Straits Times*, June 1 1997). The PAS also has the most strongly defined ideological position. Committed to the formation of an Islamic state, it espouses policies and ideas supposedly rooted in the religion. Adopting this Islamic posture, the PAS has been offering Malaysians, and Muslims in particular, a society reformed through legislative changes based on religious tenets. For the PAS, the establishment of an Islamic state will bring about spiritual upliftment and lead to the development of a more just, democratic, moral, principled, and socially conscious society, devoid of repressive legislation and unhealthy activities such as gambling. Democratic ideals, the party believes, are only acceptable within a secular context, since such ideals would automatically be a feature of a system which is inherently just within an Islamic theocratic state. Yet it has been observed that the PAS would probably reject the concepts of majority rule and individual choice, since the former allows for the possibility of morally wrong tenets being implemented, and the latter involves the assumption that individuals are all-knowing (see Jesudason 1996).

Parti Bersatu Sabah (United Sabah Party)

The multiracial PBS was formed in 1985 by dissidents from Berjaya, a BN member that then had control of the Sabah state government. The party was led by Joseph Pairin Kitingan, a Kadazan, and another notable PBS leader was Yong Teck Lee, a Chinese, and at the time the chief minister of Sabah; this helped the PBS secure a strong base among these two communities. The PBS came to power in 1986, after it narrowly defeated the Berjaya. Against this background, the PBS had an uneasy relationship with other member parties of the BN, especially UMNO, between 1986 and 1990.

Parti Rakyat Malaysia (Malaysian People's Party)

The PRM has a small membership and limited influence. Inaugurated in 1955, and hoping to derive support from rural peasants, it has, more recently, made some inroads among the urban working class. The PRM secured two parliamentary and two state seats in the first general election it contested in 1959 under the banner of the Socialist Front (SF). In the following election of 1964, the SF only secured two federal parliamentary and eight state seats. The PRM has not been able to win an electoral contest since it secured one parliamentary seat and three state seats in the 1969 general election (Vasil 1971, 167). In the elections of 1982, 1990, and 1995, the PRM collaborated with other opposition parties, including the opposition coalition Gagasan Rakyat Malaysia, formed in 1990, which had its roots in UMNO factionalism. It failed to secure representation either in the Federal Parliament or in any of the State Assemblies.

Opposition coalitions since 1987

What appeared to be a politically expedient move by Mahathir to rid UMNO of his opponents led to the emergence of the most organized opposition to the BN since the latter's formation. With Semangat in the opposition, two coalitions emerged under its leadership. The first was based on an electoral pact with the DAP, the PRM, and the Indian-based All Malaysian Indian People's Front (IPF), a breakaway MIC faction. The BN-like multiracial coalition, Gagasan Rakyat (People's Movement), primarily contested parliamentary and state seats on the west coast of the peninsula, where constituents were from all ethnic communities. In addition, on the east coast, where the constituencies are dominated by Malay Muslims, Semangat combined forces with PAS and two other small Islamic parties to form Angkatan Perpaduan Ummah (APU – Community Unity Movement) (Khong 1991).

The chief reason for creating two separate coalitions was the inability of the Islamic-based PAS and the DAP to find common ground. The DAP was opposed to PAS's intention to form an Islamic state, while PAS was not willing to renounce this goal. When both coalitions were formed just before the October 1990 general election, it was the first time in the history of Malaysian politics that all opposition parties were united and led by an established ex-UMNO Malay leader, Razaleigh. Midway through the campaign, the PBS joined the opposition, giving the Gagasan Rakyat control over Sabah even before it contested its first election.

The new opposition coalitions proved formidable adversaries to the BN. The APU resoundingly defeated the BN in Kelantan, securing victory in all the state's parliamentary and state seats. The Gagasan Rakyat narrowly failed to secure control of the Penang state government. The BN's performance in the other states, however, was much better, enabling it to retain its two-thirds majority in parliament, albeit by a mere seven seats. But it was indisputable that the BN's victory was due to its effective use of funds, government machinery, and the leading newspapers as well as television and radio networks (Khong 1991).

Subsequently, federal funds to the Kelantan and Sabah state governments were reduced. This led some PBS leaders to advocate closer ties with the BN, ostensibly to secure more federal funding, but probably also for personal reasons. After the PBS's defection to the opposition, some party leaders, including Kitingan's brother, were detained under the ISA. Kitingan was charged and found guilty of abusing his powers to channel a RM 1.4 million construction contract to family members; he was fined for the offence (*Far Eastern Economic Review*, 27 January 1994).

The PBS left the Gagasan Rakyat and attempted to return to the BN; its application was rejected and the BN secured control of the Sabah state government following the 1994 state election through questionable means, although the PBS had narrowly secured victory (Gomez 1996b). Despite the PBS's reduced electoral support in this election and the defection of key leaders to the BN, the results of the 1995 general election showed that the PBS still commanded sizeable non-Muslim support, especially among the Kadazans and Chinese (Gomez 1996a). This sequence of events revealed UMNO's use of federal government influence to undermine leaders at state level.

The withdrawal of the PBS from the Gagasan Rakyat signalled the latter's decline despite the serious electoral threat that the Semangat-led opposition coalitions had posed to the BN in 1990. Semangat was increasingly unable to sustain co-operation among the opposition parties due to political differences, while the DAP, Semangat, and IPF were themselves encumbered with internal problems. The latter two were wracked by defections to the BN. In 1995, the DAP also exited from the Gagasan Rakyat, claiming that continued membership in the coalition was being construed by its supporters as tacit support for the PAS's idea of an Islamic state. In the 1995 general election, these opposition parties competed under their own banners (Gomez 1996a).

Meanwhile, Semangat struggled to sustain support among the electorate, performing far less well in the 1995 polls than in the 1990 general elections. As Semangat's problems with the PAS in the Kelantan state government mounted, Razaleigh returned to UMNO in 1996. The ambitious Razaleigh was probably aware that he would be unable to make further political progress, let alone secure the premiership, from outside UMNO by seeking the co-operation of opposition parties professing disparate ideologies. Semangat had difficulty sustaining its membership, as many members, denied access to state rents, defected to UMNO. With the deep rifts within UMNO, by transferring Semangat's supposed 200,000 members to the party Razaleigh hoped to strengthen his own chances of making a political comeback within UMNO.

Since the smaller parties in the APU were dwarfed by PAS and since the Gagasan Rakyat depended primarily on Razaleigh's leadership to be seen as an effective alternative to the BN, both opposition coalitions are unlikely to sustain themselves and will probably disappear with Semangat.

The founding of the multiracial Gagasan Rakyat was the result of its component members knowing that they would be unable to broaden their support independently. Thus, the leaders of the DAP, professedly multiracial in outlook, found it imperative to work with the Malay-based Semangat and the Indian-based IPF, whose heads were former leaders of the BN, and with whom they differed greatly in terms of political orientation. Although the Gagasan Rakyat fared rather well in the 1990 general election, the disparate interests of its component parties, especially their leaders, eventually contributed to its collapse.

Economic governance

From 1957 until 1970, the average annual GDP growth rate in Peninsular Malaysia was 6.4 per cent, mainly due to export earnings from tin and rubber (Khor 1983). To enhance diversification, oil palm and cocoa production were encouraged, while import-substituting industrialization (ISI) was actively promoted. This attracted much foreign capital investment, although most foreign companies participating in ISI merely established subsidiaries for assembling, finishing, and packaging goods produced with imported materials. Furthermore, since the materials and technologies used were generally imported from parent companies abroad, they were poorly linked to the rest of the national economy.

Though wage rates in these capital-intensive industries rose, the industries tended to generate relatively little employment, thus not significantly reducing unemployment. Moreover, the size of the local market was limited by the level and distribution of income (Jomo 1990, 12). By the mid-1960s, many transnational corporations were beginning to relocate their more labor-intensive production processes abroad, often in East Asia or Latin America, to reduce production costs.

With the Free Trade Zone Act of 1971, the government also began to promote export-oriented industrialization (EOI). New industrial estates or export processing zones known as "free trade zones" were established to encourage investments from companies manufacturing for export. Within a decade, firms in these free trade zones came to dominate Malaysia's manufactured exports.

Despite relatively high economic growth and low inflation for over a decade after 1957, income inequalities increased and poverty remained widespread. Interethnic income differences were reduced slightly but intra-ethnic differences grew, especially among Malays. Government schemes to foster Malay capitalism had not been successful despite provisions for Malay quotas in the award of business licences and acquisition strategies to expand Malay ownership of corporate equity. Malay capital ownership stood at a scant 2.4 per cent in 1970. Most Malays were still employed in the peasant agriculture and public sectors.

In response to criticism, the government extended the work of public enterprises. There were only 22 such enterprises in 1960 and 109 by 1970. There was growing concern among the Chinese that these public enterprises would encroach into the economic sectors they controlled. This exacerbated popular discontent.

In the 1969 general election, the Alliance government recorded its worst-ever electoral performance. The Alliance was a consociational grouping of three principals: the United Malay National Organization (UMNO), the Malaysian Chinese Associates (MCA), and the Malaysian Indian Congress (MIC). The Alliance retained control over Parliament, but with a severely diminished majority. Communal tensions ran high as the results were perceived in some quarters as reflecting a diminution in UMNO's – and hence, Malay – political hegemony. This triggered off race riots on 13 May 1969.

Malaysian political economy, 1970–1990

The 1969 riots were partly ascribed to the inequitable distribution of wealth between Malays and Chinese. In consequence, in 1970, the government introduced the New Economic Policy (NEP), an ambitious twenty-year social engineering plan to achieve "national unity" by "eradicating poverty irrespective of race" and "restructuring society" to achieve interethnic economic parity between the Bumiputeras and the non-Bumiputeras.

This was to be attained by increasing Bumiputera corporate equity ownership to 30 per cent and by reducing the poverty level from over 50 per cent to 15 per cent by 1990. Many measures were taken to achieve these goals: improving access of the poor to training, capital, and land; changing education and employment patterns among Malays through scholarships and ethnic quotas favoring Malay entry into tertiary institutions; and requiring companies to restructure their corporate holdings to ensure at least 30 per cent Bumiputera ownership. Trust agencies, like the Permodalan National Bhd, or PNB (National Equity Corporation), were incorporated to accumulate wealth on behalf of the Bumiputeras. The government argued that greater interethnic economic parity would ensure stability and economic growth, but placated non-Bumiputera misgivings about the NEP by assuring them that since redistribution would be undertaken in a growing economy, no community would feel any sense of deprivation.

Public enterprises, the new engine of growth, were to participate much more in "modern-sector" activities such as finance, commerce, and industry, previously the exclusive domain of private enterprise. These new public enterprises included government-owned private or public limited companies, like property developer Peremba Bhd and food processor Food Industries of Malaysia Bhd, whose equity holdings were either fully or partially held by the government.

Between 1970 and 1990, the total number of enterprises owned by federal and state authorities grew considerably, from only 109 in 1970 to 1,014 by 1985 (Rugayah 1995, 66). Between 1970 and 1983, public-sector employment increased almost fourfold, from 139,467 to 521,818 (Mehmet 1986, 10). The expansion of the public sector was facilitated by a gradual shift to deficit financing and the fortuitous availability of oil exports off the east coast of the peninsula from the mid-1970s.

Inevitably, most public enterprises lacked a competitive, entrepreneurial ethos, which impeded profitability. They were heavily dependent on government funds and preferential access to business opportunities, while remaining immune from financial discipline and competitive market forces. Losses or low profits and wastage of investment resources increased the government's fiscal burden and slowed economic growth. For instance, in 1984 the Ministry of Public Enterprise could only report annual returns of 269 out of a total of 900 public enterprises; their accumulated losses came to RM 137.3 million (Supian 1988, 120–23).

While the government was able to absorb such costs during the 1970s when growth and revenues were high, this was no longer possible by the mid-1980s when the economy slipped into recession and official revenues fell. Falling oil prices between 1982 and 1986, the collapse of the tin market in 1985, as well as the declining prices of Malaysia's other major exports – rubber, cocoa, and palm oil – contributed to the economy registering an unprecedented negative 1 per cent growth rate in 1985. Capital flight increased as private investment continued to decline from the mid-1970s, and unemployment rose steadily when the government could no longer afford to raise public spending after 1982.

Heavy industrialization strategy

Another factor contributing to the economic malaise in the mid-1980s was the government's heavy industrialization strategy, actively promoted by Mahathir. In an attempt to diversify the industrial sector and to compensate for declining private investments with increased public investments, Mahathir launched his (import-substituting) heavy industrialization program in the face of widespread criticisms and protests, even from within his own Cabinet. Understandably, there was much reluctance on the part of private capitalists to make massive investments in heavy industries given the huge capital investments required, the long gestation periods involved, the lack of relevant technological expertise, and the expected heavy reliance on government protection and subsidies; with the NEP-inspired practice of "ethnic bypass," the government seemed reluctant to involve the Chinese in these projects (Jomo 1994).

Thus, the Heavy Industries Corporation of Malaysia (HICOM) was set up to pursue the heavy industrialization program by collaborating with foreign, mainly Japanese, companies to develop a variety of industries, ranging from steel and cement production to the manufacture of a national car. To finance these initiatives, the government resorted to massive borrowing from abroad, mainly from Japan (see Malaysia 1986, 1989).

Between 1980 and 1987, accumulated public-sector foreign debt grew from RM 4.9 billion to RM 28.5 billion. Including loans from domestic agencies, total public-sector borrowing increased from RM 26.5 billion in 1980 to RM 100.6 billion in 1986 (Jomo 1990, 186). By 1987, public enterprises accounted for more than a third of the public sector's outstanding debt, and more than 30 per cent of total debt servicing (Jomo 1990, 186).

The impact of the recession contributed to a turnaround in government policy. Influenced by neo-liberal Thatcherism and Reaganomics, Mahathir actively sought to liberalize the economy, promote privatization, augment support for the private sector, and increase investment incentives, even going so far as to relax some requirements of the NEP. To encourage foreign investment, the Investments Promotion Act was enacted, which provided generous tax holidays and pioneer status for periods of between five to ten years for investments in export-oriented manufacturing and agriculture as well as tourism. To promote domestic private investment, the government amended legislation on its stringent Bumiputera investment and employee exemption limits for licensing of manufacturing enterprises. Privatization was supposed to curb inefficiency, poor management, and weak financial discipline in the public sector.

Events abroad also helped the Malaysian economy. After the second Plaza Hotel meeting in 1985, the U.S. dollar began to depreciate heavily against major world currencies, particularly the Japanese yen. As the value of the currencies of most East Asian industrializing economies rose, raising comparative production costs in the process, the Malaysian ringgit declined, even against the U.S. dollar. This situation, coupled with the government's liberalization efforts, resulted in a resurgence of export-oriented manufacturing, largely under the auspices of foreign, especially East Asian, capital, which re-invigorated the economy. From 1986, the role and contribution of direct foreign investment (DFI) to gross domestic capital formation increased appreciably. Between 1986 and 1989, DFI increased almost fourfold from RM 1.262 billion to RM 4.518 billion, and then soared further to RM 11.200 billion in 1991 (Ghazali 1994, 42–43). With growth rates of over 8 per cent since 1988, by the mid-1990s virtually full employment had been achieved, social mobility had increased, and business opportunities had expanded.

With the incentives provided to promote EOI, the average annual growth rate of manufacturing output exceeded 10 per cent between 1970 and 1990. By 1980, manufacturing had become a major net foreign exchange earner, reducing dependence on primary exports. Manufacturing's share of Malaysia's GDP more than doubled from 13 per cent in 1970 to 30 per cent in 1993 (table 9.3).

As the NEP period came to an end, it appeared that its goals had been achieved, aided by the growth of the economy at an average of 6.9 per cent per annum between 1970 and 1990. By 1990, public-sector asset accumulation on behalf of Bumiputeras, government regulation of business opportunities and investments, and preferential policies for Bumiputera

Table 9.3 **Malaysia's gross domestic product by sector, 1960–1993** (per cent)

	1960	1970	1980	1990	1993
Agriculture	40	31	23	19	16
Mining	6	6	10	10	8
Manufacturing	9	13	20	27	30
Other	45	50	47	44	46

Source: Gomez and Jomo 1997, 20.

Table 9.4 **Ownership of share capital of Malaysian limited companies, 1970–1995**[1]
(per cent)

	1970	1990	1995
Bumiputera	2.4	19.3	20.6
Individuals and Institutions	1.6	14.2	18.6
Trust Agencies[2]	0.8	5.1	2.0
Non-Bumiputera	28.3	46.8	43.4
Chinese	27.2	45.5	40.9
Indians	1.1	1.0	1.5
Others		0.3	1.0
Nominee Companies	6.0	8.5	8.3
Foreigners	63.4	25.4	27.7

Sources: Malaysia 1976, 1996.
[1] Excludes shares held by federal, state, and local governments. Shares are taken at par value.
[2] Refers to shares held through trust agencies such as Pernas, PNB (National Equity Corporation), and the SEDCs.

businesses had all helped to augment Bumiputera equity in the corporate sector to 19.3 per cent, a remarkable increase despite being considerably short of the NEP's 30 per cent target. Of this 19.3 per cent, Bumiputera individuals held 14.2 per cent and government trust agencies the balance. The Chinese share of the corporate sector also rose, from 27.2 per cent in 1970 to 45.5 per cent in 1990 (table 9.4).

Poverty had also been cut down to a remarkable 17 per cent nation-wide, while the identification of race with economic function had also been largely reduced (table 9.5). The increasing number of Bumiputeras in middle-class occupations was particularly conspicuous.

Table 9.5 **Malaysian employment and occupation by ethnic group, 1995**
(per cent)

	Bumiputeras	Chinese	Indians	Others
Professional and technical	64.3	26.2	7.3	2.2
Teachers and nurses	72.3	20.5	6.6	0.6
Administrative and managerial	36.1	54.7	5.1	4.1
Clerical	57.2	34.4	7.7	0.7
Sales	36.2	51.9	6.5	5.4
Services	58.2	22.8	8.7	10.3
Agriculture	63.1	12.9	7.5	16.5
Production	44.8	35.0	10.3	9.9

Source: Malaysia 1996. *Seventh Malaysia Plan, 1996–2000.*

In spite of the rapid changes of the two NEP decades, some features of the economy persisted. For instance, although the NEP helped to develop a significant Malay middle class, Bumiputeras still dominate peasant agriculture and increased their domination of the public sector. Poverty is still widespread among Bumiputeras. Government attempts to redistribute ownership of corporate stock have been effective – several studies argue considerable underestimation of the actual Bumiputera share of corporate wealth – but wealth concentration has increased (see Jomo 1990; Gomez 1990, 1994; Gomez and Jomo, 1997). Income inequality and wealth differences among all communities have also increased. The Chinese continue to dominate wholesale and retail trade, despite considerable inroads by Bumiputeras (*Malaysian Business*, 16 January 1991). Indians have failed to achieve any significant increase in their share of corporate stock (table 9.4).

Bureaucrats and think tanks

The bureaucracy's influence over the state strengthened appreciably during the early 1970s, a development that was described by Esman (1972) as the rise of an "administrative state." The extent of the bureaucracy's influence over the state has, however, been qualified (see Puthucheary 1987; Zakaria 1987). Puthucheary (1987) noted that to presume that the bureaucracy's "role is so important as to make Malaysia an administrative state is to forget the strength of the ruling party which has been in power for twenty years and is likely to stay in power for some time." Another factor undermining the strength of the bureaucracy was fragmentation. Authority was distributed among competing agencies like the Malaysian Industrial Development Authority (MIDA), the State Economic Development Corporations (SEDCs), Petronas, the Ministry of Trade and Industry, and the Economic Planning Unit in the Prime Minister's Department. Although there were overlapping objectives and functions within these enterprises, there was little co-ordination among them.

The bureaucracy's influence was particularly checked after Mahathir's appointment as prime minister in 1981. It was he who began to centralize government decision-making in the Prime Minister's Department, pushing through economic initiatives with little consultation; by 1983, senior bureaucrats were reportedly concerned that "sound, practical advice is too often discouraged or ignored" (*Far Eastern Economic Review*, 16 June 1983). The establishment of numerous policy-oriented research institutions or "think tanks" in the 1980s was believed to be motivated by Mahathir's desire to undermine the bureaucracy's dominance over policy-making (Noda 1996, 408). The most prominent institutions, the

Institute of Strategic and International Studies (ISIS) and the Malaysian Institute of Economic Research (MIER), are conspicuous for their advisory role to the government. Led and staffed by foreign-educated intellectuals and former academics, the think tanks have emerged as alternative sources of technical and other competencies.

ISIS, led since its establishment in 1985 by Nordin Sopiee, a former newspaper editor with a doctorate from the London School of Economics, is reputedly one of the largest think tanks in Southeast Asia with around one hundred full-time research and support staff. ISIS contributes to policy on defence, security, and foreign affairs and is believed to have played a key role in developing the government's post-1990 economic plans, particularly Vision 2020. MIER was established in 1985 and has been led by former academics. It provides the government with economic analysis and planning, business surveys, and economic policy proposals (Noda 1996, 411–15).

UMNO's increasing hegemony over the state also progressively undermined the bureaucrats' dominance over policy implementation, especially its redistributive aspects. Executive dominance was evidenced by its ability to bend the bureaucracy to build vertical linkages with diverse groups among the Malay population. Peasant, fishermen, and business associations were often organized directly by bureaucratic agencies and became conduits for development funds and state largess to promote UMNO interests (see Shamsul 1986).

Given the increasing political exploitation of the state for vested interests, it was probably inevitable that by the early 1980s public-sector expansion under the NEP was generally deemed to have led to a bloated and inefficient bureaucracy, exacerbated by a scarcity of Bumiputera managerial expertise. Very little monitoring, let alone financial discipline, was exercised, especially when funds readily flowed in before the fiscal and debt crises of the mid-1980s.

Vision 2020

In 1991, the government outlined its long-term goals for Malaysia through its Vision 2020 statement and the National Development Policy (NDP); its emphasis was for Malaysia to achieve "fully developed country" status by the year 2020, primarily by accelerating industrialization, growth, and modernization.

Understandably, there has been some enthusiasm, especially on the part of non-Bumiputeras, for Vision 2020's explicit commitment to forging a Malaysian nation which transcends existing ethnic identities and loyalties, and for the statement's emphasis on the market rather than the public sector to encourage growth. Thus, while foreign investors continue to be courted, the government has also started to allow local Chinese capital more room to move. Chinese capital has also been encouraged by various other reforms, for example easier access to listing on the stock exchange and greater official encouragement of small and medium industries (SMIs). Local firms, especially large corporations, have been encouraged to invest overseas, where the scope for Malaysian government influence is even less; this has been perceived as a sign of good faith that the government is committed to reducing intervention.

However, whereas the NEP sought national unity in terms of improved interethnic relations to be realized by achieving interethnic economic parity, Vision 2020's "developed country" goal stresses economic growth. Other differences are more suggestive of the new approach and priorities. While the NEP envisaged progressive government intervention and a redistributive welfare role for the state, Vision 2020 has sought to shift primary responsibility for human welfare back to the family. With cuts in public expenditure, the costs of social services like education and health have been increasingly transferred to consumers in the form of higher university fees, payments for school amenities, hospital charges, and medicine fees.

Political outlook

Middle-class activism

Despite growing concentration of power in the executive arm of government, there is little evidence of much tension between the large multi-ethnic middle class that has emerged and the authoritarian state, or of growing demands for political liberalization among the Malay middle class. Rather, as the 1995 general election results indicated, the BN still enjoys a high degree of popular support, while much of the middle class believes that there has been commendable economic performance, as well as success in reducing poverty, raising real incomes, and diminishing wealth disparities among ethnic communities thanks to the existence of a strong state (see Gomez 1996a). Mahathir probably also invokes his regime's success in promoting economic growth to justify his authoritarian style of governance; he has stated that "nobody cares about human rights so long as you can register annual growth rates of 8.5 per cent" (Third World Resurgence, August 1993).

Moreover, there is still only limited interethnic co-operation among the middle class due to ethnic polarization; this has inhibited more effective middle-class mobilization. The bulk of the middle class seems quite materialistic and unlikely to face the avoidable risks of seeking reforms.

There is little evidence that the growing access of young Malaysians to higher education has led to a significant increase in democratic values and practices, as has been the case in other parts of East and Southeast Asia. This process is hampered by the rather repressive University and University Colleges Act, which forbids students from any form of unapproved (that is, non-government) political participation.

The limited reformist orientation of the middle class may also be due to the fact that the access of most Bumiputeras to higher education has been facilitated by state scholarships and ethnic quotas. Furthermore, much of the Bumiputera middle class either is still employed by the state or state-owned enterprises, or views UMNO as a stepping stone to upward social mobility; many still conceive of UMNO and the state as protectors of their interests, politically and economically.

Undoubtedly, liberalization policies, including privatization, which have entailed diminishing the role of the state in the economy, and the recent emphasis on private sector–led growth have been well received by the Chinese community, particularly its urban, middle class members. Although government patronage has persisted with privatization, inter-ethnic business co-operation has been enhanced between those Chinese capable of fulfilling contracts and those Malays who can secure them. Economically, Mahathir has realized the utility of mobilizing Chinese capital for his modernization drive. Politically, such development of interethnic economic co-operation has given him unprecedented electoral support from non-Bumiputeras, particularly urban middle-class Chinese (see Gomez 1996a).

In addition, non-Bumiputeras have gained from, and hence been appreciative of, the cultural liberalization measures instituted since the mid-1980s, especially the promotion of English language use. There has also been greater tolerance for non-Malay cultural expression, especially when politically expedient; Mahathir, for example, lifted long-standing restrictions on the lion dance, and liberalized travel restrictions to China just before the 1990 general election. Since Malaysian Chinese have historically been as concerned with maintaining their economic, educational, and cultural rights as their political rights (Lee 1987), the move by the government toward economic and cultural liberalization, though unaccompanied by greater political and civil liberties, has been politically expedient and attractive.

UMNO factionalism

The best prospects for democratic consolidation would seem to lie in growing UMNO factionalism. This has been stimulated by greater intra-ethnic problems among the Malays as evidenced in the UMNO split, which led to the formation of Semangat, as well as current developments. Already, Bumiputeras – primarily, but not exclusively, rural Malays – are assessing the BN government's performance in terms of not only economic growth but also its capacity to prevent or deal with social ills and maintain a more decent level of probity and transparency (see Gomez 1996a).

Some of the problems that have emerged among Malays appear to have to do with Mahathir's vision of development for Malaysia. His emphasis on creating a Bumiputera capitalist elite and on industrialized modernization is not consistent with the agrarian populist basis of UMNO. The Malay peasantry, long the backbone of UMNO, appears increasingly alienated from this vision (see Gomez 1996a). Mahathir's deputy, Anwar, has tried to project a more populist vision with his greater attention to such needs. Moreover, although there was some agreement among UMNO leaders over Mahathir's prescriptions to help revive the economy in recession, there now appears to be growing concern over the biases of the new policies. These different emphases of these two leaders are a reason for perceived differences between them – UMNO remains deeply factionalized. In these circumstances, and given the concentration of power in UMNO, if greater political liberalization is to emerge, it may depend primarily on machinations within the party.

The impact of such factionalism on the future of Malaysian politics is difficult to gauge. It is possible that if factionalism intensifies, another group may break away, which may lead to the establishment of another broad-based opposition coalition. Such an alternative may not be attractive given the experience of such breakaway factions in the opposition, as evidenced by the demise of Semangat. Other breakaway UMNO factions – including one led in 1951 by Onn Jaafar, UMNO's first president – have similarly failed to undermine UMNO. On the other hand, since the increasing difficulty of reaching compromises among factions may exacerbate instability in government, Mahathir may centralize even more power in his own hands. The frustrations of Anwar 's supporters in such circumstances may increase, especially since Mahathir continues to show no sign of relinquishing power. However, much will depend on their ability to persuade Anwar to take on Mahathir for the UMNO presidency – an unlikely scenario in the near future given how effectively Mahathir checked the possibility of such a challenge in 1995 and 1996.

There are a number of reasons why factions within UMNO may emerge as key players insisting on more transparency and accountability. First, the emergence of the new Malay middle and business classes with state patronage continues to contribute to friction over access to rent opportunities, which has led to intensified challenges for senior party posts. Some leaders even use the argument of the need for greater transparency to justify their decisions to contest party posts. During the 1996 UMNO election, Siti Zaharah Sulaiman successfully challenged the party's women's wing leader; she claimed that her decision to do so stemmed from her belief that the movement needed a clean and trustworthy head. The incumbent, Rafidah Aziz, had been embroiled in a scandal in which she allegedly abused her position as minister of international trade and industry to channel to her son-in-law RM 1.5 million worth of shares in a publicly listed company reserved for the Bumiputera community under the government's Bumiputera share allocation scheme (*Asiaweek*, 21 July 1996).

Second, the ambitions of those in the middle and business classes vying to climb the UMNO hierarchy may compel them to use their business influence, especially control over the media, to expose various types of transgressions, both moral and legal, to discredit their opponents. Already, there have been numerous exposés in the mainstream press of corruption and conflicts of interest involving UMNO leaders, particularly those not aligned with Anwar. The scandal involving Rafidah is believed to have been highlighted by the Anwar-controlled media. Rafidah retaliated by alleging similar allocations to family members of equity reserved by the government for Bumiputeras, on the part of Anwar, Mahathir, and other senior UMNO leaders and pro-Mahathir figures, including the former head of the judiciary. Rafidah's exposé revealed how UMNO leaders have been channelling state-controlled rents to themselves.

This series of events suggests that such UMNO factionalism may increase demands in UMNO for greater change, changes in the leadership, increased political participation, and more transparency and accountability. Some of those who feel marginalized believe that they can operate better on a more level playing field. Thus, they may desire to alter intra-ethnic allocation to enhance their access to state rents. In that case, in the event of an economic downturn, which may greatly reduce the rents that can be distributed, UMNO factionalism may be difficult to be contain.

The Malaysian case indicates that there is no simple causal link between development and democracy. Different levels of economic development do not necessarily explain why democracy has, or has not, developed as in other parts of East and Southeast Asia. Apparently, the continued institutional viability of ethno-populism has been a major impediment to democratization. However, given UMNO's hegemonic position, political and business rivalries among UMNO members may give rise to situations that may enhance democratization in Malaysia. The government may also have to concede some political liberalization in the interests of further economic growth and political stability.

REFERENCES

Alavi, Rokiah (1987), "The Phases of Industrialisation in Malaysia, 1957–1980s," M.A. thesis, University of East Anglia.

Brown, Robert (1994), *The State and Ethnic Politics in Southeast Asia*, Routledge, London.

CARPA (1988), *Tangled Web: Dissent, Deterrence and the 27th October 1987 Crackdown in Malaysia*, Committee against Repression in the Pacific and Asia, Sydney.

Chandra Muzaffar (1982), "The 1982 Malaysian General Election: An Analysis," *Contemporary Southeast Asia* 4(1), pp. 86–106.

Crouch, Harold (1996a), *Government and Society in Malaysia*, Cornell University Press, Ithaca, N.Y.

—— (1996b), "Malaysia: Do Elections Make a Difference?" in Robert H. Taylor (ed.), *The Politics of Elections in Southeast Asia*, Woodrow Wilson Center Press, Washington, D.C., and Cambridge University Press, Cambridge.

Diamond, Larry, Linz, Juan J., and Lipset, Seymour Martin (eds.) (1993), *Democracy in Developing Countries*, vol. 3, *Asia*, Lynne Rienner, Boulder, Colo.

Esman, M. J. (1972), *Administration and Development in Malaysia: Institution Building and Reform in a Plural Society*, Cornell University Press, Ithaca, N.Y.

Freeman, Michael (1996), "Human Rights, Democracy and 'Asian Values,'" *The Pacific Review* 9(3), pp. 352–66.

Goldman, Ralph M. (1993), "The Nominating Process: Factionalism as a Force for Democratization," in Gary D. Wekkin, Donald E. Whistler, Michael A. Kelly, and Michael A. Maggiotto (eds.), *Building Democracy in One-Party Systems: Theoretical Problems and Cross-National Experiences*, Praeger, Westport, Conn.

Gomez, Edmund Terence (1990), *Politics in Business: UMNO's Corporate Investments*, Forum, Kuala Lumpur.

—— (1991), *Money Politics in the Barisan Nasional*, Forum, Kuala Lumpur.

—— (1994), *Political Business: Corporate Involvement of Malaysian Political Parties*, Centre for East and Southeast Asian Studies, James Cook University of Northern Queensland, Townsville.

—— (1996a), *The 1995 Malaysian General Election: A Report and Commentary*, Institute of Southeast Asian Studies, Singapore.

—— (1996b), "Electoral Funding of General, State and Party Elections in Malaysia," *Journal of Contemporary Asia* 26(1), pp. 81–99.

Gomez, Edmund Terence, and Jomo K. S. (1997), *Malaysia's Political Economy: Politics, Patronage and Profits*, Cambridge University Press, Cambridge.

Ghazali Atan (1994), "Foreign Investment," in Jomo K. S. (ed.), *Malaysia's Economy in the Nineties*, Pelanduk Publications, Kuala Lumpur.

Haggard, Stephan and Kaufman, Robert F. (eds.) (1995), *The Political Economy of Democratic Transitions*, Princeton University Press, Princeton, N.J.

Huntington, Samuel P. (1991), *The Third Wave: Democratization in the Late Twentieth Century*, University of Oklahoma Press, Norman.

Jesudason, James (1996), "The Syncretic State and the Structuring of Oppositional Politics in Malaysia" in Garry Rodan (ed.), *Political Oppositions in Industrialising Asia*, Routledge, London.

Jomo K. S. (1990), *Growth and Structural Change in the Malaysian Economy*, Macmillan, London.

────── (1994), *U-Turn? Malaysian Economic Development Policies after 1990*, Centre for Southeast Asian Studies, James Cook University, Cairns.

────── (1996), "Elections' Janus Face: Limitations and Potential in Malaysia," in Robert H. Taylor (ed.), *The Politics of Elections in Southeast Asia*, Woodrow Wilson Center Press, Washington D.C., and Cambridge University Press, Cambridge.

Jomo K. S. and Todd, Patricia (1994), *Trade Unions and the State in Peninsular Malaysia*, Oxford University Press, Kuala Lumpur.

Khong Kim Hoong (1991), *Malaysia's General Election 1990: Continuity, Change, and Ethnic Politics*, Institute of Southeast Asian Studies, Singapore.

Khoo Boo Teik (1995), *Paradoxes of Mahathirism: An Intellectual Biography of Mahathir Mohamad*, Oxford University Press, Kuala Lumpur.

Khor Kok Peng (1983), *The Malaysian Economy: Structures and Dependence*, Maricans, Kuala Lumpur.

Lee, H. P. (1995), *Constitutional Conflicts in Contemporary Malaysia*, Oxford University Press, Kuala Lumpur.

Lee Kam Hing (1987), "Three Approaches in Peninsular Malaysian Chinese Politics: The MCA, the DAP and the Gerakan," in Zakaria Haji Ahmad (ed.), *Government and Politics in Malaysia*, Oxford University Press, Singapore.

Lijphart, Arend (1977), *Democracy in Plural Societies: A Comparative Exploration*, Yale University Press, New Haven, Conn.

Lim Kit Siang (1978), *Time Bombs in Malaysia*, Democratic Action Party, Kuala Lumpur.

Malaysia (1976), *Third Malaysia Plan, 1976–1980*, Government Printers, Kuala Lumpur.

────── (1986), *Fifth Malaysia Plan, 1986–1990*, Government Printers, Kuala Lumpur.

────── (1989), *Mid-Term Review of the Fifth Malaysia Plan, 1986–1990*, Government Printers, Kuala Lumpur.

────── (1991), *Sixth Malaysia Plan, 1991–1995*, Government Printers, Kuala Lumpur.

────── (1996), *Seventh Malaysia Plan, 1996–2000*, Government Printers, Kuala Lumpur.

Means, Gordon P. (1976), *Malaysian Politics*, Hodder & Stoughton, London.

Mehmet, Ozay (1986), *Development in Malaysia: Poverty, Wealth and Trusteeship*, Croom Helm, London.

Milne, R. S. (1986), "Malaysia – Beyond the New Economic Policy," *Asian Survey* 26(12), pp. 1366–82.

Munro-Kua, Anne (1996), *Authoritarian Populism in Malaysia*, Macmillan, London.

Noda Makito (1996), "Research Institutions in Malaysia," in Tadashi Yamamoto (ed.), *Emerging Civil Society in the Asia Pacific Community*, rev. ed., Institute of Southeast Asian Studies, Singapore, and Japan Center for International Exchange, Tokyo.

NSTP Research and Information Services (1994), *Elections in Malaysia: A Handbook of Facts and Figures on the Elections 1955–1990*, The New Straits Times Press, Kuala Lumpur.

Puthucheary, Mavis (1987), "The Administrative Elite," in Zakaria Haji Ahmad (ed.), *Government and Politics of Malaysia*, Oxford University Press, Singapore.

Rachagan, Sothi S. (1993), *Law and the Electoral Process in Malaysia*, University of Malaya Press, Kuala Lumpur.

Rueschemeyer, Dietrich, Stephens, Evelyne Huber, and Stephens, John D. (1992), *Capitalist Development and Democracy*, Polity Press, Cambridge.

Rugayah Mohamed (1995), "Public Enterprises," in Jomo K. S. (ed.), *Privatizing Malaysia: Rents, Rhetoric, Realities*, Westview Press, Boulder, Colo.

Sankaran, Ramanathan and Hamdan Adnan, Mohd. (1988), *Malaysia's 1986 General Election: The Urban-Rural Dichotomy*, Institute of Southeast Asian Studies, Singapore.

Shamsul, A. B. (1986), *From British to Bumiputera Rule: Local Politics and Rural Development in Peninsular Malaysia*, Institute of Southeast Asian Studies, Singapore.

———— (1988), "The Battle Royal: The UMNO Elections of 1987," *Southeast Asian Affairs 1988*, Institute of Southeast Asian Studies, Singapore.

Supian Haji Ali (1988), "Malaysia," in G. Edgren (ed.), *The Growing Sector: Studies of Public Sector Employment in Asia*, New Delhi, ILOARTEP.

Vasil, R. K. (1971), *Politics in a Plural Society: A Study of Non-Communal Political Parties in West Malaysia*, Oxford University Press, Kuala Lumpur.

Zakaria Haji Ahmad (1987), "Postscript," in Zakaria Haji Ahmad (ed.), *Government and Politics of Malaysia*, Oxford University Press, Singapore.

10

Indonesia

Andrew MacIntyre

This volume is concerned with the connections between the political frameworks of countries and their economic welfare, as measured by economic growth. In particular, it seeks to probe the impact of democratization on economic performance in a range of Asian countries where economic growth rates have generally been extraordinarily high. Rates of economic growth. The task of this chapter is to focus on the case of Indonesia. From one angle, Indonesia's inclusion is natural: it is a very important Asian country that has enjoyed average annual economic growth in excess of 7 per cent since 1970 – a record exceeded by only a very small number of other countries (all in Asia). From another angle, however, Indonesia's inclusion is somewhat problematic since it is neither democratic nor, apparently, on the verge of becoming democratic. And yet, I will argue, by adopting a strongly institutional focus we can still gain useful purchase on the underlying issues at stake here from an examination of Indonesia.

Careful analysis of the formal and informal rules governing electoral systems, political parties, the structure of government, and ultimately, the character of the overall policy-making process is relatively new in the study of politics for most countries in Asia. With the conspicuous exception of the literature on Japan, these political institutions have typically been overlooked in favour of questions such as the nature of state-society relations, class analysis, civil-military relations, patron-client relations, intra-elite factionalism, ethnic and religious politics, and so on. The reasons for these established preoccupations are not hard to grasp. None-theless, the field is ripe for change and this essay represents an initial step in that direction.

Overall, my concerns here are to explain how the key elements of Indonesia's so-called "New Order" political framework fit together, to examine their consequences for economic growth, and to consider some of the implications of democratization in Indonesia at some future time. I begin by focusing in particular on political parties and the electoral system, and then broaden the empirical scope in the second section to provide a complete account of the overall policy-making architecture by dealing with channels for interest representation and the structure of government. The third section draws upon various strands of the theo-retical literature on political and economic institutions to reflect upon the political foundations for economic growth. The final section offers some a priori reflections on the possible implications of democratization for economic policy-making and economic performance in Indonesia.

Political parties and the electoral system

Indonesia's party system is reasonably well institutionalized in the gen-eral sense that there is a set of established formal and informal rules that have been observed on a repeated basis for a quarter of a century. Moreover, although probably not universally accepted in Indonesia, the system is widely understood and is one which most actors have come to expect to prevail for the foreseeable future (Mainwaring and Scully 1995, 4). However, though it is well institutionalized by the standards of party systems elsewhere in the region, one could hardly describe the system as democratic. There is a very strong and systematic bias in the rules gov-erning parties and the electoral process which largely predetermines the outcome (Djiwandono & Legowo 1996; Kristiadi 1997; Siagian 1997; Sihbudi 1997). Six aspects of the party framework and electoral system require particular attention: entry and exit controls, public-sector sup-port, controls on party policy platforms, restrictions on organizational and campaign activities, unequal resourcing and media access, and a partisan electoral umpire.

Perhaps the most fundamental control is that of entry to and exit from the electoral arena. Primarily on the basis of official statute but periodi-cally with recourse to unofficial inducement and coercion as well, the government is able to determine whether a party may contest an election, whether an individual may stand for election as the representative of a party, and which individuals may serve as leaders of the parties. Since the early 1970s, only three parties have been permitted by law: the state political party, Golkar, and two small non-government parties, the Partai Persatuang Pembangunan (PPP – United Development Party) and the Partai Demokrasi Indonesia (PDI – Indonesian Democratic Party). It was not always thus. In the 1950s, during the period of parliamentary democracy, Indonesia had a highly fluid multi-party system, with nearly thirty parties being represented in the legislature. The number of parties began to decline following the country's swing to increasingly authoritarian politics when its first president, Sukarno, introduced what he termed "Guided Democracy" and proceeded to outlaw several parties opposed to his increasingly dictatorial style. This trend intensified under the next president, (former General) Suharto, who came to power in 1966 in the context of widespread political violence. With the strong support of the armed forces, Suharto purged the organized Left from the political landscape, and set about establishing a "New Order" in the late 1960s and early 1970s by building up the military-linked corporatist body, Golkar, into a dominant state political party and forcing the remaining ten parties to merge into two fractious amalgams.[1]

There are also formal exit controls on political parties. The president is legally empowered to dissolve any party not compatible with state goals (as defined by the president) or any party representing less than 25 per cent of the population. Comparable entry and exit controls apply to individuals wishing to stand as candidates for a party at election time. Under electoral laws, all candidates are subject to an approval process administered through the General Election Institute. This means that the government can readily prevent strong critics from entering the legislature, and can eliminate any incumbent legislator at the following election.[2]

Informally, the government has been able to exercise entry and exit controls on party leadership positions. Although there is often internal competition for party leadership posts, the government is able to ensure through a blend of subtle inducements and threats of blunter coercion that only individuals who are willing to accede to government wishes secure these posts. The eruption of turmoil within the PDI during 1995 and 1996 over Megawati Sukarnoputri's bid for the leadership represented a striking partial exception to this pattern. Megawati, the daughter of former president Sukarno, enjoyed a substantial mass following both inside and outside the PDI, and was viewed as a threat by the government. When normal suasion and coercion tactics failed to remove her from the party leadership, the government engineered a violent internal party takeover by those sections of the party willing to co-operate.

If entry and exit controls are one basic means by which the government manages the party system and the electoral process, a second centres on the strong formal and informal pressures that are brought to bear on public-sector employees – in the civil service, the state enterprise sector, and other public entities such as educational and health institutions – to support Golkar (Silaen 1997). All civil servants are automatically members of Korps Pegawai Negeri Republik Indonesia (Korpri – the Indonesian Civil Servants Corps), a corporatist institution that is linked directly with Golkar. In the early 1970s, all civil servants were further required to sign a letter committing their "monoloyalty" to Golkar, with those who declined being subject to dismissal (Ward 1974, 34). Subsequently, any civil servant seeking to become an official member of a political party has been required to obtain written permission from his or her supervisor (Santoso 1990, 102–3). The probability of being granted permission to join a party other than Golkar is, of course, very low. More generally, departmental heads, and the heads of state enterprises and other public-sector institutions, come under strong informal pressure to rally support for Golkar among their subordinates at election times. As one official who served as the head of a district office of the Ministry of Agriculture and, simultaneously, the head of the local Golkar chapter, candidly put it in the lead-up to the 1997 election: "Sometimes I have trouble telling the difference between my position as head of Golkar and my job as head of the agriculture department" (quoted in McBeth and Cohen 1997, 25)

This relates to a third important dimension of government control of the party system and electoral processes, namely legal restrictions on electoral campaign activities. In addition to being subject to prohibitions on various specific campaign tactics, since 1971 political parties have been prohibited from organizing at the village level in rural areas. This is of great significance because the bulk of the population still lives in rural villages rather than towns or cities. The restriction has provided a powerful advantage to Golkar since, even though it too may not set up party branches in villages, it is able to run de facto campaigns at this level because local officials such as the village head or the local police officer or representative of the armed forces are all civil servants responsible to the national government, and are thus almost certain to be Golkar members and subject to informal incentives to rally support for Golkar at election times.

A fourth control mechanism is the government's ability to heavily shape or constrain the policy platforms of the parties. Under law, all parties (along with all social organizations) must formally accept the official state ideology, *Pancasila*, as their sole ideological foundation.[3] This, together with controls on party personnel, serves to limit the public positions taken by the two non-government parties to little more than mild variations on the themes of Golkar. Moreover, even the public stance of Golkar has little specific policy content, and consists mainly of vague invocations of the importance of values such as "development" and "stability." The net effect of this is that there is little in the way of real ideological or policy differentiation among the parties; Golkar is loosely associated with authority and economic success, the PPP is linked with segments of the Islamic spectrum and perhaps a vague critique of corruption, and the PDI has come to be loosely identified with former president Sukarno and perhaps with a vague critique of authoritarianism and inequality (notwithstanding the fact Sukarno was himself authoritarian in his final decade in office). Consistent with the implied notion of something approaching ideological unanimity is the implied principle that the non-government parties are not "opposition parties," but rather amalgams of legislators representing different segments of society that work in partnership with the executive branch of government.

A further important variable is the systematically unequal resourcing and media access of the parties. All political parties receive public funding to support their operations. The non-government parties in particular depend heavily on this support to finance their campaign rallies. The PPP is able to raise modest financial support through the mosque and other Islamic institutions from devout members of the Muslim community (Liddle 1996, n. 16). Not surprisingly, businesses have little interest in giving money to parties that have no chance of winning elections, especially if they run the risk of angering the government by doing so. Where the PDI and PPP struggle for extra resources, Golkar is supported by secret off-budget public monies and large slush funds managed by shadowy social or charitable foundations that collect money from business groups with close ties to the government (MacIntyre forthcoming-a). In addition, of course, Golkar is able to draw upon the infrastructural resources of the entire state, from national-level institutions down through the provincial, district, and local levels of administration.

Paralleling the resourcing imbalance is the differential access to the media among the political parties. Television coverage has become much more important in recent years, as rising living standards have translated into more and more households owning television sets. It is estimated that TVRI, the state-owned broadcasting channel, now reaches around 65 per cent of the population (Cohen 1997). Special television programs during election campaigns are dedicated to the three parties, giving equal time to each. But these programs are highly formalistic, closely stage-managed, and probably of limited campaign value. More significant is the total coverage given to the parties in other programs, particularly news programs. According to one survey conducted from April to June in 1995, the state television channel, TVRI, reported on Golkar 98 times during its news programs, on PPP 10 times, and on PDI just twice. And although the recently launched private television stations are growing quickly, these licenses were awarded only to those associated with Golkar, including some of the children of President Suharto (Cohen 1997). Not surprisingly, these private channels offer little in the way of alternative news coverage to TVRI.

A final factor to be highlighted concerns the status of the body formally responsible for overseeing the election process and counting the vote, the General Election Institute. Far from being an independent statutory agency, the institute functions like any other branch of the executive government and is chaired by the minister for internal affairs, a Golkar member. The potential for cheating in the counting of the vote is considerable, and following every election there are complaints from the non-government parties about irregularities at some polling booths.[4] Nonetheless, Liddle (1996, 45) is probably correct to assert that with a few exceptions, there is little in the way of systematic cheating at the ballot box or in vote counting. The reason for suspecting this is, quite simply, that the whole party and electoral system is already so heavily biased in favour of Golkar that there is little need for crude last-minute mass cheating. Nevertheless, the potential for cheating is real. Ironically, perhaps the most glaring illustration of this came in the 1997 election, when the government intervened to help *boost* the PDI after it had been all but wiped out in the polls following the government's ouster of Megawati Sukarnoputri from the leadership of the party – which had caused many supporters to desert. The preliminary results from the election suggested that the PDI would fall below the threshold of 11 seats necessary for a party to function in the parliament. It was initially suggested that Golkar and the PPP each give a seat to the PDI to help it out; but the PPP refused to co-operate. Unable to find any other means to extricate itself from the massive overkill problem the government had created, the General Election Institute apparently "found" an additional 60,000 votes, which served to lift the PDI above the threshold (Reuter, Jakarta, 22 June 1997).

To summarize, the argument thus far is that although Indonesia does indeed have an institutionalized party system and electoral process in which contests are held every five years, in which three political parties compete vigorously for voter support, and in which there is relatively little gross ballot rigging or fraudulent counting, for reasons inherent to the nature of the system, it is a far cry from meaningful democracy. The party system and electoral process are extensively managed and tilted very heavily in favour of Golkar. As table 10.1 shows, Golkar has swept every election for more than three decades by a comfortably large margin – indeed, an embarrassingly large margin in the most recent election.

This is not to say that the electoral process is utterly devoid of meaning or political significance. After all, the government would be unlikely to go to such great lengths and costs to manage the process if it was unimportant. As Liddle (1996) puts it, elections in Indonesia are a "useful

Table 10.1 **Indonesian General Election Results, 1971–1997**
(per cent)

	GOLKAR		PPP		PDI	
	Seats[1]	Votes	Seats[1]	Votes	Seats[1]	Votes
1971[2]	66	59	27	26	8	9
1977[2]	64	56	28	27	8	8
1982	60	64	24	28	6	8
1987	75	73	15	16	10	11
1992	70	68	16	17	14	15
1997	76	75	21	22	3	3

Source: General Election Institute.

[1] Refers to percentage of seats in the House of Representatives set aside for elected representatives, excluding representatives appointed from the armed forces.

[2] Percentages of votes do not sum to 100.

fiction" which helps to legitimate the regime and provide scope for mass participation, albeit heavily stage-managed. Moreover, as will be argued below, in view of the institutional structure of government in Indonesia, the electoral process has little direct bearing on control of the executive branch of government.

The policy-making framework: Interest representation and governmental structure

In democratic political systems, parties play a crucial role: they provide the institutional link between voters and the machinery of government. As part of the process of competing for voter support, parties aggregate public interests and campaign on the basis of contending packages of policy proposals. In Indonesia there is indeed competition between parties, and voters are for the most part free to cast their ballots as they please; the difference is that the electoral process has little effect on government policies. This is a pattern typical of many countries in which elections take place within a more or less authoritarian framework (Hermet 1978).

That the PPP or the PDI have little impact on the policy-making process should be evident from the previous section; they have little independent political life or policy agenda, attract little support from either business or labour, and never attract more than a modest share of the vote. More remarkable is the fact that even Golkar is not a major player in the policy process. Golkar is neither a significant generator of ideas or policy preferences nor, more fundamentally, a locus of power in the

Indonesian political system. None of the most important players in Indo-nesian politics built their careers inside Golkar; while they might occupy positions within Golkar (for instance, Suharto is the head of the party's Board of Advisors) their power derives from other posts they occupy.

Golkar is the capstone of a vast network of corporatist bodies than spans the spectrum of economic and social sectors (Reeve 1985; MacIntyre 1994b). But like the political parties themselves, corporatist interest associations in Indonesia operate within a state-dominated framework. The extent to which the state intervenes in the operations of these inter-est associations varies, with the labour movement being subject to tight control. While enjoying more operational autonomy, the national Cham-ber of Commerce and Industry (KADIN) is nonetheless a lame organi-zation which plays little role as an advocate of business interests in the policy process. Although in some industries we have seen more indepen-dent and policy-oriented business associations emerge, for the most part associations across the business sector are politically inert. Indeed, in general the myriad corporatist interest associations operate primarily as institutional mechanisms for political containment rather than as institu-tions for aggregating sectoral interests and injecting these interests into the policy-making process (MacIntyre 1991, 1994c).

The point to be emphasized here is that both the party system and the associated network of corporatist interest associations serve to limit demand-making upon the state by societal groups. Put differently, they insulate the bureaucracy from collective action and broader mass political pressures. The net effect of these institutional barriers is to concentrate influence over the policy process within the structures of the state, and as will be seen, within the state power is further concentrated in the upper realms of the executive branch – particularly around the presidency.

Under the terms of Indonesia's Constitution and its various supple-mentary legal statutes, Indonesia has a highly centralized structure of government. Although the legislature, the House of Representatives, has the right to initiate legislation and must approve all legislation (including the budget), in practice it is a tame institution. It has not initiated a single bill in three decades nor has it vetoed a bill proposed by the president. Elected members of the legislature are supposedly accountable to voters, but we have already seen that the formal and informal rules covering political parties and elections give the government great control over politicians. In a very real sense then, legislators are as accountable to the executive as they are to voters. Added to this is the fact that 20 per cent of the House of Representative comes from the armed forces and is directly appointed by the president.[5]

For present purposes, the important point here is that that although there is a constitutional separation of powers between the presidency and the legislature which is supposed to provide for checking and balancing, in practice the legislature has not functioned as an independent veto gate in the legislative process as the balance of formal and informal powers is massively tilted in favour of the presidency. In addition to formal legislative arrangements, the president has very wide-ranging decree powers. Indeed, the great majority of executive action in Indonesia results not from laws ratified by the legislature, but simply from decrees issued by the president (or one of his subordinates). Between 1973–74 and 1989–90, legislation produced by the parliament constituted a bare 8 per cent of the major legal acts introduced at the national level of government (Rohdewohld 1995, 18).

Like the legislature, the judiciary also provides little check on the conduct of executive government. The Supreme Court is not empowered to review legislation. In principle decrees issued by ministers or lower officials are subject to review, though presidential decrees appear to be immune from this possibility.[6] In practice, however, the possibility of judicial review of even lower-level statutes is remote because the judiciary is wholly subordinated to the executive. The president appoints and removes justices without the need for legislative approval, and has typically appointed (legally trained) former members of the armed forces to the position of chief justice. Further, all justices are official classed as civil servants (and are thus technically members of Korpri).

If the executive is not checked or balanced by either the legislature or the judiciary, what constrains its behaviour? Constitutionally, the president is accountable not to voters at large, but to the 1,000-member People's Consultative Assembly (see figure 10.1 below). The Consultative Assembly meets once every five years and functions both as an electoral college in choosing a president and a vice-president, and to some extent as a "super-parliament" in setting (very) broad normative guidelines for state policy for the next five-year period. The Consultative Assembly is the highest state institution and has the sole authority to appoint and dismiss the president.[7] However, here again the lines of accountability are ambiguous for although it is the assembly that appoints the president, the president appoints more than half the members of the assembly! Five hundred of the Assembly's members come from the House of Representatives (including its 20 per cent membership from the armed forces) and the remaining 500 are appointed to represent the nation's regions, and its functional and social groups.[8] Thus, the president directly appoints 60 per cent of the body that appoints him, and the bulk of the remaining 40 per cent comes from his own party. At five-yearly intervals for the last several decades the assembly has had only one name placed before it and each time has unanimously endorsed the choice of Suharto.

Not surprisingly perhaps, the assembly is widely dismissed as being little more than a rubber stamp, since the president appoints most of the people who then appoint him and has very substantial influence over the behaviour of those whom he does not officially appoint. In short, the president is usually viewed as having very weak lines of accountability to the assembly.[9] More meaningful constraints on the president perhaps come from the informal but very real requirements that he maintain the support (or at least acquiescence to his continued rule) of the armed forces and, ultimately, the population at large. Even true dictators cannot survive in the face of sustained and widespread violent public protest, or focused opposition from within the upper echelons of the armed forces. However, both of these political constraints rely on extra-constitutional and probably very violent action.

Finally, it is important to consider the president's very wide-ranging and absolute powers of appointment. Without the need for confirmation from the legislature, he can hire and fire at will Cabinet members, all senior bureaucrats, all senior military commanders, all senior judges, and all senior state enterprise managers. Unambiguously then, within the executive branch all accountability lines trace back to the president. Not only is this power critical to Suharto's maintenance of authority over the armed forces, but of greater interest for present purposes are its implications for economic policy-making. Unlike in the U.S. presidential system, there is no issue of the loyalty of bureaucrats being divided between the presidency and the legislature.

To summarize, the preceding discussion has highlighted a number of features of the institutional framework of Indonesian politics. First, both the party system and the corporatist system of interest associations serve primarily to limit and contain group- or mass-based interest representation. Second, although there is a nominal constitutional separation of powers, in practice neither the legislature nor the judiciary constitutes a veto gate in the policy process. Third, the electoral college to which the president is formally accountable, the Consultative Assembly, has in fact constituted only a very weak constraint on presidential behaviour. And fourth, by contrast, the president enjoys very clear lines of authority over his agents in the executive branch: bureaucrats, military officers, and state enterprise personnel.

Understanding who is accountable to whom for their jobs (or, in the language of collective action theory, agency relationships) provides vital information about the distribution of power among different actors and institutions within a political system. Figure 10.1 condenses much of this information in simplified schematic form. It shows the presidency at the centre of the polity, and subject to no strong accountability relationship. The Consultative Assembly is depicted as exercising only nominal authority over the president, whereas the president has clear authority over

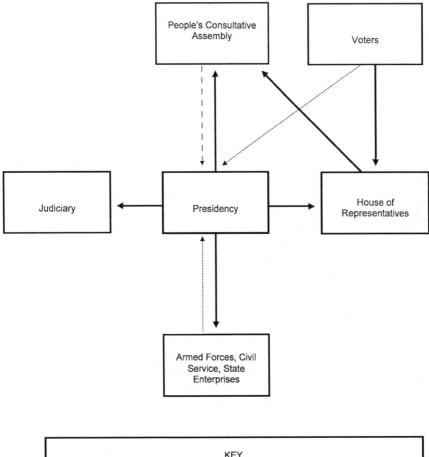

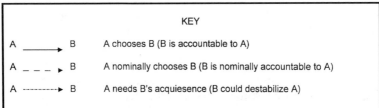

Figure 10.1 **Accountability and delegation relationships in Indonesia**

it (by virtue of his appointing 60 per cent of its membership, with the remainder coming from the House). The figure does indicate, however, that to survive the president needs to maintain acquiescence to his rule on the part of the armed forces (and other civil servants) as well as, ultimately, the public. By contrast, the judiciary, executive branch employees, and even members of the legislature (both elected and appointed) have quite clear accountability relationships to the president.

Political institutions and economic outcomes

In the two preceding sections, we have examined the nature of the party and electoral system, as well as the framework of interest representation and the structure of government. In this section we seek to link these institutional factors to economic outcomes. In so doing, we are operating on the basis of an assumption that national economic policy settings have an important bearing on aggregate economic outcomes: that is, that government policy is a large part of the explanation of a country's economic growth rate.

Within the broad institutionalist literature pertaining to political economy, two separate but strong theoretical currents stand out. Reduced to their essence, one focuses on what might be termed decisiveness, and the other on what might be termed commitment. Both have important consequences for economic policy-making and economic performance.

The former body of literature is concerned with the extent to which political institutions promote qualities such as efficiency in policy-making and implementation or the ability to make and carry out difficult policy decisions that are necessary to maintain an environment conducive to economic growth. The literature concerned with state "autonomy," "capacity," and "strength" falls into this category (see, *inter alia*, Katzenstein 1978; Johnson 1982; Deyo 1987; Wade 1990; Haggard 1990; MacIntyre 1994a). This macro-institutionalist literature all relates directly to the experiences of the high-growth economies of Asia. A logically parallel body of literature has been concerned with the efficiency of political institutions in advanced industrial democracies, but rather than being pitched at a macro level (the state) it has focused on the consequences of variables such as the division of governmental powers, the type of electoral system, and bureaucratic delegation for policy-making (see, *inter alia*, Weaver and Rockman 1993; Cox 1987; Cox 1997; Moe and Caldwell 1994; Kiewiet and McCubbins 1991; Shugart and Carey 1992) Typically, the political economy implications of the institutional framework have not been the primary concern of this literature, though recently this has begun to change (Haggard and McCubbins forthcoming).

Uniting this diverse literature is its attention, on the one hand to the way in which institutional design can facilitate or hinder decisiveness in the policy process, and on the other, to the way in which decisiveness can facilitate economic policy management. For instance, a polity in which there is a separation of powers between the executive, legislative, and judicial branches, in which the legislature is separated into two houses, in which the electoral system encourages either weak party identification on the part of legislators or perhaps multi-partyism, in which bureaucrats are accountable to both the executive and legislative branches, and in which subnational regional governments have significant economic powers, is likely to respond much less rapidly and decisively to an economic policy problem than one in which veto points are fewer and authority is more concentrated.

By contrast, the literature I have characterized as dealing with commitment has had almost the opposite preoccupation. Instead of seeing executive autonomy and institutionally rooted decisiveness in policy-making as a boon, this second approach views it as a problem. A number of influential studies have argued that it was firm institutional constraints on leaders which were critical in solidifying property rights and thus permitting the expansion of investment and growth in Europe (North 1981, North and Weingast 1989; Weingast 1995; Root 1989), in Asia (Root 1996; Montinola, Qian, and Weingast 1995), and, cross-nationally, in the telecommunications sector (Levy and Spiller 1996).

Precisely the same institutional conditions which permit a leader to take difficult but economically necessary decisions, can just as readily permit a leader to take arbitrary, capricious, and even predatory decisions which undermine the property rights of investors, and thus by extension, investor confidence and economic growth. If leaders are subject to little or no institutional constraint by the political framework, investors cannot be confident that the policy environment will not change quickly in ways which erode or eliminate their profits. In this view, what is needed above all else for robust economic growth to emerge is that private investors should feel confident that the policy commitments leaders make are credible, and this is only possible if leaders are subject to institutional constraints which remove the possibility of arbitrariness. In short, political autonomy is viewed as the enemy of long-term investor confidence and thus economic growth.

The arguments pertaining to both decisiveness and commitment are based on powerful logic and substantial empirical evidence. And yet, clearly, there is a tension between the two – even if it is a tension that is seldom discussed. It is useful to think of there being a trade-off between decisiveness and commitment: both conditions carry important benefits for economic governance, but an excess of one can also be highly prejudicial to growth. How should we interpret the Indonesian case in light of these considerations?

It should be immediately apparent from the earlier discussion that Indonesia's party and electoral systems, its framework for interest representation, and its constitutional structure all combine to produce a very

high level of decisiveness. The party and electoral systems, the corporatist framework, and ultimately, the existence of a potent coercive capability in the armed forces has served to reduce greatly the scope for
organized demand-making by societal groups. In practice there is only a
weak division of governmental powers, with the executive branch thoroughly dominating the legislature and the judiciary. Lines of executive
accountability are very clear, with bureaucrats being responsible only to
the presidency. And the presidency itself is only weakly accountable to
the Consultative Assembly.

This has meant that the president and his ministers have not had to
bargain with any other branch of government over economic policy; that
the bureaucracy has (relatively speaking) been a compliant administrative tool; and that there has been little real scope for public resistance to
government action. As a result, when economic challenges or crises have
arisen, the government has been able to move swiftly, take difficult and
unpopular policy decisions, and implement them. There is no need to reproduce the history of the New Order's successfully overcoming the economic chaos of, for instance, the late 1960s, or the sharp downturn of the
mid-1980s arising from the collapse of international commodity prices;
that story has been told already in many places (Hill 1996; Booth 1992;
Battacharya and Pangestu 1993; Woo, Glassburner, and Nasution 1994;
Azis 1994; MacIntyre 1992). Suffice it to say that the relative autonomy of
the political executive and the decisiveness of the policy process have
greatly facilitated the task of maintaining a generally sound macroeconomic framework as well as liberalizing trade, investment, and financial regulations when this became necessary.

This much is not surprising. But what of commitments? How has Indonesia managed to sustain investor confidence if the political authority
has been so centralized, so unconstrained? As figure 10.2 shows, levels of
private investment in Indonesia have indeed been high, indicating that
uncertainty about commitments from unconstrained government has not
been a major deterrent to investors. Even if we allow a very substantial
discount for expectations of high rates of return, it seems likely that there
is still a residual puzzle to be explained. I have argued elsewhere that the
explanation for this lies on the one hand with the government's long-
established track record of sound macroeconomic management, and on
the other, with specific policy measures (most notably an open capital
account since 1970) which, in effect, constituted an unbreakable commitment on the part of the government to that most fundamental investors'
interest – the ability to get money out of the country at will (MacIntyre
forthcoming-b).

In sum, although the predominant institutional characteristic of the
Indonesian case is, without question, decisiveness, it is important to rec-

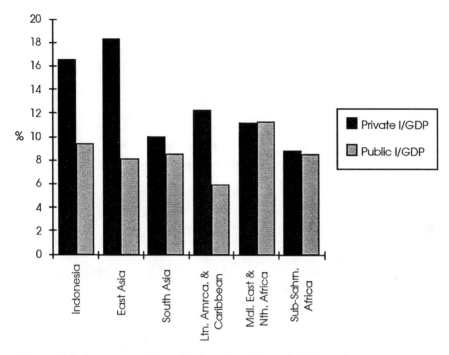

Figure 10.2 **Average public and private investment in Indonesia as a percentage of GDP, 1980–1994** (Source: Jaspersen, Aylward, and Sumlinski 1995)

ognize that there have also been factors providing a significant counter-vailing effect. That is to say, while decisiveness has been the predominant feature, this has not been to the complete exclusion of commitment. The net effect has been a policy environment sufficiently flexible to respond to exogenous economic shocks when necessary, and sufficiently stable to provide longer-term confidence for investors.

For many years this combination has proved very conducive to economic growth. And yet this unusually long-lived framework for success has, from the outset, been vulnerable to change. This has been powerfully and dramatically illustrated by the collapse in value of the Indonesian rupiah in 1997 as part of the wider Asian currency crisis, and the economic destruction this has unleashed. In the early months of the crisis Indonesia fared relatively well, with the government moving quickly to take decisive pre-emptive measures, before calling in the IMF once it became clear that the scale of the crisis was such that Indonesia could not manage it alone. However, because Indonesia's institutional framework concentrates so much authority in the office of the president, when he was reluctant to cut back on the business privileges enjoyed by relatives and close associates as currency markets seemed to demand, and even more so when he became seriously ill, the policy process became frozen. As doubts about Suharto's willingness to take decisions painful to his family businesses and doubts about his health were added to long-standing uncertainty about the process of political succession in Indonesia, the confidence of foreign and local investors (together with that of Indonesians at large) quickly evaporated. Like other countries in the region hit hard by the currency crisis, Indonesia cannot now escape several years of economic hardship. For our purposes, though, the key issue is whether the policy environment the government produces is conducive to making a swift recovery.

At the time of writing, it is too early tell how this economic crisis will play through in Indonesia. Nonetheless, it neatly illustrates the trade-off between decisiveness and commitment. It was the extreme centralization of power – the decisiveness of the system – which enabled Suharto in early 1998 to announce (under pressure from the IMF and the country's parlous economic condition) a truly stunning package of economic reforms which promises to radically hack back the worst crony business privileges, to give the central bank operational autonomy, and to radically reduce off-budget fiscal activity. However, the very centralization of the system which makes it so decisive also leaves it vulnerable to commitment problems: will Suharto in fact implement the reforms he has promised? how much longer will he survive? what will be the mechanism for political succession? In a system so centralized, much rides on whether investors continue to trust the president's ability to provide economic leadership.

Indonesia has been very lucky that three decades of authoritarian politics have been accompanied by remarkably good and sustained economic progress. Unfortunately, this is not true of most developing countries with highly centralized political systems. Regardless of whether Suharto is able to salvage his reputation for effective economic leadership, it remains the case that the existing framework in Indonesia is very fragile because it is so sensitive to the behaviour of the occupant of the presidency. Even if it is not brought down by the political ramifications of the current economic crisis, the institutional framework Suharto has built up cannot have a long shelf-life.

Democratization and economic growth

One of the essential themes of this volume is the impact of democratization upon economic growth in Asia. When considering this question in the context of Indonesia the obvious complication we immediately confront is that it is not democratic. And yet sooner or later the nascent pressures for democratic change in Indonesia are likely to produce results.[10] Inevitably, decades of sustained rapid industrial change have economic, social, and ultimately political consequences.

This is not the place for an extended discussion of the causes and dynamics of democratization. Nor will it be particularly fruitful to try to speculate on the timing or form of democratization in Indonesia, for the possibilities are myriad. But it does seem reasonable to assume that at some not too distant point, Indonesia will have a much more democratic framework of government in place. Can we say anything about the implications of such a political transformation for the country's economic growth prospects?

While we cannot know what precise constitutional form democratic government in Indonesia might take, if a presidency is retained we can be reasonably sure that it will be much more strongly accountable than at present, and that the fundamental line of accountability will be directly to voters. We can also be reasonably confident that a more effective separation of powers between the executive and legislative branches of government will emerge as electoral rules are modified to provide for more independent political parties and an unorchestrated electoral process. (Indeed, even under the existing constitutional framework, the legislature would become important if electoral and party rules were freed up.) While there are many possible variants on this theme, these fundamental changes would be inherent in any democratic form of presidential government.[11]

What would changes to the institutional framework of this magnitude mean for the pattern of economic policy making, and thus the likely economic growth trajectory? Or, couched in a somewhat more tractable form: what would such changes mean for the trade-off we have postulated between decisiveness and commitment?

If democratization in Indonesia proves to be a relatively smooth process, that is, if it does not lead to fundamental fragmentation and conflict along ethnic, religious, or regional fault lines,[12] we can reasonably expect that over time commitment will become a stronger feature of the policy-making framework. As the executive branch becomes more democratically accountable it will become more constrained by the need to satisfy the preferences of median voters. This will reduce the likelihood of rapid swings in policy orientation. And as the executive is forced to share control of the policy-making process with the legislature and perhaps the judiciary, this effect will be intensified because policy change of any sort (that entails legislation) will become more difficult as the number of veto points in the system increases. As change becomes more difficult, government policies gain credibility; they become more meaningful commitments because it becomes increasingly difficult for the government to reverse itself should it so wish. Relatedly, as the legal system becomes more independent, commercial contracts become more meaningful and there may be options for legal redress against the government itself. In short, all of these developments would tend to produce changes to the policy process which the stream of the institutionalist literature concerned with commitments would regard as highly beneficial to long-term economic growth prospects. Investors could be increasingly confident about the security of their capital and the impact of the policy environment on business conditions, because these would be less uncertain.

But what of decisiveness? Might not democratization produce an institutional framework which so prejudices commitment over decisiveness that policy-making becomes paralyzed? Legislative gridlock is certainly a possibility, and within Southeast Asia, one needs only to look at the experiences of Thailand under the successive governments of Chuan, Banharn, and Chavalit to see a striking illustration how some democratic institutional configurations can be so inimical to decisiveness as to cripple economic management.[13] A much less extreme example of the effects of democratization on economic policy-making is provided by Mexico, where for the first time, governments are now having to bargain with the legislature over the budget.

Whether or not economic management in Indonesia would suffer a crippling reduction in decisiveness will depend very heavily on the precise institutional arrangements that emerge in the process of democratization. As Cox and McCubbins (forthcoming) demonstrate, decisiveness in a democratic polity depends heavily on the precise combination of institutional features that pertain, notably whether or not the constitutional structure is presidential, is bicameral, is federal, and has judicial review; and whether party and electoral rules promote many or few parties, and cohesive or atomistic parties. Shugart and Carey (1992) and Haggard and Shugart (forthcoming) focus more specifically on presidential systems, extending this logic to show how specific institutional features affect the policy process and policy outcomes. In short, there is wide variation in the extent to which democratic frameworks promote or inhibit decisiveness, and the specific institutional features in each case have a critical bearing upon this. In principle, it is possible to specify the likely effect of different institutional arrangements, but such an exercise would be more than a little artificial for Indonesia given the current political realities.

Sooner or later Indonesia is likely to democratize. The political framework that emerges from this process may well be presidential in form, but if so, it will be configured in ways that differ fundamentally from the status quo. These institutional changes will have important consequences. As far as the country's economy is concerned, the most important effect will be on how the polity is repositioned in terms of the trade-off between decisiveness and commitment. No less naive (and dangerous) than the claim that Indonesia's economic well-being will be jeopardized by democracy is the opposite claim; that Indonesia's economic well-being will necessarily be advanced by democratization. Democratic political systems vary greatly, and it is thus to the key institutional features that we will need to direct our attention when change gets under way.

Postscript

This chapter was completed in early January 1998. In the five months since then much has happened in Indonesia: Suharto's New Order regime has collapsed, amidst turmoil a process of political reform is underway, and the country's economy has been utterly devastated. Happily, the analysis in the body of the essay has stood up well. This short postscript is intended to review briefly the main developments over the past five months and to reflect on where this may lead.

Suharto resigned the presidency on 21 May as it became clear that one after another of his key supporters was abandoning him. The proximate causes of this were large-scale student demonstrations (including student occupation of the parliament) and, more destructively, an orgy of mob rioting and looting which left parts of Jakarta in smoking ruins. Behind these events, however, lay the collapse of the country's economy and with it the evaporation of any remaining legitimacy the regime enjoyed. And behind these developments lay the institutional framework of the regime. Although Indonesia's (and Asia's) economic crisis was ignited by events in Thailand and fuelled by a number of economic policy problems, the extraordinary degree of damage that has descended upon Indonesia's economy is largely a function of the way in which the government managed the crisis from late 1997 onwards, and this in turn, reflected the institutional trade-off between decisiveness and commitment. Following the initial depreciation of the rupiah in mid-1997, it plummeted to economically devastating levels in late 1997 and through 1998 because local and foreign investors lost confidence in the government. In essence, investors believed that the president was no longer sufficiently committed to maintaining the sort of policy framework necessary to promote profitability. Confidence in his leadership was undermined first by the stroke he suffered in early December, and then by mounting concern that he was not committed to implementing reform measures agreed upon with the IMF as members of his family and other close business associates succeeding in exempting themselves from austerity measures. These fears were reinforced in early 1998 by a budget which was seen to be out of touch with economic realities, and by ensuing presidential manouvers which appeared extraordinarily capricious (e.g., the nomination of B. J. Habibie as vice-president and the flirtation with the idea of a currency board). In a political system so highly centralized – a system which so prioritized decisiveness – there were no institutional checks on the president. Thus, if the president was not willing to implement reform measures, there was ultimately no means of constraining him to do so, short of removing him from office. Once local and foreign investors abandoned Indonesia – and this was clearly the case by mid- to late January – it was simply a matter of time before the resulting pressures forced political change.

In the wake of Suharto's fall, Vice-President Habibie succeeded him as president, as provided for by the Constitution. Few expected Habibie to survive, though he has done so now for a month, largely because in the circumstances he has proved an acceptable transition figure who has responded successfully (even if opportunistically) to demands for reform. Having freed the press, labour unions, and a number of political prisoners, and having committed to a process of constitutional reform and a timetable for fresh elections, Habibie has set in motion processes which may yield major political change. Whether he is able to survive these processes of change himself remains to be seen.

Although the process of democratic reform in Indonesia will be multi-faceted, one of its most important aspects will be changes to the institutional framework, that is, the Constitution and related political laws. Habibie has appointed a small but capable political reform commission (comprising academics, bureaucrats, and a military officer) which is to report back to him within a short time frame. He has then committed to submit recommendations for reform to the House of Representatives and the People's Consultative Assembly. Although there are certainly some popular demands for far-reaching democratization, to date the focus of discussion appears to be limited to modifying laws controlling and restricting political parties, modifying the closed-list proportional representation electoral system, and possibly modifying the selection process of the president (through a reduction in the number of appointees to the Peoples' Assembly, which would give the political parties in the House of Representatives a much louder voice in the choice of the president).[14]

The main concern in debates about constitutional reform thus far has been to bring about real democratic change while at the same time ensuring that Indonesia does not return to the volatile multi-party chaos of the 1950s. In this respect, the electoral laws will be very important. Another remarkable feature of the reform process is that, thus far at least, there has been no serious discussion within the political elite about either eliminating armed forces representation in the House or, more importantly, moving toward a system of direct presidential elections. This no doubt reflects the fact that it is the state elite which is dominating the redesign process.

It will be some months before the outcome of the process of political reform becomes clearer. Further, it is no doubt very likely that this will be only the first step in a longer process of democratization which is likely to stretch over a decade or more, reflecting long-term processes of socio-economic change. In the near term, however, a critical factor bearing upon the success of this first round of democratization will be the country's economic fate. Indonesia has suffered a truly devastating economic setback. The most optimistic scenarios now suggest that it will be three to five years before the economy again finds its feet. Quite apart from the governance consequences of the new configuration of political institutions to emerge from the current reform process, and quite apart from the coalitional character of the government that Habibie (or a successor) constructs, investors are likely to be very wary of the risk of further political instability in Indonesia. The longer it takes for Indonesia's political framework to stabilize, the further off economic recovery will be. Compounding this problem is the fact that Indonesia's economic fortunes are now also seriously constrained by developments elsewhere in Asia – most notably Japan. The danger for democracy in Indonesia is that the longer the country's economy remains depressed, the more social and political instability is likely to result, and thus the greater the probability of some form of military coup in the name of restoring order and progress. This seems a quite remote prospect at the time of writing, but if the economy continues to slide the political landscape is likely to deteriorate with it.

Indonesia has now entered a period of major political flux, the outcome of which is as yet far from clear. Our understanding of the pattern of governance and economic performance under the New Order regime and of the collapse of this regime has been powerfully aided by an analytical focus on the underlying political institutions. Similarly, a careful analysis of the institutional framework of the newly emerging environment will powerfully illuminate our understanding of its politics and economics.

Notes

1. The PPP comprised several rivalrous Muslim parties and the PDI comprised a number of nationalist and Christian parties. Not coincidentally, the natural ideological and personal divisions within these artificial amalgams helped to keep them from developing into more potent political organizations.

2. This can be achieved in more or less subtle ways, depending on the urgency of the situation. Because Indonesia uses the closed-list proportional representation system, party leaders determine the rank order of all their candidates for each district – and thus also determine which ones have a high probability of being elected, or are placed in an unwinnable position. The government can thus bring pressure to bear upon party leaders

to place critics low on the candidate list, or if necessary, the government (through the General Election Institute) could declare the person unfit to stand as a candidate for election. In extreme cases, sitting members of the legislature can be removed, as happened in 1996 to Sri Bintang Pamungkas.

3. Taken literally, *Pancasila* (the Five Principles) is quite benign. The principles are: belief in God, humanism, nationalism, popular sovereignty, and social justice. In practice, this seemingly inclusive set of ideas is used as an instrument for political control as the government requires that everyone be "for" *Pancasila*, and that anyone deemed by the government to be operating outside its hazy parameters (e.g., a militant Muslim or trade union leader) is in breach of the law.

4. During the 1997 election an independent volunteer election watchdog committee, KIPP, was established to watch for irregularities. Despite government objections, KIPP was able to monitor activities in at least some voting districts (Van Klinken 1997, p. 5).

5. The share of appointed seats reserved for the armed forces was reduced from 25 per cent to 20 per cent in the early 1990s.

6. Personal communication from Daniel Lev.

7. Interestingly, the fact that the legislature is directly involved in choosing the president (by virtue of its making up half of the Consultative Assembly) means that Indonesia's system of government cannot, strictly, be considered presidential. (I am grateful to Matthew Shugart for drawing this to my attention.) This taxonomical dilemma is intensified once we recognize that the legislature can, technically, shorten a president's term by calling a special session of the Consultative Assembly to review the president's performance.

8. Technically, the president does not personally or directly appoint all of the remaining 500 members of the Assembly (i.e., those not from the House). Under Law no. 16 of 1969, as amended in 1975 and 1985, the president is authorized personally to appoint 100 delegates to represent social and functional groups. Each province is entitled to 4–8 delegates (depending on its population). In 1997 the number of provincial delegates totalled 149. The remaining delegates – 251 in 1997 – are divided among the political parties and the armed forces, based proportionately on their numbers in the House. Although, technically, the president selects only the 100 delegates from the social and functional groups, in practice he also has control of the remainder by virtue of the formal and informal authority the executive branch has over the political parties and provincial governments. (I am grateful to Bill Liddle for a number of these points.) For a breakdown of the 1997 membership of the Assembly, see *Suara Pembaruan Daily*, 20 September 1997.

9. It may be that this relationship deserves closer investigation. An interesting point of comparison here is with the relationship between the leadership of the Communist Party and the Central Committee in both China and the former Soviet Union. The Central Committee is formally responsible for selecting the party leadership, but is itself chosen by the party leadership. Susan Shirk (1992) has argued that this is less lopsided than often realized, and that while the party leadership does hold the upper hand, its activities are nonetheless constrained by the re-election imperative. Philip Roeder (1993) tells an equivalent story for the former Soviet Union. Two notable points of difference that seem to separate the situation in Indonesia from that in China (or the former Soviet Union) are that the Consultative Assembly meets very rarely, and that it is a much larger body (and thus less hospitable to collective action). This is a topic that requires further investigation.

10. There is now a sizeable scholarly literature on issues pertaining to democratization in Indonesia (Morley 1993; Alagappa 1995; Rodan 1996; Taylor 1996; Anek 1997; Uhlin 1997; Djiwandono and Legowo 1996; Kristiadi 1997; Siagian 1997; Sihbudi 1997; Schwarz 1994).

11. Alternatively, Indonesia could develop a parliamentary or even a hybrid premier-presidential system of government (Shugart and Carey 1992). Neither would, at this stage, seem as likely as a presidential system. Nonetheless, the same fundamental variables would pertain: greatly increased accountability of the executive, and more independent elections and political parties.
12. This is a far from trivial possibility. Much discussion of democratization ignores the reality that democratic change can unleash violence, suffering, and illiberalness far worse than that which previously prevailed. The fate of the former Yugoslav nations provides a clear illustration of this, but by no means the only one (Zakaria 1997).
13. An excellent and innovative analysis of the institutional dynamics of Thailand's political malaise is provided by Allen Hicken (1997).
14. Interestingly, if this came to pass, it would heighten the taxonomical problem of classifying Indonesia's political system noted above in note 8. If the fate of the political executive – the president – is primarily in the hands of the legislature, the system becomes much closer to a parliamentary one than a presidential one, formal labels notwithstanding.

REFERENCES

Alagappa, M. (1995), *Political Legitimacy in Southeast Asia: The Quest for Moral Authority*, Stanford University Press, Stanford, Calif.

Anek L. (ed.) (1997), *Democratization in Southeast and East Asia*, Institute of Southeast Asian Studies, Singapore.

Azis, I. (1994), "Indonesia," in J. Williamson (ed.), *The Political Economy of Policy Reform*, Institute for International Economics, Washington, D.C.

Battacharya, A. and Pangestu, M. (1993), *The Lessons of East Asia: Indonesia's Development Transformation and Public Policy*, World Bank, Washington, D.C.

Booth, A. (ed.) (1992), *The Oil Boom and After: Indonesian Economic Policy and Performance in the Soeharto Era*, Oxford University Press, Singapore.

Cohen, M. (1997), "On-Air Campaigning: Politicians Reach out to Voters via Television," *Far Eastern Economic Review*, May 15.

Cox, G. (1987), *The Efficient Secret: The Cabinet and the Development of Political Parties in Victorian England*, Cambridge University Press, New York.

——— (1997), *Making Votes Count: Strategic Coordination in the World's Electoral Systems*, Cambridge University Press, New York.

Cox, G. and McCubbins, M. (forthcoming), "Structure and Policy: Institutional Determinants of Policy Outcomes," in S. Haggard and M. McCubbins (eds.), *Structure and Policy in Presidential Democracies*, Cambridge University Press, New York.

Deyo, F. (1987), *The Political Economy of the New Asian Industrialism*, Cornell University Press, Ithaca, N.Y.

Djiwandono, S. and Legowo, T. (eds.) (1996), *Revitalisasi Sistem Politik Indonesia* [Revitalizing Indonesia's political system], Centre for Strategic and International Studies, Jakarta.

Haggard, S. (1990), *Pathways from the Periphery: The Politics of Growth in the Newly Industrializing Countries*, Cornell University Press, Ithaca, N.Y.

Haggard, S. and McCubbins, M. (eds.) (forthcoming), *Structure and Politics in Presidential Democracies*, Cambridge University Press, New York.

Haggard, S. and Shugart, M. (forthcoming), "Institutions and Public Policy in Presidential Systems," in S. Haggard and M. McCubbins (eds.), *Structure and Politics in Presidential Democracies*, Cambridge University Press, New York.

Hermet, G. (1978), "State-Controlled Elections: A Framework," in G. Hermet, R. Rose, and A. Rouquie (eds.), *Elections Without Choice*, Wiley, New York.

Hicken, A. (1997), "Political Parties and Elections in Thailand," unpublished paper, Graduate School of International Relations and Pacific Studies, University of California, San Diego.

Hill, H. (1996), *The Indonesian Economy since 1966: Southeast Asia's Emerging Giant*, Cambridge University Press, Melbourne.

Jaspersen, F., Aylward, A., and Sumlinski, M. (1995), *Trends in Private Investment in Developing Countries: Statistics for 1970–94*, Discussion Paper no. 28, International Finance Corporation, The World Bank, Washington, D.C.

Johnson, C. (1982), *MITI and the Japanese Miracle: The Growth of Industrial Policy, 1925–1975*, Stanford University Press, Stanford, Calif.

Katzenstein, P. (ed.) (1978), *Between Power and Plenty: Foreign Economic Policies of Advanced Industrial States*, University of Wisconsin Press, Madison.

Kiewiet, D. R. and McCubbins, M. (1991), *The Logic of Delegation: Congressional Parties and the Appropriation Process*, University of Chicago Press, Chicago.

Kristiadi, J. (ed.) (1997), *Menyelenggarakan Pemilu yang Bersifat Luber dan Judul* [Organizing a free and fair general election], Centre for Strategic and International Studies, Jakarta.

Levy, B. and Spiller, P. (eds.) (1996), *Regulations, Institutions, and Commitment: Comparative Studies of Telecommunications*, Cambridge University Press, New York.

Liddle, R. W. (1996), "A Useful Fiction: Democratic Legitimation in New Order Indonesia," in R. H. Taylor (ed.), *The Politics of Elections in Southeast Asia*, Cambridge University Press, New York, pp. 34–60.

McBeth, J. and Cohen, M. (1997), "Winner Takes All: Golkar's Dominance Leaves Little Room for Other Voices," *Far Eastern Economic Review*, 30 January.

MacIntyre, A. (1991), *Business and Politics in Indonesia*, Allen and Unwin, Sydney.

——— (1992), "Politics and the Reorientation of Economic Policy in Indonesia," in A. MacIntyre and K. Jayasuriya (eds.), *The Dynamics of Economic Policy Reform in Southeast Asia and the Southwest Pacific*, Oxford University Press, Singapore, pp. 138–57.

——— (ed.) (1994a), *Business and Government in Industrializing Asia*, Cornell University Press, Ithaca, N.Y.

——— (1994b), *Organising Interests: Corporatism in Indonesian Politics*, Working Paper no. 43, Asia Research Centre, Murdoch University, Perth.

——— (1994c), "Power, Prosperity and Patrimonialism: Business and Government in Indonesia," in A. MacIntyre (ed.), *Business and Government in Industrializing Asia*, Cornell University Press, Ithaca, N.Y., pp. 244–67.

——— (forthcoming-a), "Funny Money: Fiscal Policy, Rent-Seeking, and Economic Success in Indonesia," in K. S. Jomo and M. Khan (eds.), *Rent-Seeking in Southeast Asia*, Cambridge University Press, Melbourne.

—— (forthcoming-b), "Investment, Property Rights, and Corruption in Indonesia," in J. E. Campos and D. Leipziger (eds.), *The Institutions of Rentseeking and Corruption in East Asia*. The Brookings Institution, Washington, D.C.

Mainwaring, S. and Scully, T. (1995), "Introduction: Party Systems in Latin America," in S. Mainwaring and T. Scully (eds.), *Building Democratic Institutions: Party Systems in Latin America*, Stanford University Press, Stanford, Calif., pp. 1–34.

Moe, T. and Caldwell, M. (1994), "The Institutional Foundations of Democratic Government: A Comparison of Presidential and Parliamentary Systems," *Journal of Institutional and Theoretical Economics* 150(1), pp. 171–95.

Montinola, G., Qian, Y., and Weingast, B. (1995), "Federalism, Chinese Style: The Political Basis for Economic Success in China," *World Politics* 48(1), pp. 50–81.

Morley, J. (ed.). (1993), *Driven by Growth: Political Change in the Asia-Pacific Region*, M. E. Sharpe, Armonk, N.Y.

North, D. (1981), *Structure and Change in Economic History*, Cambridge University Press, New York.

North, D. and Weingast, B. (1989), "Constitutions and Credible Commitments: The Evolution of the Institutions of Public Choice in Seventeenth-Century England," *Journal of Economic History* 49, pp. 803–32.

Reeve, D. (1985), *Golkar of Indonesia: An Alternative to the Party System*, Oxford University Press, Singapore.

Rodan, G. (ed.) (1996), *Political Oppositions in Industrialising Asia*, Routledge, London.

Roeder, P. (1993), *Red Sunset: The Failure of Soviet Politics*, Princeton University Press, Princeton, N.J.

Rohdewohld, R. (1995), *Public Administration in Indonesia*, Montech, Monash University, Melbourne.

Root, H. (1989), "Tying the King's Hands: Credible Commitments and Royal Fiscal Policy During the Old Regime," *Rationality and Society* 1(2), pp. 240–58.

—— (1996), *Small Countries, Big Lesson: Governance and the Rise of East Asia*, Oxford University Press, Hong Kong.

Santoso, A. (1990), "Government and Constitution: The Case of the 1945 Constitution in Indonesia," in C. Sison (ed.), *Constitutional and Legal Systems of ASEAN Countries*, Academy of Asian Law and Jurisprudence, University of the Philippines, Quezon City.

Schwarz, A. (1994), *A Nation in Waiting: Indonesia in the 1990s*, Allen & Unwin, Sydney.

Shirk, S. (1992), *The Political Logic of Economic Reform in China*, University of California Press, Berkeley.

Shugart, M. and Carey, J. (1992), *Presidents and Assemblies: Constitutional Design and Electoral Dynamics*, Cambridge University Press, New York.

Siagian, F. (1997), "Pemberdayaan Organisasi Peserta Pemilu (OPP) pada Pemilu 1997" (Organizational dynamics of parties in the 1997 general election), *Analisis CSIS* 26(2), pp. 137–49.

Sihbudi, R. (1997), "Mengkaji Ulang Praktek Pemilihan Umum Kita" (Reex-amining our electoral practices), *Analisis CSIS* 26(2), pp. 150–61.

Silaen, V. (1997), "Korpri-Golkar, Pemilu 1997, dan Demokrasi" (Korpri-Golkar, the 1997 general election, and democracy), *Analisis CSIS* 26(2), pp. 162–67.

Taylor, R. H. (ed.) (1996), *The Politics of Elections in Southeast Asia*, Cambridge University Press, New York.

Uhlin, A. (1997), *Indonesia and the "Third Wave of Democratization,"* Curzon Press, Surrey.

Van Klinken, G. (1997), "Citizens Organise Themselves," *Inside Indonesia* 51, p. 5.

Wade, R. (1990), *Governing the Market: Economic Theory and the Role of Government in East Asian Industrialization*, Princeton University Press, Princeton, N.J.

Ward, K. (1974), *The 1971 Election in Indonesia: An East Java Case Study*, Centre for Southeast Asian Studies, Monash University, Melbourne.

Weaver, R. K. and Rockman, B. A. (1993), *Do Institutions Matter? Government Capabilities in the United States and Abroad*, Brookings Institution, Washington, D.C.

Weingast, B. (1995), "The Economic Role of Political Institutions: Market-Preserving Federalism and Economic Growth," *Journal of Law, Economics, and Organization* 11(Spring), pp. 1–31.

Woo, W. T., Glassburner, B., and Nasution, A. (1994), *Macroeconomic Policies, Crises, and Long-Term Growth in Indonesia*, World Bank, Washington, D.C.

Zakaria, F. (1997), "The Rise of Illiberal Democracy," *Foreign Affairs* 76(2), pp. 22–44.

11

Singapore

Khong Cho-oon

Introductory: The dog that did not bark

"Is there any point to which you would wish to draw my attention?" "To the curious incident of the dog in the night-time." "The dog did nothing in the night-time." "That was the curious incident," remarked Sherlock Holmes.
                              – Sir Arthur Conan Doyle, "Silver Blaze"

Politics in Singapore ticks over with the efficiency of the proverbial Swiss watch. Technocrats scan the horizons of the global economy; ministers read the entrails, pronounce their pragmatic policies, thereupon swiftly implemented by an efficient bureaucracy; and a covey of government-sponsored committees chivvies the public in support. Singapore, as one of the original "Asian Tigers," must, on the face of it, be an exemplar of the connection between the political management of the economic system on the one hand, and the legitimation of the ruling political regime by an impressive rate of economic growth on the other. It is also, apparently, a practice of politics so inimitable that Singapore must constitute a unique test-bed for political ideas, at a time when political regimes everywhere are having to measure up to the challenges of globalization, liberalization, and a new revolution in technological advancement.

Yet, while politics across Asia is in turmoil, the political system in Singapore lies quiescent. What accounts for this condition? What led growth to assume its central importance within that political system, what were the political elements that needed to be put in place to ensure the delivery of growth, and what have been the subsequent ramifications of that growth?

In any comparative study of the relationship between democratization and economic growth, Singapore would be an intriguing case – marked by many seemingly inexplicable paradoxes in the way its political processes function.

Historical origins

Lee Kuan Yew and his People's Action Party (PAP) came to power in 1959, in a newly autonomous, though not yet quite independent Singapore. The Singapore society of the time was economically extremely divided, and communally fragmented and inchoate, with a multitude of political groupings, each representing a specific economic or ethnic identification. These groups manoeuvred, plotted, and struggled against each other in a protean political soup, creating the semblance of democratic discourse, while each secretly aimed to seize power for its own exclusive use and to eradicate its rivals, in what was in reality a Hobbesian political struggle. As it turned out, it was Lee Kuan Yew who came to power at the head of a small Western-educated group of intellectuals, quite atypical of the Singapore society of the time, and with a mass following of workers and Chinese middle-school students gained only through a tactical alliance with Communist forces. On attaining power, Lee first distanced himself from his radical populist support, and then proceeded to cut his links from and then to eliminate his erstwhile Communist allies. Yet Lee himself shrewdly observed at the time:

The mass of the people are not concerned with legal and constitutional forms and niceties. They are not interested in the theory of the separation of powers and the purpose and function of a politically neutral civil service under such a constitution.... if the future is not better, either because of the stupidities of elected ministers or the inadequacies of the civil service, then at the end of the five-year term the people are hardly likely to believe either in the political party that they have elected or the political system that they have inherited.[1]

Lee Kuan Yew's words reflected the political conditions of the time and the particular circumstances of his ruling party. Yet his words provide a revealing insight into his political beliefs. They set out a political creed that was to inform the process of creation and construction on which Lee was then to embark, a process whose end result is the modern city-state that is Singapore today. In his relentlessly unremitting drive to improve the material circumstances of his people, Lee Kuan Yew in his practice of politics has not allowed himself to be bound by the principles or prejudices of any particular political model, democratic or otherwise. Instead, he has drawn ideas, in eclectic fashion, from whichever political model suited his purposes at any one time, upholding those ideas passionately and persecuting opponents of them with ruthless zeal; yet discarding those ideas without compunction in favour of something else, should circumstances so dictate.

Without a mass base of populist support, and confronted with the need to gel together his disparate populace, Lee Kuan Yew turned to the civil service, an organization imbued with an elitist ethos and a technocratic bias against political bargaining and compromise. These technocrats were like-minded in seeking economic growth, and like Lee, the civil service was sufficiently removed from, and indeed above, the demands of ordinary people, that it could maintain its autonomy to act and to implement policies with little or no popular support. Lee and his civil service allies had a window of opportunity to act, but they had to move quickly and to show results rapidly if they were to secure their position in power. As a governing elite, they could secure their political survival only by persuading the people that, despite their composition being distinctly different from that of Singapore in general, they nevertheless represented the people's interests and could ensure their material welfare.

The conditions of the time were extremely turbulent, with social unrest, high unemployment, and uncertainty over the nature and dimensions of the state. The political factions squared off against each other at the time of Singapore's joining the new Malaysian Federation in 1963, and again after its ejection in 1965, with political arguments over its ability to forge an independent course as a separate and distinct nation state. Such turbulent conditions provided the grounds for the PAP leadership to suppress destabilizing political opposition in the interests of securing political stability.

Other former colonized states may have secured their independence, perhaps after bitter struggle against their colonial masters, in a burst of euphoria, later to be dampened as the hard realities of economic development dawned on leaderships and peoples. Singapore became an independent nation state in polar-opposite conditions. Independence was neither sought nor fought for, but rather thrust upon a reluctant and fearful state on 9 August 1965, when Singapore was expelled from Malaysia. The political tears of frustration and fury which Lee publicly shed on that day were shared by both leadership and people, faced with an uncertain political future as an island nation state and enclave within Southeast Asia. Politically, the imperative was to secure social cohesion in the face of perceived external threats, and the path chosen was a nation-building programme which emphasised modernization, social reform, and economic development, reinforced through ideological imposition and political institutionalization.

The changing social structure

The major indices of social stratification in the late 1980s were education level, citizenship status, sector of the economy where employed, and the number of employed people in each household.[2] Here, sharp differentiations open up, for example, in levels of education. In 1980, 44 per cent of the population aged 25 and over had no educational qualifications whatsoever, 38 per cent had a primary school education, 15 per cent had a secondary school education, and only 3.4 per cent had a tertiary education. While these figures must obviously have improved since then, there will for many years continue to be a significant proportion of the adult population with only an extremely limited education – this in a society where wages are fairly closely correlated with educational attainment. The stress on individual competition, rather than inherited status, makes education a keenly prized good in Singapore society, which is seen as the key to upward social mobility.

The uppermost levels of Singapore society are occupied by an elite group comprising high-level civil servants, business managers, and professionals, many working for large foreign-owned companies, together with a coterie of wealthy Chinese businessmen, leading the various associations which represent the Chinese-speaking community. The former have an extremely cosmopolitan outlook, apparently distinctively different from the bulk of society, and both groups tend to vigorously support values of competition, economic advancement, and social mobility through education.

There has, however, been significant alleviation of poverty, which by one measure fell from 19 per cent of households in 1953–54 to 0.3 per cent in 1982–83. In part this is a consequence of the general economic growth over the period – though a leading direct cause of poverty alleviation must surely have been the increased participation of women in the workforce, as households typically improved their material circumstances through having more than one wage earner (and also fewer children to support). Whatever the cause, household income distribution in Singapore in 1982–83 was roughly equivalent to that of the United Kingdom – a country which in the 1980s prided itself on encouraging individualistic values, led by a prime minister who stated publicly her disbelief that there is any such thing as "society" – and very much more equal than in Latin American countries such as Brazil and Mexico, though significantly more unequal than in developed countries such as Germany and Japan.[3] The evidence supporting the application of communitarianism in Singapore, so far as the statistics are concerned, does not therefore appear conclusive.

Finally, ethnicity is an issue of extreme sensitivity whose dividing lines cross potential fracture points in Singapore's plural society. The official ideology is multiracial – even if in practice, the government sets out its own agenda of how multi-ethnicity should play out, an agenda fraught with its own internal contradictions. The government has tried to narrow the gap between English-educated and Chinese-educated within the majority Chinese community, while paying special heed to the minority Malay community, because of the country's geopolitical situation.

The institutions of politics

A two-party system would put us on the dangerous road to contention, when we should play as one team.
 – Commodore, now Minister for Education and Second Minister for Defence
Rear Admiral Teo Chee Hean, 1992[4]

The conditions from which Lee Kuan Yew and his PAP sprang were such as to lead him and his party away from what they viewed as the degenerate compromises of "Western-style" liberal democracy, so inimical to economic development, and also away from blatant appeals to populist sympathies. Indeed, rather in the manner of an oriental Churchill, Lee pledged his equivalent of blood, sweat, and tears – establishing political order through an extremely efficient and relatively incorrupt government, and securing material welfare for the citizenry through a benevolent, if not entirely benign, paternalistic government. Any measure in the political and economic armoury that suited these purposes was taken without compunction, and applied without reservation. National survival and political survival for the PAP (for by then the two were inextricably interlinked in the minds of the ruling elite, as they are indeed now in the minds of many of the populace) brooked no half-measures.

These governing measures were tempered from the 1980s by the grooming of a successor political generation, chosen from the ranks of the technocrats within the bureaucracy, socially and politically cosseted, and to some degree rather like the mandarins of yore, without the close ties to the grass roots that many of their predecessors in the founding political generation possessed. This change took place at a time when the general populace was becoming noticeably affluent, with the spread of greater material comforts. And, in the face of continued unremitting pressure from the political leadership to strive even harder, these people were beginning to raise demands which were seemingly for a more tolerant liberal political practice, and exhibiting behaviour patterns at odds with the austere living style exalted by the political leadership as the appropriate model to follow.

The leader of that successor political generation, Goh Chok Tong, formally assumed the prime ministership in November 1991, and seized the opportunity to show a more human face by adopting a more common and sympathetic manner. This different style of leadership, it was believed, would help check the rising alienation by bridging the gulf between rulers and ruled. Goh had earlier declared his intention to work toward a "kinder, gentler society" and to introduce policies that have "a human face," though adding that "this does not mean that the society under Mr. Lee has not been kind and gentle."[5]

The experience of this successor political generation has been mixed. Opening up a political "discussion space" in society has inevitably entailed the flowering of a diverse range of views and expectations of governance, not all of which could be met, or indeed were deemed desirable. And while exercises in consultation have an air of contrivance about them, the government remains closely aware of political opinions "on the ground."

In thinking through the key elements of politics in Singapore, a number of puzzling contradictions present themselves. For a start, we need to move away from the conventional notion that increasing economic affluence somehow leads to social change, which in turn compels a move from authoritarian to more democratic structures, cognisant of individual human rights. Having made that point, neither can we assert that the reverse is strictly true – that material affluence and globalizing trends have not led to increasing tensions between individuals and the state. Globalization challenges the adaptability of traditional patterns of hierarchy and elite status. The Singapore picture presents elements which seemingly support both notions, so how do we reconcile such contradictory trends?

To begin with, we need to make the point that what you see is not necessarily what you get. In form, if we accept a minimal procedural definition of democracy, we may identify a structure of democratic procedures in the Singapore polity, with political parties competing for power (albeit one dominant over the others, hence the term "one party dominant system" or "hegemonic party system" applied by a leading political scientist),[6] in elections held periodically, in which the government pledges that the ballot is secret. In turn, there is widespread acceptance of governmental authority. Yet these procedures have been so constrained by a range of restrictions and limitations – and, perhaps even more important, by a fear, held by many in society, of actively supporting opposition politics) that the democratic nature of these procedures loses much of its validity.

The electoral process and its characteristics

In elections through the 1980s and early 1990s, the PAP steadily lost ground, first losing its parliamentary monopoly in a by-election in 1981, and then seeing a steady fall in its share of the vote in subsequent general elections. The turnaround in the PAP's electoral fortunes only came with the general election of January 1997, when Goh Chok Tong explicitly repudiated a more liberal political line and set out a much less compromising political style. In this most recent election, the PAP's share of the vote in constituencies where there was an electoral contest (less than half of parliamentary seats was contested, so the PAP was already returned to power at the start of the election campaign), rose from 61 to 65 per cent[7] – not a substantial rise, but nevertheless significant in the face of what many had expected would be a continuation of its earlier electoral decline. Why the PAP, and Goh Chok Tong's coterie in particular, should have recovered political ground by threatening tougher governing measures, is an issue which must hold significant lessons for the future direction of politics in Singapore.

To take one example, there was supposedly a fear that "unsophisticated" Singaporean voters, unschooled in democratic practice, would somehow come to believe that their vote could be traced back to themselves.[8] The voting system in use in Singapore derives from the British model, with numbered ballot papers linked to voters' names on the electoral register (though the number on the ballot paper is different from the identity card number of the voter recorded on the electoral register). The government claims that all votes are sealed and destroyed after counting, and has invited opposition representatives to witness the process. Increasingly, over successive elections, the fear of traceability of the vote has gradually diminished. Nevertheless, it may well be that a residue of that fear still remains. The critical issue is therefore not one of the secrecy of the ballot, but rather of the perception of the voter that there remains a possibility that his or her vote can be traced if the authorities so decide. This fear was heightened during the 1997 elections, when Goh Chok Tong declared that with vote counting being decentralized (in the interests of giving out the results more rapidly), it would then be possible to quickly establish how individual precincts voted (each with around 5,000 votes) and to reward those who most strongly supported the government.[9]

Certainly, Singapore's political evolution has not gone down the trailblazing democratic path set by Taiwan and South Korea. But to the question, why did the dog not bark? The answer (as Sherlock Holmes made clear) is that it was in perfectly familiar surroundings and that it recognized the object of its actions. It is not that the government formulated communitarianism in order to deny democracy; on the contrary, what is clear in the practice of politics in Singapore today, is the seriousness with which the government treats the exercise of formal democracy, where every percentage point lost in electoral support (from what is, at over 60 per cent of the vote, a very high level of support) is worried over by the government precisely because it rests its claim to power on a communitarian ideology. If this government claims to embody the collective interests of society, such a claim to power would sit uneasily with an apparently increasing dissension within the ranks of that society.

What Goh Chok Tong did, in the January 1997 elections, was to turn around this general expectation of the electorate, by spelling out his intention to link government public-spending programmes to the extent of voter support of the government, not just in individual constituencies, but also in individual wards within constituencies.[10] Rather than the government being accountable to the people, the people were now explicitly made accountable to the government.

What, then, of the constraints which the Singapore government places on the mass media and on the voluntary associations of civil society? Rather than being symptoms of a transitional political phase to full democracy, these constraints are instead the means by which the government imposes its view of what the communitarian consensus should be. Communitarianism may have a soft centre – the desire to build and to live in stable communities, and consideration and responsibility for the wider community to which one belongs viewed as a social virtue (shades of Francis Fukuyama) – but it also has a hard edge, emphasizing duties and responsibilities rather than rights. Illiberal measures which restrict the public expression of individual interests are part of the expression of this hard-edged communitarianism. People have to recognize that they may need to make sacrifices for the greater good, rather than pander to their own individual gratification.[11]

The communitarian ideology and its role

Throughout the whole period of independence, there has been a tension in the Singapore polity between the competing claims of communitarianism and individualism – which evokes a familiar argument over supposed "Asian values." Superficially, the Singapore government may be seen as the guardian of communitarianism, against the apparent erosion of those values by more self-centered individualistic concerns. Communitarian values did indeed underpin popular support for the government's initial decision to legitimize its rule through economic growth. The government and civil service had to have in place mechanisms and institutions which the disparate elements making up Singapore society could believe would spread the benefits of growth. Only then did a groundswell of support build up which created sufficient socio-political stability to sustain the economic policies that were put in place. Without this communitarian reassurance, it would be safe to say that there would not have been the co-operation between groups which would have allowed the social stability to give these policies time to take effect.

One striking feature of politics in Singapore is the way that ideology has been defined by the government so as to reinforce its claim to power and the duty of citizens to obey. Motivated by concern that people were being overly influenced by ideas seeping in from abroad, influences that were difficult for the government to monitor and control, the government directed a lengthy public debate over the relative merits of "Asian values" (good) versus "Western values" (bad). The "Asian values" espoused were the alleged values of Confucian high culture, to which the cultural distinctiveness of Asian politics is nowadays fashionably attributed. Asian politics has everything to do with the Asian spirit, defined as a belief in strong authoritarian control, respect for bureaucracy, and emphasis on the group at the expense of the individual. Lee Kuan Yew, incidentally, is often characterized as advancing this view, but a close reading of his public pronouncements shows a rather more sophisticated appreciation: disclaiming that an "Asian model" exists, accepting that value systems do change, and criticizing Western society, interestingly enough, for a perceived erosion of individual responsibility and for an over-reliance on government to solve social problems.[12]

The ideas propagated by Confucius and the school of thought he established were ideas for a governing elite, at a time when cities were being built and states being established in China. It took centuries – almost right down to our own time – for these ideas to percolate down to the common people, and in doing so they became mixed in with all sorts of local folk traditions and practices. This is not the popular Confucian ethos innate in that part of Singapore's population that is immigrant Chinese. What we see at this populist level is not the high Confucianism of the intellectual elite (actually extremely stifling towards entrepreneurial initiative and innovative ideas), but the vulgar Confucianism of ordinary people (best exemplified in the networking of overseas Chinese). It is this lower form of Confucianism which shapes the values and the political choices of many ordinary people from among the immigrant Chinese community in Singapore. At this level, the pontificating of Asian elites becomes irrelevant; and we need to discard all those abstract concepts of high Confucianism such as loyalty and filial piety.

Strangely enough, the Singapore government had to sponsor the study of Confucian ethics through the setting up of an Institute of East Asian Philosophies, staffed by eminent academics brought in from abroad, to define Confucianism for the citizens of Singapore. Indeed, although Lee Kuan Yew once confidently asserted that "for most Chinese students, Confucianism not Buddhism will be what parents would prefer their children to study,"[12] in the event, a survey of student preferences in 1989 gave Buddhism 44 per cent, bible knowledge 21 per cent, and Confucianism a mere 18 per cent. The presumed role of Confucian values in Singapore's economic development is indeed an intriguing issue, which certainly deserves detailed consideration.

Popular Confucianism, as it affects the man or woman in the street, is far removed from high Confucian theory. It is perhaps no more than a vague amalgam of residual ethical beliefs and a bias towards particular practices – not amenable to rational analysis, but nevertheless prompting certain attitudes towards the family, education, social responsibility, and government. The family is the focus of attention and close affections, education is respected, public service honoured, but government viewed with a measure of suspicion. There is a concern to keep some distance between one's family on the one side, and the state – whose intentions cannot, in the last resort, be fully known – on the other. Such attitudes are neither obviously democratic, nor readily authoritarian. They do, however, lend themselves to participatory politics which is very much locally focused.

In Singapore, the ruling party constantly reworks its legitimizing ideology to suit changing economic circumstances. The advocacy of Confucianism has since moved on, with the evolution of a form of communitarianism, through a process by which the PAP has repeatedly repackaged and redefined a national ideology to serve as its *raison d'être*. It has been argued that the objective of ideological reformulation in Singapore's case has been to obstruct and to deny any logical linear move to liberal democracy, as exemplified by the experiences of Taiwan and South Korea.[13] Yet it could be even more plausibly argued that this constant redefinition by government of the basis of its legitimacy is a measure of its adaptability to a rapidly changing society. Indeed, this capacity to continually reinvent itself in the perceptions of the electorate could well be the key to the government's long-term survival.

The Singapore government's interpretation of communitarianism is a doctrine in which government, as custodian of the communitarian will, ineluctably imposes a set of civic values on individual behaviour. By emphasizing the community and telling us how things should be for the greater good, this form of communitarianism curbs egocentric behaviour and asserts that responsibilities to the wider community coexist with individual rights. In any society where there is a range of personal moral and religious beliefs (and in Singapore, this range is even wider than is usually the case, given the plural nature of its society), any assertion of a common standard of behaviour must involve a measure of coercion. The Singapore government might presumably assert that all states (even the most supposedly liberal) coerce, but the question is: to what end is that coercion addressed?

In the case of Singapore, the aggregate effect of the government's communitarian style, however illiberal it may be characterized as being, is to consolidate the politics of the middle ground, deliberately excluding what are perceived to be political extremes. Goh Chok Tong's own declared intention has been to enlarge the middle ground through a more accommodating and participatory style of government, and he has clearly moved to include the greatest number of Singaporeans in the political process, rather than to exclude them from it.

Indeed, communitarian ideology renders the Singapore government, despite its authoritarian tag, even more vulnerable to electoral rebuff than so-called democratic governments elsewhere. If communitarianism is defined in terms of a common national will, any dissenting political activity must call into question the extent of that common will. The Singapore government must therefore constantly be acutely sensitive to the varying shades of public opinion, and act quickly to deal with contrary views, either through suppressing them or through going some way to meeting them. Fully conscious of the position the government is in, Singaporeans are perhaps even more sophisticated than their Western counterparts in exercising their voting rights. Because opposition parties recognize the general sentiment that there really is no practical alternative to keeping the PAP in power, and therefore do not contest the majority of seats in general elections (giving these general elections a by-election flavour), Singaporeans vote, not to change the government, but to register dissatisfaction with its policies – and to express their expectation that the government, precisely because of its communitarian legitimizing ideology, will act to redress the grievances raised.

The institutions of economic policy: Chasing bubbles of value

Exceptional returns arise from exploitation of market, political and technological discontinuities.... Successful companies pay inordinate attention to identifying discontinuities early on, as well as predicting their implications for money making opportunities that may be short-lived.

– *McKinsey Quarterly,* 1994

When Singapore gained its independence in 1965, it was burdened with an economy seemingly in terminal decline. Forced out by Malaysia and still in confrontation with Indonesia, the new state confronted an external environment that appeared darkly threatening. There would, apparently, be no regional common market of which Singapore could be a part, and its own domestic market was minuscule. So the import substitution policies of growing nascent industries that were the economic development fashion of the day were obviously inappropriate. The economy, meanwhile, was burdened by a declining entrepot trade, dependence on British military spending, low productivity, and chronic unemployment – the seeding ground, together with latent irredentist sympathy by elements within the majority ethnic Chinese community for the People's Republic of China, of much of the support for radical Marxist political opposition depicted in the above.

Given that all economic paths being pursued at the time led to obvious dead ends, there was no alternative to a complete restructuring of the Singapore economy to force it in a direction which it had never taken before. The private sector would not take the lead, with foreign capital being repatriated abroad in the face of such poor economic prospects, with no large agglomerations of domestic capital given the small scale of Chinese family businesses and local banking houses, and with little prospect of raising much more money from a profoundly non-egalitarian society. The state, therefore, was forced to pursue policies of massive economic intervention, in a bid to re-align the domestic economy. The result was an example of economic development cited by economists worldwide, however inappropriate Singapore may be to their own particular preoccupations, as a growth model to emulate.

This irony is compounded by the fact that economic policy in Singapore is characterized by – to use the government's favourite term of approbation – "pragmatism." The economy has been shepherded along by the state – first surmounting one challenge, next another – not according to rigid principle, but rather, in a spirit of willingness to adapt and change according to what circumstances require. The domestic economy, because of its small size and responsiveness to government control, has proved manoeuvrable and quick to change – swiftly moving out of one area where its competitive advantage is being eroded, to seize "bubbles of value" in another, and to build a position to exploit them rapidly before, ineluctably, other competitors come in to squeeze it out.

Lee saw that the only possible economic strategy he could pursue would be to create an investment climate conducive to foreign investors, since only they could grow the economy. To do so, Singapore offered a range of inducements, though these proved less significant in the long run than sound government, a stable currency, a lavishly supportive and reliable physical infrastructure, and a dependable workforce, disciplined by government injunction and easily controlled because of its urban character and the small size of the state.

Most of all, however, by plugging into the emerging global economy, Singapore benefited from the favourable economic situation of the time. The 1960s were a period of rapid economic growth for all industrialized countries, and the Vietnam conflict also provided an economic stimulus for regional states (much as Japan had benefited in the 1950s from the Korean War). So also did the 1973 oil crisis, which led to a heightened search for oil reserves in Southeast Asia.

Initial industrialization was based on labour-intensive heavy industry, such as shipbuilding and the processing of oil products – activities then not to be found in neighbouring countries. "Heavy industry ... swept the whole economy along in its wake throughout the 1970s, energy products alone serving as the driving force for manufacturing industry and exports and becoming the primary focus of Singapore's activities."[14]

The Singapore government's management of multinational companies played a key role in shaping the policies of the political leadership, and in nurturing large state-owned companies run by the civil service bureaucracy. These state companies (comprising three large holding companies for a diverse range of small to medium-scale enterprises), together with multinational enterprises, provided the main thrust for the economic development that was the leadership's primary objective. The foundations of a much-expanded role for multinational investment in the domestic economy were laid by the labour legislation of 1968, which, by establishing the rights of managers while limiting the employment protection of labour, shifted the balance of power between employers and employees. In particular, the Industrial Relations (Amendment) Ordinance set out the prerogatives of management and removed a range of contentious issues from labour-management negotiations.[15] The managers of multinational enterprises, though not part of the governing elite, found themselves playing a more significant role in government policy formulation, through their links with government statutory boards and state-owned companies, than they might have expected to play in most other countries.

The aim of the new labour laws was to assure employers, especially potential employers from multinational companies, that labour in Singapore was disciplined and provided a reliable low-cost resource. It should be stressed that in the view of the political leadership, these laws did not leave labour unprotected. Rather, given the critical, importance of export-oriented investment in the leadership's development strategy, trade unions could not be expected to carry out their labour protection function while giving due regard to the government's, and hence the country's wider interests. Labour interests were therefore yet another responsibility that the government arrogated to itself, using a corporatist, rather than a legalistic, approach to managing relations between employers and labour by carefully regulating wage levels through a National Wages Council, in consultation with both employers and labour.

Economic growth therefore allowed the civil service bureaucracy to consolidate its power and influence within the Singapore polity. A range of statutory boards was set up, mostly during the 1970s, to guide government involvement in the economy in a diverse range of seemingly unrelated activities. Lawrence Krause observes: "there appears to be no ideological barrier preventing the government from entering any economic activity."[16] These organizations, staffed by government employees and directed by top-level civil servants with direct access to the prime minister's office, have played a key role in enhancing the power of the civil service within the governing coalition and in impelling the coalescence between political leadership and high-level bureaucrats.

From 1979 to 1981, the government began a new drive to push the economy up the technological ladder, impelled by increasingly effective competition in labour-intensive industry in neighbouring countries. The rising costs of doing business in Singapore meant that it was losing its ability to compete in manufactures where cost of factors of production was the primary consideration. New priority economic sectors were identified: precision engineering, electronics, information technology, optics, chemicals, pharmaceuticals, aeronautics, telecommunications, and biotechnology. The government-run National Wages Council decreed a substantial increase in pay for labour, ranging up to 20 per cent, with the intention of forcing out labour-intensive industries which added little value to gross domestic product. Other measures were also introduced to enhance skills and to raise labour productivity. This policy tipped the Singapore economy into recession: it moved from a growth rate of 8.3 per cent in 1984 to minus 1.6 per cent in 1985. Yet the economy was to stage an extraordinary recovery in two years, with growth rates reaching 9.7 per cent in 1987 and 11.6 per cent in 1988.[17]

An Economic Committee under the chairmanship of Lee Hsien Loong, Lee Kuan Yew's son, aimed at charting a course of action to end the recession. But equally important in turning around the recession was the impact of external developments – in particular, an influx of Japanese investment brought about by a rapid appreciation of the yen and encouraged by government-imposed cuts in local employment and operating costs (a consequence of the Economic Committee's deliberations).

Nevertheless, the recovery from the late 1980s led to a rethinking by the state of its appropriate role in the economy. In 1986, the government began a programme of deregulation and privatizing public enterprises, first with obviously commercial enterprises which had private-sector competition (such as Singapore Airlines and Neptune Orient Lines), and then with other companies (such as Singapore Telecoms). The government, though, retained a minimum participation of 30 per cent in each and every case, and hence a voice in management. The government also began a programme of supporting local industrial entrepreneurs with financial and technical assistance, a programme too recent for its long-term results to be assessed, though the initial impressions are very mixed.[18]

Singapore therefore faces new challenges, if it is to maintain its remarkable economic growth. The lesson of the 1980s was that the economy is too small to stand on its own, but will have to continue to adapt to trends in global and regional markets – trends which are increasingly swift-moving, turbulent, and unpredictable. Singapore will also have to be adept at seizing the new technologies which are rapidly becoming available, as its own regional competitors grow in economic and technological sophistication. Rather like the Red Queen in *Through the Looking Glass*, the Singapore economy will have to run very fast just so as not to slide backwards. If it is to continue to push ahead, the pace at which it needs to go will be positively breakneck.

If the Singapore economic development model is an exemplar, it is through the role of the state, led by a political-bureaucratic alliance, akin to the management of a business enterprise, operating in the global economy. While almost everywhere else, the state has been much diminished by globalizing forces of political change, the internationalization of financial markets, and rapidly cumulative increases in technological capability, there is an alternative by which the state can build up its strength vis-à-vis the domestic economy and polity – through going along with and feeding, rather than vainly attempting to counter, those forces of globalization. Singapore provides an example of such a "competing nation."

Rather than try to "pick industrial winners" and build up large national companies behind mercantilist barriers, as Japan and South Korea have done, Singapore recognizes that capital is mobile; that companies are increasingly thinking in global terms; that governments have little talent for picking winners (particularly as they move ahead of the rest of the competition or if their circumstances – like Singapore's small size – are such that meaningful comparisons with other countries are difficult); and that there is intense competition between companies – which countries can exploit to their own advantage. A sense of national economic purpose can be created around this idea of competitiveness – with the government implementing proactive non–laissez-faire policies to create a pool of highly educated and flexible workers, an extensive and efficient infrastructure, and a sound and stable currency. If the government can set up such a base of economic support, then the nation it governs is well placed to operate as an open economy, attracting mobile financial and human capital to a place where the environment is conducive for business and where people can live in material comfort. The government still plays an extremely active role in controlling social behaviour, and in policing the outer boundaries of the state to keep out not goods, but illegal immigration; while the economy is extremely open to trade flows, all factors of production crossing into or out of its territory are kept under tight control. Such is the Singapore model.

Conclusion: The future of the state

"You want to go into the world and you are going empty-handed, with some promise of freedom, which men in their simplicity and their innate lawlessness cannot even comprehend, which they fear and dread – for nothing has ever been more unendurable to man and to human society than freedom!"

– The Grand Inquisitor in Fyodor Dostoyevsky, *The Brothers Karamazov*

Fire is fierce, and people feel fear at the sight of it. So they seldom die of it. Water, on the other hand, is gentle, so that people are inclined to play in it. As a result, many of them drown.

– Traditional Chinese saying

Singapore politics is not in a transient phase, evolving towards a future, more liberal form. Rather, the current formally democratic yet illiberal political style, whatever tension it may breed in parts of the populace, is likely to prove fairly resistant to change. Singapore resents comparisons with Western models. Indeed, at a time when the Western political vision has itself become clouded by alienation and uncertainty, and many people in those countries are engaged in a search for new political forms and values to revitalize existing structures, the Singapore government would presumably argue that its version of imposed communitarianism has managed, by whatever means it was done, and however tenuous the result, to strengthen weak civic bonds in a plural society (formerly fractured), and to instil a sense of belonging to the majority of the population.

Furthermore, for a country pursuing a "competing nation" strategy in the global economy, the Singapore government's willingness to spell out and to successfully impose on everyone a common view of how people should live together, achieves a sense of cohesion, of trust within society, and of an intrinsic civic justice, which helps oil the wheels of business and commerce. That this imposition requires a hard edge is due to the apathy of many people, who do feel a vague sense of commitment to their own community, but are not prepared to do much about it – a hangover, perhaps, from their immigrant origins. As writers like Robert Putnam and Francis Fukuyama assert, a high level of interpersonal trust in society provides a critical competitive advantage, and leads to high rates of economic growth.[19]

A corollary to the strategy of playing as a "competing nation" in the global economy is the need for periodic acts of symbolic nationalism – to reinforce national cohesion and purpose, against the dissolving influences of global internationalism on the loyalties of the domestic population. Hence, Singapore has emerged as a strident champion of Asian Confucian values in the global ideological debate, neutered since the collapse of Soviet communism. The advocates of Asian values point to the inherent cultural advantages of countries such as Singapore, imbued with Confucian values, over a declining and degenerate West.

Political tensions will persist, and we will see a new younger generation of voters make increasing demands on a not too flexible political system. But as beneficiaries of the steely-eyed paternalism which characterizes that system, they will generally seek to maintain the status quo, as change is threatening and uncertain. A few may take upon their shoulders the mission of acting as a conscience for their society, asserting individual rights and calling for a greater sense of responsibility towards the disadvantaged. But the majority have made a pragmatic calculation, and will continue to uphold it, that swings the other way, toward calculated inaction. However enticing ideas of liberal individualism may be, why rock the boat when it is moored in such comfortably familiar waters? It would take a tropical typhoon to strike sparks off these people, to galvanize them into attempting to shift Singapore politics onto a completely different course.

Notes

1. Lee Kuan Yew, *Text of a Speech by the Prime Minister, Mr. Lee Kuan Yew, at the Official Opening of the Civil Service Study Centre* (Singapore government press statement, 15 August 1959).
2. Measures cited in U.S. Library of Congress document addressed hup lllcweb2 loc gov/ cgi-bion query D/cstdy:2:./temp/-ffd_MKZf, from which the figures for educational levels come.
3. Data from World Bank, *World Development Report 1997* (New York: Oxford University Press, 1997).
4. *Straits Times*, 12 December 1992.
5. Ibid., 27 September 1990.
6. Change Heng Chee, *The Dynamics of One Party Dominance: The PAP at the Grassroots* (Singapore: Singapore University Press, 1976); and "Political Parties," in Jon S. T. Quah, Chan Cheng Hee, and Seah Chee Meow (eds.), *Government and Politics of Singapore* (Singapore: Oxford University Press, 1987), pp. 146–72.

7. hup://www.sintercom.org//election96/results97.html (13 February 1997).
8. From discussion in http://www-leland.stanford.edu/-chongkee/sef96/vote_trace.html (31 December 1996). See also Derek da Cunha, *The Price of Victory: The 1997 Singapore General Election and Beyond* (Singapore: Institute of Southeast Asian Studies, 1997), p. 64.
9. *Straits Times*, 1 and 12 January 1997.
10. Da Cunha, *The Price of Victory*, pp. 40–41.
11. Thus in the debate on emigration by Singaporeans to Australia, Canada, and other countries, the argument is even made that people have a patriotic obligation to remain in Singapore, even if they feel that they and their families would do better elsewhere.
12. Fareed Zakaria, "Culture Is Destiny: A Conversation with Lee Kuan Yew," *Foreign Affairs* March–April 1994; 73(2): 109–26.
13. See Beng-Huat Chua, *Communitarian Ideology and Democracy in Singapore* (London: Routledge, 1995).
14. Philippe Regnier, *City-State in Southeast Asia*, trans. Christopher Hurst (Honolulu: University of Hawaii Press, 1991), p. 55.
15. See Pang Eng Fong, Tan Chwee Huat, and Cheng Soo May, "The Management of People," in Kemial Singh Sandhu and Paul Wheatley (eds.), *Management of Success: The Moulding of Modern Singapore* (Singapore: Institute of Southeast Asian Studies, 1989), pp. 129–30.
16. Lawrence B. Krause, "Government as Entrepreneur," in Sandhu and Wheatley, *Management of Success*, p. 439.
17. International Monetary Fund, *International Financial Statistics Yearbook 1998* (Washington, D.C.: Publication Services, IMF, 1998), pp. 154–57.
18. See Lee Tsao Yuan and Linda Low, *Local Entrepreneurship in Singapore: Private and State* (Singapore: Institute of Policy Studies, 1990).
19. Robert D. Putnam, *Making Democracy Work: Civic Traditions in Modern Italy* (Princeton, N.J.: Princeton University Press, 1993); and Francis Fukuyama, *Trust: The Social Virtues and the Creation of Prosperity* (London: Hamish Hamilton, 1995).

12

Hong Kong

James T. H. Tang

Introduction

The minimalist state of Hong Kong is under transformation in the brave new post-colonial world. On 1 July 1997 British rule ended. China resumed sovereignty over Hong Kong and granted it the right to self-government for at least 50 years, except over diplomatic and defence matters. Under an arrangement described as "one country; two systems," Hong Kong has become a Special Administrative Region (SAR) of the People's Republic of China. As an administrative state, colonial Hong Kong had been at the forefront of the East Asian economic "miracle" between the 1970s and the mid 1990s. Colonial Hong Kong, however, was an exception in a region where economic developments have been largely propelled by state-led strategies.[1]

That East Asian states have been able to develop their economies rapidly has been attributed to state capacity in the region. Works on industrializing Asian economies such as South Korea and Taiwan have emphasized the existence of effective states with well-developed bureaucracies capable of formulating economic policy without being captive to rent-seeking societal groups. While the political elite did form alliances with business interests, the relationship was highly unequal, with the state acting the dominant partner. Most of these states have been described as "strong states" which were willing to coerce business groups to move towards economic objectives formulated by the government.[2]

The colonial Hong Kong state, however, was widely seen to be minimalist. The government was not regarded as a dominant partner in its infamous alliance with the business community. In fact a popular characterization of the government-business relationship was that Hong Kong was ruled by the "Royal Hong Kong Jockey Club, Jardine Matheson and Co., the Hongkong and Shanghai Bank, and the Governor – in that order."[3]

Institutionally, major business interests had been very much an integral part of the system of governance in colonial Hong Kong. A closer look, however, suggests that Hong Kong could hardly be considered a "weak state" in terms of its autonomy against society, its organizational capacity, and its effectiveness in implementing policies. The territory's well-established economic philosophy of "positive non-interventionism" was not simply the outcome of a pro-business agenda, but also a deliberate choice by a colonial administration whose *raison d'être* was almost completely commercial. In fact, colonial Hong Kong was a dominant state. Formal political authority was concentrated in the hands of the governor, a representative of the queen of England whose formidable powers were comparable to those of the monarch in pre-democratic England; and the governor was appointed by London from the ranks of the Colonial Service and, after the demise of the Colonial Office, the Foreign and Commonwealth Office (Chris Patten, the last governor, was the only exception). In addition, colonial Hong Kong was served by a well-developed and highly efficient bureaucracy when the city went through its industrialization stage during the 1960s and 1970s. In practice the administration ruled in coalition with the major British business corporations and with the support of prominent local Chinese.[4]

The political system of colonial Hong Kong had remained more or less unchanged and not directly challenged (apart from an interruption of three years and eight months of Japanese occupation between 1941 and 1945) for almost one and a half centuries until the Sino-British talks on the future of the territory began in the early 1980s. Hong Kong experienced rapid economic expansion between the 1960s and 1980s despite a brief period of political turbulence in the late 1960s when the Cultural Revolution swept through mainland China. Although Hong Kong was not immune from the upheaval, the Chinese leadership made no attempt to challenge the territory's status and Hong Kong remained British.[5]

Hong Kong's economic performance remained impressive without political change until the 1980s when, fearful of an uncertain future under Communist rule, the people of Hong Kong became more assertive politically. The political turbulence in the 1980s, however, did not make any major impact on Hong Kong's prosperity. Difficulties did occur in early

1983 when the government had to peg the Hong Kong currency to the U.S. dollar at a fixed rate to maintain economic stability.

According to the 1984 Sino-British Agreement on Hong Kong's future and the constitutional arrangements in the form of the Basic Law, Hong Kong's political and economic system are to be preserved. Some have argued that Hong Kong is merely being transferred from one type of authoritarian rule (in the form of British colonialism) to another (in the form of Chinese communism). Economically, given the integration of the Hong Kong and mainland China economies, many have maintained that the economic situation in Hong Kong would not be affected by the handover. In fact the SAR administration uses the expression, "business as usual" to describe post-handover Hong Kong.

This chapter suggests that internal political developments in Hong Kong since the mid-1980s have made a significant impact on economic management in the territory, and that this trend will be accentuated in Hong Kong's search for a post-colonial order after China's resumption of sovereignty. Although the democratization process which began in the 1980s was temporarily reversed when colonial Hong Kong became a Chinese SAR, the political system in Hong Kong had already undergone important changes prior to the political handover. This chapter examines the impact of democratization on Hong Kong's economic governance and the implications of such changes for post-colonial Hong Kong.

Economic growth without democracy

The administrative state of colonial Hong Kong adopted a pro-business stance. Local business elites exercised influence over government through representation in the Executive Council (the highest advisory body in the colony), and the Legislative Council was dominated by civil servants up to 1976. Even by the mid-1980s the membership of both councils was entirely appointed by the government. The colonial administration also set up a consultative system in the form of committees to advise the government on matters related to the economy.[6]

Unlike with neighbouring Southeast Asian states, decolonization did not come to Hong Kong following the end of the Second World War as China plunged into civil war almost immediately after Japan's defeat. The leadership of the People's Republic of China then decided that British Hong Kong would serve as a window for the newly established communist state which was isolated by the West because of Cold War politics. Hong Kong faced major political challenges in the 1950s, with an uncertain political future, a massive influx of refugees from across the border, and economic difficulties when the colony's entrepôt trade collapsed following the United Nations sanctions against China as a result of the Korean War. The colony, against all odds, managed to survive when it became clear that China had no intention of taking over the city. Strategically located, with a liberal economic policy and stable political order, Hong Kong managed to survive and prosper.

Within a 36-year span from 1961 to 1997 Hong Kong rose to be one of the richest territories in Asia, and its average wealth even surpassed that of its colonial master when the British departed. The economy took off in the 1960s, and expansion was at its most dramatic during the 1970s. During the 1960s economic growth averaged 11.7 per cent per year and international trade expanded four times at an annual rate of nearly 10 per cent. The 1970s saw Hong Kong's economy growing at an even faster pace, with an average annual increase of 21.1 per cent. Hong Kong's economic expansion was less spectacular in the 1980s, but still impressive by any standards with a 6.3 per cent average annual growth rate. The first half of the 1990s saw continuous expansion of the economy and a steady climb of per capita income. By the time that the territory turned into a SAR in 1997, Hong Kong had maintained an annual growth rate of 7 per cent for two decades, twice as fast as the world economy. Its GDP per capita, which grew at an average rate of 5 per cent per year, also doubled in the same period to reach US$26,400. Hong Kong's average wealth was second only to that of Japan and Singapore, and surpassed not only that of the U.K. but also that of countries such as Canada and Australia.[7]

Unlike other East Asian economies, Hong Kong did not begin its industrial development with a phase of import substitution. In the 1950s Hong Kong's economy was based on entrepôt trade; it shifted to export-oriented industrialization in the 1960s, to internationalization of the financial sector in the 1970s, and to expansion of the service sector as well as relocation of its manufacturing sector in the 1980s. As a leading economist observed, all these phases took place without government plans or directives.[8] The government, confined its role to exercising varying degrees of microeconomic control over essential public services including transportation, postal services, and public utilities such as water, electricity, and land supply, and to providing regulatory frameworks. It followed a non-intervention approach to the development of private industries. In macroeconomic terms, the colonial government also resisted employing fiscal policies to accommodate the different stages of the business cycle. But the government did follow a stabilizing budgetary policy reminiscent of the Keynesian model, with budget surpluses during periods of fast growth and deficits during periods of recession.[9]

A number of theories have been advanced to explain why Hong Kong stayed politically stable under colonial rule for so long when turbulence swept through neighbouring countries in the form first of the anticolonial struggle for national independence and then of internal struggle for democracy. The administration was able to provide an economic haven for both people and capital from the political and economic turbulence in China. With a stable political environment and a common law system as well as an efficient public service, the British government was able to keep its rule in the territory. Hong Kong was part of China when Britain took over and the local population has always been largely Chinese, but there was little support for independence. When the Chinese Communists took power in 1949 they deliberately kept Hong Kong as a window to the world because of economic and strategic considerations.

If China's decision not to challenge colonial rule provided the external context for political stability without independence, the absence of a strong political demand for democracy in Hong Kong has been explained with reference to specific historical circumstances, the bureaucratic polity, and the political cultures of the population.

Decolonization did not come to Hong Kong, partly because the people in Hong Kong did not see themselves as a separate nation from mainland China, and many went to Hong Kong for temporary refuge from the upheavals in the mainland and considered the British-administered territory as a place of transit from where they would move on once they secured the economic means to do so. By the 1970s, however, the local population, better educated and with a stronger sense of belonging, began to demand more political involvement in the governmental process. When Sino-British negotiations began in the mid-1980s Hong Kong society was further politicized by the uncertain prospect of reunification under Chinese Communist rule. A democracy movement developed rapidly.

During the Sino-British talks the people of Hong Kong were often relegated to the position of bystanders, but many did make their views known and political groups were formed to champion their political demands. By 1984 when the Sino-British agreement on Hong Kong's future was reached, the political system was being gradually liberalized. Political reforms in the 1980s began at the local level with the establishment of district boards with elected members to advise the government on matters affecting the welfare of the district. The government subsequently not only further broadened the base of citizen representation at the level of local and district administration, but also introduced elected seats to the Legislative Council as the British and Chinese governments negotiated for Hong Kong's future in the early and mid-1980s.

Although the Chinese government remained suspicious of British intentions, it accepted limited democracy for Hong Kong. By 1991 the people of Hong Kong had already taken the first steps towards democracy by directly electing their representatives to the Legislative Council which was moving towards a fully elected legislature. Sino-British confrontations over the pace and scope of the democratization process, however, marked much of the final phase of Hong Kong's existence as a British colony with the arrival of the last British governor, Chris Patten, in July 1992.

In the aftermath of the 1989 Tiananmen crackdown on the pro-democracy student movement in Beijing, the British government attempted to restore both the confidence of Hong Kong and its international reputation as a responsible colonial power by pushing for faster democratic reform and introducing a higher degree of representation in the last colonial Legislative Council elections in 1995. Following the introduction of a constitutional reform package, which was vehemently opposed by the Chinese government, the people of Hong Kong cast their votes for a fully elected Legislative Council in September 1995. Electoral politics and political parties have also emerged in the political landscape of Hong Kong politics where the voices for labour and other grass-roots groups and demands for more government action to improve the livelihood of the people have become important elements in local politics. The Hong Kong government's traditional hands-off approach to economic governance was increasingly challenged towards the end of colonial rule.

Hong Kong under Chinese sovereignty

The first Hong Kong SAR government under Tung Chee-hwa's leadership is widely expected to be a pro-business administration. The fact that Tung Chee-hwa comes from the business community himself and is supported by prominent businessmen in the territory has given rise to suggestions that Beijing's promise of "Hong Kong people ruling Hong Kong" (*gangren zhigang*) would turn out to be "business people ruling Hong Kong" (*shangren zhigang*). Moreover, the rationale for Hong Kong's existence as a SAR and the privileges granted to the territory in maintaining a high degree of autonomy is based primarily on economic considerations. Although the "one country, two systems" formula is also used by the mainland government as a solution to the problem of reunification with Taiwan, Beijing obviously would like to see an economically thriving Hong Kong dominated by business interests rather than a politically active Hong Kong dominated by popularly elected democrats and grass-roots leaders.

Tung Chee-hwa himself has repeatedly asserted that Hong Kong became too politicized during the decade or so of political transition since the signing of the Sino-British Joint Declaration on Hong Kong's future in 1984. He would, presumably, prefer the return of the old political order which was characterized by "administrative absorption of politics," with the top echelon of government working closely with the business elite, and a restoration of the pre-Patten colonial government's laissez-faire approach to economic governance. In fact a few months after the reversion of sovereignty the SAR administration under Tung Chee-hwa insisted that things had remained unchanged in Hong Kong. If that is the case the departure of the British simply represents the replacement of one business elite group by another. The only difference would be that instead of having a pro-British business orientation, the SAR would shift towards a more pro-mainland orientation.

While the business community cannot expect the same degree of domination in Hong Kong's economic governance as it had in colonial times, it has regained its prominence as a central political force in the SAR. The chief executive is a former businessman. His closest advisers in the form of the Executive Council are also dominated by people from the business community and professionals. Among the members only Tam Yiu-chung, a trade unionist and member of the Democratic Alliance for the Betterment of Hong Kong, comes from a grass-roots background. Many executive councillors also have close connections with the mainland.[10]

Beijing loyalists were also able to dominate the provisional legislature established by the Beijing government following the collapse of the Sino-British talks regarding the Patten reforms. While a majority of the Provisional Legislative Council members served in the 1995 Legislative Council under the former colonial administration, political dynamics have undergone significant changes. The Democratic Party, the largest political force in the 1995 Legislative Council, was out of the provisional legislature. Political parties and other groups such as the Democratic Alliance for the Betterment of Hong Kong, the Hong Kong Progressive Alliance, and the Liberal Party, which had good relations with the leadership in Beijing during the territory's transition, became dominant forces in the legislature.

While pro-democratic forces returned to the first SAR Legislative Council following the May 1998 elections, the number of Democratic Party councillors has been reduced by 6 from 19 to 13, and the overall political strength of pro-democracy forces is short of one-third of the legislature (see table 12.1). The electoral arrangements for the first legislative elections in the SAR had the effect of ensuring that the Democratic Party and other pro-democracy groups such as the Frontier would be only a minority in the first Legislative Council in 1998. Of the 60 council seats only 20 were to be filled by direct elections based on geographical areas. Thirty seats, or half of the total, were to be filled by professional and business groups which were formed into functional constituencies, and

Table 12.1 **Political party/group strengths in Hong Kong's legislature, 1995–2000**

	Legislative Council (1995–1997)	Provisional Legislative Council (1997–1998)	First SAR Legislative Council (1998–2000)
Democratic Party	19	0	13
Liberal Party	10	10	9
DAB/FTU	7	11	10
ADPL	4	4	0
HKPA[1]	2	6	5
LDF[1]	1	3	n.a.
NHKA	1	2	n.a.
123 DA	1	0	0
Citizen Party[2]	n.a.	n.a.	1
Frontier[3]	n.a.	n.a.	3
NWSC[4]	n.a.	n.a.	1
Independents	15	24	19
Total	60	60	60

Source: Compiled by the author based on electoral results supplied by the government.

123 DA: 123 Democratic Alliance.

ADPL: Association for Democracy and the Development of the People's Livelihood.

DAB: Democratic Alliance for the Betterment of Hong Kong.

FTU: Federation of Trade Unions.

HKPA: Hong Kong Progressive Alliance.

LDF: Liberal Democratic Foundation.

NHKA: New Hong Kong Alliance.

NWSC: Neighbourhood and Workers' Service Centre.

[1] The HKPA and the LDF merged on 26 May 1997.

[2] The Citizen Party, formed in May 1997, did not take part in the Provisional Legco elections.

[3] The Frontier, formed on 26 August 1996, did not take part in the Provisional Legco elections.

[4] The NWSC candidate was also a Frontier member but decided to run under the NWSC banner.

10 seats were to be filled by an electoral committee. Motions, bills, or amendments of government bills introduced by individual Legislative Council members can only be passed with the support of a majority of members from both categories. This effectively imposes limitations on the power of the Legislative Council. Pro-Beijing forces, well represented in the functional constituencies and the Election Committee seats, have remained dominant in the legislature.

With more pro-Beijing businessmen gaining political prominence, and as mainland China becomes one of the leading investors in Hong Kong, a key question is: will various state enterprises from the mainland and other business ventures funded by mainland China–related organizations become the new *hongs* – firms owned and managed by British interests, which dominated the territory in colonial times? Chinese state enterprises had a long history of business activity in Hong Kong when the China Merchants Corporation was established. From 1949 to the late 1970s most mainland enterprises in Hong Kong were primarily trade agents without local business interests. By 1978 there were only 122 mainland enterprises in the territory. Their number expanded dramatically during the 1980s when a large number of provincial governments, major cities, and ministries set up companies in Hong Kong. By 1989 mainland enterprises registered in Hong Kong reached over 2,500. Between 1989 and 1991 the central government weeded out those considered not to have the necessary management and business capacities and the number was reduced to 1,500, before rising steadily to 1,830 in 1996.[11]

By the mid-1990s the mainland had already become a significant economic force in Hong Kong. In 1995 the gross asset value of mainland enterprises was estimated to be more than HK$1,300 billion (US$170 billion). Altogether there were 11 mainland conglomerates in Hong Kong with over HK$10 billion (US$1.2 billion) gross assets. Since May 1994 the Bank of China also become a Hong Kong dollar note issuing bank. With 11 sister banks, the Bank of China group has become the second largest banking group in the territory after Hongkong Bank. In addition to the financial sector, mainland enterprises have also penetrated into all the other major sectors of the Hong Kong economy, including trading, transportation, construction, real estate, hotels, retailing, and tourism.[12]

Many mainland enterprises also made use of the capital market in the territory by seeking public listing in the stock market. By mid-1997 the 63 listed enterprises, with a total share value of almost HK$390 billion (US$50 billion), were popularly referred to as "red-chip companies." The red chips achieved record highs in the run-up to the handover. In fact share prices for blue chips also went up whenever rumours about the injection of capital from mainland enterprises were reported. Some observers are referring to such companies as "pink chips." The expansion of mainland businesses in Hong Kong and their penetration of the economy have been extensive.

Representatives from major mainland enterprises are becoming not only more influential in the boardrooms of Hong Kong's corporate world, but also in public institutions. One example is the Exchange Fund Advisory Committee. The Exchange Fund reserves are a key element in maintaining Hong Kong's financial stability. On 17 October 1983 the Hong Kong government adopted a linked exchange rate system at a fixed rate of US$1 to HK$7.80. The core feature of the arrangement is the full backing of domestic currency notes by a foreign currency. In the foreign exchange market, the Hong Kong dollar exchange rate is determined by supply and demand. The rate has remained remarkably stable since 1983 largely because of Hong Kong's large official reserves. The reserves forming the Exchange Fund, managed by the Hong Kong Monetary Authority (HKMA), reached HK$535 billion at the end of 1996, or HK$83,316 per person in the territory. According to the Exchange Fund Ordinance, the financial secretary exercises control of the fund in consultation with an Exchange Fund Advisory Committee chaired by himself, with other members who are appointed by the governor. The committee advises the financial secretary as controller of the Exchange Fund on general policy relating to its deployment.[13] While the committee members sit in a personal capacity, they represent major banks in the territory.

In 1997 the membership consisted of the financial secretary, the chief excutive of the Hong Kong Monetary Authority, and top management representatives from major banks in Hong Kong, including the Hongkong and Shanghai Banking Corporation, the Bank of East Asia, the Standard Chartered Bank, the Chase Manhattan Bank, the Hang Seng Bank, and the Bank of China. Many members are also politically influential. Anthony Leung of Chase Manhattan is a member of the SAR Executive Council; the Bank of East Asia's David Li, who served on the SAR's selection and preparatory committees, represents the Financial Constituency in the Legislative Council. All are prominent figures in the field of finance who have spent most of their careers in the territory, with the exception of Bank of China's Liang Xiaoting.[14] Mr. Liang's membership clearly has do with his position at the Bank of China. More representatives from major mainland banks and other enterprises are likely to be appointed to important advisory bodies. The formation of the Hong Kong Chinese Enterprises Association in 1991 gave such enterprises a collective and distinct political voice. It is perhaps not surprising that as mainland business activities in the SAR expand, representatives from the more powerful enterprises will be appointed to major advisory bodies and play a more influential role in Hong Kong's economic governance.

However, the mainland Chinese enterprises are unlikely to play a role similar to that played by the *hongs*. The domination of British business interests was evident in the days of colonial rule. In 1965 over one-third of the seats of the Executive, Legislative, and Urban Councils were occupied by British businessmen. In 1976 all but two of the major business groups were owned and controlled by expatriate business families. But the *hongs* have been on the decline since then. By 1986 Chinese businessmen such as Li Ka Shing and Y. K. Pao had taken over a number of British firms, and expatriates occupied only 13 per cent of the council seats. The steep decline of the British businesses and their political influence reflected structural changes in the Hong Kong economy. A number of local Chinese firms have become immensely successful. The structural diversity of the Hong Kong economy, which consists of international businesses, a number of large Chinese firms, numerous small and medium-sized enterprises, and Chinese enterprises which are in turn diversified in nature, means that business interests are not always coherent, and this would make it hard for mainland Chinese enterprises to acquire the kind of dominance that the *hongs* once possessed.[15]

Moreover, the political elite from the pro-Beijing business community may also encounter resistance from the ranks of the bureaucracy. Unlike their counterparts elsewhere, as the elite of an administrative state Hong Kong's top civil servants have been both politicians and administrators responsible for formulating and implementing policies. Therefore they have had power to make policy choices as well as to explain government policies to the public. The rise of the new elite is threatening their positions.

Although pro-China and pro-business interests will be influential forces in shaping the economic governance of the Hong Kong SAR, the diverse economic structure and fragmentation of business and pro-China interests as well as resistance within the administration are likely to limit their influence. The introduction of electoral politics in Hong Kong also means that labour and welfare interests cannot be easily brushed off. While the institutional machinery which serves the new political elite in the SAR has become more powerful, Hong Kong's democratization in recent years has injected new elements into government-business relations as the territory transforms into a SAR within the PRC.

Only a few days before the political handover, on 25 June 1997, the Legislative Council hastily passed new labour laws to provide workers with the right of collective bargaining and better conditions of work. The government was opposed to the introduction of such laws, arguing that they had not been properly discussed in the normal consultative channels such as the Labour Advisory Board. The secretary for education and manpower, Joseph Wong, suggested that the laws would adversely affect industrial relations in Hong Kong with far-reaching consequences. The members of the Liberal Party, which represents business interests, walked out of the council meeting in disgust when their opposition to the bills was ignored by other legislators representing grass-roots and labour interests.[16]

Major chambers of commerce in Hong Kong expressed their opposition to the new labour laws in a joint newspaper advertisement, and many expect the SAR government to repeal the laws. Chairman of the Hong Kong General Chamber of Commerce James Tien wrote on 29 June 1997 that Hong Kong had been polarized by labour issues and policies under the last colonial administration. Tien, who is also a member of the Liberal Party, expected that "In the SAR era, employers and employees, instead of resorting to collective bargaining, strikes, union militancy and private members' bills will resolve their differences through reason, dialogue and compromise, and work towards a common goal – maintaining stability and prosperity for Hong Kong." He further maintained that "we need to ensure the executive administration is not overwhelmed by populist politicians who entice voters with free lunches and welfare promises. The representation in the legislature needs to be more diverse and reflective of the wide range of views in our community." He predicted that "In the SAR era, with economics taking precedence over politics, we will return to a more orderly and productive environment which we had during the time when our GDP growth was double what it is today."[17]

When the SAR government introduced the Legislative Provisions (Suspension of Operation) Bill 1997 to freeze seven laws passed by the former Legislative Council, including those related to labour matters, members of the Provisional Legislative Council raised objections.[18] The government's unprecedented move to suspend ordinances already in operation was seen as a departure from usual practices.[19] The Provisional Legislative Council supported the administration's position on four ordinances related to labour matters with 40 votes, but not the other ordinances. The council also extracted a promise from the government not to extend the freeze beyond 30 October 1997 without its approval.

There is little doubt that the business community has maintained its influence and indeed reasserted itself as the central political force under the Tung administration. This is demonstrated by the reversal of the democratization process with the establishment of a more pro-business and pro-Beijing Provisional Legislature. Pro-Beijing political forces continued to dominate the first SAR Legislative Council, helped by the new electoral arrangements, and pro-democratic political forces were left with 19 seats following the elections.

Unlike in the old colonial days, the legislature will not be dominated by the business elite alone. Not only will a significant minority voice in the form of the Democratic Party be likely to persist, but some of the pro-China groups such as the Democratic Alliance for the Betterment of Hong Kong, and the Hong Kong Federation of Trade Unions, are also strongly oriented towards labour and grass-roots interests. The labour laws passed by the Legislative Council were the result of a coalition among groups with different positions on the Beijing government. Furthermore, according to the Basic Law additional directly elected seats will be gradually introduced in the legislature: half of the 60-member assembly will be returned by direct election by 2004. With the introduction of competitive electoral politics, even in a limited form, and with a much better-developed political culture of open debate and discussion, even under constraints, the political landscape of Hong Kong has undergone fundamental change. The conditions for restoring the old intimate business-government relationship no longer exist.

Towards the end of colonial rule the administration had come under increasing pressure to re-define "positive non-interventionism." Political changes following the Sino-British negotiations for the return of Hong Kong to Chinese sovereignty have opened up a political system which was remained closed to those outside the establishment. As a commercial centre Hong Kong has also faced tougher competition from neighbouring industrializing economies. This chapter examines changes in the business-government relationship in the Hong Kong SAR by examining three interrelated issues: economic ideology, institutional and policy developments, and the political environment in the territory.[20]

Economic ideology in flux

Hong Kong's minimalist approach, originating in the nineteenth-century British tradition of allowing free play to market forces, has guided the government's economic policies ever since the establishment of the colony. In 1997 the territory won the title of the world's freest economy, according to the Heritage Foundation's index of economic freedom, for the third time in a row. In its 1997 review the foundation declared: "There is little government interference in the marketplace; taxes are low and predictable; increases in government spending are linked closely to economic growth; foreign trade is free; and regulations, in addition to being transparent, are applied both uniformly and consistently. Hong Kong now has the world's freest economy."[21]

The colonial administration's last annual report stated that "the government advocates free and fair competition. Business decisions are left to the private sector, except where social considerations are over-riding. It is considered that the allocation of resources in the economy is best left to market forces. Adopting this free-market philosophy, the government has not sought to influence the structure of industry through regulations, tax policies or subsidies." The government also held to a low tax regime and contained the growth rate of public-sector expenditure.[22] A recent analysis of the strength of the Hong Kong economy contains the following observation: "The clear separation in Hong Kong between the role of the government as referee, and the role of private companies as active players in the economy, is unique in Asia and rare world-wide."[23]

Although the Chinese system is officially socialist, the Chinese version of socialism clearly embraces the principles of a free-market economy. At the time of the political handover in July 1997, the arguments for believing that Hong Kong's economy would continue to prosper under the same model of economic governance were very powerful. The Hong Kong economy remained robust, and the economic fundamentals were strong. The new administration's more pro-business outlook as well as Beijing's economic interests in Hong Kong should also ensure that the political transition would not bring economic disruption, and that the ideology of a free-market economy would continue to guide the SAR. The major concern seemed to be arising from the growing presence of mainland enterprises in the SAR and whether the administration could maintain the integrity of its legal system without special privileges for Chinese enterprises in the territory.[24]

The constitutional arrangements for the Hong Kong SAR, as promised by the Joint Declaration and confirmed by the Basic Law, are meant to ensure the continuation of the existing system in Hong Kong which was guided by a liberal economic ideology. The Basic Law stipulated: "The socialist system and policies shall not be practised in the Hong Kong SAR, and the previous capitalist system and way of life shall remain unchanged for 50 years" (Article 5).

The framework of economic governance as provided for under the Basic Law included the following elements: independence, preservation of the present economic and legal framework, development of appropriate policies to maintain the current financial system which is both liberal and highly open, and maintenance of the existing international network. These features are stipulated by various articles in the Basic Law:

- The Hong Kong SAR shall have independent finances. It shall use its own financial revenues without contributing to the central government. The central government also cannot levy taxes in the SAR. (Article 106.)
- The SAR shall practise an independent taxation system and continue to pursue a low-tax policy. (Article 108.)
- The Hong Kong SAR shall provide an appropriate economic and legal environment for maintaining Hong Kong's status as a financial centre. (Article 109.)
- The Hong Kong SAR shall formulate its own monetary and financial policies, and safeguard the free operation of financial business and markets with proper regulations. (Article 110.)
- The Hong Kong SAR shall ensure the continued free convertibility of currency with no foreign exchange control, and the free flow of capital in and out of the territory. (Article 112.)

- The Hong Kong SAR shall maintain its status as a free port, remain as a separate customs territory, and pursue a policy of free trade. (Articles 114, 115, and 116.)

In a study of the legal order of the SAR, one of Hong Kong's most prominent public law experts states that "the intention in the Basic Law was to entrench the existing capitalist system."[25] The reference to previous/existing practices and policies suggests that the SAR government would have to operate within the economic framework that was in place prior to the signature of the Joint Declaration between the two sovereign governments. While the legal framework stipulated in the Basic Law has guaranteed the independence and liberal orientation of the economic system in Hong Kong, the SAR would still be able to pursue broad economic objectives using different instruments and with varying degrees of involvement in macroeconomic management.

Hong Kong's 1997–98 budget, which is a product of joint Sino-British consultation, confirmed that the capitalist system will remain unchanged, and the commitment to Hong Kong's role as an international business and financial centre was demonstrated by the administration's decision not to increase business and profit taxes. In 1998, when the financial secretary announced tax cuts and increased benefits for the public in the first budget that was prepared wholly for the SAR, he also maintained that the SAR government remained small and efficient, with total public expenditure kept below 20 per cent of GDP.[26]

At the time of the political handover, the administration was set to carry on the laissez-faire tradition of the previous administration. The SAR inherited a very strong economy. In 1997 Hong Kong was the world's fifth largest banking centre for external financial transactions, the fifth largest foreign exchange market, the seventh largest stock market, the seventh largest trader, and the busiest container port. It was ranked as the second most competitive economy in the world in 1997 after Singapore by the World Economic Forum, and reclassified as an advanced economy by the International Monetary Fund. In Financial Secretary Donald Tsang's words, "Hong Kong is already the best place in the world in which to do business. The Government is totally committed to ensuring that it remains so."[27]

In February 1998, outlining some of the economic problems Hong Kong could have to weather in 1998 and 1999, the financial secretary remained optimistic about the SAR's economic situation. Acknowledging the economic pain resulting for the SAR from a sharp decline in stock-market and property-market values, he nevertheless remained optimistic about Hong Kong's economic outlook. While the government recognized that the financial turmoil would damage the territory's external trade growth and that unemployment would likely rise, the financial secretary forecast a modest yet positive GDP growth of 3.5 per cent for 1998. He also predicted a solid 4.8 per cent growth in exports of goods and a 3.5 per cent growth of exports of services, as well as an inflation rate at around 5 per cent.[28]

In choosing "Riding Out the Storm: Renewing Hong Kong Strengths" as the title of his speech, the financial secretary maintained that he was guided by two principles: assurance of continuity matched with incentives for new growth. The chief executive has also repeatedly affirmed that "we practise a sound macro-economic policy of small government, with strong support for the free market."[29] This seemed consistent with the economic policy of previous administrations. In short, the new SAR government indicated that it would continue a pro-business and laissez-faire economic policy, i.e., "business as usual."

But as Norman Miners has pointed out, the government's belief in the free market is not absolute. Sir Philip Haddon-Cave, financial secretary of the territory during the 1970s, who coined the term "positive non-intervention" to describe the government's approach to economic management, clearly felt that the administration did have a role in the management of Hong Kong's economy. His view was that the government would provide the basic legal framework and infrastructure to facilitate the operation of market forces.[30] From the 1970s onward, however, the growing sophistication of the Hong Kong economy, and rising protectionism in the form of non-tariff barriers in the industrialized world as well as the intensification of competition from neighbouring countries, have eroded the liberal economic ideology of the administration.[31] In fact the business community, which had in past always endorsed the liberal economic ideology of the government, has urged the government to provide more support to business.

While the government has continued to adopt a hands-off approach to economic management, a number of economic crises have forced the government to step up regulatory actions and provide more direct support to local industries. For example, the government established the Securities and Futures Commission in 1989 to regulate the trading of securities, futures, and leveraged foreign exchange contracts in response to the exposure of deficiencies of regulatory framework following the market crash of 1987.[32] Reflecting growing pressure on the government to assume a more active role in regulating economic activities and providing more support to local businesses, the Hong Kong 1997 yearbook proclaimed that the government's policy was "minimum interference and maximum support."[33] In fact the market crash of 1997 prompted the government to conduct a comprehensive review of the financial markets in Hong Kong. Although the report maintained that the economic system in the territory was sound and the regulatory mechanism had worked during the financial crisis, it also made specific recommendations to tighten the regulatory framework further.[34]

In his first policy speech as chief executive of the SAR, Tung Chee-hwa suggested that under his leadership Hong Kong's development strategy would be based on a free-market economy and a prudent fiscal policy. But he obviously considered that a new strategy would be required to push Hong Kong forward. He announced that a commission on strategy development would be set up to "conduct reviews and studies on our economy, human resources, education, housing, land supply, environmental protection, and relations with the Mainland, to ensure that our resources are well used, and that we keep up with the world trends in competitive terms, and that we maintain the vitality of Hong Kong's economic development."[35] Thus while Tung preaches the same fundamental economic philosophy as previous administrations, he obviously also wants to adopt a more proactive approach in developing a new economic strategy for the SAR.

From a different direction, the introduction of a more representative Legislative Council since the early 1990s has also generated more pressure for the promotion of labour and welfare rights, which in turn has led to more intense pressure on the government from the business community to protect business interests in Hong Kong.

In general, the number of public institutions involved in developing government economic policies, maintaining the regulatory framework for the economy, and promoting economic growth and better opportunities for Hong Kong businesses has grown steadily in recent years.

Institutional and policy changes

The Hong Kong state has been described as weak not because it has an ineffective administration or one with limited autonomy vis-à-vis society, but because it has kept government involvement in the economy to a minimum in the past. The weakness of the Hong Kong state was therefore the result of a policy choice guided by a liberal economic ideology and other political considerations. In terms of resource and capacity the bureaucratic machinery of Hong Kong is by no means weak.

The chief executive of the SAR took over a powerful bureaucratic machinery when he assumed office on 1 July 1997. Under colonial rule, political power was always concentrated in the hands of the governor. The governors were advised by the Executive Council and implemented government policies through the policy branches which were in turn supported by government departments and agencies. A parallel network of statutory bodies, many directly answerable to the governors, also existed to support or implement government policies when direct governmental control was regarded as inappropriate.

When the SAR government came into existence in 1997 there were 15 policy and resources bureaux,[36] 71 government departments and agencies, plus a number of statutory bodies.[37] The government employed over 180,000 civil servants, or about 6 per cent of the labour force. Until the 1980s the legislature was an appointed body dominated by the civil service and business. The formal governmental and public agencies or corporations were supported by 500-odd boards, councils, and advisory committees composed of civil servants and members of the public appointed by the government.

It is not my intention to review comprehensively all the institutions involved in the economic governance of Hong Kong. This section highlights the role of some of the more important institutions and assesses the impact of Hong Kong's political transition on such institutions.

Of the three major categories of public institutions – government branches and departments, other public agencies, and advisory committees – those in charge of financial matters and trade and industry are the most relevant in the present context. The Finance Bureau (formerly the Financial Branch) plays a critical role, being responsible for overall resource planning including drawing up and applying overall public expenditure guidelines. It manages and co-ordinates the annual resource allocation exercise, and compiles the annual estimates. In addition, the bureau also manages the government's revenue policy and administration, both to ensure that sufficient revenue is raised, and to keep the tax system as simple, stable, and productive as possible. It lays down and implements policies and procedures to ensure effective control and management of public revenues and expenditure, including assets and investments. Its other roles include: exercising policy responsibility for taxation, rates, fees, and charges; government accounting arrangements; procurement and tendering; land transport; printing; information technology; and the government estate. Finally it also serves as the formal interface between the administration and the legislature on all financial matters.[38]

Other government bureaux and departments such as the trade and industries departments also play important roles in economic governance and in facilitating the expansion of the economy. The Trade Department, for example, proclaiming its mission as to be a driving force in liberalizing world trade, plays a key role not only in the promotion and protection of Hong Kong's economic and trade interests, but also in ensuring compliance, and in safeguarding the integrity and credibility of Hong Kong's trade regime. The department has to make sure that Hong Kong industrialists and traders observe the textiles control policy in accordance with the World Trade Organisation Agreement on Textiles and Clothing. It also imposes licensing control for pharmaceutical products and medicines on health and safety grounds, and ensures the availability of essential foodstuffs for emergency situations. It exercises licensing control over local consumption of controlled substances as agreed under the 1987 Montreal Protocol on Substances that Deplete the Ozone Layer. The department also imposes licensing control over strategic commodities to prevent Hong Kong being used as a conduit for the proliferation of weapons.[39]

The Industry Department is responsible for facilitating the further development of manufacturing and service industries. While the department has declared that its commitment to promote manufacturing and service industries will not lead to interference with market forces, it has become more active in developing closer relationships among government, business, education and training institutions, and industrial support bodies. Its priority areas include "physical, human and technological infrastructure; productivity and quality; applied research and development of products and processes; technology upgrade and transfer; and monitoring and informing industries of world-wide developments that may impinge on their competitiveness in the global market."[40]

Although the government does subscribe to a liberal economic ideology, it is clear that the government cannot be truly laissez-faire as the Hong Kong economy becomes increasingly complex and sophisticated. In recent years the Hong Kong government's role in macroeconomic management has become far more visible. A large number of government departments and other public corporations have been set up to regulate the economy and provide more support to local industries, to ensure the territory's compliance with international agreements.

One example is the Intellectual Property Department. As intellectual property has become an important element in the world trade regime, the government established the department on 2 July 1990. It is the focal point in the review and enforcement of Hong Kong's intellectual property legislation. The department also administers the system of registration of trade marks and patents.[41] Of the numerous institutions established in recent years in economic governance, the most important is the Hong Kong Monetary Authority. It was established on 1 April 1993, by merging the Office of the Exchange Fund with the Office of the Commissioner of Banking. The primary monetary policy objective of the HKMA is to maintain exchange rate stability within the framework of the linked exchange rate system which is set at the rate of approximately US$1.00 to HK$7.80. The authority is also required to promote "the safety and stability of the banking system through the regulation of banking business and the business of taking deposits, and the supervision of authorized institutions; and to promote the efficiency, integrity and development of the financial system, particularly payment and settlement arrangements."[42] In defence of the Hong Kong currency in October 1997, the HKMA adopted measures which led to increased interest rates in the territory. The attack on the Hong Kong currency has prompted debates in Hong Kong about the link system. While a majority of Hong Kong analysts and the public support the system, some economists have argued that the HKMA should not rely solely on interest rates to defend the Hong Kong currency. But after the HKMA's review of the currency defences, the government decided to continue with the existing linked exchange rate mechanisms.[43] In August 1998, however, the government decided to intervene in the stock market to prevent "speculators" who were engaged in double play – selling Hong Kong dollars to force a higher interest rate and selling short in the stock market anticipation of a fall in stock prices as a result of an interest rate increase.

The government's more proactive approach to economic management is reflected by the establishment of organizations such as the Hong Kong Industrial Technology Centre Corporation, the Hong Kong Industrial Estates Corporation, a Software Industry Information Centre and Cyberspace Centre, and efforts in promoting research and development as well as the establishment of the Government Task Force on Services Promotion.

The financial secretary in the 1997 budget reaffirmed the proactive approach. He identified government efforts in four areas: manufacturing, services, the financial sector, and infrastructure. In his speech he announced the government's plans in support of the manufacturing sector which included: HK$410 million earmarked for Science Park Phase I; planning for a second industrial technology centre; planning work started on a fourth industrial estate; applied research and development schemes to support technology ventures with HK$250 million seed money. In the area of services promotion, the government announced the formation of a new Services Promotion Strategy Group, bringing the government and the private sector together. The government also concluded negotiations on all major air services agreements and issued six new licenses for personal communications services. The Export Credit Insurance Corporation is to introduce a specific insurance policy for small and medium enterprises. Through the Services Support Fund, the government committed HK$28 million to help 14 projects. The Trade Development Council is to spend another HK$30 million in 1997–98 to promote exports of services. The financial sector is supported through the introduction of legislation to permit development of a captive insurance industry. A Mortgage Corporation is to commence operation in 1997. The government is also to develop a Mandatory Provident Fund to spur creation of new financial products, and launched 10-year Exchange Fund Notes. A large number of infrastructural projects have also been completed or are about to be finished, including the Western Harbour Crossing (HK$7.5 billion) the Ching Ma Bridge, the world's longest road/rail suspension bridge (HK$7.9 billion), the Convention Centre Extension, the new international airport with a second runway, and plans for the Western Corridor Railway and commuter railway extensions.[44]

The government also formed a Business Advisory Group on 1 December 1996, and established three subgroups in February 1997 to examine issues such as deregulation, cost of compliance assessment, and transfer of services to the business sector. The new Business and Services Promotion Unit was formed in May 1997 to provide executive support. A one-stop Business Licence Information Centre in the Industry Department was opened in September 1997.

In its policy programmes for 1997–98 the Tung administration committed about US$64 million to support the commercialization of research in information technology and other high technology fields," and US$6.4 million to "finance initiatives which help sustain and improve the competitiveness of the service sector." The government also moved ahead with the development of the Science Park at Pak Shek Kok, and the establishment of a second technology centre as well as a fourth industrial estate in Tuen Mun, and explored the need for the establishment of a business park.[45]

The last colonial administration had set in train a proactive approach and gradually developed a set of institutional arrangements which have become more complex and much wider in scope than before. Instead of reversing the trend in economic governance, the Tung administration has maintained a strong element of institutional continuity and strengthened the government's role in economic affairs.

Conclusions

Political developments in Hong Kong since the 1980s have altered the framework of economic governance which once served the colonial state well. Towards the end of Hong Kong's colonial days, its liberal economic ideology had already been eroded not only by a deteriorating international economic environment and increased competition from neighbouring economies, but also by a more politicized domestic environment. While the government still maintained a policy of minimum interference, positive non-interventionism was re-defined. The institutions involved in economic governance have become more powerful as a result of new regulatory requirements created by the increasing sophistication of the economy as well as international developments.

The "weak state" of Hong Kong has tried to become more assertive since the establishment of the SAR by attempting to restore the pre-Patten political framework. The new political framework which has emerged in the SAR, however, is far more complex than the old days. The dominance of the bureaucrats is being challenged by the new pro-Beijing business elite in a system which is marked by the growing importance of competitive politics. Internationally, the globalized nature of the world economy has reinforced the vulnerability of an open and relatively small economy like Hong Kong and the importance of keeping the territory competitive. The SAR economy has been badly shaken by external economic forces. The Asian financial crisis, precipitated by the collapse of Southeast Asian currencies in the second half of 1997, subsequently led to a wider financial turmoil in the region and crippled most East Asian economies. The transfer of sovereignty and domestic political changes have also led to the reconfiguration of economic and political interests.

While mainland Chinese enterprises are becoming more important in the territory, they do not seem to have acquired special privileges. To what extent influences from Beijing would in the long run eventually alter the rules of the game in Hong Kong still remains unclear. For the time being, however, the central government has adopted a hands-off approach to the SAR. The more immediate challenge to the Tung administration is that on the one hand it has to respond to popular demand for improving the livelihood of the people, and on the other hand it must face the business groups' misgivings about turning Hong Kong into a welfare state as well as their demand for more resources during a major economic downturn. The government's approach to economic management is evolving within the framework of domestic and international political and economic situations which have been changing rapidly. As Hong Kong becomes more politicized and the contradictions in the political system surface, it is hardly surprising that the model of economic governance as practised in colonial days has become inappropriate. Unfortunately, the Hong Kong SAR will only be able to develop a coherent approach to economic governance after it establishes a stable political order.

Notes

1. A comparative study of the different paths of economic and political development in East Asia is Anek Laothamatas (ed.), *Democracy in Southeast and East Asia* (Singapore: Institute of Southeast Asian Studies, 1997).

2. See discussions in Andrew MacIntyre (ed.), *Business and Government in Industrializing Asia* (Ithaca, N.Y.: Cornell University Press, 1994), pp. 3–4. The standard work on the subject is Frederic Deyo, *The Political Economy of The New Asian Industrialism* (Ithaca, N.Y.: Cornell University Press, 1987). See also Yu-han Chu, "State Structure and Economic Adjustment of the East Asian Newly Industrializing Countries," *International Organization* 43(4); Stephan Haggard, *Pathways from the Periphery: The Politics of Growth in the Newly Industrializing Countries* (Ithaca, N.Y.: Cornell University Press, 1990).

3. Norman Miners, *Government and Politics of Hong Kong* (Hong Kong: Oxford University Press, 1994), p. 46.

4. A comprehensive account of how Hong Kong was governed is Norman Miners, *Government and Politics of Hong Kong*, 5th ed. with post-handover update by James T. H. Tang (Hong Kong: Oxford University Press, 1998).

5. One detailed study of the Chinese Communist leadership's attitude towards Hong Kong from the 1940s to the late 1960s is Gary Wayne Catron, "China and Hong Kong, 1945–1967" (Ph.D. diss., Harvard University, 1971). For a more general account of the evolution of China's policy towards Hong Kong, see Kevin Lane, *Sovereignty and the Status Quo: The Historical Roots of China's Hong Kong Policy* (Boulder, Colo.: Westview Press, 1990).

6. For a discussion of the history and nature of the colonial government's consultation with the business community, see Norman Miners, "Consultation with Business Interests: The Case of Hong Kong," *Asian Journal of Public Administration* December 1996; 18(2): 246–56.

7. Government of the SAR, *Estimates of Gross Domestic Product 1961–1997* (Hong Kong: Census and Statistics Department, HKSAR, 1998); Bod Howlett, ed., *Hong Kong – A New Era: A Review of 1997* (Hong Kong: Information Services Department, HKSAR Government, 1998), p. 43.

8. Edward K. Y. Chen, "The Economic Setting," in Ng Sek Hong and David G Lethbridge (eds.), *The Business Environment in Hong Kong*, 3d ed. (Hong Kong: Oxford University Press, 1995), p. 34.

9. Ibid., pp. 35–40.

10. The members of the SAR government's first Executive Council are: Chief Executive Tung Chee-hwa; Chief Secretary for Administration Anson Chan; Financial Secretary Donald Tsang; Secretary for Justice Elsie Leung; Sze-yuen Chung (convenor), Nellie Fong, Rosanna Wong, Henry Tang, Charles Lee, Tam Yiu-chung, Yang Ti-liang, Leung Chun-ying, Antony Leung, Raymond Ch'ien, and Chung Shui-ming.

11. A useful account of the development of mainland economic interests in Hong Kong is Wulan Mulun (ed.), *Maixiang ershiyi shiji de xianggang jingji* [Hong Kong's economy towards the twenty-first century] (Hong Kong: Hong Kong Joint Publishing, 1997), pp. 583–613.

12. Ibid., pp. 585–605. See also Hong Kong Trade Development Council, *Economic Information on Hong Kong and China*, 4 September 1998. For an analysis of mainland China–Hong Kong economic relations, see also Yun-Wing Sung, *The China–Hong Kong Connection* (Cambridge: Cambridge University Press, 1991).

13. Hong Kong Monetary Authority Website, Hong Kong Government Information Centre.

14. Ibid.

15. Wong Siu-lun, "Business and Politics in Hong Kong during the Transition," in *Hong Kong in Transition 1992* (Hong Kong: One Country Two Systems Research Institute, 1993), pp. 489–514, esp. pp. 491–500.

16. See *South China Morning Post*, 25 June 1997; *Wen Wei Po*, 24 June 1997; and *Ming Pao* editorial, 25 June 1997.

17. James Tien, "Playing to Our Strength," *South China Morning Post*, 29 June 1997.
18. Protection of the Harbour Ordinance 1997; Employment (Amendment) (No. 4) Ordinance 1997; Occupational Deafness (Compensation) (Amendment) Ordinance 1997; Employment (Amendment) (No. 5) Ordinance 1997; Employees' Rights to Representation, Consultation and Collective Bargaining Ordinance 1997; Trade Unions (Amendment) (No. 2) Ordinance 1997; and Hong Kong Bill of Rights (Amendment) Ordinance 1997.
19. Press release by the government, 8 July 1997.
20. The discussion here is inspired by Jagdish Bhagwati, *Protectionism* (Cambridge, Mass.: MIT Press, 1988).
21. The Heritage Foundation, *1997 Index of Economic Freedom*.
22. *Hong Kong 1997* (Hong Kong: Information Services Department, 1997), p. 64.
23. Michael J. Enright, Edith E. Scott, and David Dodwell, *The Hong Kong Advantage* (Hong Kong: Oxford University Press, 1997), p. 30.
24. See, for example, Yasheng Huang, "The Economic and Political Integration of Hong Kong: Implications for Government-Business Relations," in Warren I. Cohen and Li Zhao (eds.), *Hong Kong under Chinese Rule: The Economic and Political Implications of Reversion* (Cambridge: Cambridge University Press, 1997), pp. 96–113.
25. Yash Ghai, *Hong Kong's New Constitutional Order: The Resumption of Chinese Sovereignty and the Basic Law* (Hong Kong: University of Hong Kong Press, 1997), p. 152.
26. Donald Tsang, *The 1997–98 Budget: Continuity in a Time of Change*, 12 March 1997 (Hong Kong: Hong Kong Government, 1997); *The 1998–99 Budget: Riding Out the Storm, Renewing Hong Kong Strengths*, 18 February 1998 (Hong Kong: Hong Kong Special Administrative Region Government, 1998).
27. Tsang, *The 1997–98 Budget*.
28. Tsang, *The 1998–99 Budget*, pp. 8–9.
29. Speech by the Chief Executive, Mr. Tung Chee-hwa, at a lunch hosted by the Hong Kong Trade Development Council and the Conseil National du Patronat Français International (French Employers' Association), in Paris, Wednesday, 11 March 1998.
30. Miners, *The Government and Politics of Hong Kong*, 5th ed. p. 47.
31. For an analysis of the impact of protectionism on the world trading system, see Jagdish Bhagwati, The *World Trading System at Risk* (Princeton, N.J.: Princeton University Press, 1991).
32. For a brief official history of the Hong Kong Securities and Futures Commission see the Commission's website: http://www.hksfc.org.hk/eng/about/backgrnd.htm, "Historic Background to the SFC," June 1997.
33. *Hong Kong 1997*, p. 64.
34. *Report on Financial Markets Review* (Hong Kong: Hong Kong Special Administrative Region Government, April 1998).
35. *Building Hong Kong for a New Era: Address by the Chief Executive, the Honourable Tung Chee-hwa, at the Provisional Legislative Council Meeting on 8 October 1997* (Hong Kong: The Hong Kong Special Administrative Region of the People's Republic of China, 1997), para. 16.
36. Broadcasting, Culture and Sport Bureau; Civil Service Bureau; Constitutional Affairs Bureau; Economic Services Bureau; Education and Manpower Bureau; Finance Bureau; Financial Services Bureau; Health and Welfare Bureau; Home Affairs Bureau; Housing Bureau; Planning, Environment and Lands Bureau; Security Bureau; Trade and Industry Bureau; Transport Bureau; Works Bureau.
37. Agriculture and Fisheries Department; Architectural Services Department; Audit Department; Auxiliary Medical Services; Buildings Department; Census and Statistics Department; Civil Aid Services; Civil Aviation Department; Civil Engineering Depart-

ment; Civil Service Training and Development Institute; Companies Registry; Correctional Services Department; Customs and Excise Department; Drainage Services Department; Education Department; Electrical and Mechanical Services Department; Environmental Protection Department; Fire Services Department; Government Flying Service; Government Laboratory; Government Land Transport Agency; Government Property Agency; Government Supplies Department; Health Department; Highways Department; Home Affairs Department; Hospital Services Department; Housing Authority; Housing Department; Immigration Department; Industry Department; Information Services Department; Information Technology Services Department; Inland Revenue Department; Intellectual Property Department; Labour Department; Lands Department; Land Registry; Legal Aid Department; Legal Department; Management Services Agency; Marine Department; New Airport Projects Co-ordination Office (Hong Kong Airport Core Programme); Official Language Agency; Official Receiver's Office; Planning Department; Post Office; Printing Department; Public Records Office; Radio Television Hong Kong; Rating and Valuation Department; Regional Services Department; Registration and Electoral Office; Royal Hong Kong Police Force; Royal Observatory; Social Welfare Department; Student Financial Assistance Agency; Telecommunications Authority; Office of the Television and Entertainment Licensing Authority; Territory Development Department; Trade Department; Transport Department; Treasury; Urban Services Department; Water Supplies Department. Airport Authority; Hong Kong Broadcasting Authority; Consumer Council; Employees Retraining Board; Equal Opportunities Commission; Hong Kong Arts Development Council; Hong Kong Council for Academic Accreditation; Hong Kong Council on Smoking and Health; Hong Kong Examinations Authority; Hong Kong Export Credit Insurance Corporation; Hong Kong Industrial Estates Corporation; Hong Kong Industrial Technology Centre Corporation; Hong Kong Monetary Authority; Hong Kong Productivity Council; Hong Kong Sports Development Board; Hong Kong Tourist Association; Hong Kong Trade Development Council; Hospital Authority; Independent Commission against Corruption; Independent Police Complaints Council; Kowloon-Canton Railway Corporation; Legal Aid Services Council; Mass Transit Railway Corporation; Occupational Safety and Health Council; the Ombudsman; Port Development Board; Privacy Commissioner for Personal Data, Office of the Public Service Commission; Securities and Futures Commission; Standing Commission on Civil Service Salaries and Conditions of Service; University Grants Committee; Vocational Training Council.

38. The official description of the various roles of the bureau is at its website, Hong Kong Government Information Centre: http://www.info.gov.hk/fb.
39. Details of the Trade Department's work are at the department's website, Hong Kong Government Information Centre: http://www.info.gov/trade/department/.
40. Industry Department website, Hong Kong Government Information Centre: http://www.ingo.gov.hk/id/.
41. Hong Kong Monetary Authority website, Hong Kong Government Information Centre: http://info.gov.hk/hkma/.
42. Hong Kong Monetary Authority website, Hong Kong Government Information Centre: http://info.gov.hk/hkma/.
43. For a discussion of the issue by Joseph Yam (Chief Executive, Hong Kong Monetary Authority), see *The Hong Kong Dollar Link* (Speech at Hong Kong Trade Development Council Financial Roadshow in Tokyo) 3 March 1998.
44. Tsang, *The 1997–98 Budget.*
45. *The 1997 Policy Address: Policy Programmes* (Hong Kong: Hong Kong Special Administrative Region Government, 1997), p. 308.

Conclusion

13

Conclusion

Jean Blondel and Ian Marsh

By the end of the 1990s, East and Southeast Asia were sharply divided between those countries which had experienced a major political change and had moved, in some cases repeatedly, from authoritarianism to liberal democracy, and those which had experienced no change and had been for a period – often a long one – partly democratic and partly authoritarian. There was little ground for suggesting that change was about to occur in this second group of countries, except perhaps in Indonesia, though there was also little expectation that changes which have begun to occur in that country would quickly bring about a genuine form of liberal democracy.

To this extent, the countries of the region were providing only limited evidence for the prevailing view in the political science literature according to which socio-economic well-being was highly likely to be connected with political liberalization. This relative "exceptionalism" of East and Southeast Asia has perhaps not been given the attention which it deserves, although exploration of the roots of this state of affairs could well provide an indication as to what tends to occur at the border of the area in which liberal democracy is strongly and even permanently associated with socio-economic well-being.

However important such a problem may be, another was felt to be more pressing, given the strength of political opinion on the subject, in some quarters at least: namely whether liberal democracy, achieved by whatever means and in particular independently or not from socio-economic development, was likely to impede further "progress" in the direction of economic well-being. There was a clear need to explore the validity of the very strong claim made by a number of leaders of the region that the Asian "miracle" was due to "Asian values" and that these values did not coincide at all with liberal democracy. Indeed, these claims were echoed to an extent, if perhaps with more subtlety as well as a degree of ambiguity, by a substantial number of Western scholars working on the region: it was often regarded as axiomatic that certain characteristics of the work ethic and perhaps of the family structure were in part responsible for the success of the economies of the region, following that of Japan. It was also regarded as axiomatic that this success was due in part to the strength of the civil service, with the corollary that such strength was dependent, on the one hand, on the level of education of the citizens, but also, on the other, on the propensity of these citizens to "accept" what was suggested to them by authority. Views of this kind were adhered to widely, perhaps even universally, in the West, indeed typically with a tinge of envy: this envy surely explains in part the degree of condescension of many comments made about the region's plight in 1997 and later.

It is therefore perhaps not too much of a caricature to summarize the commonplace notion of the relationship between the politics and economics of the area in the following way. By and large, citizens of East and Southeast Asia do not seem to be "inherently" and "naturally" as disposed as those of the West to adopt liberal democratic formulas; to an extent, this characteristic accounts for or at least contributes to the extraordinary speed at which the Pacific fringe of Asia developed economically in the second half of the twentieth century. Thus it is not only because some leaders of the area have emphatically stated that "Asian values" were antinomic to liberal democracy that the question of the impact of liberal democracy on economic development needs to be explored: this is also because variations on this theme were found to be expressed in many quarters.

Yet the underlying hypothesis was rarely explored, let alone tested. This was in part, as was pointed out in the introductory chapter, because it was difficult to undertake such a test, although efforts were made in this direction, in particular by Feng;[1] but these efforts were focused primarily on other regions, Latin America in particular, since outside Europe and North America, only in Latin America was it possible, up to the 1980s, to find a sufficient number of countries which had been liberal democratic for a period: East and Southeast Asia were naturally ruled out, as only from the second half of that decade did liberal democracy begin to spread, Japan having previously been the only country of the area belonging to that category. However, given that the characteristics with which Latin America was typically associated in respect to its socio-economic values were vastly different for those of East and Southeast Asia, it seemed difficult to believe that what might be true of the former would also be true of the latter. Moreover, since the tests which had been applied to the Latin American case were contradictory or inconclusive, it seemed pointless to extrapolate to East and Southeast Asia what could be concluded about Latin America.

Given this situation, the only way to begin to make some progress in assessing the possible impact of liberal democracy on economic performance in East and Southeast Asia was to examine what had indeed been happening in that region once liberal democracy had begun to spread beyond Japan from the mid-1980s – for the first time in Taiwan, for almost the first time in Korea and Thailand, and after over a decade of dictatorship in the Philippines, while Malaysia, Singapore, and Indonesia maintained their traditional political characteristics.

An enquiry of this kind was littered with difficulties, however. First, the number of countries was obviously too small for statistical tests to be applied: the case-study method had to be used, with the consequence that there was never any question of "proving" what the impact of liberal democracy on economic development might be. Second, this small number of countries was strongly divided economically into two groups. Two countries, Korea and Taiwan, had been part of the first flock of "geese" to follow Japan; the other were part of the second flock, indeed to a large extent because Japan had been instrumental in their economic progress. Third, this division into two groups was underlined by the fact that the two groups differed rather strongly with respect to what was usually regarded as the key intermediate variable, namely the strength and capacity of the bureaucracy. What was clear was that the countries of East and Southeast Asia benefited from bureaucracies which were markedly more efficient and markedly more penetrating than those in the rest of Asia including China, in Latin America, or in Africa; but what was also clear was that the bureaucracy displayed more of these qualities in East Asia than in Southeast Asia. If the bureaucracy was the intermediate variable and if, perhaps, the characteristics of the bureaucracy, including the characteristic relationships between people and bureaucracy, accounted for the "miracle" which the region underwent, there should then be some differences between East and Southeast Asia. Thus the very nature of the impact of liberal democracy on economic development, as diffracted by the bureaucracy, was rendered more difficult to assess and even to identify.

As if the question were not already sufficiently complex, matters were made more problematic by the outbreak of the economic crisis of 1997. At one level, the crisis could be regarded as being somewhat irrelevant to the problem under investigation, first because it was manifestly a second-order problem which did not affect the fundamental point that the region had developed markedly more quickly than any other part of the world since the end of World War II, and second because the crisis affected both "rather authoritarian no-change" countries (Indonesia, Malaysia) and countries which had become liberal democratic (Korea, Thailand). Yet even if democratization was not to be viewed as the "cause" of the crisis, the crisis could not be regarded as irrelevant, both because of its major impact on the economies of the countries concerned and because the methods adopted to move out of the crisis might differ depending on whether the countries were or were not liberal democracies. It could of course be argued that this last point was beneficial for the study, since it could provide a further means of assessing whether liberal democracy was more or less favourable to economic development than authoritarianism; but the hope of being able to use such a characteristic was limited by the fact that the freedom of action of all the countries of the area was markedly restrained by decisions of international bodies, the IMF and the World Bank in particular, by Western governments, and by Japan, as well as by private banks. All the countries would therefore be likely to follow a similar path, whether or not they had become liberal democracies.

There was nonetheless no other way but to undertake case studies of the countries of the region if some conclusions, albeit tentative, were to be drawn about the problem at hand. The eight case studies which have been presented here indicate what was clear from the start, namely that the evidence which could be provided did not lead to straightforward conclusions. Yet by the same token this evidence does lead to the conclusion that moves towards liberal democracy have "caused" neither the end of the process of economic development nor even its slowing down. Moreover, the case studies did more than provide such a negative, if basic, conclusion: they provided a rich set of insights into the nature of liberal democratic changes where they were taking place, as well as about the nature of the political process where authoritarianism continued to prevail. Similarly, the case studies provided important insights into the characteristics of the bureaucracy and into the nature of the relationship between the political authorities (as they had been all along or as they had become) and the bureaucracy. The case studies therefore constitute important sources: they make it possible to describe more accurately both the political and the politico-administrative processes of the countries of the region. Moreover, since the eight countries have been examined on the basis of the same general framework, they provide a more solid basis than hitherto for a truly comparative analysis.

The aim of this conclusion is therefore in the first instance to bring together and reflect on the political and politico-administrative characteristics of the countries concerned. Then, on the basis of the examination of these characteristics, as well by assessing how far the economic crisis of 1997 can be handled differently in a liberal democratic and in an authoritarian context, reflections will be made about possible future trends, in particular about the extent to which liberal democracy is likely to be consolidated in the region; and, if so, about the effect that such a development may have on the region's economic well-being.

Political and politico-administrative processes

The political process and the role of parties

On the political plane, as was pointed out in chapter 2, the emphasis of the present inquiry has been on drawing a concrete picture of the political process in the countries of the region. This has meant first and foremost describing how parties function. Whatever may be said about their limitations, parties justifiably occupy not merely a key position but the key position in the political life of all types of modern societies.[2] On the one hand, they help to maintain (for a long while at least) authoritarian and even totalitarian governments, as has been demonstrated by Communist regimes; on the other hand, they help to maintain, indeed constitute the only way of maintaining, liberal democracies. Yet, as was pointed out in some detail in chapter 2, parties may vary from being internally very divided and even almost inchoate, to being united and well structured. If the first type of situation obtains, their capacity to link the people to the government is limited: in such cases, most of the power is at the level of local cadres or notables; the relationship between these notables and the electors is clientelistic while the link between the notables and the national organization is loose. Influence does not therefore move freely between the bottom (the voters) and the top (the national party elite). The national policy-making process of these parties is almost non-existent; indeed the national organization is so weak that the party itself is unlikely to remain in existence unscathed for more than short periods.

The maintenance or at least the healthy development of liberal democracy does therefore hinge on the characteristics of the parties: parties are inchoate and dominated by local bosses when no national social cleavages prevail in the polity or when these social cleavages are weak. Where, on the contrary, class, religion, or even ethnic differences cement party members and party supporters together, the party system becomes national and clientelism ceases to prevail. These opposing characteristics are naturally more or less marked according to the distance of the two types of parties from the polar extremes of the continuum. Moreover, the problem is particularly serious as a country moves towards liberal democracy, for these characteristics are crucial at the beginning of the process. If the faith of citizens in a given party has once been firm, its effect will continue to be felt even after it has ceased to be so intense. This has been true of supporters of socialist, Christian Democrat, conservative, agrarian, and Muslim parties who have at one time (or whose parents have at one time) truly identified with the party in question.

Given this premise, the main question to be examined in relation to East and Southeast Asia is how far, both in the countries which have become liberal democratic and in those which have remained authoritarian or semi-authoritarian, parties can be said to be well implanted because of the strength of the social cleavages from which they originated. In this respect, the eight studies which have been conducted provide substantial, if rather worrying, information. For in only two of the countries of the area is there evidence that the parties are well implanted, while in at least five of the others the implantation is weak and in the sixth there is only a scant hope that the parties will be strong in the future.

The two countries in which parties can be said not to be inchoate, because they have strong roots in the social structure, are Malaysia and Taiwan. It may seem surprising that these countries should belong to the same category since Malaysia is generally regarded as being semi-authoritarian if also rather consociational. Its authoritarianism is shown by the fact that there is no likelihood that the opposition will be able to replace the coalition in power in the short or medium term. The same can of course be said of Switzerland or could have been said of Austria in the 1950s; in the Netherlands, one and the same party was a "pivot" of coalitions between 1945 and 1994, and in Belgium continuously since 1945 to the present, except for one four-year period. The permanence of a party in government takes place in a democratic context, however, only if electoral practices give equal chances to governmental and opposition parties, if the campaign is not unduly short, if the opposition's rights are not curtailed, and if the media are not slanted in favour of the government. None of these characteristics obtains in Malaysia, while they all obtain in the European consociational countries. Yet the main parties of the Malaysian governmental coalition are rooted in the social structure: class may not play much of a part, but ethnicity does, together with religion. This is shown by the large membership of the parties as well as by the close links which at least a substantial proportion of the population has with the parties. Malaysian parties are unquestionably lively organizations.

The same can be said of Taiwan parties, despite the fact that the development of parties occurred since the late 1980s only, at least with respect to the second party. The end of the single-party system did not result in a variety of rather inchoate political groupings emerging in the society: it resulted, on the contrary, in the growth of a major party, the Democratic Progressive Party, which rapidly gained ground and, unlike the opposition in Malaysia, has appeared poised to win power at the centre, as it already did at the local level in the late 1990s. Taiwan politics has come to be "adversarial" rather than consociational. This adversarial system may not be a "pure" two-party system, but few two-party systems are pure: they tend to be often of a "two-and-a-quarter" variety, as in Britain, New Zealand, or Australia.

What rendered the Taiwan party system strong and consolidated has been, in an analogous manner to that of Malaysia, the existence of a cleavage between the indigenous Taiwanese part of the population and the part of the population whose roots are on the mainland. As in Malaysia, the main cleavage is not based on class, and in Taiwan it is not even based on religion: instead, it has an ethnic or pseudo-ethnic character. As in Malaysia, too, this cleavage is sufficiently profound to lead to a genuine sense of difference, and this sense is likely to be long-lasting. However, in part because the general political framework is freer than in Malaysia, the basic political cleavage which characterizes Taiwan has led to the emergence of two blocs: as in Britain and other "two-party adversarial countries," the battle is fought on the lines of "ins" and "outs," with the bulk of the population being associated with one or the other camp. For a polity which lived under a single-party system with strong military undertones as late as the early 1980s to have been able to move rapidly and peacefully towards a lively competitive party system is almost as "miraculous" as the economic development of that country has been "miraculous."

This "miracle" contrasts with the markedly more limited progress of party development in three of the other six countries, and with the lack of any progress at all in at least two of the remaining three. The countries which have made limited progress are those in which liberal democracy has been introduced or restored in the mid-1980s, Korea, the Philippines, and Thailand. The countries where there has been no or almost no progress in the strengthening of the bases of the party system are Indonesia and Singapore, and also Hong Kong, where the party development which had begun to occur came to be in question when the area ceased to be a British colony.

In Korea, the Philippines, and Thailand, the installation or restoration of liberal democracy has not been accompanied by the development of a well-structured party system as in Taiwan. What has emerged or re-emerged, on the contrary, has been a number of inchoate bodies, as the chapters relating to these countries clearly show. Parties are tied to the support of presidential candidates in Korea, and this support is neatly circumscribed geographically; parties in Thailand and the Philippines lack even minimal permanency. Clientelism prevails, in the absence of any national social cleavage broad enough to override localism. The parties of all three countries have more in common with French parties before the advent of the Fifth Republic in 1958 than with parties in other Western countries; they have even little in common with Japanese parties, as the parties of that country, despite their divisions, are national in character. This was not the case in France, at least among parties of the Right and Centre before World War II and even to an extent before 1958. The lack of a national party system in the three countries, as indeed in pre-1958 France, should not be regarded as being due to the absence of a feeling of national identity, however. As a matter of fact, Korea is a highly homogeneous country; Thailand and the Philippines are less homogeneous, but the feeling of national identity of both of these countries dates back for centuries. Yet this is associated in all three cases with a high degree of local or parochial "patriotism" which determines the patterns of political allegiance.

Thus liberal democracy cannot be said to be consolidated in these three countries; nor can it be even said that it is undergoing a process of consolidation. The political game is open, but it takes the form of a drama in which there are many minor parts, but no major ones; indeed, those who have the minor parts replace each other rapidly and in an obviously unpredictable manner. Thus these countries are not consociational in the true sense, despite efforts in this direction which have sometimes been made, as in the case of the "growth coalition" which emerged in the Philippines in the middle of the 1990s and lasted about a year. But politics in these countries is not adversarial either, as there are no party alignments analogous to those of Taiwan. The structuring which parties could provide being non-existent or almost non-existent in these three countries, the form which politics takes is likely to oscillate sharply depending on circumstances.

The lack of national party structuring suggests that liberal democratic life in the three countries has not found a "natural" equilibrium: many of its characteristics – and perhaps its very maintenance – depend on accidents, such as the emergence of a strong leader. This is what may render a presidential or semi-presidential system appropriate, as was suggested in chapter 4. That system is indeed better able than the parliamentary system to provide both leadership and policy consistency where both would otherwise be lacking as a result of the weakness of the parties. The contrast between Korea and the Philippines, on the one hand, and Thailand, on the other, is illuminating in this respect. Ostensibly at least, politics has been more coherent in the first two countries than in the third, while the only partial remedy for the absence of strong leadership in parliamentary Thailand is the fact that the monarch can and indeed does play a part in situations of real emergency; but this remedy is more in the nature of a medicine designed to lower the temperature than one that eliminates the causes of that temperature.

Yet the presidential system provides a temporary solution only: in both Korea and the Philippines it buttresses liberal democracy somewhat artificially. Whether the presidential system will give these countries a breathing space during which a well-implanted party system will emerge is doubtful. Parties in the Philippines have not shown any noticeable tendency to become more solid, quite the contrary; and parties in Korea seem to continue to be appendages of presidential candidates. The consequences of such a situation may well be serious. In the 1990s, the global political environment has been broadly unfavourable to coups and to authoritarian rule in general, but if this were to change, parties might not be sufficiently consolidated in Korea, the Philippines, and Thailand to prevent a return to authoritarianism.

Meanwhile, parties are so superimposed on the political system in the last three countries, Indonesia, Singapore, and Hong Kong, that it is difficult to regard them as being more than marginal and symbolic elements, as the chapters relating to these countries indicate. Of the three, Hong Kong is the closest to being a pure "administrative state," but an administrative state in which the bureaucracy is rather low-key, as we shall see shortly. Singapore is in all but name an administrative state as well, and a strong one at that, and the dominant party is little more than a mechanism aiming at formally legitimizing what the administration does, without in fact having the authority to provide real legitimacy. Parties are a little more alive in Indonesia, in part because they are officialized and include an opposition whose (tiny) role is formally recognized. Yet the apparently solid structure of the main party is so artificial and its capacity to hold the nation together is so problematic that that party has to be regarded as little more than a symbolic superstructure which, like its counterpart in Singapore, though in a different manner, formally but not really legitimizes the regime. Following the collapse of the Suharto regime, parties have now proliferated in Indonesia. The political outlook remains uncertain. Indonesia is likely to encounter major political difficulties if only because of its size, as the Soviet Union did. Meanwhile, Hong Kong might have gradually acquired a well-implanted party system on the model of Taiwan, based on the distinction between the indigenous population and the population coming from China proper. But the end of the colonial period stopped this development and made an administrative state formula the only practical solution.

Bureaucracies and politico-administrative structures

The eight country studies survey economic governance, the roles and effectiveness of the bureaucracy in this area, and the institutions through which policies are devised, co-ordinated, and implemented. These data allow patterns of economic governance in the countries concerned to be evaluated and compared. The picture that emerges is extremely varied and, as a result of the financial crisis of 1997, extremely volatile, particularly in the affected states of Korea, Indonesia, Thailand, and Malaysia.

The first contrast between the eight states concerns the scope of economic, industry, and technology policy. Economic policy covers the role of the state in fiscal, monetary, and trade policy; industry policy the degree to which the state attempts to manage industrial structure outcomes; and technology policy its programs to foster productivity and the progressive development from wage cost–based industrialization, through catch-up, to innovation. At least three factors influence the experience of individual states: their expressed economic ambitions; the duration of their experience of rapid growth; and the relative roles of domestic and foreign capital in the initiation and maintenance of growth. The first factor affects the overall complexity of bureaucratic policy-making and implementation tasks; the second affects the precise nature of these tasks; and the third affects technology strategy and business-government relations.

In terms of these three variables, the eight states fall into three broad groups. The first is constituted by Korea, Taiwan, Hong Kong, and Singapore. These countries progressively entered the world production system from roughly the 1960s. With the exception of Hong Kong, they have all attempted to influence industrial structure outcomes. The state conceived and initiated a growth strategy and mobilized, at least initially, the resources – capital, human, and technological – to implement that strategy. This initial role coloured the subsequent development of economic governance. The state has continued to aspire to a catalytic role in relation to markets. While Singapore and Hong Kong have drawn heavily on DFI, Taiwan and Korea, but Korea up to the 1990s only, have relied primarily on domestic capital mobilization.

The challenge for these states has been to adapt to their changing external and domestic contexts. Externally, they have become progressively more implicated in global production, and save for Taiwan, in global financial systems. Domestically, they have had to integrate at least business and labour interests and to move from catch-up technology strategies towards innovation. For example, the crisis in Korea reflected, among a number of factors, the progressive weakening of that state's ability to manage the integration of labour, to curb the power of the chaebols, and to progressively augment catch-up technology strategies with innovation. By contrast, Taiwan and Singapore are perceived to have succeeded in all these tasks – albeit by varying means.

Three of the states of Southeast Asia – Indonesia, Thailand and Malaysia – constitute a second group. These states experienced rapid industrialization from the late 1980s as they became more integrated in Japanese and other MNC production systems. Thailand has never sought to manage structural outcomes, whereas Malaysia and to a lesser degree Indonesia have both augmented macroeconomic management with plans to develop particular sectors or capacities. The declared aim, at least in part, has been to build local technological capacity and to progressively boost productivity, thus permitting advance from low wage–based industrialization. Further, these latter two countries have deliberately sought to protect national sovereignty by building a local entrepreneurial class to partner foreign investors and to stimulate indigenous managerial capacity. Some interpret these efforts in a less public-spirited light: they see state patronage primarily as a device to consolidate the power of authoritarian regimes.

The Philippines occupies a third category since its economic expansion did not commence until the early 1990s. This state broadly exhibits the same characteristics as its Southeast Asian neighbours – except that here economic governance is being practised at an earlier developmental stage. The state has sought to establish a basic "market-friendly" framework and to influence, indirectly, productivity gain.

Another point of contrast concerns the degree of bureaucratic autonomy. This refers to the ability of the state's professional managers to formulate and implement chosen policies. Taiwan provides the most developed example of persisting autonomy. The state's ambitions to guide structural development continue; but business and labour interests have both acquired more independence as the process of economic development has advanced. Democratic consolidation has here worked to reinforce bureaucratic autonomy. The KMT has played a larger role in integrating business interests while the state has developed arrangements to integrate labour. In other words, the state's directing and facilitating role has become progressively embedded in more collaborative structures. How these arrangements would fare if the opposition DPP gains power remains to be determined.

In Korea's case, by contrast, a shallower democratic consolidation had opposite effects. The concentration of economic power in the chaebol progressively insulated them from state influence, a process that was reinforced by their internationalization and by the weakness of the parties which rendered them unable to integrate interests; nor was labour integrated either. Yet democratization enhanced the veto power of both groups. The autonomy of the elite bureaucratic agencies was thus progressively reduced as democratization has stopped short of bringing about a genuine party development.

In Singapore's case, the state's co-opting powers have not changed and bureaucratic autonomy has been preserved. Hong Kong has progressively moved towards a more elaborated industrial policy but there has been no attempt to influence industrial structure outcomes.

In the case of Indonesia, Thailand, Malaysia, and the Philippines, bureaucratic autonomy has hitherto resulted from the reputation and roles of the limited number of elite agencies which basically managed fiscal and monetary policy. The insulation of these agencies from the political system was the key to their strength. In the first three, this insulation has been eroded and the political system has progressively emerged as a major constraint. In Indonesia, the focus of authority on the president, the adoption of dirigiste approaches by particular ministers and/or in particular sectors, and the allocation of production licenses to members of President Suharto's family and other favoured citizens has qualified the autonomy of the elite agencies. In MacIntyre's judgement, "the existing framework is very fragile because it is so sensitive to the behaviour of the occupant of the presidency." The political and economic aftermath of the Suharto resignation is unclear – but the outlook remains grim. In Malaysia, bureaucratic autonomy has been compromised by the progressive expansion of the influence of the prime minister and by the extension of patronage through the majority party: the bureaucracy has mostly been a secondary actor in these processes. In Thailand, corruption has penetrated the hitherto insulated elite economic policy-making institutions: for example, the reputation of the Bank of Thailand for impartial action was severely compromised by the scandals in 1996. Only in the Philippines does there appear to have been a positive relationship between the political and administrative system. Here the short-lived but critical "growth coalition" of the mid-1990s was the occasion for significant structural change. This strengthened the position of elite bureaucrats in national economic management.

The evidence on bureaucratic quality also points to variation between states. Korea, Taiwan, Singapore, and Hong Kong all recruit extensively from elite universities. Their bureaucracies generally retain their high reputations. In Southeast Asia, only the elite agencies enjoy a reputation for high-calibre staffing. This has been compromised in Thailand's case by scandals and other allegations of corruption in prudential and supervisory agencies.

The crisis of 1997 resulted in a special focus on the quality of economic governance of the financial sector in affected states and on the appropriate state roles in this sector. The practices of individual states had varied in relation to the openness of their financial sectors to international participation, their prudential requirements and monitoring practices, and their general requirements in relation to the transparency of corporate activity. Progressive liberalization of this latter sector in Korea has been said to be one of the causes of the crisis in that country: prior to liberalization the state oversaw the level of chaebol borrowing. Taiwan has retained tight controls, and this has insulated that country from the constraints that economic globalization otherwise imposes on domestic freedom of manoeuvre. By contrast, the city-states of Singapore and Hong Kong have managed their financial sectors with a degree of transparency and with prudential and supervisory arrangements sufficient to satisfy the global financial community. Such arrangements have been absent in Thailand, Indonesia, and Malaysia: their absence and the resulting excesses are held to have contributed to the crisis of 1997. The Philippines has adopted relatively more stringent monitoring policies. To be noted in passing is that the presence of such arrangements is not associated with the absence of crises, as is shown by the U.S. savings and loans episode and by the British abandonment of the EMS. Perhaps the best that might be claimed is that such arrangements help to confine such crises to the financial sector.

In sum, only Taiwan and Singapore broadly retained in the late 1990s the framework of classic developmental states; democratization, in the first case, is also leading to a reconfiguration of the institutional context. The institutional forms remain in Korea, but the capacity to influence, directly or indirectly, industrial structure outcomes has been undermined: to an extent at least, this has been due to political developments. Malaysia and Indonesia, in very different contexts, adopted limited programmes to shape the industrial structure; but this policy was pursued through special-purpose agencies and through direct political linkages rather than through a coherent state apparatus. Hong Kong has also introduced policies designed to encourage technology development in the electronics and information technology sectors, but as an augmentation of existing "followership" policy, not through the reshaping of the industrial structure. The Philippines and Thailand have not generally sought to influence industrial structure outcomes; in the latter case the reputation of the elite bureaucracy has also been compromised by bribery scandals.

Finally, the consequences for economic governance of the financial crisis of 1997 should be noted. This crisis, and the subsequent interventions of the IMF and the World Bank in affected states, put a number of facets of economic governance under the spotlight. They demonstrate the limitations on economic governance, at least in the financial sector, and perhaps more generally, that are imposed by substantial reliance on international capital. The OECD move to introduce an investment code reflects the same pressures in production sectors. The crisis has given fresh impetus to arguments concerning the desirability, from the perspective of national sovereignty, of financial liberalization, and of other international regulatory codes framed in accordance with Western norms. The financial crisis has also stimulated debate about the value of the remedies routinely sponsored by the IMF and the World Bank and about the potential for more elaborated regional co-operation to insulate states better from international investor sentiment, such as the setting up of a regional monitoring authority or of a regional yen bloc. In sum, the events of 1997 and their aftermath, no less than democratization in Taiwan, Korea, and Thailand, have meant that economic governance in individual states is subject to an array of volatile pressures.

Liberal democracy and economic performance in East and Southeast Asia

It is possible at this point to attempt to summarize the evidence which has been collected in the course of this volume about the possible impact of liberal democracy on economic performance. To do so, it is best first to locate the eight countries analyzed in this volume in the matrix derived from Shefter and described in chapter 4 (see figure 13.1, and compare figures 4.1 and 4.2). The evidence suggests that, whereas no Western state falls in the right-hand column of "weak and internally divided" parties, three of the countries examined here, Korea, Thailand, and the Philippines, are located in that column; furthermore, a fourth column covering "countries without a freely developed party system" has to be introduced on the right of the matrix to accommodate Singapore, Hong Kong, and Indonesia. Only Taiwan and Malaysia are to be located in the middle column of party strength. With respect to administrative structures, Taiwan and Singapore are located in the top row as their bureaucracy is strong, while the other six countries are located in the middle row as their bureaucracy is intermediate in strength; however, some change may be occurring since Hong Kong may be in the process of moving up while Indonesia may be in the process of moving down, and Korea has already moved from being characterized by a strong bureaucracy to being characterised by a bureaucracy of intermediate strength. Only Taiwan and Malaysia have party and administrative characteristics which render them comparable to Western countries, as they have both relatively strong parties and strong bureaucracies, the Taiwan bureaucracy being the stronger of the two.

On the basis of the way in which countries of East and Southeast Asia are located on the matrix, a set of conclusions can be drawn about some aspects of the impact of liberal democracy on economic development.

Political Parties

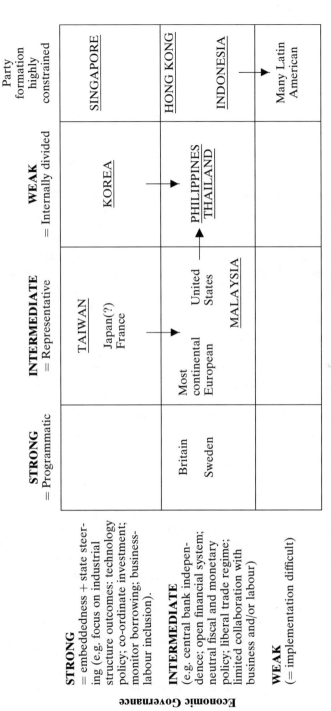

Figure 13.1 **Political parties and economic governance in East and Southeast Asia**

347

The question is better examined successively in two ways, however, as this impact can be expected to be different, to a degree at least, when there is an economic crisis of the magnitude of that which hit the region in 1997, than when economic development takes place without major national or international impediments.

Liberal democracy and economic performance in general

Although the impact of liberal democracy on economic performance in the context of East and Southeast Asia, even outside economic crises, clearly cannot be strictly speaking "measured," a number of conclusions can be drawn from the evidence of developments which took place from the mid-1980s to the mid-1990s. The first and most immediate piece of evidence is constituted by the fact that during these ten years, there was no sign of a decline in rates of economic growth in any of the countries which became liberal democratic at the time, Korea, Taiwan, the Philippines, and Thailand. The "economic miracle" continued in these countries as it did in those in which there was no break in authoritarian rule. It may be, admittedly, that this state of affairs simply results from the fact that there can be a substantial lag for the effect of a change of political regime to be felt: it manifestly takes time for the attitudes of the actors concerned, entrepreneurs, employees, and members of the bureaucracy, to be modified. But it is surely fair to conclude that the installation of liberal democracy has not immediately and directly destroyed economic performance.

The analysis needs to go further, however. Three types of considerations, which have been highlighted in the course of this volume, both in the general and in the country chapters, need to be taken into account. First, is there a direct and concrete effect of the installation of a liberal democratic regime on the part which the bureaucracy is able to play in a country? Do administrators continue to be able to initiate policies and to follow these through on the scale to which they were accustomed in an authoritarian regime? Second, is there a consensus among all relevant parties and politicians on continuing with a policy of economic growth, or are there divisions among these parties and politicians with respect to the fundamentals of economic policy-making? Third, conversely, do bureaucrats recognize that parties and politicians have a part to play in the development of the nation, including in its economic development? Do they feel deficient in "legitimacy capital," so to speak, and do they need to rely on the legitimacy of parties and politicians to achieve their own goals, or do they, on the contrary, consider that parties and politicians (or at least some of them) prevent them from achieving these goals?

The last two aspects of this problem form part of a kind of trade-off between the two sides. Parties and politicians may have to accept to exercise a degree of self-restraint in terms of their own involvement in economic policy-making if a high level of economic performance is to be maintained; bureaucrats may have to agree to involve parties and politicians in policy-making, and indeed to bow to the desires of these parties and politicians, in order to reap the benefits of the legitimizing umbrella which parties and politicians can open above them.

1. On the first point, a mixed answer can be given for East and Southeast Asia. The role of the bureaucracy remained unchanged in two of the four countries which moved towards liberal democracy, Taiwan and Thailand, while some changes occurred in Korea and the Philippines. The differences between Taiwan and Thailand, in the involvement of administrators in policy-making, pre-dated liberal democracy: in Taiwan, the involvement of administrators in sectoral economic management continued; the fact that the bureaucracy was only basically concerned with macroeconomics in Thailand is a reflection, not of the change in the political regime in the country, but of the fact that the civil service never was deeply involved in microeconomic initiatives, perhaps because of its more limited capacity.

In the Philippines the involvement of the bureaucracy in microeconomic management which characterized the second period of the Marcos dictatorship was markedly reduced when liberal democracy was restored and a policy of privatizations and economic liberalization was adopted; but that change followed a period during which the economy had ceased to grow and had even gone into decline. Moreover, the policy of microeconomic management which had been introduced by Marcos during the second phase of his dictatorial rule was more designed to enable the president and his close business associates to exploit the economy than to give the bureaucracy a key role in the management of the economy. Thus the failure of the policy was perhaps due, in part at least, to the predatory aims of the Philippine power elite, although it may also have been the case that, as in the rest of Southeast Asia except Singapore, the bureaucracy did not have the required technical competence to undertake successfully a detailed supervision of the different sectors as its opposite numbers in Korea or Taiwan had been able to do. Thus the Marcos policy of sectoral intervention had analogous characteristics to that of Suharto in Indonesia: in both cases, it is difficult to dissociate the microeconomic aims from the desire to provide benefits to the immediate entourage of the leader. The change of policy after the return to democracy is not therefore an indication that the role of the bureaucracy was being "ideologically" reduced.

However, while democratization may not be regarded as having "caused" a decrease in the involvement of the bureaucracy in three of the four countries of the area which did democratize, the same does not appear to be the case in Korea. Admittedly, the strengthening of some of the non-state economic actors, businesses in particular, was not due to democratization, but to the increase in the power of the chaebols. Yet the loss of influence which the bureaucracy suffered as a result was not compensated by an increase in the ability of parties to channel demands coming from these bodies; nor did demands from employees and in particular from manual workers come to be channelled by the parties either. The rather limited extent to which the presidency can compensate for the inability of parties to play a part in the polity is thus manifest in the Korean case. Korea constitutes therefore an instance in East and Southeast Asia where democratization may have contributed to a reduction in economic performance, while this cannot be deemed to have been the case for the other three countries of the area which became liberal democracies.

2. Second, there appears to be a consensus on the part of parties and politicians in the countries in which liberal democracy was installed or restored about the need to pursue policies of economic growth. As a matter of fact, in the specific case of the Philippines, as we just saw, the authoritarian regime of Marcos proved increasingly unable to bring about economic growth. Thus, in this respect at least, liberal democracy did influence economic development positively. Moreover, in all the four countries which installed or restored liberal democracy, a consensus has existed among parties and politicians on maintaining the policy of economic growth. This has been particularly manifest in the Philippines, where a "growth coalition" brought together most parties in the mid-1990s; and in Korea, where successive presidents, including the president elected in 1997, have been at pains to state and prove that they believed in continuing existing economic policies. However, in both countries, as well as in Thailand, the weakness of parties means that a commitment to growth on their part has little significance. As parties in these countries count for very little, it cannot be claimed that these would have been in any real sense in a position to affect the impact of the bureaucracy on policy-making even if they had wanted to. But as we noted in the Korean case, the weakness of parties may indirectly have contributed to a reduction of the general role of the state in supervising economic actors.

The only one of the democratizing countries of the region where the position of parties on the question of economic growth could be said to have a real relevance is Taiwan, since it is the only one in which the parties have acquired genuine strength: on coming to power, the DPP might be able to introduce different policies, if it wished to do so. Yet this does not seem likely, not merely because the views of the DPP on economic policy do not appear to differ markedly from those of the KMT, but also because the DPP has begun to represent to a substantial extent the interests of the large group of small businessmen on which the economic performance of Taiwan has been based. Admittedly, it might be that the coming to power of the DPP would have such consequences for foreign policy developments that the economic performance of the country would be adversely affected, but this means going beyond the economic area proper and therefore outside the parameters of this study.

Overall, there is thus consensus among parties and politicians in the region on the need to pursue a policy of strong economic growth, but except for Taiwan, there remains some doubt as to whether parties are sufficiently alive to be regarded as reliable agents in this respect. It may therefore be that, if parties were to become stronger, or if new and stronger parties were to emerge and be successful, a challenge to the policy of economic growth would also emerge and the consensus would be broken. All that can be said is that there are no signs that any party is about to take such a line, as there are no signs that any party (except in Taiwan) will be in a position to adopt, let alone maintain, a definite and coherent policy line.

3. If it is unclear whether parties might emerge which might challenge the policy of economic growth, it is even more unclear whether bureaucrats will develop attitudes which would be antagonistic to liberal democratic parties and politicians: for what needs to be determined to give definite answers to such a question is evidence about what the reactions of civil servants might be if confronted with situations in which the economic performance of their countries was impaired under a liberal democratic regime. To an extent, the crisis of 1997 constitutes an instance of such a situation, and its potential consequences in terms of the impact of liberal democracy on the economy will shortly be examined; but there could be other circumstances in which the problem might arise since there could be many situations leading civil servants to mistrust liberal democratic parties and politicians and to favour a return to authoritarian rule.

In the absence of detailed studies of these potential attitudes of civil servants in each country, the points which can be made have to be general. Three of these appear to be particularly important. First, if what is feared by civil servants is undue manipulation of economic policy by the political masters, it is not clear that there is less of this kind of manipulation under authoritarian rule than under liberal democratic rule. The cases of Marcos in the Philippines and Suharto in Indonesia have already been mentioned; in Singapore, Lee Kuan Yew has more than occasionally acted over and above his civil servants; the part played by Malaysian political leaders, above all Mahathir, in economic policy-making has been very significant. In contrast, liberal democratic leaders are likely to be anxious to avoid giving too often the impression of intervening, for instance, to please their constituents: civil servants may even be able to resist these interventions more effectively in a liberal democracy than in an authoritarian regime.

Second, however, such restraint on the part of liberal democratic leaders may be felt to be temporary and to result from the desire to appear morally superior to authoritarian rulers: liberal democratic leaders may be more disposed to look after their interests and those whom they wish to help when their rule becomes better established. Indeed, civil servants may worry about the potential meddling of liberal democratic politicians regardless of its actual extent, and be therefore somewhat uncommitted to liberal democratic rule. Furthermore, bureaucrats may be only temporarily restrained in their desire to bring about more "order" in society, so long as the view prevails in the world at large that liberal democracy is to be preferred. Such a view may not prevail indefinitely: by the end of the 1990s its strength had already somewhat diminished. This may affect the commitment of civil servants to liberal democratic politics in the longer term.

Yet, third, the problem may gradually take a different shape as co-operation between the two sides comes to be regarded as normal. Civil servants in the area may be impressed by the fact that, in the West and in Japan, a working relationship does exist between politicians and bureaucrats. They may also come to note that such a relationship has the advantage of taking away from civil servants the burden of having to justify what is done on the economic front, including of having to defend any mistakes which may be made. Moreover, if bureaucrats accept liberal democratic rule as given, they cease to have to ask themselves difficult questions about the costs and uncertainties connected with regime change.

At this stage, it can at least be concluded that the impact of liberal democracy on economic performance is not necessarily negative. More specifically, while more needs to be done to examine in detail how economic policies are being affected by democratization, it seems that in the particular case of East and Southeast Asia, that impact has proved to be at least neutral in the short term. The future is not as clear, however, given the problems posed by the consequences of the economic crisis of 1997.

Liberal democracy and economic crises

Independently from its importance for the region as a whole and indeed for the world, the financial crisis of 1997 constitutes a test case of the relationship between politicians and civil servants in both a liberal democratic and an authoritarian context. This crisis has constituted a major upheaval for East and Southeast Asian countries, though the extent of the upheaval has been different from country to country; the different origins of the crisis in each country may account in part for its different effects. The problem has arisen in Korea primarily because of the extent of borrowing by the major companies, and in Southeast Asia, because of an internal collapse of major banking institutions and the lack of regulation of the financial system: this means that, as was pointed out at the beginning of this chapter, whatever the extent of the consequences of the crisis, the cause of the trouble cannot be attributed – or at least, not directly attributed – to moves towards liberal democracy. Indeed, a country such as Indonesia has been affected as much as, if not more than, any liberal democratic country of the area.

What does remain in question is whether a liberal democratic framework is likely to help or hamper the management of the crisis. The crisis renders more acute the dilemmas of both politicians and civil servants regarding the extent to which they should respect each other's domain. On the one hand, the bureaucracy needs to enjoy considerable autonomy in order to be able to play its full part in the policy-making process; but it also needs to be buttressed, on the other hand, by politically authoritative institutions – primarily parties, or failing these, by institutional devices such as the presidency. There has to be a good mix of or trade-off between administrative involvement and political support, as political support must not be overshadowed by administrative involvement if crisis management is to proceed smoothly. Let us therefore return to the positions occupied by the various countries of the area on the matrix derived from Shefter as shown in modified form in figure 13.1.

If we consider the location of the countries of East and Southeast Asia in the matrix, these are exposed to two types of risks. Polities in the two right-hand columns would appear likely to suffer because of the lack of strength of their political institutions; polities in the lower part of the matrix are also in danger because of the weakness of their administrative apparatus. Thus countries in the bottom right-hand corner, such as Latin American countries outside the area, have tended to be particularly at risk.

None of the countries of East and Southeast Asia is in the same box as the Latin American countries, but Indonesia comes close to that position: the ability of its political institutions to relate to the people via the parties and even the presidency is almost non-existent; the ability of the bureaucracy to manage the economy and the society is the weakest of the countries of the region and its performance is in question. Admittedly, this is in part due to the difficulty of administering a vast country in which there is considerable ethnic diversity; but problems have been compounded by the fact that the autonomy of the bureaucracy had come to be somewhat hampered by the actions of Suharto in favour of his business associates. As a result, the Indonesian presidency had ceased to provide help to the politico-administrative system and had come to be a handicap. Indonesia appears therefore to be the polity of the area least likely to surmount the crisis.

In the other countries, the risk represented by the crisis would in theory seem to be greater as a result of legitimacy being low than as a result of the weaknesses of the administrative apparatus, since, in East and Southeast Asia, the administration is always at least able to see its decisions implemented relatively efficiently. Thus the countries in which parties display intermediate strength (Taiwan and Malaysia) would appear more likely to control the effects of the crisis than the countries in which parties are weak (Korea, Thailand, and the Philippines) or almost nonexistent (Singapore and Hong Kong).

Two points modify this conclusion, however. First, in relation to a crisis, the "accidental" coming to power of a president has the effect of increasing, albeit perhaps only temporarily, the capacity of the political system to resolve the crisis or at least reduce its impact, since a crisis, financial, economic, or otherwise, is itself an event or a situation of an "accidental" character which is by its very nature "abnormal." The reasoning which can be made in this context is analogous to Max Weber's reasoning about charismatic leadership:[3] in a crisis, if a truly popular leader happens to come to power, the society may be able to overcome the problem and return to "normalcy." This means, in practice, that not only should Taiwan be able to surmount the crisis – as it might in any case be able to do given that its party system is relatively strong – but that Korea and the Philippines may also be able to do so, if and so long as these countries are ruled by a strong and popular president who is willing to support the bureaucracy and protect it if it comes under attack because of the severity of the measures which are taken. We noted earlier that there was some doubt in this respect in the case of Korea; yet the country most at risk in the group of those which have become liberal democratic seems to be Thailand, as parties in that country are inchoate and the parliamentary system does not provide "artificially" and automatically mechanisms through which to build as strong a leadership as the presidential system.

Second, while Singapore and Hong Kong would appear to be politically weak because they lack the legitimizing impact of parties, the special characteristics of these two polities renders them appreciably less vulnerable. They may be both almost pure administrative states, but they appear nonetheless able to surmount without great difficulty any crisis which they will have to face, as, in sharp contrast with Indonesia, they operate within the narrow geographical compass of city-states with relatively small populations.

Parties may play an important part in city-states; but the limited size of these polities and the fact that they are wholly urban mean that relationships between people and government are facilitated, whether parties exist or not. These two factors also make it possible for the government to control citizens more adequately. Moreover, the two Southeast Asian city-states, probably like all city-states, are threatened by neighbours which are larger in size and in population; and in societies at risk the government can more easily use the argument of patriotism to ensure that its decisions are obeyed and that dissent is restricted. It may seem paradoxical to come to this conclusion, in view of what Rousseau once stated, but a city-state is perhaps less likely to be or remain a liberal democracy in the context of a crisis than a larger polity.[4]

As a result, first, an authoritarian state such as Indonesia is less likely to manage effectively a major crisis than the states which became liberal democracies in the 1980s. Second, the two relatively authoritarian city-states of the region are likely to surmount the crisis better than those which became liberal democracies, except that Taiwan, too, as a consolidated liberal democracy with a strong bureaucracy, is also likely to come out of the crisis without having suffered major damage. The three liberal democracies which are not consolidated, and are perhaps not even in the process of being consolidated, are between these two groups. Among them, those in which liberal democracy, despite the absence of lively parties, has been accidentally and probably temporarily "saved" by a popular president (Korea and the Philippines) are more likely to surmount the crisis than Thailand where the absence of effective parties is not compensated in this way, in part at least. That country would therefore seem to be, after Indonesia, the one in which liberal democracy is least likely to be able to control the crisis.

The question of the possible impact of liberal democracy on economic performance, whether in East and Southeast Asia or elsewhere, poses such complex problems that it may not be surprising that some leaders should have peremptorily affirmed, more or less honestly but clearly conveniently for themselves, that liberal democracy is detrimental to the economic well-being of citizens. A definitive answer to this question may never be given. It is clearly unrealistic to attempt to give such an answer at this early stage in the examination of the role of liberal democracy in economic life, let alone one that is valid for all times and all regions, given cultural differences and differences in living standards. It may not be as unrealistic to attempt to give an answer for a particular region at a particular point in time, however: indeed, an effort has to be made to give such an answer within the circumscribed context of East and Southeast Asia, as "answers" have been offered frequently by politicians and observers of political life in the region.

The most straightforward point to make is that there is no manifest evidence that liberal democratic rule is directly and obviously detrimental to economic well-being. There is at least enough support for the view that economic performance has flourished under liberal democratic regimes in East and Southeast Asia that the overall verdict must be the same as that given for Latin America on the basis of systematic statistical analyses relating to the 1960s and 1970s: that democracy can help economic growth, even if authoritarian rule can also do so.[5]

Beyond this general point, detailed case studies provide more specific insights into the nature of the variations in the impact which liberal democracy may have on economic performance. The extent to which parties are strong or weak is an important factor, since the coherence of policies pursued by governments under liberal democratic rule is heavily dependent on parties being well structured: in the absence of such parties, the presence or absence of a strong presidency may constitute a partial and somewhat temporary substitute. Case studies make it possible to assess whether parties and/or presidents are in tune with the bureaucracy on economic goals, and thus help to determine whether or not there are grounds for doubting the positive or at least neutral effect of liberal democratic rule on economic performance. Case studies also offer evidence about the extent to which the bureaucracy is able to steer the economy, although more thorough analyses of the attitudes of civil servants are needed if one is to discover whether these are likely to recognize that parties and politicians provide legitimacy to their actions. The debate about the impact of liberal democracy on economic performance does remain open; but the parameters within which the problem is to be addressed have become more definite and more precise. This, in turn, will help to throw light on whether East and Southeast Asia are likely to remain economically buoyant while also being one of the areas of the world where liberal democracy has become firmly established.

Notes

1. See Yi Feng, "Democracy, Political Stability and Economic Growth," *British Journal of Political Science* 1997; 27: 391–418.
2. For references on the role of parties see chapter 2.
3. Max Weber, *The Theory of Social and Economic Organization* (New York: Free Press, 1947).
4. Jean-Jacques Rousseau, The *Social Contract* (London: Penguin, 1974).
5. See Feng, "Democracy, Political Stability and Economic Growth."

Contributors

Ahn Chung-si, Professor, Seoul National University, Korea.

Jean Blondel, Professor, Robert Schumann Centre, European University Institute, Florence.

Cheng Hsiao-shih, Associate Research Fellow and Head of the Third Division of the Institute of Social Science and Philosophy, Academia Sinica, Taipei.

Edmund Terence Gomez, Lecturer at the University of Malaya, Kuala Lumpur. He is the author of *Politics in Business*, *Political Business: Corporate Involvement of Malaysian Political Parties*, *Chinese Business in Malaysia* and the co-author of *Malaysia's Political Economy: Politics, Patronage and Profits*.

Hsin-Huang Michael Hsiao, Research Fellow at the Institute of Sociology and Director of the Program for Southeast Asian Studies (PROSEA), Academia Sinica; Professor of Sociology, National Taiwan University.

Takashi Inoguchi, Professor at the Institute of Oriental Culture, University of Tokyo.

Jaung Hoon, Associate Professor of Political Science, Chung-Ang University, Korea. His research interests include political parties and elections in Western European democracies and in Korea.

Jomo Kwame Sundaram, Professor in the Faculty of Economics and Administration, University of Malaya.

Khong Cho-oon, Senior Analyst with Shell International Limited. London.

Dan King is currently an equities analyst in Chicago. He spent six years in Thailand (1992–98) conducting field research, and with

357

the Asia Foundation and other local financial firms. He holds a Ph.D. from the University of Wisconsin-Madison.

Andrew MacIntyre, Professor, University of California, San Diego

Ian Marsh, Associate Professor, Australian Graduate School of Management, University of New South Wales.

James T. H. Tang, Professor at the Department of Politics and Public Administration, University of Hong Kong.

Renato S. Velasco, Associate Professor of Political Science, University of the Philippines. On secondment as Director for Policy and Technical Services at the Office of the Vice-President of the Republic of the Philippines.

Index